D0062384

BUFFALO WOMAN COMES SINGING

THE SPIRIT SONG OF A RAINBOW MEDICINE WOMAN

BROOKE MEDICINE EAGLE

BALLANTINE BOOKS NEW YORK

Copyright © 1991 by Brooke Medicine Eagle

All rights reserved under International and Pan-American Copyright Conventions. Published in the United States by Ballantine Books, a division of Random House, Inc., New York, and simultaneously in Canada by Random House of Canada Limited, Toronto.

Grateful acknowledgment is made to the University of Nebraska Press for permission to reprint excerpts from *Black Elk Speaks* by John G. Neihardt. Copyright © 1932, 1959, 1972 by John G. Neihardt. Copyright © 1961 by the John G. Neihardt Trust. The poem "Tampons" reprinted by permission of Ellen Bass.

Library of Congress Catalog Card Number: 91-91879
ISBN: 0-345-36143-1

Cover painting by Rick Faist
Cover design by James R. Harris
Text design by Holly Johnson

Chapter opener and spot illustrations
copyright © 1991 by Prudence See
Lightning Buffalo copyright © 1991 by Greg Jahn
Medicine Wheel copyright © 1991 by Lynn Peck

Manufactured in the United States of America

First Edition: October 1991
20 19 18 17 16 15 14

*This book is dedicated to
those who have been my teachers:
both those who modeled what to do,
and those who demonstrated what not to do.*

*It is dedicated as well to
Father Spirit and Mother Earth;
to those who are awakening to heal themselves and the Earth;
and to All My Relations.*

ACKNOWLEDGMENTS

First of all I want to acknowledge my family, who see me very little because of my commitment to teaching and sharing with others, and also to thank them for their support and caring. Many thanks go to my agent Wabun Wind for helping get this book started; to Melane Lohmann and Marion Gracen for their splendid assistance on this project, which made it easy on me and the editors; to Lynn Peck for her artistic rendering of the Medicine Wheel I use; to Rick Faust for his beautiful cover art; and to Sondra Kate and Alan Geller for the lovely retreat they offered at Hedgerow. Deep appreciation goes to my partner, Alvin EagleSmith, who provided the solid ground of home for me to stand on during these years of writing.

I realize that much of what is contained in this book emerged through interacting with you who are my students. My thanks goes to every one of you, and especially to those who offered their comments on my work for this book.

And most of all, I want to thank my editor, Cheryl Woodruff, who helped me turn a wobbly first draft into a very special communication for All My Relations. Her thoughtful criticism and challenges not only helped me grow a better book, but also to become a more integrated author!

CONTENTS

Prologue		3
Introduction		9
Part One: Reclaiming the Lineage		15
Chapter 1	The Woman Who Knows Everything	17
Chapter 2	The Quickest Zipper on the Reservation	35
Chapter 3	Lessons of the Buffalo Lodge	53
Chapter 4	On My Way to the Sacred Mountain	77
Chapter 5	The Heart of Black Hand	93
Chapter 6	Rainbow Woman Comes	113
Chapter 7	The Flaming Arrow	131
Part Two: Walking the Rainbow Path		153
Chapter 8	Fighting the Dragon	157
Chapter 9	A Chalice Overflowing with Light	173
Chapter 10	An Old Samurai Moves Me	189
Chapter 11	The Heaviest Sword and the Sharpest Razor	215
Chapter 12	A Northern Face, A Southern Heart	235
Chapter 13	A Crystal Among Them	257
Part Three: Dancing Under the Teaching Shawl		275
Chapter 14	Around the Rainbow Wheel	281
Chapter 15	Healing Through Ritual Action	307
Chapter 16	The Mysterious Feminine	327
Chapter 17	Dancing Awake the Dream	345
Chapter 18	At Camp on the Deerborn	363
Chapter 19	Embodying Spirit	403
Chapter 20	Carrying Her Pipe of Oneness	429
Glossary		447
Appendix 1:	Resources and Ordering Guide	455
Appendix 2:	Suggested Reading: A Selected Bibliography	459
Appendix 3:	Information on Brooke Medicine Eagle	469
Appendix 4:	A Reference to Works by and about Moshé Feldenkrais	480
Index		483

LIST OF EXERCISES

Chapter 1
Creating a Sacred Space 28
Smudging 29
Calling Your Teachers 30
Chapter 2
Connecting to the Great Spirit Within 47
The Golden Seed Atom 48
Connecting to Spirit Through Sacred Words and Sounds 49
A Ritual for Spiritual Cleansing 49
Chapter 3
Creating the Necklace of Connectedness 72
Chapter 4
Fasting—A Pathway to Spirit 88
Alternate Fasts 89
A Turning of Attention 90
Chapter 5
The Tree of Family Patterns 105
The Law of Seven Generations 106
A Ceremony of Release 108
The Paraphernalia Purge 110
Chapter 6
Exploring the Feminine 123
Drumming the Heartbeat 126
A Simple Drumming Ceremony 127
Chapter 7
Reenacting Your Vision 144
Pursuing the Symbolic Guide 147
Bring the Vision to Life 148
The Medicine Bundle 148
Vision in Action 149
Chapter 8
Assessing the Outer (Right-Sided) World 168
The Inheritance Suitcase 169

Chapter 9
   The Names You Carry   183
   The Search for Your True Name   183
   A Ceremony for Taking Your New Name   185
Chapter 10
   Awareness Through Movement: Tension Check   207
   Awareness Through Movement: Noticing Habitual
     Patterns   208
   Awareness Through Movement: Moving Blindfolded   209
   Awareness Through Movement: Breathing   210
   Awareness Through Movement: Reality Shifts   211
Chapter 11
   The Absolute Yes!   230
   The Integrity of Feeling   231
Chapter 12
   Recapitulation   252
Chapter 13
   Nurturing Our Crystals   269
   Cleaning Your Crystal   270
   Filling Your Crystal with Intention   270
Chapter 14
   Honoring the Six Directions   288
   Walking the Wheel of Relatedness   296
   Around Your Personal Medicine Wheel   303
Chapter 15
   Having Your Cake and Eating It, Too!   311
   Taking Ritual Action   322
Chapter 16
   Moon Time Awareness   340
   Moon Staff   342
Chapter 17
   Manifesting Through the Four Winds   359
Chapter 18
   Support Hoop   387
   Power Leaks   388
   Acts of Power and Beauty   389
   Action Contract for Acts of Power   391
   Action Contract for Acts of Beauty   392
   Earth Action Contract   395
   Outer Earth Walk   396
   Medicine Wheel Walk   397
   Earth Medicine Contract   398

Chapter 19
The Right Questions   422
Finding Your Holes—and Filling Them   423
Accepting Your Mantle   424
Earth Medicine Contract: "One Block at a Time"   426

In black, there are all colors.
Where darkness, always the light.
Iridescent the raven's wing in sunlight.

—BROOKE MEDICINE EAGLE

BUFFALO WOMAN
COMES SINGING

PROLOGUE

Although this story is my story, told through the metaphors of my own personal experience, my hope is that it is more than just a personal recounting. My prayer is that it will stimulate understanding, growth, and healing in your own life, which in turn offers healing to our Mother Earth. In this time of our maturing as a species of two-leggeds (humans), the messages, the spirit, *the energy of our great teachers is calling to be lived out into the world through our own bodies and our own experience,* through you as well as through me. I call my work EMBODYING SPIRIT, in honor of this understanding.

In thinking about this, I want to share with you a song I wrote some time ago with one of my spiritual benefactors:

❤ THE RETURNING ❤
White Buffalo Calf Pipe Woman is a day woman,
a day woman,
a woman of Light.
Her Lightness makes her white,
shows her white,
crystal bright.
We want her here,
we call her here,
White Buffalo Calf Pipe Woman
Buffalo Woman of Light.

Through my heart she comes;
she comes
in soft white glow,

she shines out
through my heart,
Buffalo heart,
Buffalo Hat,
Sacred Tipi.
White Buffalo Calf Pipe Woman
is returning through me.

This song speaks to that very experience—of embodying the energies of the great teachings, which is not only mine but many others' as well. Within the last two years, I have had women of every race and walk of life come to me saying, "There has been a woman in my dreams, a beautiful native woman walking beside a white buffalo, who seems to be calling me. This is puzzling, because I don't know what this image means. Yet I sense it is a very important message. Can you help me understand?" And thus it is that White Buffalo Woman comes singing into our present experience.

So that you might know and understand her song more deeply, let me briefly share her story. For more depth, read Joseph Eppes Brown's *The Sacred Pipe,* in which he shares the account from Black Elk, the Lakota holy man, visionary, and leader who died in the early 1950s; or the beautiful artistic rendering of that same story in Vera Louise Drysdale's *The Gift of the Sacred Pipe.*

A long, long time ago our Lakota people—now popularly known as Sioux, a nation of Plains Indian tribes now living primarily on reservations in the Dakotas—lived settled, agrarian lives in the woodlands, and came out onto the Prairies to hunt buffalo. Two young men from a small hunting encampment were out scouting across the rolling hills covered with long, soft grasses waving in the breeze. They moved with focused awareness—on the lookout for game or the presence of other people, possibly enemies. Their practiced eyes swept the horizon. Suddenly they noticed, in the far distance, something moving. They stopped and looked more closely, aware that a strange aura seemed to surround whatever was there.

The mysterious figure was coming directly toward them, and as it approached, the two scouts could see that it was a two-legged (a human being), still surrounded by a bright and beautiful light. They watched in fascination as this person came closer, and soon perceived it to be a woman with long flowing hair, who carried a bundle of some sort on her back.

The men in this archetypal story were two very different sorts. The first man looked upon her with lust. He saw that not only was she a woman, she was a beautiful woman. And not only was she a beautiful woman, she was alone and undefended. He went toward her with intent to take advantage of her. And this mysteriously radiant woman opened her arms and her shawl and drew him to her. The other young man simply watched and saw a mist swirl about and surround them, and after a while, when the prairie breezes blew away the mist, he saw the woman open her arms. What fell from them were his companion's skull and bones. The bleached skeleton fell into the dirt—some even say that snakes crawled through it. The bones then crumbled into dust, and were scattered by the winds. Thus was his selfish intention broken apart and dispelled.

The second young man, the kind of person my people call a true warrior, looked with awe upon this beautiful, mysterious woman and her powers. As with all true warriors, his intent was not to harm or take for himself, but to serve All Our Relations, and the whole Circle of Life. Seeing her power and beauty, he wished to share her with his people. And so he spoke to her, saying, "Oh, woman of power and mystery, will you come and teach my people?"

"Yes," she replied to the good man. "Go before me to prepare a lodge [tipi], and I will come."

And he did this, gathering the people of his camp in an enormous lodge made of the skins of many tipis. So she came among them, revealing from her bundle the catlinite pipe with a long wooden stem, *whose high purpose is use in sacred rites to bring about a reunion with all things in the Circle of Life—a re-membering of ourselves as one with all things, with All Our Relations.*

Holding the stem of the pipe toward the heavens, she said, "With this sacred pipe you will walk upon the Earth; for the Earth is your Grandmother and Mother, and She is sacred. Every step that is taken upon Her should be as a prayer. The bowl of this pipe is of red stone; it is the Earth. Carved in the stone bowl and facing the center is this buffalo calf who represents all the four-leggeds who live upon your Mother. The stem of the pipe is of wood, and this represents all that grows upon the Earth. And these twelve feathers, which hang here where the stem fits into the bowl, are from *Wanbli Galeshka,* the Spotted Eagle, and they represent the eagle and all the wingeds of the air. All these peoples, all the things of the universe, are joined to you who smoke the pipe. All send their voices to *Wakan Tanka,* the Great Spirit. When you pray with this pipe, you pray for and with everything."

This version of the story comes from Black Elk's account in *The Sacred Pipe,* recorded by Joseph Eppes Brown.

White Buffalo Woman reminded the people then, and reminds us today, of the intricate web of life of which we are a part, and that our honoring of the holiness—the wholeness—of that web is the only way we will be able to move through this crucial time into a new era of harmony, beauty, and abundance. Her words spoke of each thing and each day as holy, and thus to be treated by us as such. Creator's law of oneness, given us when the world was formed, is that *we must be in good relationship with all things and all beings—with All Our Relations.*

The phrase, "All Our Relations," is used to represent the full Circle of Sacred Life, of which we are a part. This sacred circle includes not only two-legged relatives of all colors and persuasions, but also all the peoples with four legs, those with wings and fins, the green standing (tree and plant) people, the mineral and stone people, those that live within and crawl upon the Earth, those in the starry realms, and those ancestors who have gone beyond, as well as those children of generations to come. Everything, both known and unknown, is included in this phrase of wholeness and holiness. The corollary to creator's law, brought by this mysterious holy woman, is that *whatever we do to any other thing in the great web of life, we do to ourselves, for we are one.*

When she left the people and walked out over the prairie, one of her final acts in the far distance was to roll in a buffalo wallow—a hollowed-out place in the ground, made by buffalo rolling. When the dust cleared and she ran off again across the prairie, the people saw that she had become a white buffalo calf. Thus, those Lakota named this mysterious holy woman, "White Buffalo Calf Pipe Woman." And she continued to communicate with them through visions she sent—visions that guided and gifted them with new and powerful rituals for living in harmony. She is to us Elder Sister, who first appeared a very long time ago, calling us to live a life of deep ecology upon Mother Earth, for ourselves and the generations of children who follow us. It is obvious that she continues to send visions to us in this modern time. The critical nature of the issues we two-leggeds have brought upon Earth call White Buffalo Woman to speak now with special urgency to people of all colors and religions, to awaken truth and harmony within us all.

I, as many others, have heard within myself and my visions the pulsing rhythm of her song, its truthfulness and beauty. I have answered that call through my own continuous learning and transformation, and through sharing those understandings I have reached with others who have, in turn, called out to me. My story, and your story if you so choose, is one tiny part of the unfolding of White Buffalo Calf Pipe Woman's story, a small yet significant part of our coming into oneness with All Our Relations.

This song came to me as a part of that learning and sharing:

> Buffalo Woman is calling. Will you answer her?
> Buffalo Woman is calling. Will you answer her?
> She's calling light; she's calling peace.
> She's calling Spirit; she's calling you.
> Buffalo Woman is calling. Will you answer her?
>
> Buffalo Woman is calling. Will you answer her?
> Buffalo Woman is calling. Will you answer her?
> She's calling light; she's calling peace.
> She's calling Spirit; she's calling you.
> Buffalo Woman is calling. I will answer her!
> We will answer her!

I have been answering her in my own way, and you will answer her in yours. This book is a sharing of part of my quest to embody these teachings and share them with others. A primary note in the song of all my questing has been a search for the ancient truths that ring down through time to form a foundation for present and future truths, from wherever these might come. I am drawn more intensely to the truly old ways of my native people than to the teachings of many modern elders who have been deeply influenced from childhood by outside cultures, foreign religions, and values. I am more interested in the spirit of ancient *living* tradition rather than in the set forms and structures of any one period. What you will find here may be more real than romantic, more experience than ideal; more universal than Native American. And yet, through it all, I hope the ancient truths I have found will speak.

Although my racial background contains Native American blood of several tribes through both my mother and father, and I am on the official tribal rolls of the Crow people—the registry of all those who belong to a given tribe—I am a mixed blood, a *métis* (a French word for *half*); thus, in common terms, I am a half-breed. This has been both a challenge and a gift, making it less than comfortable in either world, and yet creating within me the metaphor of the rainbow bridge, which has become my outward teaching. Spiritual elders have indicated to me that I will never have a traditional form—*that mine will be a formless form that breaks through form into Spirit.*

As is respectful among Native peoples, the names of people, sacred places, articles, and lineages have been purposely fogged to protect those concerned. After all, the specific people and location of the stories are not so important as the lessons learned through our interaction— lessons that, hopefully, will stimulate your awareness of the great songs of truth wanting to sing out through you.

My continuing prayer for you and for All My Relations is that we will listen to White Buffalo Woman as she comes singing a holy song among us, and that we learn to live her truths through our lives for the benefit of All Our Relations.

Ho!

Brooke Medicine Eagle
Sky Lodge, Montana
Time of the Colored
Leaves Falling, 1991

INTRODUCTION

In our present time of ecological and social crisis, all of humanity is looking for new ways to move forward, ways that will solve current problems without creating new ones (as we have in the past with gasoline engines and other technological "advances"). One place it has been obvious to turn is the native peoples of our lands, whose ancient ways reveal a deep ecology that is at once both physical and spiritual, even though their practice is varied in the hundreds of tribes on this continent. *These ancient teachings call us to turn primary attention to the Sacred Web of Life,* of which we are a part and with which we are so obviously entangled.

This quality of attention—paying attention to the whole—is called among my people "holiness." Holiness is never understood to be focusing attention on a white-bearded old man figure as God, or on any specific spiritual figure, but rather enlarging our awareness to consciously include and respectfully consider All That Is, All Our Relations—all beings, energies, and things in the larger Circle of Life.

This sacred focus on holiness as an integral part of everyday life is central to Native American teachings, and is of great value to us today. White Buffalo Calf Pipe Woman, the mystical woman who came long, long ago to bring the sacred pipe as a symbol and reminder of the holiness, stands today as a central figure in the spiritual way of the Lakota Sioux and many other native tribes. The symbolism of the two men in the story of White Buffalo Woman told in the Prologue, as well as her pipe and teachings, are clear metaphors about how we are to approach life on Mother Earth if we two-leggeds—we humans—are to make it through this next century and create a new way of being on Earth that will open us to our full human-ness.

Central to White Buffalo Woman's message, and to all native spirituality, is also the understanding that the Great Spirit lives in all things, enlivens all forms, and gives energy to all things in all realms of creation—including Earthly life. Several things follow from this understanding:

▶ *We, and all things in the web of life, are related.* We are not only children of our Mother Earth, but also of our Father, the Great Spirit. And thus we are all each other's brothers and sisters.

▶ *Primary to our beingness, and to our relationships in the larger hoop, is the feminine energy of nurturing and renewing*—of ourselves, each other, and all those peoples in our Sacred Circle of Life, especially the children.

▶ *Each of us has Spirit within us to develop and bring forward.* Each thing and being contains Spirit's living flame—consciousness and aliveness—and thus has the right to be respected and honored for its unique power and gift.

▶ *Through each of us Spirit can speak, and thus guide us and our people.*

▶ *Each of us is a small, yet significant part of the wholeness and at the same time contains the wholeness.* As in a hologram, where each piece contains the whole picture yet the picture becomes clearer as more and more pieces are joined together, so our harmony, unity, and cooperation with All Our Relations are necessary for the full picture of life to be revealed. It is only through this harmony that we will be able to move forward.

▶ *Our participation with the Great Creator in the continuing unfoldment of life is essential.* Thus, renewal dances, such as the Corn Dance among the Pueblo peoples of the Southwest, and the Sun Dance among the Plains peoples; the harvest dances and honoring dances of other peoples in the Circle of Life, such as animal dances; plus all the other ceremonies honoring the cycles of the seasons and of life, are both our duty and our joy. These rituals focus participants toward the unfolding unity that can create life anew.

Interestingly enough, the various native tribes or groups practiced these principles within their own group and with Mother Nature, yet they seldom extended this practice to other groups or tribes. A unified dance of all people, a rainbow dance of creation, did not occur to them. This is why the sacred dream of the Lakota visionary, Black Elk, was so important. When he was only nine years old, in the late 1800s, he had a vision of all races and colors dancing together to renew the Tree of Life. (This story is told in *Black Elk Speaks* by John Neihardt.) He was so uncomfortable with what had been revealed to him that he did not even speak of it until later in his life when urged to do so by an elder. Yet Black Elk's vision of a universal, global dance of creation and celebration that will be *required* in order for life to continue is absolutely vital to us all in this present day. In fact, *we must not only renew the dances of creation, we must also extend them to include All Our Relations.* This is the task before us, and it cannot be completed until we all join in a joyful dance of life.

In our process of transforming and healing ourselves and the world in the present, it seems important that we understand something of our place in North American history. We need to know where we are and who we are being called to be, whether or not we are Native American. Let us first look at one of the structures used by many early native peoples as they attempted to create a peaceful and harmonious life.

From the earliest times, our native people have had councils—often comprised of all males or all females—each holding a powerful focus of energy for the people. In many tribes, the men had an impressive war council—but they also had a peace council as well. During the latter years of the fighting between Indians and whites in the late 1800s, the finest of our Native prophets began to receive information from Spirit. They were told that their people must make peace and eventually come into spiritual unity with the oppressors, in order for anyone—most especially their own children of coming generations—to have a good life, and for the Tree of Life to blossom again for all.

At that time, the war councils and warrior societies, which were devoted to conflict and did not serve the people, essentially became obsolete. Our world was changing rapidly. The intention of Peace was set within the deep spirit of the Americas, and yet our struggle since then has been to make it real in our daily lives. The great prophets from time immemorial spoke to our people of returning to the oneness—the brother/sisterhood that was modeled on this continent at the time of the great Sun centers in the South, when the Dawn Star walked among the people (see chapter 7). But for the most part, our Native people, as well as those from across the waters, engaged in divisiveness, warring, and separation, and in conflict over territory. Thus Indian and white alike were joined in a karmic endeavor to complete the warring and return finally to oneness and peace.

To give an example, in his classic work, *The Cheyennes,* E. Adamson Hoebel speaks about the Cheyenne tribal council of peace chiefs. He explains:

> The keystone of the Cheyenne social structure is the tribal council of forty-four peace chiefs. War may be a major concern of the Cheyennes, and defense against the hostile Crow and Pawnee a major problem of survival, yet clearly the Cheyennes sense that a more fundamental problem is the danger of disintegration through internal dissension and aggressive impulses of Cheyenne against Cheyenne. Hence, the supreme authority of the tribe lies not in the hands of the aggressive war leaders but in the control of the even-tempered peace chiefs, all proven warriors.

Yet this peace council of male elders eventually failed to control the Bow Society, the warriors who wanted to go to war indiscriminately, without consulting their spiritual sources or the council of elders. In the subsequent fighting with other Indian tribes, a third of all the warriors and most of the chiefs on both sides were killed. The Sacred Bundle of Arrows—the central sacred object of the tribe, representing masculine, procreative power—was lost to the Cheyennes. Other serious physical and spiritual calamities befell them as well, all of which clearly pointed out the danger of indiscriminate warring, when what actually should have been happening was the making of peace and the nurturing of the people. Because of all this, the male Cheyenne peace council eventually lost its power and function.

The message here is the primacy that the pursuit of peace and holiness must have in the minds, hearts, and actions of the people. In days of old, this concern extended only to those within the tribe. Now we have matured into a new time of understanding: we realize that peace and harmony must be generated not only within the entire family of two-leggeds but within the full Circle of Life as well.

In the time since the degeneration of the male councils, the female elders, whom we might call spiritual Grandmothers, have stepped forward in spirit with intention as peace councils. Their actions have not been so public. Rather, they centered their spiritual work in small quiet groups or "hoops," circles of women who have come together with intention to nurture and protect. Their functions have included:

▶ Holding all peoples together in their hoops of Oneness.

▶ Weaving their spider-web tapestries of peace among the peoples.

▶ Encouraging use of the plant medicines that help us create patterns of harmony within ourselves.

▶ Struggling over marriage baskets whose power is the melding of the poles within us, whether male/female, left/right, or Indian/white.

▶ Creating shielding hoops of women in a world circle devoted to prayer for all peoples.

These Grandmothers have taken the banner of peace and woven its spirit into reality on hundreds of looms. In modern times they have stimulated the creation of books and other media to awaken all peoples to their golden destiny as family upon Mother Earth under Father Sun. They have echoed into the spirit of our time, the song of oneness sung for us by White Buffalo Calf Pipe Woman as she gifted the Lakota—and others who learn from them—with her pipe of peace. *The spirits of the Grandmothers have been strong, moving through time and space to touch the spirit of anyone in our time who has been ready to carry the banner, to continue the weaving, to speak the unity. They have touched Native, half-breed, and white alike with their haunting call.* Now the living Grandmothers of holy stature are few, and those of us who hear their call must answer.

It is now time for me and for you, whatever our race, color, or background, to learn this song of unity and to sing it out—time for us to carry it forward in beauty another seven generations to touch *all* the children of our Mother Earth and Father Spirit. A traditional song, created from White Buffalo Woman's words, says,

> *With visible breath, I am walking.*
> *With visible breath, I am walking.*

I sense that this is her way of saying that she is walking through her life with the smoke of the sacred pipe being sent out with every breath. This smoke represents our prayers and respect for everything in the Circle of Life. We must do this, not by getting caught in the romanticism—"the beads and feathers of the paraphernalia path"—but rather by living these values in our everyday lives.

Buffalo Woman Comes Singing is a sharing of stories from my own quest to make these teachings real in my life—to embody spirit and holiness in my work and in my personal experience. Although these values and ways did not always surround me, even in childhood, I have always carried a deep and quiet trust that they might live again. It is my sense that my stories may parallel your experience and so let you know you have a compatriot in your own quest—or even more positively perhaps, someone to help create a useful map for parts of your journey that you have not yet walked into reality.

May these words serve you and All My Relations.

PART ONE

RECLAIMING THE

LINEAGE

Grounding myself in the roots of my native background—after having been taken away from them in adolescence—has been one of the most powerful aspects of my spiritual quest. I had been actively seeking spiritual teaching and guidance since my youth, yet I had not found anything to satisfy me as I approached my late twenties. In these beginning chapters, I share with you my seeking of a medicine teacher, and finding one; my seeking of life's direction, and being set firmly upon the path.

CHAPTER ONE

THE WOMAN WHO KNOWS
EVERYTHING

Grandma gave me, even more than a personal relationship with her,

a relationship with the power she served:

the Sacred Bundle of the Lodge and its feminine nurturing and

renewing power.

Her people called her The Woman Who Knows Everything; I
guess that's why my dad advised me to come home to the reservation
area in Montana to talk with "this little old lady" when I asked him
questions about his experience of some of the spiritual practices of our
Apsa Indian people. The whole thing was odd to begin with, first of all
because I had not really been around Dad for twenty long years, not
since my folks divorced and we left our home ranch. Secondly, I had just
moved to San Francisco into a new flat with a new telephone number
that almost no one had. And still my dad called to chew me out for not
staying in touch! Spirit was already moving in mysterious ways, yet I had
no idea what lay in store for me in the northern mountains of my home
reservation country.

I was in my late twenties at the time, and in the full power of my
first Saturn return—a twenty-eight-year astrological cycle said to be a
powerful and challenging time to make the first transition into full
adulthood or other life changes. Having just cut myself free from years
of working as a teacher, counselor, and administrator in the academic
world, I had come to California to take the next step in my life—
opening to new experiences and possibilities, both within and outside
myself.

My academic career had not given me the opportunity to facilitate
the kind of healing and transformation I desired for my students. In fact,
it felt as though all the rigid rules actually blocked such things from
happening. It seemed I had always been a teacher, having for short

periods taught every level from first grade to college. Yet, somehow, it was always rote, always a dead form instead of truly living education. There just had to be something more, both for myself and for those I served!

So I headed for the West Coast where things were popping and crackling with an awakening consciousness; and now here I was, in the early seventies, enrolled in one of the newly formed and very open humanistic doctoral programs. Although I had been awarded a scholarship to attend Stanford University's prestigious clinical psychology program, I had turned it down because they required that new doctoral candidates work on someone else's project for two years before getting started on their own. This was absolutely horrifying to me, for although I hoped to gain good credentials, what was first on my list was an intense desire to get on with finding out who I was and what I personally could offer the world! So I chose a new and untried program where my own experience was the major factor. And that's where I was when my dad called—newly set up in a Noe Valley flat with a hippie boyfriend known as Lucky.

For years of my life, I had longed for a personal "Medicine" teacher, someone highly developed spiritually, who would help me develop my sacred uniqueness and gifts; someone who would teach me magic, who would help me develop the healer I had always known was there inside me. My sense is that each of us yearns for an elder who will focus personal attention on our special gifts and challenges because our current educational system of teaching has none of this. We all know the need within us for this kind of devoted attention from someone wise and loving, most especially someone who will pay attention to our spirit and its development. In times past, this would have been a grandparent, an aunt or uncle, a neighboring godparent, perhaps a tribal shaman. However, with the new mobility of the fifties, which led to the separation of extended families, very few of us had this cohesiveness.

Certainly, at the time of my childhood on the reservation, much of the Native culture and spirit had already been shattered. Although a few families held strongly to the old ways, many were torn by the shift to a radically new milieu in which alcohol seemed to stand out and beckon as a solution to the dissolution. This was also nearly three decades before the Indian Freedom of Religion Act was passed by Congress in 1978, when many of our spiritual and ceremonial ways were still actually illegal. The Act at long last re-established the right of Native people to practice their religion—practices that had been made a federal offense in the late nineteenth century in order to suppress the culture and way of life of a conquered people—something totally antithetical to our

Constitution. Had the old ways been functioning fully and available in my growing-up years, it is clear to me that I would have been chosen for my path when I was five years old and my already blossoming spirit would have been trained. But no one saw. And a little renegade girl, raised in the hills far even from the Apsa reservation village, slipped between the cracks.

I was left, however, with the beauty of Spirit's aliveness in Mother Earth. It was all around me on the chokecherry-lined creeks running north out of the reservation's Pryor Mountains, where my Nez Percé grandfather had created big ranches over several decades. When my older brother Tom, my only sibling, and I were not working on our parents' self-sufficient ranch, we were running the nearby hills in search of the sweet wild strawberries, and riding our ponies into the aspen groves above the ranch looking for fat blue-black gooseberries along the spring-fed streams. I would lie for hours in ancient buffalo wallows where cool spring breezes blew above me, and the warming sun fed my body and soul. Around me were fields of crimson shooting-star blossoms, their exquisite fragrance wafting to me on the breeze. And in nearby marshy ponds, blackbirds kept up a constant chorus. I told my mom once, "Heaven is just like this, except that the animals are not afraid of us." I've come many miles and years since then, and that child-envisioned heaven is still what I long for and pursue.

In my first free year after leaving my professional job in Minnesota, I studied and played in the fading bouquet of San Francisco's flower-child days. Janis Joplin was gone, Vietnam had released our young men, and Carlos Castaneda's stories of plant medicines and magic in the Sonoran desert were on everyone's mind. And certainly the old medicine woman up north was on my mind, for my spirit had longed since my early childhood for a wise elder to guide and teach me. Dad had invited me up for the next summer, and I'd made plans to be there on quarter break. I was excited and yet a bit nervous, since I had not seen Dad in so many years. Nor had I met my stepmom and my new relatives, members of the neighboring Shinela tribe on whose adjacent reservation they now lived. I looked forward to seeing them, and yet, my focus of attention was on the Woman Who Knows Everything.

As soon as I arrived in Lone Deer, my stepmom, Ella Jay (also called E.J.), began preparations for me to meet "Grandma Rosie." Ella Jay was a tall, smiling woman with a deep and beautiful spirit. She was thrilled to have me in her family, happy for Dad that I was here, and joyous about my spiritual intentions. The old medicine woman was Ella Jay's aunt, and yet in the traditional way, she was called Grandma, so she became Grandma Rosie to me as well. Our first meeting was to be a dinner at our house, and Ella Jay was preparing the meal. Ella Jay's daughter Heta (which means Loving Child in Shinela) and I were sent off to get Grandma from her relatives' place.

I nervously knocked on the door of the trailer house, which was opened by some young people with a slightly hostile attitude toward this blue-eyed, half-breed stranger from their old enemy nation who was picking up Grandma. The Apsa and the Shinela had lived close to each other, vying for the richest buffalo country in the world, for many decades. The Shinelas had been allied with other Indian nations, all of whom then attempted to take away the exquisitely beautiful mountain area of Montana, the home country of the tiny Apsa tribe. These allied nations had never conquered the fierce Apsa, yet every family on both sides remembered very clearly those of their ancestry who had been killed in the mutual fighting. Those old animosities were fueled anew when the U.S. Government placed the Apsa and Shinela on adjacent reservations—and I was facing them now.

Grandma Rosie came hobbling toward me across the small room, a bent and wrinkled woman in a traditional flowered calico dress that hung loose on her slight frame. She walked with a cane to help her crippled leg; her blind eye was white and the other one misty as she looked up at me, turning her head in a birdlike fashion from her bent position. But at eighty-five years old she still had her raven black hair, liberally sprinkled with white. Because I had been told that she did not speak English, and was very hard of hearing besides, I simply reached out my arm to give her support. Her frail arm rested on mine, and down the steps we went. Her summer moccasins, made of white canvaslike, tennis-shoe material rather than of leather, padded softly beside me. The journey—which still unfolds before me in beauty—had truly begun!

We did not speak on the way back to the house. I wanted to study her out of the corner of my eye, yet out of respect I kept my eyes on the road. Anxious thoughts raced wildly through my mind about how I would possibly be able to learn from this person whose language I did not speak, and whether she knew everything going on in my tumbling mind, and if there would be time enough in my very limited days to touch her magic—forgetting that the essence of magic is that it requires no time. I helped her up the steps to where Ella Jay was waiting. When we were all inside, my formal introduction to the Woman Who Knows Everything began.

I was so startled I almost jumped as Ella Jay cupped her hands and literally SHOUTED into Grandma's ear in her native tongue, telling her who I was, about my wanting to receive blessing and learning—all the while gesturing toward me. As Grandma Rosie nodded and Ella Jay shouted, I had a terrible sinking feeling that I would never be able to communicate with this wise old woman.

"Ahhhhhhhhhhhhhhhhhh," Grandma crooned, acknowledging the introduction in an incredibly long glissade. When the shouting was finished, Grandma carefully laid her cane aside, slowly reached to shake my right hand with hers, and gently grasped my forearm with her left hand. The touch of this frail and bent little woman was amazingly soft and warm, and yet some deep part of me knew she had the strength within her to move mountains!

Then all thoughts were swept from my mind in amazement, as this tiny, frail, wizened woman began to shine with golden light and un-folded out of herself into a radiant woman of light towering above me, pouring golden rays of love and wisdom upon and through me. All else in my surroundings fell away as I looked up into the face of an angelic presence, awed by the beauty and stunning transformation. Moments of such grace have no time, and I bathed in that light until I was filled. Then the light began to fade, she began to fold into herself again, and soon my eyes perceived again the outer form I would grow to know so well. She released my hand and arm, picked up her cane, and walked to the dinner table. I recall looking sideways at my dad with a *"some* little old lady!!" look on my face as I joined them at the table. He had gifted me with a priceless and life-altering presence, and my communication with the Woman Who Knows Everything had begun.

As we sat down, Grandma Rosie prayed over our meal for ten minutes with words I could not understand. Once again I tasted the frustration I would continue to experience in our daily contact. Only twice in my presence did she ever break her vow never to speak English, for I found out many years later that she did know English. She had taken this vow after being forced into a white school as a child, and beaten for speaking her own tongue. On her death bed she spoke to me in English, and before that on a somewhat humorous occasion when she was quite frightened. This occurred several years after I first met her, while I was driving her back from her relatives in Lone Deer to her own home in the nearby village of Benney.

The old, narrow road wound up a valley and over high open meadows surrounded by towering evergreen trees; then it fell, winding down into another valley and out onto the open plain along a cotton-wood-lined river. Just as we dropped over the far side into the sharp, blind curves, an enormous logging truck rushed at us, then roared past—its size, speed, and the wind it created around it almost pushing us off the road. Grandma Rosie's eyes got as big as saucers, and she blurted out, "Big truck!" Then, very embarrassed, she did not speak again.

Off and on for many years, Grandma had been the keeper of the most powerful Sacred Lodge among her northern people, a Buffalo Spirit Lodge. It consists, in essence, of a tipi surrounding a bundle containing the buffalo relic that represents the nurturing and renewing power of the feminine, one of the most revered sacred articles of this tribe. It is much like the Sacred Arrow Bundle, representing the male procreative power, held by a southern group. In olden times these Lodges were held jointly, and so a balanced power was available to the people in times of need. Such Lodges and their bundles of sacred objects can perhaps be likened to the altar of a church, where people go to pray and gain spiritual blessing. A similar bundle might be held by a tribe, a clan, or an individual, often having come to them through spiritual questing. Such bundles are held and used as a continuing form of guidance and blessing.

Traditionally, such Lodges and their Sacred Bundles were kept by a man and wife. But in this case, no couple had been able to meet the standards for very long in the years since Rosie's husband had died. The ideal was for this couple to measure up to very high standards, both in their understanding of the sacred object and its use to benefit the people, and also in their exemplary conduct as models for the tribe. It would have been likely that this couple would have been younger and stronger than Grandma Rosie, so that she would have had an honorary rather than everyday working connection with the bundle.

Yet, the federal government's purposeful breakup of the culture—or breakdown, as it might be more aptly called—occurred at every level of tribal life. Held captive on small reservations, men accustomed to lives as nomadic hunters, warriors, and shamans no longer had roles to play. Instead of a natural, healthful diet of gathered plants, and hunted meat, and herbal medicines to feed and nurture their families, the women were rationed white flour, sugar, coffee, beef, and perhaps beans—if they were lucky.

All their religious practices were outlawed. Whiskey and smallpox-infested blankets were issued to the people by the conquering oppressors. These actions were a means to genocide. And to add insult to injury, the agents assigned to care for the people were often corrupt and mean-spirited, selling the people's supplies for their own profit. Extended families were broken up first by keeping the people in small, separate groups with no interaction allowed and, second, by forcibly taking the young away from their families to be taught in missionary boarding schools where they were often treated like dumb, superstitious animals. Most of the younger elders now of eligible age and wisdom to act as keeper of a Sacred Bundle were those who were taken away to white schools as young children, indoctrinated in a new religion, and taught that the old ways were superstition and foolishness, then sent off with shortened hair into the competitive, material-first world to raise and feed their families. Few had even been around the Sacred Lodges— beyond the occasional emergency situation when prayer was desperately needed—let alone spent the days and years of devotion to its service that would prepare them for its keeping. And even fewer had the necessary interest for such full-time service to the people. Being Lodge keepers not only required them to be exemplars of traditional values, it also meant rising at dawn to open and smudge the Sacred Bundle with cleansing herbal incenses like sage, sweet grass, or cedar (see pages 29–30 and pages 49–50). Then it was necessary to be available all day, every day, for those coming to be blessed in its presence; to carefully put the bundle away in the twilight hours; and to guard it through the night. Grandma, old and frail though she was, still received the bundle back into her keeping again and again, when others failed at the task through lack of knowledge and dedication, or through behavior unworthy of the keeper of a sacred lodge.

Although Grandma Rosie and I had continuing contact from the very beginning of our acquaintance, what she gave me, even more than a personal relationship with her, was a relationship with the power she served—the Sacred Bundle of the Lodge and its feminine nurturing and renewing power. And this was very difficult for her because, although I was related to her through marriage, I was still a member of a tribe of traditional enemies with whom her people had fought for generations.

She had very likely had a similar experience to mine at that numinous moment of our first meeting and so knew deeply my spirit, and my intention to heal and serve. And yet Grandma Rosie found it hard in her daily life to share her knowledge with this young "enemy woman." This amazing elder had been for all the years of her life a shining light to her own people. In her younger days, she had been a strapping, big-boned woman who was a healer, teacher, and spiritual leader among her people. The dimming of her bright eyes, the stoop and frailty of her body did not lessen the light she shed upon the Shinela. Yet her medicine was only for her own people. She had no sense of the "rainbow medicine" that is now awakening us to our oneness with all the two-legged family. Like Black Elk, when given the vision of all peoples dancing together, she could not find this in her experience. The under-standing of what I call rainbow medicine was not yet alive in the spirits of the people.

This rainbow medicine way teaches that, in order to step across the gap that lies between this age and a new age of harmony and abundance, we must make a bridge, and that bridge must be made of light. In order for the light to become a rainbow powerful enough to arch across the chasm, it must contain all colors—all peoples, all nations, all things. If any one color is left out, it will not have the strength to become the arching rainbow bridge upon which all of us will walk into a new time. This, in essence, is the same teaching given us by White Buffalo Calf Pipe Woman: the teaching of oneness, of unity, cooperation, and har-mony. Living this new way into reality seems to be the challenge of those of my generation, rather than of Grandmother's. And so, her best course was to turn me over to Spirit, to the Sacred Bundle, to the higher power. There the truth would out.

Letting the Spirit be the judge was a traditional practice of Native people in the distant past. If someone from outside their clan or tribe came to them seeking spiritual knowledge, they knew that they had no right to judge this person or their spiritual intent. That was for Spirit to decide.

They also knew that Spirit needs no police: The truth of what is in the person's heart will eventually show itself, and the Circle of Life will serve them what they have coming. If these seekers come with a good heart, clear mind, and deep intention—if they come taking care of themselves and helping others—then Spirit will be moved through the sacred forms to bless them and encourage them no matter what their outward appear-ance. Then, the tribe can follow suit. However, if they come with a bad heart, a deceiving mind, and an intention to destroy—taking rather than giving, serving only themselves—then they will receive in like manner from Spirit. The people will not need to stop them or deter them ahead of time. The old ones trusted Spirit's ability to deal with such things and were glad to have it that way.

Nowadays, due to the breakdown of the traditional culture and its spiritual values—as well as to the overwhelming intrusion of outsiders into their lives at all levels—many Native people have come not to trust Spirit's ability in such matters. They feel that they themselves must police the sacred ways. This is a very pompous and burdensome place to put oneself—unless, of course, one has an impeccable spirit, an open heart, and an absolutely unfailing perception of the deeper spiritual intentions beyond a seeker's surface. In my experience, few if any have those credentials.

One of the most powerful aspects of Native spirituality in its myriad forms among many different tribes is that it is a mystical tradition, rather than a priestly one. Let me explain the difference as I see it.

In a priestly tradition there is a human lineage down through which the teachings and powers are passed. Perhaps it began with one especially enlightened being, and it has come down through time via the spoken or written word. Lineage holders are acknowledged by certain initiations such as the laying on of hands. This kind of religion has a priesthood of men and/or women, and these special ones are the spiritual teachers and authorities. Often in this kind of religion, a common person must come to the priests or priestesses for intercession with God, or the gods. They are told they cannot communicate directly, or receive directly from Spirit. Often, the enlightened one at the beginning of the lineage has spoken or written of the way. Over time, this becomes the given word. Anyone presuming to communicate with Spirit thereafter is often seen as an imposter.

Mystical religion, on the other hand, understands that the Great Spirit lives within each and every thing, Earthly or otherwise, and so teaches that communication with Great Spirit/Source/God is a completely natural part of all beings. Those who are especially trained or experienced in spiritual matters can provide a roadmap or a model of what has worked for them—and has perhaps worked for others seeking communion with the Great Spirit. They become like elder brothers or sisters on the path. They can guide and assist others, yet would never presume to require another person to go through them to reach Spirit. Their calling is to assist, rather than to intercede. Their intent is empowerment, not disempowerment.

The mystical peoples realize that God speaks to each of us, if we will but listen; and that, in fact, God often speaks through one of us to all other people. Thus, the "Bible" is continually being written. It is a living, growing revelation; it is not a closed book. For example, the old-time Lakotas listened to the vision of Black Elk, which he received when he was only nine years old, and literally danced it into their mythology—their ever-growing "Bible." It was a revelation not only for them, but for people of all races upon Mother's breast. Rather than being excluded by a structured and "complete" past, this new vision was honored and made a part of the vital, living tradition.

Since Black Elk's time, though, several things have happened to profoundly influence our native spiritual ways. The first is that there are always natural human tendencies at work that want to formalize things, to get final answers, and to gain power by having exclusive access to these "final answers."

The second influence is that our Native American people were defeated in a war that was almost a genocide, and their spiritual ways were forbidden them by the conquerors. Since our Northern Plains people were forbidden purification (sweat) lodges, vision quests, and sun dances—all of which were means of touching the Great Mystery—fewer and fewer were able to touch into vision. Because of this, only a tiny portion of the people remained strong in their old ways through clandestine practices in the far back country of the reservations, away from the government agencies. When the living tradition of mystical revelation was broken, the most natural thing in that situation was to hold tenaciously to what had already been given. Those elders who had the strength of spirit to carry the knowledge and to practice the old ways eventually became more and more like a priesthood.

The third crucial influence on Native spirituality is that there are only rare individuals among the elders of our time who were not uprooted and taken away from their ancient spiritual ways, and who were not beaten for speaking their language or for daring even to speak of their former culture or spirituality. In addition, in the mission-run schools, the Native children were indoctrinated into priestly religions—largely Catholic, but other European religions as well.

I remember one Hopi couple speaking to me of their own personal challenges with this. The wife was raised in a Catholic missionary school and indoctrinated with the idea that the old Hopi ways were superstitious at best, and the ways of the Devil at worst. This had made her both fearful and disdainful of the ancient ways. Her husband, on the other hand, somehow managed to escape that upbringing, and continued to be a strong practitioner of the old ceremonial life. When they fell in love and married, it took many years for them to resolve this deep conflict, and for her to become comfortable with the old ways, to understand them, and to come to know their deep beauty and purpose.

Although Grandma Rosie had also been taken away to missionary schools, she had likely already had some training in her people's spiritual ways. And when she was able to leave that schooling, she resolved to reintegrate herself into the Native ways—cultural, linguistic and spiritual. Also she obviously had the strength of spirit and intention to do just that. I'm sure that her heart longed for more young people of her tribe with whom to share her knowledge, yet she was able to share it with those from whatever race or background Spirit directed to her. Grandma's way was not to judge, or turn away, but to give that seeker over to Spirit through the Sacred Lodge. Thus, she chose to open every opportunity possible for Spirit to speak to and through that seeker, in service of All Her Relations. And this she did for me.

ABOUT THE EXERCISES

These exercises I offer you in each chapter are an opportunity for you to deepen my story by making it yours as well. You may wish to create a special journal or notebook in which to keep your work on the exercises.

To begin with, I want to acquaint you with the form I will frequently use. The first step we take in any of our learning is a step of awareness, of focusing attention on what is true for us now without judgment or denial. Too often we want to jump ahead to something considered more ideal. And yet we cannot reach that new place because we do not know where we are standing right now, what influences have formed our experience, or what powerful beliefs we hold that have brought us to exactly where we are.

Taking this inventory is of utmost importance because it is clear to me that these beliefs, attitudes, and influences determine most of our experience. If we attempt to learn by turning outward, before we establish where we are within, we deny ourselves the firm ground upon which to build the rainbow bridge of transformation. All changes begin within us and proceed outward: we do, in fact, create our own reality.

Once we take our inventory we have a better idea of who, what, and where we are now, and what we actually want to be different in our lives. Once we reach this point, it is time to create a dream, an image, a feeling, a vision that we can project clearly into our future without reservation or fear. **The least reservation or fear will stop the mechanism of creation, so we must find ways to clear hesitations of any kind.**

If we find ourselves unable to do this, perhaps we're not ready for what we thought we wanted, for this means we still have work to do in the area of our reservation or fear. However, if our reservations make sense upon examination, then perhaps all we need do is slightly alter our image so it more truly corresponds to our inner truth.

Not until this clearing is complete will it be time for us to take action on any other—especially outer—changes that need to be made. Once completed, though, the image or dream we hold in our hearts will have become so clear as to take on a very powerful reality. When we arrive at this point, getting what we're asking for cannot be very far off.

TAKING INVENTORY

In many of the exercises I offer, I will very likely ask you to go through the following steps in some form. Internalizing this method, which can be applied to any form of learning, is a powerful gift we can give ourselves, one that can move far beyond our work together in this book. These steps are:

1. Assess past history and present truth, without judgment or denial, of the internal beliefs, attitudes, and influences that have brought you to where you are.

2. Consider new possibilities, and put out a clear projection of what you want without reservations or fear.

3. Realize what changes must be made within you in order to invite and make real what you desire—especially how to clear up any reservations or fears.

4. Clear the reservations and create the changes, or accept the present situation with grace.

You might want to record your perceptions in your journal and/or you might want to talk them over with a trusted friend or a professional counselor. These exercises can take you very deeply into yourself. They will prove to be remarkably transforming—if you give them the time required to make them real for you. You will very likely run into areas where a great deal of personal growth work is stimulated. At such times you may want to reach out for help with your process. For many people, self-help groups and individual professional therapy can be of great benefit during such deep shape-shifting.

CREATING A SACRED SPACE

Before you begin the exercises, it is important to establish a safe and sacred space for yourself. It needs to be a place where you can close the door and have time in private to devote to your own inner process. Although it is beneficial to have one specific place where you can build the energy of your inner work, it is not necessary.

Whenever you take time to go inside for your processing, first establish your outer space. Decide where to be and how long you will be there. Let others in your environment know of your need for privacy and how long they must respect that "closed" door. Then find a comfortable place to sit, stand, and move in whatever way you wish.

Stand in the center of this space for a few moments, close your eyes, and concentrate on bringing full, deep, relaxed breaths all the way down into your belly, your center. Draw those breaths until you have left everything outside yourself behind, and can focus on your own experience and feelings. Then open your eyes, and using your right index finger, a feather, or a wand as a "pointer," draw a circle around the area that is to be your sacred space. Say, quietly but out loud, something like, "With this circle, I create for myself a safe and sacred space for the work I now wish to do. Only that which is beneficial and useful will enter this circle. Ho!" In this place, then, you can set about your work.

Each time you complete your sacred work, express your gratitude. Then, as though you're exiting through a door, step outside your sacred circle. Sweep your hand around the circle as before, this time "erasing" the circle. Know that you can open it again each time you need it. However, if you have a permanent altar and/or sacred place, you can simply close that energetic door, sealing the sacred circle and its energy until you come once again.

SMUDGING

Another simple ritual which can be used to prepare for inner work and for cleansing your own energy, that of others, a room, or area of open space, is smudging. You can use any of a variety of herbs for your smudge; sage and cedar are commonly used by many Native people (see Glossary for their specific properties). Sweet grass is another smudging herb. It is found in northern swamps, and retains a wonderful aroma when dried and braided. It is burned ritually to bring sweetness into one's life and surroundings. I often use it as a prayer, asking it to bring sweetness and beauty into the space I have cleared with sage. You may use sticks or braids of these plant incenses, which you can simply light and hold, or you can burn loose herbs in a container. Many modern people use an abalone shell as a container. My elders say the water element represented by the shell cancels out the energy of the fire, so it would be better to use a fired earthen pot. I use simple fired clay bowls—just be sure that the intense heat will not break them.

In some stores where incense is available, you can buy little round charcoal "bricks" that will start easily and stay lit so that your smudge will keep burning. It is best to light your smudge with a simple wooden match, representing fire as it was naturally given by Spirit—lightning struck trees and set them afire. Even if you use the stick form, it is best to carry a plate of some kind under the lighted smudge to catch the burning pieces that will likely fall from it.

To smudge yourself, set the lighted herb in front of you and use both hands—or a feather, if you prefer—to gather the smoke and bring it over yourself in a symbolic "washing." If you use an incense stick, you can simply move it over and around you. Each person finds a different way that feels right to them to do this ritual cleansing. I personally often use a movement that brings the smoke up the front of my body and down over my back, covering me fully. It is traditional to do this four times.

Begin alone, and find your own way—one that feels good and clearing to you. Then when you are with others who are smudging, drop your eyes and give them the private space to do it as they feel comfortable. Staring at such times is very impolite. Remember that you do not have to copy anyone—it is a question only of your feeling inside. To smudge others, you can simply hold the smudge out for them to pull over themselves, or you may use a feather to move it over them yourself.

For smudging a room or area, light the smudge and carry it all around. I often start in one particular place, frequently near a door, and go around the room working with the smudge as though gathering the old energy ahead of me and pushing it eventually out the door when I come full circle. If there is especially negative energy, I make sure to get into all the corners and stagnant areas. This same thing can be done energetically with an open area, if you sense a natural "door" into it.

However or wherever you use the smudge, get comfortable enough with the actual procedures so that you can focus your attention on the process of cleansing and keeping that intention clear. It is always powerful to add words of intention aloud.

CALLING YOUR TEACHERS

The story of this chapter tells of my meeting Grandma Rosie, who became a major teacher, guide, and spiritual influence in my life. Let us, then, deepen your personal experience of these learnings as they apply to you.

These exercises call for you to make a personal assessment—without judgment or denial—of your past and present experience of seeking for or having a major spiritual teacher in your life.

Step I: List the five most important spiritual lessons you have experienced so far.

▶ Were they created by a formal teacher outside yourself, or did you draw them to yourself directly?

▶ In the past, have you recognized a major teacher in your life? What did you learn? How was the teaching accomplished?

▶ What beliefs and attitudes do you carry about the teachers who have shaped your experience up to now, and might influence your having and interacting with a teacher in the future? For example, "I'm afraid a good teacher will see all my bad points and make me feel worse." Or, "I feel unworthy of a special teacher." Check in with yourself about fears you may have, lack of self-worth, negative attitudes toward authority figures, etc.

▶ List six truths you believe about teachers:

Teachers are _____

Teachers think _____

Teachers offer _____

Teachers deny _____

Teachers help me _____

Teachers bring _____

▶ What is your definition of a good teacher? Can they be from your own culture, or do you think another perspective is needed? Who do you expect your teacher to be—and what do you expect of this person?

I need a teacher because _____

I want my teacher to _____

I don't want my teacher to _____

I'm afraid my teacher will _____

My ideal teacher is someone who _____

Step II: Teachers sometimes model what *not* to do, rather than offering help in the way we think they should. Notice how much you learn from watching others attempt to live their lives in ways that don't work.

It is important to be grateful for these "inside-out" lessons and to learn them well, even when you don't like what you see or what has happened to you. Such learning gives us the chance to avoid experiencing these hard lessons in our own lives! Although it may not seem so at first, such learning offers us a very special blessing.

▶ List three disappointments, disillusionments, or hurts you encountered with teachers in the past.

▶ What did you learn from these experiences? How have they framed your present reality?

Step III: Do you recognize your teachers in All Our Relations—in all their surprising forms? Do you take to heart the profound wisdom voiced from time to time by the little children in your life? Are you willing to learn from the simple grasses of the Earth about the importance of flexibility and tenaciousness? What have you learned from your family pets? For example, our dog Bud has taught me more about love and open-hearted devotion than any human teacher. And my crystals have been some of the most powerful teachers I have ever known.

▶ Is there anything currently in the way of your learning from your own experience? From your deep Self? From Mother Earth? From the Great Spirit?

▶ Name three important teachers in your life who have not been two-leggeds.

▶ What have you learned from them? How does this learning manifest itself in your life today?

Step IV: Now that you've taken your inventory of the past and present, what are you ready to project as your new options for the future?

▶ Are you ready for a strong teacher, knowing that they will challenge your weaknesses and make you uncomfortable, even as much as they enhance your strengths and make you feel good?

▶ What do you fear the most about change?

▶ What do you enjoy the most about change?

▶ What does being a student or apprentice mean to you?

▶ What commitments are you ready to make?

▶ What changes are you willing to make in your life just to be with this teacher?

▶ Are you willing to let go of having a major teacher and instead learn your lessons in other ways more appropriate for you at the present? It isn't necessary for you to have a major teacher in your life in order to grow—although at certain times they are very appropriate and helpful.

▶ Do you want to call a major spiritual or medicine teacher into your life? Why?

▶ Are you ready for the possibility that your teacher will not look at all as you imagine, or perhaps not be who you think he, she, or it should be?

▶ Are you willing to work on your next personal growth steps with this teacher, who will very likely challenge you to confront the unworkable parts of your present life, and make changes that will affect your entire experience—not just one isolated part?

▶ Can you embrace this challenging and wonderful possibility as real for you, without reservation?

Step V: Calling your teacher:

▶ Do you want a spiritual teacher now? Why do you feel you need one in order to grow?

▶ What changes must be made within you before your teacher can become real in your life?

▶ What additional steps will bring the clarity you need to clear the space for your teacher? Remember, if you were perfectly clear about all this now, your teacher would already be in your life.

Step VI: Preparing for your teacher:

▶ List the changes you must complete to prepare for your teacher.

Then get ready for some intense and gratifying times. Keep remembering when the going gets rough that *you* asked for this!

You may have discovered through your personal reflections, as I did with Grandma Rosie as my first major Native spiritual teacher, that you have been quite naive about what it means to summon a major teacher, and that you have not considered all the ramifications for your larger life. When I came to Grandma Rosie, I came in youth and innocence for blessing, seeking learning that would develop my ability to create a healing way for All My Relations. I certainly encountered more than I ever expected. Spirit had plans for me that I would have cancelled immediately had I but known what they were and what they would require of me.

Yet, at that moment, I came in excitement, joy, and anticipation of the goodness to come, unaware, as I looked up toward the shining mountains and smelled the sweet scent of pine outside our door, of the quagmire I'd be asked to walk through on my path. Buffalo Woman was singing her song of Spirit, and my heart was singing too, for I had found at last The Woman Who Knows Everything.

CHAPTER TWO

THE QUICKEST ZIPPER ON THE RESERVATION

Know that when you stand before the Sacred Bundle,
you stand before Truth.

The buffalo stood still, quiet, and focused, as though
hearing the deepest wishes of my heart, as though its brain and my
heart had become one.

Heading north that first time to meet Grandma Rosie and my Shinela family, I was in a state of anticipation and wonder, like a kid at Christmas. As I look back on it now, I can see the childlike innocence and purity of intention I carried into that experience. I could feel my spirit pulsing and shifting, lifting to a new level of awareness.

What was in fact happening was the grounding of my spirit in a Native traditional form through contact with a very developed spiritual being. Although I had been deeply interested in healing, in Spirit, and in religion from the time I was very small, I had not yet found a place of spiritual power in which to stand.

My family expressed belief in Creator, but did not formally practice a spiritual way. As a child, my healing interests were stimulated by all the veterinary work we did ourselves on the ranch, since it was sixty miles over bad roads to a vet, and we had no money to pay one anyway. I helped with surgery, assisted in difficult births, cleaned wounds, bound injuries, and gave injections—dealing with everything from newborn pigs to two-thousand-pound bulls. My brother Tom and I took special joy in caring for injured birds and foundling cottontails.

Yet other than this healing practice, there was little stimulation of my spiritual self except for the beauty of Spirit alive in the land and its creatures. Since we lived five miles from the nearest ranch, and ten miles from our little Indian village, we were seldom able to get to town to participate in any gatherings and ceremonials. Although both my parents were half-breed and living on the reservation, neither had been given a strong spiritual tradition to hand down to us. So, when in our early childhood Mom took us to a town off the reservation for better schooling, I was very curious about churches and their spiritual possibilities. I would attend church with my Catholic friend, or my Lutheran friend, or my Methodist friend, or with my mom's Episcopalian friends. I'd sit wide-eyed, observing the proceedings, Sunday morning after Sunday morning.

Although I was not overly impressed by the services, something did finally catch my eye. The choir director at the Methodist Church was wonderful, the harmony of the chorus exquisitely beautiful, and I loved to sing! So I became a Methodist. I would dress up each Sunday morning and trot off to church by myself. As soon as they would let me, I joined the choir. All this was well and good, and something of my spirit was stimulated. Yet, a lot more was missing in a way that I could not have articulated then. I'll never forget the look on our pastor's face one day when, out of the blue, I told him that I attended the Methodist Church because there was no Buddhist shrine in our town! Except for the sweet, lifting inspiration of the rich harmony of the voices in the choir, I seemed to find more depth of Spirit and beauty in the Sundays when we went back to the ranch, and I touched again the wild lands and the living things there. I yearned toward a deepening of Spirit and understanding, but there was no adult in my life who could provide it.

In later years, after I had left both home and the reservation for college, I was still searching. But I found less and less that served me in any traditional religion from the wider culture. I studied, read, awakened, and developed my consciousness in many ways; yet still, somewhere, a piece was missing. And that immensely important piece was growing more and more important to me.

Then came the call from Dad, and my journey to meet Grandmother. Something deep inside me was in fact moving and connecting in a whole new way. Although I could not have put it in words then, the connecting of Spirit and All My Relations—*all* things in the Great Circle of Life—rather than the separation between them was a large part of what was missing. The Native understanding and daily practice of a philosophy emphasizing that *the Great Spirit lives in everything, including ourselves, and can be touched through all things,* not just through church, was finally made conscious in me even though it had been an unspoken part of my childhood.

My numinous meeting with the Woman Who Knows Everything, and the light and love generated in that connection, were a dream come true for me. At last, I had been led to a person of deep Spirit to guide me and help me groom my own spirit! And I also realized how much support my Shinela stepmom, Ella Jay, was offering me as well. She took me seriously, seemed to understand my spiritual longings, and made the steps to move me forward in my quest. From the very first day we met, she has stood like a tall tree on my left side—that aspect of myself which is non-linear, non-rational, and open to spiritual images. She and I were forced to deal with some difficult issues before we even knew each other well, and she stood strong and courageous beside me through it all.

The first difficult incident arose on my second visit to Lone Deer, only a few months after meeting her and Grandma Rosie. Grandma had been ill and was staying in Lone Deer with her relatives for a while when I first met her. Back in her home village of Benney, someone else was keeping the Sacred Lodge. Now she was feeling better and wanted to go home, so we volunteered to take her. It was also an opportunity for my first blessing in the Lodge, and Grandma was to accompany us and formally introduce me there.

I put on a very conservative ankle-length cotton skirt, a long-sleeved white shirt, and a pair of moccasins. I brushed my shoulder-length hair until it shone, and was ready to go. We stopped downtown to buy tobacco and meat, to make an offering to the Buffalo Spirit, and one-yard squares of cotton for prayer cloths—pieces of cloth used to symbolize certain prayers. In this instance, I brought a black cloth as an honoring for the buffalo energy of the bundle, a red cloth to symbolize my prayers for All My Relations, and a white cloth as a remembrance of my wish for purity and clarity. Then we picked up Grandma Rosie with her small, beat-up cardboard suitcase, and we were on our way.

The day was sunny and beautiful. The cooling breeze through the open windows whipped our hair as we wound up through the little evergreen-filled valley and over the top of the divide that would become so familiar to me. Everything seemed fresh and clear; flowers filled the meadows as they did Grandma's neat print dress. Ella Jay told stories and joked, and we all laughed and enjoyed ourselves on the way. Yet behind Grandma's clouded eyes, her thoughts were difficult to judge. She seemed somewhat preoccupied, and she and Ella Jay spoke briefly in Shinela about the man who was now keeper of the Lodge. In an aside to me, Ella Jay explained who they were speaking about, but she gave me no idea of what they were saying. I was glad for her light talk and banter, because my stomach was all butterflies, thinking about my first Lodge blessing and wondering if I would know what to do, to not embarrass my relatives.

We went by Grandma's old log cabin to check on things, and then we continued a mile or so up the river to our destination. Traveling along the edge of a plain, I could see that near us, on the left side, there was an embankment that dropped down to the level of the river. Through an occasional dip in the terrain, I could see lush pastures and fields of alfalfa growing below. It wasn't until we turned off the plain and down into the keeper's yard that I saw the Lodge. It was a simple tipi of white canvas, enclosed by a fence of two strands of barbed wire to keep large animals out.

"What is really in that tipi?" I wondered. And especially, "What is in there for me?"

We went into the house to announce our arrival and to ask for a blessing. Other than simple introductory hellos, the conversation was carried on in Shinela, so I just leaned against a door frame and observed. The family that now cared for the Sacred Lodge was named Sand Crabs. They seemed reserved, yet glad to see Grandma. I suppose when she came, it felt to them like being observed in student teaching, since they were new at the procedures, and Grandma a past master. They were both slight of build. Mrs. Sand Crabs, like Ella Jay, had permed hair and wore slacks. Sand Crabs himself was a man between forty-five and fifty, with jet black hair, smooth skin, slightly puffy eyes, and a little paunch. Children and grandchildren played about the house and sat on everyone's laps, round-eyed and curious, happy to be the center of a moment's attention.

From indications of their hands and other gestures, I could tell the conversation had turned to me. Feeling a subtle assessment going on by all in the room, I wished as always in such moments that I was not so much of an oddity, an outsider, in a small parochial community. Glancing sideways at Ella Jay, I smiled nervously. She nodded encouragement with her head as though to say, "Everything is all right."

Soon everyone got up and went into the kitchen, where Sand Crabs's wife put cedar needles in a coffee can on the stove and smudged each of us. Needles from cedar trees are used as a cleansing incense.

When burned or smudged, the needles give off a fragrance that has long been known to be cleansing of our emotions and actions (see pages 29–30 and pages 49–50).

Then Sand Crabs led our family out of the house, through a gate into the enclosure, and into the Lodge. Holding the tipi flap up, I helped everyone else enter until only Sand Crabs was left standing beside me. Looking at me intently, he said something that snapped me to immediate attention: *"Know that when you stand before the Sacred Bundle, you stand before Truth. Be very sure and clear about what you say and do."*

With that he nodded for me to enter and followed me in, guiding me to the left around the circle. I saw that my relatives were seated on the ground in a semi-circle to my right. Skirting a pallet covered with Pendleton blankets, I stood in front of the Sacred Bundle. During these first brief moments inside the Lodge I had been madly reviewing my intentions, remembering that I had come for blessing to deepen my own spirit, and to help me in the teaching/healing work that was my professional practice. I checked my motivations and found them pure. I was as ready as I could be.

Covered with a buffalo robe, the bundle before me stood as high as the back of a chair. It seemed to be wrapped around a three-pole stand, the tops of the poles extending beyond the bundle. I knew this sacred object was Buffalo Medicine, but I knew little about its real contents or function. Then Sand Crabs stepped in front of me, made a short offering of prayer, and placed the colored cloths we had brought upon the bundle. Then, sitting down behind me on the pallet, he said, "You can go ahead now."

My first inner response was, "Go ahead and do what?" I wasn't sure whether to pray out loud, sit, stand, or what. So I simply stood for a few minutes, centering myself, taking deep breaths and opening my heart, soon dropping within the aura of the bundle until all else seemed far away. Then I began to speak, talking to the spirit of the ancient bundle, telling it why I had come and asking for blessing for myself, my family, and my work.

My statements were very simple, and I spoke slowly and clearly. "O Great and Sacred Power of the Buffalo, you who have helped the Shinela people down through time, I come in humbleness to ask for blessing— to ask for blessing for myself, my family, and my work in the world," I began, continuing on with the specific requests that were current for me at that time.

At the same time, other things began to take shape in my left-side awareness. It seemed that, from within the bundle, something infinitesimally small emerged and whistled through the air. It reminded me of a balloon when the air is let out, making that high-pitched sound and whipping rapidly around in random circles. Only whatever this was, it grew larger and larger rather than smaller, moving so fast my eyes could not keep up with its movement or rapid growth. I felt something hit my chest, and instantly I was looking up over the humped shoulders and back of a full-grown buffalo, whose head was inside my chest cavity! My eyes must have been popping out of my head, yet I continued with my prayer.

My rational mind screamed, "How can this be? A buffalo's head is enormous!" Yet there it was, and I felt an intense pressure that seemed to expand my heart area to make room for this huge, shaggy head. I smelled the musty odor of buffalo and saw clearly the old rust brown fur that hung in pieces and strips along the sides of its hump. And the buffalo stood still, quiet, and focused, as though hearing the deepest wishes of my heart, as though its brain and my heart had become one. It *heard* my feelings, listening at a level I had never experienced, and I drifted into the joy of this unfathomable connection.

With my outer ear, I heard myself finish my prayer, and then I stood silent again. At this, the buffalo withdrew its head from my chest, and again whistled rapidly around in front of me. This time it was exactly like a balloon losing air, quickly diminishing in size and disappearing again into the Sacred Bundle. My chest felt enormous and hollow, yet my heart was rich and full.

As I gave my head a rapid shake, blinking my eyes and turning my attention to the others in the room, my family got up and filed back past me, shaking Sand Crabs's hand and thanking him. I followed suit and ducked out through the tipi flap into the bright sunlight. The meadowlarks singing in the sweet-smelling alfalfa fields seemed to declare the happiness I felt in my heart. Everyone else seemed a little "ho-hum" at the experience, but I was bursting with joy as we walked back to the house. I wished I could stay there beside the Lodge for a while to catch my breath. I wanted to integrate my experience without the presence of others, but I wasn't sure that would be acceptable and didn't want to make waves. I wanted to dance and sing for joy! I had not only made it through the experience without embarrassing myself or anyone, I had actually had profound contact with the Spirit of the Lodge! I could hardly wait to share this with Ella Jay. However, Sand Crabs was holding the gate open for me, so I too left the enclosure.

As we came into the kitchen, Grandma noticed that the ground meat we had brought was still lying on the table, and pointed it out to Sand Crabs. He had obviously forgotten to include it in the offering to the Lodge, and grabbed it nervously. A short conversation ensued in Shinela, after which Ella Jay motioned for me to follow Sand Crabs out with the meat offering while they stayed inside and visited. I felt strange following this man who seemed to walk so stiffly and nervously back into the enclosure. He started around the outside of the Lodge, offering tiny pieces of meat at each of the poles, and offering me meat and indicating that I should do the same. I was never told the meaning of this ritual, and no subsequent keeper ever used it again.

We turned left, making our offerings all around the tipi, up to the door flap. He seemed agitated and tense. When we got to the door, he looked around a few times, as though undecided or checking for the presence of someone else. Then he lifted the flap and motioned me in. He pushed me gently ahead of him and indicated that I should sit down on the pallet, directly in front of the bundle but with my back to it. Expecting him to sit down too, I was staring at the blanketed pallet, deep in thought. Then I heard something and looked up. He was standing directly above me, with his pants already unzipped, and taking them down.

"Oh, my God!" My mind was racing. "What is going on here? Does he think we're going to have intercourse?" I did not want to be offensive, and I felt terribly disadvantaged by not knowing the Shinelas' ways. I remembered reading once about a practice of ceremonial intercourse in their tradition—although this didn't seem appropriate for the Shinela— and I tried frantically to remember if it had anything to do with initiations. No, no. His energy felt so sneaky I decided that was not the case now. Our coming into the tipi was obviously an afterthought; the blessing had been over when we left the first time.

Yet I still wanted to act appropriately. Thankfully, the Sacred Bundle blessed me with an idea for an easy way out. I wanted to leave at least the appearance of choice up to him, and so, looking up past his now bare legs and jockey shorts, blurted out to him my white lie, "I don't think this is a good idea—I have a very bad infection."

I knew that if this was an appropriate ritual he would be protected by Spirit, and continue with what was necessary. But, as I'd suspected, he managed to say through a very tight throat, "Oh!! We better go back in." And he jerked his pants up, tucking in his shirt on the way to the tipi opening. He looked surreptitiously around as he stuck his head out, and seeing no one, strode to the house on thudding boot heels.

By the time we reached their door the shock of what had happened, the deep betrayal, was sinking in, and I fought to hold back the tears. I nodded to the family and went outside to the car. Grandma Rosie, Ella Jay, and the others soon followed. We drove silently to Grandma's house and said good-bye to her. I looked hard at her, wondering if somehow she knew, as her bent figure climbed up the two steps by hanging on to the door frame, and she turned to wave from the shadowed doorway.

"Oh, man! What now? Should I tell Ella Jay? Will she believe me, as little as she knows me? Why did he do that?" My feelings tumbled in bewilderment, until finally a flash of anger burst inside me. "Of course! He did it because he thought he could get away with it. By all that's sacred," I said to myself, "I will not be quiet and make it easy for him!" Behind the anger, the deep sadness came again, and I burst into tears.

"What's wrong?" Ella Jay asked in alarm, and I told her exactly what had happened. "Aaaiiiii!!" she cried, her hand over her open mouth and a look of horror on her face. "Oh, no. Oh, no," she said, "I'm so sorry. It's hard to believe he would do something like that in the Lodge!" Although some tribes are very relaxed about sexual matters, the Shinelas are known as "the prudes of the Plains." Among them this was an especially despicable act, and the fact that he was the keeper of a Sacred Bundle made it all the worse. Ella Jay then explained in detail to me what I have already expressed: the necessity for a tribe's holy people to be exemplars and living expressions of its highest ideals.

When she had recovered from her initial shock, she asked me what I had done when I realized he had his pants down. I told her what I had said, and how fast he had jerked his jeans up. And she laughed and laughed, saying how much he deserved it. "If he has the quickest zipper on the reservation, then you have the quickest wit!" And she cackled on, holding her sides.

E.J. now felt at liberty to tell me what she and Grandma Rosie had been talking about on our way over the divide that morning. They had been discussing this man's capabilities as keeper. Although not really formally trained, Sand Crabs as a young man had learned the sacred ways by being around his grandparents who then kept the Lodge. But mostly Ella Jay and Grandma had spoken of his personal behavior, and what a shame it was that a man who ran around on his wife, drank and debauched, was the only one available to take the Sacred Lodge when Grandmother couldn't handle it. Ella Jay, although usually very easy and fair in judging people, obviously did not approve of this man in the least. That was why she could laugh and enjoy the joke of my response to him so much. She finally even got me laughing, and that's when my healing began.

The incident, however, was not yet over. As soon as we arrived in Lone Deer, Ella Jay asked that we go to see her parents, who were members of the society that oversees the Sacred Buffalo Lodge. We stepped across a rickety porch into their small log home, and they both smiled in toothless delight to see us. Grandma Shell was a tiny, wizened woman whose one bad eye caused her to cock her head to the side. She wore traditional braids, a calico dress, and an ever-present scarf on her head. In contrast, Grandpa Big Man was very tall and stooped—walking in a manner that suggested an injured back.

They offered us coffee, asked where we had been, and we visited casually for a few minutes. After a moment of silent tension, Ella Jay told them why we had come. "Aaaeeeiiiiii!!" they cried in turn, their hands flying to their mouths, and their eyes widening in alarm. Their outrage was voiced in Shinela, and I could only guess what they were saying. But my new grandparents both dropped their eyes in shame for what had happened.

Their Sacred Lodge is a spiritual center for the entire Shinela people, and to have it desecrated by such an act was a grave matter. From the energy of the exchange, I sensed that they had been afraid such a thing might happen because of the present keeper's reputation. Yet, they had been in dire need of someone to be caretaker of the Sacred Bundle. The pain in their eyes went far beyond this particular situation. It touched on the breakdown of their traditional ways and the dearth of dedicated people to carry on what little was left. My heart fell with theirs.

Grandmother and Grandfather cleansed me with burning cedar incense. Then they prayed for me, and sent me on my way with the assurance that they would take care of the situation. They and Ella Jay instructed me to release this incident to Spirit and go forward in beauty.

I later heard that their guardian society for the Sacred Lodge had met and had taken its keeping from Sand Crabs. Remembering the lessons portrayed by the foolish, lustful young man in White Buffalo Woman's story, I was reminded that all of us must be very aware of what we are doing under the guise of spirituality. I wondered what other lessons might come to Sand Crabs as a result of his actions. It was obvious that he had not been listening to his own medicine when he cautioned me: *"Know that when you stand before the Sacred Bundle, you stand before Truth. Be very sure and clear about what you say and do."*

With gratitude, I at last turned my attention to the gift of vision I had received, and to the profound connection with the Buffalo Spirit I had experienced. Even though I was still grieving that so much attention had been spent on the negative aspect of the experience rather than on counseling me about the beauty of my vision, I felt happy. No matter what tests had been given in the external world, Grandma's intention to connect me with the Sacred Buffalo Spirit had carried the day.

The buffalo is seen as one who gives away everything for the people, and thus blesses them. The buffalo gave its body to the Native people not only for food, but for clothing, shelter, implements, and many other things. It thus symbolizes serving others by giving of oneself. In addition, the buffalo object contained in the bundle itself comes from a cow (female) buffalo. This symbolizes the nurturing and renewing power of the feminine. It was clear that the buffalo's brain had become a part of my heart. My wit had outrun "the quickest zipper on the rez," as E.J. said. My initiation had begun.

I have spoken in many different ways of the lack of spiritual guidance that I experienced as a young person. And I know I am not alone in that experience—I see it in a majority of my students. A longing for their own spiritual development is palpable, even though sometimes they might not know to call it that.

The ancient ways of working with a child's developing spirit, which came down through many cultures in response to our human spiritual nature, are similar across many different peoples. At the time of birth, there is a tremendous opening of the wings of spirit. Those of you who have been present at a birth know that a numinous force fills the room— Creation and the Great Mystery overflow. No matter how messy the child may be from the birth, a radiance glows from that little being. The newborn is almost total spirit, coming awake in unknown flesh.

Then those wings of spirit tuck themselves back in and are not seen again so clearly until around the age of five. Spiritual elders watch the children closely, and observe them at this next opening of their spiritual intent. Those small wings flutter and open, flap and stretch in a brief display, and are then quiet again. The way this numinous force shows itself—the amount, the direction, the strength of it—helps determine how the elders work with that child.

In Tibet, the high incarnates will have revealed themselves by this time, and their spiritual education for this lifetime will have begun in earnest. Among Native American people, the strength of spirit of some of the children marks them as the spiritual leaders of their generation, and their training begins as well.

I know two different Cherokee people who were recognized at this age to be carriers of the spiritual lineage and then began their training. One is a crystal woman—a carrier of the spiritual practices of her people. Her knowledge has passed through many generations of teachers. The other spiritual leader is a doctor, one who is put in charge of his patient's full well-being, whether spiritual, physical or otherwise. His gifts were recognized when he was five years old. As a result, he was kept hidden away from the white man's schools, and taught Cherokee medicine and healing ways. He began his full apprenticeship at seventeen, and after the age of thirty he was given charge of his people's well-being.

In the stages of spiritual development, another opening of the wings of spirit comes at puberty. In cultures where the spiritual ways are still intact, this is a time when the young people are given full initiation into the ceremonial life of the people. They are sometimes brought into *Kivas,* or Sacred Lodges for training and initiation. They are sometimes taken up on a sacred mountain for a vision quest. And they are sometimes accepted within a Moon Lodge at the time of their first menstrual blood. But they are always formally acknowledged to be part of the spiritual life of the people.

And this is certainly not the end of it. These young people have examples around them of their elders who have practiced the ways of Spirit for ten years, twenty years, thirty years, fifty years, eighty years. This allows them to see that the development of their spirit is a continuing process. Spirituality grows like a flowering plant—a sturdy stalk, with flower after unique flower developing as an expression of their inner beauty and gifts.

Our generation has yearned for this guidance, yearned for it with the fullness of our humanity even if decades have passed since this kind of assistance was given to children. It is still our birthright, and we feel it deep within ourselves as a natural longing. We reach out for it wherever it may seem to be offered.

One of the things I consider the most damaging of what I have seen among our generation is the practice some elders make of expecting sexual favors in return for spiritual teaching. I have dealt with it again and again in my own seeking. I see it happening in circles where I am teaching. And I hear reports of it in every tradition from Buddhism to Catholicism, from Jungian therapy to New Age teachers, as well as in Native American circles.

Many who carry the teachings of Spirit, traveling alone on the road without mate and family, reach out for physical comfort and release to their students. Many of these young people so desperately want the attention and teachings of the elders that they are willing to make the trade. Some are even proud of the "special" attention they are getting. I have never seen this kind of bartering deepen anyone's spirit—and I have held countless shattered young people as they told their stories about it. Very likely many of you, especially women, have similar stories to tell.

This brings up the question that lies deep within each of us: "How do I reach Spirit and develop that connection into a powerful force within my life?" Around that cry of the heart circle many other questions, some of which have already been addressed: Does that power of Spirit and the possibility of its development lie within me? Do I need someone else to assist me? Where and from whom do I find the guidance that will enhance my journey? What do I need to give in return for this guidance? Is the sacred pipe a phallic symbol? Or does it represent the golden open line to be cultivated between each person and the Great Mystery? What if I turn down the connections that are offered through sexual intimacy? Will I ever find another teacher?

These questions are important, not only for you personally, but for all our transitional generations—all peoples alive today. I have seen many instances where young women are reaching out for guidance, and the only mentors available to them are male elders who are on the road teaching. If these male elders are suspected by their wives and families at home of sexual dalliance with all their young female students, then the families' hearts turn against those young women. When and if these students ever have the opportunity to go to the reservations or homes of these teachers, they often find a solid wall of anger and hurt standing between them and the very people who could be their finest teachers: the elder women. I have experienced this myself. I have been cut off from some of the women elders of my blood lines because they assumed, without any evidence, that I had been sleeping with their husbands, most of whom I appreciate as teachers but who held not the slightest sexual interest for me.

I have come to understand that confronting these issues was a powerful part of my learning. And yet, to this day, I grieve that this kind of thing seemed again and again to turn attention away from the beauty of Spirit's messages to me. However, today Sand Crabs has been left far behind me, and Sacred Buffalo Medicine lives with me daily. The power of the Buffalo Spirit entered my heart, regardless of who and what was happening in my outer world at the moment of that first visit to the Sacred Lodge.

This points out very clearly Spirit's ability to transcend the limits of our teachers' personalities, or personal issues. *The intention carried by the seeker is of paramount importance, for that establishes the pathway upon which Spirit and the seeker walk toward each other.* What challenges and learnings stand in or along that path cannot stop that connection, unless the intention is lost. Yet certainly, when elders or teachers are fully attuned and connected to Spirit, they use their own energy to open the pathway even wider, thus modeling that powerful link-up with Spirit.

CONNECTING TO THE GREAT
SPIRIT WITHIN

Connecting with the Great Spirit within is a profound and absolutely vital task if you are to pursue a spiritual path. To begin the quest by thinking that someone else has the connection—that power lies outside of you—means that you are not even on the path.

So take time now to really reflect on how it is for you. Do it without any harsh judgments on any of the choices you may have made up to now. If you find that you choose to move toward a different way of being, then taking this assessment of your current personal belief structure will give you a foundation on which to stand as you begin to encounter the currents of change.

Ask yourself:

▶ Is it possible for me to communicate with the Great Spirit?

▶ Does that power of Spirit connection and the possibility of its development lie within me?

▶ How do I reach Spirit and develop that connection into a powerful force within my life?

▶ Do I simply desire a teacher/elder/guide in my life—or do I feel that I truly need one in order to develop spiritually?

▶ Where and from whom do I find the guidance that will enhance my journey?

▶ What do I need to give in return for that guidance?

THE GOLDEN SEED ATOM

This exercise is designed to help you develop your own inner connection to Spirit and, since this communication is based on love, it is natural for us to begin with the heart. Lying within the left auricle of our heart is what might be called a Golden Seed Atom, which contains within it the remembrance of all your soul's past experience in many lives and situations.

The Golden Seed Atom is the repository of incredible wisdom, built over perhaps eons of time. It is the place we tap into when we realize that we come into this life with incredible abilities, or when we realize that we know things that we could not from this one life experience.

1. Begin by creating and dedicating your sacred space, which we discussed on page 28. Now, sit quietly in meditation, body relaxed, and center yourself. Take several deep breaths, pulling each breath down to your navel, which is your symbolic and physical center.

2. Allow yourself to go within and begin to visualize that Golden Seed Atom within your heart. What is its shape? How do you experience it? If you are not good at visualizing, then try creating a fantasy of how it might be.

3. Then spend fifteen minutes tuning in to that part of yourself, that ancient repository of knowledge.

4. When that is complete, create or imagine a golden line, extending from the Golden Seed Atom in your heart to the heart of the Great Mystery—the Great Spirit, God, Source, All That Is. Meditate upon this flowing connection, realizing that not only can you send prayers, thoughts, communication to Source, but also that you can receive abundantly through this same line.

5. Take another fifteen minutes to establish this golden line of communion.

6. Then, once you have set that pattern in your consciousness, spend five minutes a day on each part of the exercise. Give yourself five minutes to quiet yourself and connect with your own ancient knowing, and then five minutes to open your golden line of communications with All That Is.

7. Learn to rely on this connection and communion, rather than on someone outside yourself, for the deepening of your spirit and wisdom.

CONNECTING TO SPIRIT THROUGH SACRED WORDS AND SOUNDS

There are other ways of opening and maintaining communications between you and your highest self, between you and the Great Spirit.

1. Simply meditating to quiet and center yourself is very powerful all by itself. Breathe deeply and pull each breath down to your navel—your symbolic and physical center. Continue this until you feel a better sense of yourself.

2. Create a mantra or affirmation—a brief, simple positive sentence to speak or chant again and again—to help you feel that special connection with Spirit. It should always be in your own words, but it could be something like, "Great Spirit, you are within me, and I am within you, now and always."

3. Make an altar for yourself to represent the Great Spirit in your life (for more information, see page 72). Spend time there each day meditating and perhaps repeating your sacred sounds to honor your connection to All That Is.

A RITUAL FOR SPIRITUAL CLEANSING

Many of us do not have the living spiritual teachers and guidance to ease and clarify our path, yet all of us do have the life of Spirit living within us. Our challenge is to develop that connection, that renewing communion. Whether this guidance comes outwardly or inwardly in the form of invisible teachers, helpers or healers, great benefits come to us from this practice. For instance, a deep connection to Spirit can help us avoid taking inappropriate actions in our attempts to meet our spiritual needs.

On your own spiritual path, you too will very likely be tested on the issue of right action—even though it will probably take a different form from mine. But such testing will very likely incorporate all the exhilarating highs I experienced in my first meeting with the Sacred Buffalo Spirit, as well as the devastating lows brought about by the inappropriate actions of the keeper of the Sacred Lodge. And yet, because of my inner connection to Spirit, I managed to move through my experience in balance without doing harm to myself or others.

Such testing has arisen for me, again and again in many guises, because *the lesson of relying on and trusting the Great Spirit living within us—rather than looking outside ourselves—is so essential for each of us to learn!* Yet, having learned it, we can then benefit from the teachings and sharings of others, without having to feel dependent upon them.

If you have had some inappropriate contact with an elder or teacher—or even simply feel the pull of a deeply imbalanced relationship—you may wish to do a cleansing or releasing ceremony. One way to begin any cleansing, releasing, or healing ceremony is the act of ritual purification called "smudging" (as discussed on pages 29–30). Then do what follows.

1. Take yourself to a place in nature where you can speak out loud without anyone overhearing.

2. Dig a hole in the Earth into which you can put all the experience and energy you no longer need. Think of it as creating compost for Mother Earth.

3. Get down on your belly or hands and knees so you can send your words into the hole. Then make a full statement of what your experience has been and how you have felt about it. Realize that some of your feelings may be negative, such as feeling used or deceived, and some may be very positive, such as feeling cared about, feeling special, and so on. Speak them all into the hole.

4. Now, into this Earth bowl, add any objects or other things connected to this issue that you wish to release.

5. Sit back, close your eyes, and sense any "strings" that are still attached to this issue. You may be able to sense these energy bonds as spider webs between you and it. Taking a very deep breath, blow intensely out through your pursed lips, blowing away all the attaching strings. Do this until you sense yourself completely separate from what you wish to release.

6. Sprinkle cornmeal over the hole and what it contains, making a prayer/statement about your willingness to let all of this go. Offer it to Mother Earth as compost, so that other life might be nurtured through the transformation of this energy.

7. Cover the hole, giving thanks to Mother Earth and Father Spirit. Forget where you made the hole.

8. If, in succeeding days or weeks, you find yourself feeling attached again, simply take a few minutes to center yourself and do the releasing ritual with the breath. Do not stop until you again have completely cleared the space between you and what you wish to release. It may take a long while to reach the point where the old energy no longer calls you; just keep at it any time it comes up. Take your power back, and use it actively in this way.

LESSONS OF THE BUFFALO LODGE

The buffalo placed fully within me this understanding of
magnanimous giving away for the life of the people.

My giveaway, however, was not to be one of flesh,
but of heart and of spirit.

"A buffalo head in my chest. A buffalo brain in my heart. What do these things mean?" I asked myself these questions again and again as I contemplated the vision I had received in the Lodge. I had known immediately that it was a powerful confirmation of my connection with the Buffalo Spirit. However, there had been so much anxiety and trauma around that first visit to the Sacred Lodge that the joy of my initiatory experience—the power of it—had been overshadowed. When I asked Ella Jay or any of my elders about the meaning of my numinous experience, they would just shake their heads and smile, as though to say, "It's your vision. You work it out."

With time and experience, I began to understand some of what this powerful and numinous event might mean to me. In thinking about the buffalo, I remembered how central these great shaggy creatures had been to the lives of our Northern Plains people, as well as to Native peoples all across Turtle Island—the North American continent. The buffalo gave of themselves in a profound way that the people might live. Our sheltering tipis were made from their hides, as were our robes, moccasins, bags, and shields. Their meat fed the people, who often used spoons and other utensils carved from their horns. Their hooves made glue, their sinew a strong thread. The buffalo had been the primary means of sustenance for the people. The U.S. Army policy of slaughtering the buffalo was a devastating blow to the Plains people. When millions of buffalo lay rotting on the Plains, one of the major life supports of the people was gone. This killing was so depraved and evil, it must have struck a certain terror and despair in their hearts. The buffalo symbolize for us that which nurtures and helps renew our lives. And, too, the "buffalo hat" contained within the Sacred Bundle of the Lodge is the skull of a female buffalo, which deepens the sense of nurturing and renewing represented there. In the magnitude of its giveaway, the buffalo also symbolizes the abundance that is possible when we all give away at our highest capacity. This abundance, and our gratitude for that richness, are all part of the Buffalo's medicine.

The Buffalo Spirit instilled within me this understanding of magnanimous giving away for the life of the people. I had stood before the bundle, praying for my work to be blessed, and I had received not only a blessing, but also a challenge to use myself to my highest potential. My giveaway, however, was not to be one of flesh, but of heart and of spirit. I have come to see that, in our time, this kind of nurturing, this spiritual offering, is the heart of what people need. We have fallen far into the gross thinking that makes us believe we have life only through the physical, when what is absolutely necessary if we are to move forward in our human evolution is a return to the knowledge of ourselves as Spirit, of our oneness with all of life. I had been shown that Spirit is present, awaiting our call.

Another profound aspect of my Sacred Lodge experience was graphically illustrated—that important initiations do not necessarily consist of words but of a deeper experience. This buffalo experience was real in my body. It grounded me in the Sacred Lodge in a way that remains true over time—beyond changes in Lodge keepers, beyond Grandma Rosie's eventual death, and beyond many other changes in my own life. Within the Buffalo Lodge, there is represented a great abundance of Spirit, waiting for me to call upon and share it.

And call upon that Spirit I did. As often as I could get home to the reservation, I asked my family to take me for blessing and re-connection with the Lodge. Each time, as the keeper prayed and I opened myself to the Buffalo Spirit, I was given vision. Although some of these inner teachings were very personal, others I am able to share.

One time Ella Jay, her daughter Heta, and I came to the Lodge for blessing. Driving along a cottonwood-lined river on the other side of the Wolf Mountains, we found the Lodge in the keeping of Strongly Bears the Spirit, at his home in an area of small buttes that rose into evergreen hills. I had brought three prayer cloths as a symbol of my prayers and offerings: a black one for the Bundle; a red one for All My Relations; and a white one for my own purity and clarity. Strong Bear (as his name was sometimes shortened) took the cloths and went inside the Lodge, gently opening the tipi flap and closing it behind him.

After praying there, he emerged holding only the red and white cloths. Then he beckoned me and I stood before him, facing east with my back to the entrance, while he used the cloths to cleanse me, pulling them from toe to head in passes up the front and back of each leg, then up the center of my spine and body, over the back of my heart. After each pass, he shook out the cloths as though freeing static electricity. Then he beckoned Ella Jay, and I stood aside as she, then Heta, was cleansed. By the time he had pulled and flicked those cloths over all of us, they were standing almost straight out, flaring with energy. At this point his family and some neighbors came out of the house to be cleansed in the same manner, then went back outside the white-pole fence surrounding the Sacred Lodge.

Strong Bear motioned us in and I led, stooping and stepping in, moving around to my left past the Sacred Bundle, to sit on a robe spread at the center back of the tipi. My family followed me and sat beyond me to my left. All became quiet, everyone with lowered eyes, touching into the Buffalo Spirit. At length, the keeper asked me why I had come. "To serve the light and to serve my people in the highest and best way I know—to be supported and blessed in that work," I replied to him, to everyone there, and to the Bundle.

Nodding, he began his prayer in Shinela, the sound rising and falling, drawn out in unfamiliar cadences, rhythms that stirred my memory and soothed me deep inside. Yet the words were ancient, and somehow I knew them in my heart. First for me came the sounding prayer—to bless and guide me and serve the light in me. Then for my family present and for those not present. Then for all the Shinela people, all the peoples of Turtle Island, and all the peoples of the world.

Formal Shinela prayers are long, and I knew from experience that this was my time to say my silent prayers in accompaniment to his. So I began, asking for guidance and clarity for myself, then bringing in all my loved ones, my friends, those in need, my students, those I wished to support—bringing them clearly into my mind and thus into the tipi, to be blessed there with me. When I felt complete, I sighed and focused attention again on the drone, the cadence that had formed a background for my prayers.

Prayer among our Native people is more personal and direct than I have experienced it in other cultures. It is a conversation, a friendly and intimate exchange with Spirit. It is not only about asking for things but also about acknowledging Spirit in all things and situations; and certainly it is used to express honoring and gratitude. These prayers are a continuing process, a habit of expression, rather than being something reserved for times of dire need or official religious functions. Often, prayers are spoken, or "cried," aloud, to bring our expression into reality, rather than keeping it only within us. This way of praying is in keeping with the deep awareness that Spirit is present with us at all times—in ourselves as well as in all other things.

I sat quietly, breathing gently. And in this uplifted space, I saw, as though right in front of me, an old wooden frame—perhaps the window, weathered and gray, of an old barn. Through it I could see something not immediately identifiable. I leaned forward and looked more closely. But I still could not identify what I saw. It seemed to be green tiles laid sideways and reminding me of red-tiled Spanish roofs. Then I noticed the tiles were moving—just slightly, and quite regularly. I continued to study them, but they revealed no more.

So I thought, "Aha, I'll move back to get a wider view." Stepping quite a few paces back in this envisioned space, I looked up again and saw before me an ancient and very huge iridescent female dragon! The tiles were the scales on her sides, gently lifting and falling with each breath. She appeared so soft—little iridescent wings lay against her back. I was open-mouthed with awe, both at her beauty and at her very presence. "A dragon? Here? In the Sacred Lodge? She seems so out of place. . . ." My mind spun.

Then the dragon began to flick her tail. Although it was huge it came to the finest point, almost heart-shaped, at the tip. Then with a powerful movement, seemingly effortless, she flung her tail around behind her in an enormous circle, stretching clear to the horizon far, far away. Then it curled back around, drawing nearer and nearer until the tiny heart-shaped tip settled, oh so softly, upon her front paws, pointing upward toward the inside of the circle, now gold-lit by the sun. In the center of the circling tail I could see the hoops of all the nations. The bright, glowing hoop of the Shinelas—the Morning Star People—was the nearest to me. Then came the hoop of the Apsa. And on and on . . . more and more warm, glowing circles until all the peoples of all the kingdoms of Earth could be seen there in that beautiful place, laughing and joyful in the Sun.

I looked back at the dragon herself, and she appeared snug and contented, like a mother hen settled on her nest of eggs. She blinked her large slanted eyes, and slowly fluttering them, laid her head gently back along her flank, like a cow, restful. As her head settled upon her soft-scaled side, she breathed out balls of liquid fire—light, almost blue-white. They rolled along her back and tail, around and around and far around, coming back again and again, faster and faster. Soon their path was only a blur—a thin sheet of iridescent light that rose, spiralling higher and higher until it formed itself into a cone. Then it spread again, like a tipi, its poles rising out the top. To the tips of the poles were tied the seven pastel colors of the rainbow, gently rippling in a slow southerly breeze. I suddenly realized that the old one, the Great Mother, had disappeared—transformed into that radiant tipi, inside which the light had become an exquisite glow that shimmered like a halo on the blades of grass and trees and all the smiling faces.

That vision remained with me for some time. I felt myself bathed in its beauty, serenity, and light. Then I was whisked outward far, far from the radiant tipi, and I saw that it covered the entire Earth. I observed it as it seemed to melt and slowly close itself around Mother Earth—warming, protecting, clearing, healing. All was well with All Our Relations.

Then I was drawn out of vision back to the Sacred Buffalo Lodge, for the others had begun to stir; I realized that Strong Bear's prayer was over and the blessing complete. Shaking hands with him, I emerged into the late afternoon light, coming back to myself fully. On the way home, I checked in with Ella Jay about the vision, knowing that her knowledge of the sacred ways had come through her grandmother and grandfather, very traditional Shinela people who had long passed beyond this life.

"E.J., you'll never guess what I saw this time!"

She perked up her ears, lifted her dark eyebrows, and asked, *"Henawat?"* (meaning "What?" in Shinela).

"A huge old dragon!" I said, still amazed that a dragon, of all things, should appear to me.

"The old female?" she asked, with interest.

I was stunned! "Yes, the old female," I said. "The Great Mother Dragon. How in the heck did you know that?"

"She's been with the Shinela people down through time," Ella Jay replied. "She's our protectress. I can show you where she lives, or at least where she used to live. She hasn't been seen in about fifty years."

Again, I was stunned. But E.J. continued to surprise me, revealing where the dragon lived—a cavern that was now caving in. She described the exact place, right beside the road to Ashfield—a place I know well, as there are picnic tables near there now. I was already confused enough by how this strange vision was being tied more and more securely into my "real" world. Yet, Ella Jay regaled me with more humorous stories about how the Great Mother had frightened people in bygone days.

"One time," she said, "a Shinela family camped near her cave in a beautiful spot. They went to bed, some in tents and some under the stars. In the dark of night, the old dragon roared. Everyone jumped and let out a shriek—including all the birds and animals in the forest! A wide-eyed silence followed."

I too, was left in wide-eyed silence, wondering whether they packed up and left right then, or stayed to wander around in the night. It seemed such a crazy image that I laughed, letting go of my intellect, enjoying the usual result of E.J.'s stories—me being amazed, laughing, and lightening up.

In reflecting on this vision, I remembered a photograph I'd seen once of a Tibetan woman. Her black braided hair was only slightly streaked with silver, although she appeared to be very old—a twin, an exact lookalike of my Lakota grandmother! The same pug nose and gentle eyes, standing there dressed in bright, natural colors. I thought to myself, Well, they probably are related. The old ones have told me that peoples not only crossed from east to west via the Bering Strait, but also criss-crossed back and forth over the ages. They're all related in some not-so-distant past. So, why not a dragon crossing along with them to protect them on their journey down through time?

The beauty of that image of the universal Great Mother, protecting her hoops of all peoples, and shedding healing rainbow light over the whole Earth, would stay with me, reminding me of the healing that comes from the universal love. She remains a symbol to me of making my circle large enough to hold All My Relations within it in a healing and nurturing way.

Of course, another lesson of the vision was that, for me, truth is often limited by the boundaries I construct myself. It's very likely that I allow myself to live in only a small corner of the infinite vastness of truth. The image of the dragon urged me to continually open my mind to all the possibilities of surprise and mystery, rather than limiting it with my ideas of what belonged where, and what I should or should not see in a certain situation; what I had decided, with my limited experience, could or could not be true. This was a lesson I evidently needed because I had received it several years before this dragon vision, on the very first, very informal, vision quest I had ever done.

Vision quests, or fasts as my people call them, are an age-old human practice for the grooming of one's spirit—some religious traditions might think of them as an intense retreat.

The central idea of such a fast is to leave behind the everyday world—what one of my lineages calls the "right-side" world. This represents the material world, the world of our work, our relationships, our possessions, and our thoughts and feelings about them. Because of the cross-over of the nervous system pathways from brain to body, the right side has more to do with the left hemisphere of the brain, and the left side with the right hemisphere.

Leaving behind this ordinary worldly reality opens our attention to the "left side," which contains everything else. It is the side of Spirit rather than externals—the space of dream, vision, fantasy, other dimensions, non-ordinary realities, and extraordinary perceptions. The left side is where we most easily touch Spirit and receive vision.

On a fast, then, we leave behind our everyday surroundings, our interactions, our work. We strip down our normal clothing to wear only what is needed for protection from the elements. In the old days, for instance, a man might have stripped down to his breech cloth and taken only a buffalo robe to wrap around him for warmth or to sleep on. Everything is left behind, with the exception of a sage or sweet-grass smudge (sage, cedar, and sweet grass are herbal incenses used for cleansing and for calling sweetness into one's life—see pages 29–30), a sacred object such as a pipe, or a small offering to the spirits. There will be no food, no water, no outer distractions. What is left is basically oneself—one's own physical presence and inner realms.

I had gone up for a one-day fast to a place above our little Apsa village, called the Medicine Rocks—three sentinels jutting out of the rolling plain. These castle-like rocks have long been experienced as sacred, for the Little People who are the Spirit helpers of the Apsa are said to live on top of these forty-foot granite cliffs, which are very difficult to scale. No one I knew of in my time had seen the Little People there, yet the area was still favored for vision quests, and I felt very drawn there.

Finding a place on a large flat rock about fifty feet below the base of the cliffs, I laid my few things out and rested from the long climb up.

I had brought only a robe to sit on, and some sage and sweet grass to smudge with. Now I used the smudge to cleanse myself, and settled down to wait.

I looked out past the little pine tree beside the rock over the mountains stretching far southward, and over Arrow Creek, on which I had played as a child during summer outings when my folks came fishing here. Minutes passed. Then half an hour. I was already getting impatient. More time passed, and I began to fidget, expecting something numinous to happen soon. All my life, I had heard stories of the old ones and their vision quests—of the Spirit beings who came to them bringing profound messages and awakening them to new possibilities within themselves. They were often visited, as well, by animals and birds, who spoke to them, giving them personal messages and prophecy. Now, several hours had passed and nothing had yet happened—except the flies and the wind that moved around me. I was practically tapping my fingers with impatience.

Those of you who know anything about vision quests will find the same humor in this situation that I now do. Most of those traditional people of whom I remembered stories had very likely gone through much training, much cleansing, and preparation—and still sat on the mountain for three to four days without food and water before they received their visions. And here I was, an impatient youth, wanting something spectacular to come to me in just a few hours!

It was well into the afternoon before something finally happened! A magpie—a black and white bird about the size of a crow—flew into the little pine tree that grew beside the flat stone on which I was sitting. She perched just out of my reach and scratched herself. I watched intently and cocked my ear to listen—I was so sure she would speak. Of course she has come to speak to me, sitting there so close, I thought. But she just hopped around on the little pine, acting very much like a normal magpie, except for being so very close to me. She completely ignored me, and soon flew off. I was crestfallen. No message.

Some time later, as I looked south over Little Mountain, I saw two dots far away in the distant sky. With little else to do, I watched them grow larger as they came closer to me. They were two big birds. Finally, I could just make them out—a pair of spotted eagles flying directly toward me! In our way of speaking, golden eagles are called "spotted eagles" because of the mottling on their bodies, especially when they are young. Now this was exciting! I waited and called out to them in my heart. But they flew right past me around the Medicine Rock where I was sitting. "Oh well, I guess it was not meant to be," I said to myself, feeling pretty discouraged.

Yet, soon there was more activity from the winged tribe. Three beautiful little mountain chickadees alighted in the tree. They stayed on the branches closest to me, hopping about picking at twigs, hanging upside down as they do, and twittering. Again, I watched closely, almost holding my breath so I would hear when they spoke to me. Nothing happened. Except that they, too, totally ignored me—acting, in their carefree behavior so close to my fingertips, as if I did not exist. Then, in a flutter, they were gone.

In the quiet after they flew away, my mind turned to the birds who had visited me. Suddenly, it dawned on me that a pattern was forming: one magpie, two eagles, three chickadees. Maybe there was a message after all! The magpie made sense because I had been blessed in the Sacred Buffalo Lodge before I had come to the mountain. The magpie is symbiotic with the buffalo, often sitting upon the buffalo's back pecking about for grubs for food. In return, the magpie acts as an early warning system for the large near-sighted friend upon whom it sits— flying up and squawking to alert the buffalo of anything unusual in the distance. I had loved magpies with their iridescent black-on-white colors since childhood, although my folks had not appreciated their scavenging ways. So yes, this made sense—a sign from the buffalo spirit that all was well.

And the two eagles, of course, made sense. The eagle is very strong medicine for me. I had been named Medicine Eagle after a visionary experience of becoming a spotted eagle in the primary, numinous event that had led me back to the path of my Native people. (The full story of this experience begins on page 176 of chapter 9.) Perhaps the pair of them nested near here, and I had come to their aerie to seek vision. A feeling of happiness flooded me, and I thanked the spirits of the spotted eagles and magpie.

Then the chickadees came to mind. First it had been the Medicine of the Sacred Lodge that had come to me, then my personal Medicine, and now here was the Medicine of the last traditional chief of our Apsa people. That chief, Plenty Coups, which meant "Many Achievements," had been a powerful leader. He helped our Apsa people move through the time of defeat into some semblance of normal life on the reservation, dying just before I was born. In a very significant vision he had come here to this same area, the Medicine Rocks, and the chickadee had brought him a profound message. And now chickadee had come to me, bringing me his Medicine and symbolizing the Apsa people. Things were beginning to make sense!

One magpie, two spotted eagles, three chickadees, and four _____? What would be the fourth kind of bird to appear? I was very excited at the thought of another visit to come. And this one would likely be the whopper, the big one, the extra special one, because of the number four's special significance of completion and fullness in Native symbology. I waited, again impatient, looking around me hopefully. Nothing had happened for almost an hour, and I was beginning to get discouraged. Then I heard something behind me—a flutter of wings— and I turned to see who was there. Coming from over the Medicine Rocks were five pigeons, fluttering and diving to alight on a big stone about thirty feet above me.

Well, I was disgusted. Pigeons, yuk! Walking around on the stone, cluck, cluck, cluck. They reminded me of all the big cities I had left behind for this sacred quest—of messy ledges and public statues. Most especially they reminded me of a time in El Paso, Texas, when I had just come out of a clothing store wearing a brand-new white summer outfit. Since I had very little money at the time, this was a big deal. Then, plop! Right on my shoulder came a giveaway from one of the pigeons flying overhead. Yuk, pigeons! I didn't like them. They surely couldn't be a part of my sacred quest, and I turned my back on them in disgust. But they continued to cluck.

Then things got strangely quiet. So I turned around again to see what was happening. One pigeon was perched on the near edge of the stone, ready to fly. As I turned, he dropped off the stone, flapped his wings a few times, and sailed directly at me. Then, *poof,* he was gone! I was stunned. My rational mind raced to explain this—I looked on the ground for him; I tried to find him in the air nearby; I kept looking around me for explanation. There was none. He had disappeared into thin air. Wow! And as I looked around again at the stone, there sat my four magical birds—pigeons clucking on the stone.

When the pigeons finally flew away, and I had time to meditate upon my lessons during the remaining hours of my stay on the mountain, I really laughed at myself. I had been so impatient and so self-righteous, so judgmental and haughty. I had thought I was right about everything—that I knew how the vision quest should be. Those "disgusting" pigeons had given me a powerful lesson in expectation, judgment, and the limited nature of my thinking. All the birds had come to gift me with a beautiful lesson about not deciding ahead of time what should be happening. I went down from the mountain just a little more open to what might be given by the Great Mystery, and not so sure of what I knew. It reminded me of an old friend who used to say that the worst state a human being could be in was the state of being "right." "That's the worst dead end I know of," he would say. "Keep away from being right." Yet obviously I needed more lessons about it, and the dragon vision in the Sacred Lodge was certainly one of them.

I would like to share with you the vision that Plenty Coups was given at the Medicine Rocks because it helped me make sense of another vision I received in the Sacred Lodge. (For the complete story and other wonderful tales of this great chief's life, see Frank Linderman's *Plenty Coups*.)

While he was still a young man roving with his band, Plenty Coups was brought to these sacred rocks for his clearest, greatest vision. He had begun his fast in the Crazy Mountains of southern Montana, about 150 miles from the Medicine Rocks. After several days of deprivation and prayer, he dreamed, hearing a voice telling him that he was wanted. He went, traveling almost instantaneously over the long miles between the Crazies and the Pryors, to where he could see a buffalo. At that instant, the bull changed into a man-person wearing a buffalo robe, and when Plenty Coups approached him, he sank slowly into the ground at a place on the plains below the Medicine Rocks.

Plenty Coups was then beckoned underground and led toward a light at the far end of a tunnel, which he knew was in the direction of the Arrow Creek mountains. All that night and the next day he traveled through countless buffalo, smelling their bodies and hearing them snorting, ahead and on both sides of him. Finally, he emerged from the hole at the western Medicine Rock, which is called the Fasting Place. The man-person then shook his red rattle and commanded young Plenty Coups to sit and look.

Before him, Plenty Coups saw buffalo—bulls, cows, and calves— coming out of the hole in countless numbers, spreading far and wide until they blackened the Plains. When at last they ceased coming out of the hole, all the bison vanished. All were gone. Only a few antelope remained on a hillside.

Then the man-person shook his red rattle again and commanded Plenty Coups to look. Out of the hole in the ground came countless spotted creatures, which he later identified as cattle. These, like the buffalo, scattered and spread across the Plains. Though the man-person did not tell him to look this time, Plenty Coups watched all the spotted creatures go back into the hole in the ground until, again, there was nothing but a few antelope anywhere in sight.

After the last animals disappeared, Plenty Coups followed the man-person back through the hole in the ground until they came out in the same spot where they had entered. Plenty Coups was then shown a house by a spring, and an old man sitting alone in front of it under a shade tree. The man-person told him, "This old man is yourself, Plenty Coups." Following this explanation, the man-person disappeared, as did the vision of the old man.

Now Plenty Coups saw a dark forest. A fierce storm was gathering on the horizon, the sky blackened with mad colors. The Four Winds— the circling pattern that moves through the cross-quarterly directions: southeast, northwest, northeast, southwest, and symbolizes all action and manifestation in the world (see chapter 17, pages 351 and 359, for more information)—gathered and struck with terrible force. Plenty Coups stood powerless, with pity in his heart for the beautiful trees and for all things that lived in the forest.

In the wake of the Four Winds making war together, trees twisted like blades of grass and fell into tangled piles. Where the forest once stood, only one tree remained standing. A voice then whispered to Plenty Coups, "In that tree is the lodge of the chickadee. Though the chickadee is least in strength, he has the strongest mind. He is willing to work for wisdom, and he is a good listener. He gains success and avoids failure by learning how others succeed or fail." The voice further instructed Plenty Coups to follow the chickadee's example—to develop his body but not to neglect his mind, for "It is the mind that leads a man to power, not strength of body."

Later, the wise elders among his Apsa tribe interpreted Plenty Coups's vision. In it they saw a prophecy of the buffalo disappearing, to be replaced by the cattle of the whites. The Four Winds represented the white man and those who helped him in war. The trees of the forest signified that the tribes that fought the white man would be beaten down and wiped out. However, the wise ones predicted that, by listening and becoming wise like the little chickadee, the Apsa would escape this impending doom and keep their lands. The one tree left standing would be the Apsa.

Plenty Coups's vision shaped his tribe's future response to the whites as they began settling the Plains. In time, Plenty Coups became a great chief who advocated that his people adopt some of the white man's ways in order to survive. Plenty Coups lived to see the buffalo disappear from the Plains, and to know himself as the old man living in the house by the spring. The Apsa were one of the few tribes to retain their ancestral lands.

One of the visions I was given seems to be a contemporary reaffirmation of the message Plenty Coups received nearly a century ago. Once again I had come to the Sacred Lodge to ask for support in my teachings. The appropriate ceremony was performed, and the keeper of the Sacred Hat said his lengthy prayers in the lilting rhythms of the Shinela. Tuning myself to the revered presence of the Sacred Bundle and the timbre of his voice, I said my own silent prayers, asking for global cleansing and for a healing of Mother Earth. Bringing these images into my mind, I completed my prayers and focused my attention on the varying tones of his voice and Native tongue.

Suddenly, a space opened before me—a vision space. I found myself standing high on the cliffs of a box canyon—beautiful red sandstone cliffs circling around in a horseshoe. This "box" had only a small opening on my left, out onto the Plains. Through it ran a small stream that originated in a lovely stand of quaking aspen trees at the back of the canyon. I could feel the breeze blowing up out of that canyon, stirring my hair. When I looked down again I saw, standing on my side of the stream, an old bull buffalo, an ancient one, much larger than those we see now, since the white men almost destroyed them, killed the largest for trophies. He was a powerful, wise, ancient one. His neck was stretched out toward the opening to the Plains, and he was lowing softly, yet with penetrating strength, a deep and rumbling call. Then, on the other side of the stream, behind the old one, there appeared a young modern buffalo bull, perhaps three years old, powerful even though he had not yet reached full maturity. He, too, was calling, neck outstretched toward the opening in the red canyon walls. Above me an eagle circled, a messenger from Spirit. I watched it slowly riding the thermal breezes coming up off the canyon walls. Looking down again, I saw behind the old bull, across from the young one and near this side of the stream, the bleached skull and horns of a steer.

The scene held for a few moments, then I looked toward the Plains, where the buffalo were facing. Far in the distance, at the very horizon, I could make out a small dark dot. As that dot grew larger, even from a far distance I could see it was a buffalo, then more and more of them, slowly moving and spreading out onto the Plains, until again the buffalo were numerous, countless. Then the scene faded, and my blessing in the Sacred Lodge was concluded.

Coming out of the tipi, I left the area in somewhat of a hurry, excited about seeing friends in another village. I was thinking more about a young Shinela man than my vision. On the way there, I made a rest stop, walking down through a little meadow to a stream that seemed to run parallel to the road. However, as I approached the creek, I was surprised to see what seemed a magical doorway, a small opening to my left in the brush along the stream which made a full circle curve here, invisible from a distance. I turned and, ducking my head, entered the doorway. Down to my left lay the bleached bones and skull of a steer! I did a double-take, and recalling the steer skull in my vision, I picked up the skull (still not thinking about the meaning in my hurry); holding it in my arms, I reemerged from the hidden cove. It was just after sunset. Twilight—two-light, the magic time—the setting sun still pink against the scattered clouds. As I came through the "doorway," I looked up in awe at the sky. Before me on high appeared the skull of a steer, emblazoned in a pink/gold cloud formation that filled the whole northern sky.

In many of my dreams and visions, like the one Plenty Coups told, the meaning is not immediately evident to the dreamer. Its meaning flows into me in various ways—from my own thought and reflection; from connections made by wise ones and others who hear the story; from reading and listening. But whatever meaning would emerge, on that evening I realized that I was being told very forcefully, "Pay attention to the skull!" Finally consciously waking up, I laughingly shouted to the universe, "Yes, yes, I hear you. I hear you. . . . no more signs are needed!"

Plenty Coups's watching the cattle leaving the Plains after they filled it? My vivid experience of the steer skull? What meaning do these visions have? It seems to me that what is being communicated is something about the end of an era, the end of the time when we can depend upon those things that have been imported, that are not native to this land, that require our work and care—domesticating, herding, controlling, and manufacturing, that require our dependence upon something or someone outside our native soil—be it cattle or oil or papayas. Perhaps that which can return to nurture us, what we must support and cultivate inside and outside ourselves, what we must renew our ability to use and sustain ourselves with, are those things that are native to this land and to our own particular area.

We depend now upon imports, not only from other countries, but from other areas of our country; on manufactured goods; on food and vitamins from the store; on oil from the Persian Gulf. What we will have in the future, if I interpret my vision correctly, will be only those things that we have at hand. Instead of going to the grocery store, we must learn to use the herbs and food that grow on our land. Instead of getting our vitamin C from Florida oranges, we'll have the rosehips that grow so abundantly outside our doors. Instead of cattle, buffalo. Instead of tearing up the Mother Earth, we'll learn to use the incredible resources and technology we have developed inside and outside ourselves to live on this Earth. We must work not only to use, but protect and renew the natural life gifted us by Mother Earth and Father Spirit. We must learn to use such freely given power sources as the Sun; to offer free to the public the many patents for simple, economical technologies that have been bought up and suppressed by large corporations fearful of competition from things that work well and cost very little. Plenty Coups's vision implies using our minds, spirits, and internal resources as well as our bodies to bring ourselves back into harmony with the land and with each other, using the powerful tools that are inexhaustible.

A clear example of this is our use of sunglasses to shield our eyes from the light. Based on the assumption that we were not naturally equipped to deal with the Sun, we developed means outside ourselves that necessitated tearing up Mother Earth's surface for petroleum to make plastic, metal for machinery, fuel to power it and to deliver the product. We forgot that we have been given the ability to deal internally with the bright rays of the Sun. We simply have to close our eyes, raise our face up to the Sun, and roll our head from side to side in an arc so that the Sun touches one eye and then the other through the thin eyelids. Doing this just a few times triggers the constriction of the pupils of the eyes. When the eyes are then opened, less light is allowed in, there is no strain, and all is well. (However, with pollution tearing away Earth's ozone layer, perhaps our natural means of dealing with the incoming rays will no longer be enough!)

How poorly we use ourselves and our resources. How quickly we forget the amazing abilities within ourselves and how well suited we are for this place we were given to live. We know only how to search outside ourselves for answers—cumbersome, incomplete, inharmonious answers. Now that time is nearing its end.

These stories of the Medicine Rocks remind me of yet another time during my series of vision quests, several of which took place in that area. I was still living in California, and on the way north for one of my fasts on the mountain, I decided to touch into my Nez Percé lineage. My dad's people are Apsa, but his grandpa Charlie had come to our reservation very early in his life from his home on the Nez Percé reservation in Idaho. He came to spend time with a distantly related "shirt-tail" relative among the Apsa, a fine old man named Shot in the Hand. (Edward Curtis, a famous photographer of Native peoples in the early 1900s, took a beautiful photograph of Shot in the Hand.) Grandpa Charlie stayed on to live among the Apsa, and when Native people were assigned a reservation, he was assigned on the Apsa registry. Family stories told of Grandpa Charlie being descended from Old Joseph, father of the famous Chief Joseph, the legendary leader, military strategist, and champion of the Nez Percé people during the early reservation days. Grandpa Charlie and Chief Joseph had different mothers, which made Joseph Charlie's step-uncle. Before my California journey, when I lived and worked in Minnesota, Chief Joseph had stepped forward in vision to take my hand. I began reading about him, everything I could find, and came to admire him for his loving heart and the courageous ways he tried to take care of his people.

I had never been to the beautiful area in Oregon where Joseph and his Nez Percé people had lived before they were moved to the barren reservations they now occupy. Desiring to touch his spirit and the spirit of those ancient people through their original homeland, I drove up the coast from California to Oregon, then crossed the Cascades and the plains beyond them. In the distance I could see the magnificent Wallawas, the mountains of Joseph's home. Driving through them and beyond, I began to see why Joseph and his people had loved this place so much. High above the plain with its lake stood the snow-capped mountains—they would have provided a cool and beautiful summer place. The people journeyed down in the fall, passing over the area of plains and on down, to the cottonwood-lined valley of the nearby Snake River for winter. Within a present-day county or two, they had a magnificent, nourishing, cradling home that included low river to high alpine—a rich and gracious land.

During my stay, I saw thunderclouds frequently rolling up over the Wallawas, building high into magnificent white shapes: each time they reminded me of Chief Joseph's Nez Percé name, which translates into "Thunder Rolling to Loftier Heights in the Mountains." After exploring the Wallawa area for several days, I followed the old peoples' trail down, down, and down across the Snake River to visit one of their reservations in Idaho. Feeling sad that this tribal lineage had also been lost to our family over the decades since Grandpa's time, I drove on through Idaho and into Montana.

But all the while, the huge splendid thunderclouds—and Joseph's spirit—rode with me. Close to home, I passed through the arid high farming country bordering the Apsa Reservation. I was getting eager to look down from the top of the highest hill and see before me the green, rolling pastures and mountains of Apsa country, so radically different from the farms with their dryness.

When I topped the hill, I was looking directly at the Medicine Rocks, far out across the rolling hills—the place where I would sit again to call vision. And I saw, directly over the spot where I would sit for my fast, an incredibly large, white, and radiant thundercloud. Joseph's spirit had gone on before me on this sunny day to provide a "welcome home" at my visioning place! During the entire time of that fast, his spirit was with me. The fast was a very personal one, in which I worked on many family issues, and Joseph came within me again and again to guide and counsel.

His thunderclouds in the blue skies, and his wise counsel within, have come to me a number of times since at very crucial junctures of my life and in times of need. One such reassuring visit was when I returned to Shinela country for the first time after the Sand Crabs incident. I wanted so much to be blessed in the Sacred Lodge, and yet I felt sick to my stomach whenever I thought of seeing him again—I hadn't yet heard the news of his removal. This time I approached the Benney area, where the Lodge was usually kept, by another route. My stomach was knotted with anxiety as I drove up from the south across the low pine-covered hills, following the river running beside the fields to the Lodge. As I came over the top of a long red hill, and could see down across the country where I knew Benney to be, there—over the area where the Lodge likely sat—was not only a huge thundercloud, but also, arching high in the sky over it, a rainbow. I let out a sigh, knowing Chief Joseph had signaled me that all was well. When I talked to my folks I learned that, indeed, there was a new keeper, a fine and highly spiritual man. In this way and countless others, Chief Joseph continues his loving guidance to this day.

A humorous vision came to me when I went into the Sacred Lodge that time. I needed something to release me from the memory, and to lighten me up so I could be free within the Lodge again. As always, there were the prayers: mine, my family's, the keeper's. I completed my prayers before the keeper, and I sat listening quietly, in a very left-sided state. Suddenly, there stood over me a huge buffalo bull. He seemed to fill the entire tipi, with his head near the eastern door and his tail behind me in the west. I could even smell his intense musty odor.

And then I realized what part of his anatomy I was near! I was seated in just such a position that his huge testicles hung right where my head was! I contemplated this strange state of affairs for a moment, until I noticed him begin to sway. I swayed and moved with him. In the swaying and moving, multicolored lights began popping and snapping all around in my head. Then I began to see my head, which also seemed to be his testicles, as a large rattle. The popping lights were the tiny stones in the rattle swirling and striking the hard rawhide of the rattle. As this continued, the sound of the rattle grew louder and louder. It felt as though the rattling was grabbing hold of all my thoughts, all that was in my brain, and shaking them—loosening and opening them.

This shake-up went on and on until I heard the keeper end his prayer. When I opened my eyes, the huge buffalo was gone. But my mind now felt open and clear. I smiled to myself about this funny yet powerful incident, realizing how much the Buffalo's Medicine had relaxed me in this place where I had formerly felt such deep anxiety.

While working with rattles in the months following this vision, I began to realize that one of their functions was to do exactly what I had experienced in the Sacred Lodge. Rattles do, in fact, pull our attention to them and shake it up; thus, they are excellent tools for clearing our rigidity, limitations, and old forms. I often use them in meditation, and occasionally take one to my fasting (vision questing) place to help me release the old and open to the new.

It became clear to me that all these happenings, all these experiences and many more, were grooming me, building a pathway of Spirit in my consciousness. These experiences were very different from the events of my ordinary world, and were invaluable in creating a map of inner awareness and vision. Seeking and finding Grandma Rosie had set me on a path that now widened itself step by step into a whole new territory of consciousness.

STRINGING THE PEARLS OF ONENESS

Although we often don't even realize it, the primary experience we two-leggeds are searching for is a perception of ourselves as Spirit, of ourselves connected with all things. Occasionally, we have the good fortune to touch those numinous moments of oneness with all of life that make White Buffalo Calf Pipe Woman's teachings come alive in our minds, hearts, and bodies.

And, yet, it is the day-to-day practice of connecting to Spirit within ourselves that solidifies the bridge of light and allows us to cross over into that place of oneness. So often we focus on looking for that "big moment" to transform our experience—not realizing that these extraordinary events have been made possible by the less momentous learnings and experiences that built toward them. And so, in order to continuously strengthen our connectedness with All That Is, we must create a consistent place and time for our spiritual practice, one that will allow us to move gently along with small, incremental steps.

The image I often receive in my practice is of a golden ray, a loop, of warmth and light coming to me from a Great Central Sun—the Source of All Life. Each time I make a bond with Spirit, a beautiful pearl of awareness and recognition is added to that golden loop of light creating, pearl by pearl, the necklace of mutual consciousness that connects us.

Of late, we seem to have strung so few pearls along the golden loop that there have been great gaps, great lapses, between them. But in my meditations I have discovered that regular attention to our spiritual practice continuously adds these luminous pearls of conscious connectedness. Over time, the pearls begin to mount up. And the more of them there are, the faster and faster others move toward the circling loop of oneness. The pearls seem to exude a sort of magnetic energy—as soon as they come near each other they are drawn closer and closer together until they eventually fill the loop. The necklace can then be fastened, and the circuit between Spirit without and Spirit within is complete. Suddenly, we experience the numinous moment when our connection with Spirit and all things becomes obvious to us. We realize that we have never simply been isolated pearls, but that we were always a necklace, scattered, and now come together again.

As we tie the tiny knots between one pearl and another, we are enlightened with another realization. All the pearls are the same size! The ones closer to the ends—the ones "closer to the realm of Spirit," we thought—are not larger, heavier, more beautiful, or more important than any of the others. The pearls of "our" human side are exactly the radiance, beauty, and size as all others. At this point an even deeper realization of the oneness of all things is made abundantly clear to us.

CREATING THE NECKLACE OF CONNECTEDNESS

If you would like to open yourself to the creation of such a necklace, then come with me into practice.

1. First, and most importantly, create a special place and a regular time for the creation of oneness.

▶ Decide upon a time when you will devote yourself to this practice. Although it will initially take great discipline, stick with this time in order to create in yourself and the larger life around you a readiness as this time approaches.

▶ The more often you meditate, the more quickly the additions are made. However, if your "meetings with Spirit" are unrealistically close, you may find the practice difficult to keep up, and you will drop away from it. But staying away too long means the pearls develop very little magnetism for each other. Find the right interval for you. It may take several tries to find the correct one, so do not "make yourself wrong" for this—just don't quit. It is all a part of the process.

2. Create an altar in your special "meeting" place.

▶ My suggestion is to clear a rectangular space about eight by twelve inches for your altar. Upon it, place a beautiful scarf or woven piece that is not too distracting. It should give the impression of being a space made ready to place something upon—open and receptive. I use small weaving from the Ortega family weavers of Chimayo, New Mexico (see appendix 1, page 457).

▶ Over time, you may realize that there is something you can place there to remind you of that connection. But often only Spirit resides there. It is important that if you do add an object, it should not distract your attention from the realm of the non-material. Remember that each physical thing is somewhat bound in time, space, and our experience, and we do not want to place limits on our experience of All That Is, of the oneness of Spirit.

▶ Have a cloth or scarf to cover the altar when you are not doing your practice. This keeps it from being associated with daily and outward things. Make it a special moment when you remove the cover. Do not remove it casually—have respect for this place of Spirit.

▶ It is best if this altar sits at a level where you are either looking up to it or down at it at a 45-degree angle. This helps your eyes trigger an internal state of receptivity. I find that looking down at the altar is the most balanced placement for me. That way, I can keep my back and neck tall and straight—simply dropping my chin, head, and eyes a bit. This also functions to open the area between the back of your skull and your neck—another eye or window to Spirit.

3. Create a comfortable place to sit, unless standing for extended periods is not tiring to you. You need to be relaxed yet alert, so something that helps you sit up straight and breathe deeply is very helpful. Make sure your back, hips, knees, ankles, and feet are comfortable and restful.

4. Clear your mind. Fill it with the empty space on your altar.

▶ Initially it is very helpful to use sound. I have been given a simple chant that works beautifully for me. It is a waiting song, meant specifically to be used for someone asking entrance at a Sacred Lodge, an elder's home, or the Lodge of the Great Spirit/All That Is. (You will find "The Waiting Song" on my cassette, *Singing Joy to the Earth:* See appendix 3, page 473.) Learning these simple notes and singing them continuously can be very useful to you in this process. Another sound that helps me greatly in this context is heartbeat drumming. I have recently created, for my own use and for distribution, a cassette tape that contains half an hour of the heartbeat on a rawhide drum. (See *Drumming the Heartbeat* in appendix 3, page 473.) You may use other sounds or music that feels helpful to you, such as Tibetan bells, or Native American flute songs, or chanting (see Canyon Records in appendix 1, page 456). Just remember to use sounds that open up that inner space, rather than fill it.

5. Soften your eyes. You can accomplish this in several ways:

▶ Feel what it's like to look outward as a kind of reaching with your eyes. It may cause you to lean forward, as though you are actually physically reaching for something. Notice the rather "grasping" energy that accompanies this kind of looking. Now, shift into a different mode of seeing. Let the light bring the objects in to you. Spirit knows when your eyes become receivers rather than graspers, shells catching the breeze rather than hands trying to grasp the wind. This receptive seeing is what I call "soft eyes."

▶ Although you are looking toward the altar, loosen the tight focus of your eyes; allow your vision to spread peripherally, seeing softly from the outer corners of your eyes.

▶ Now, relax your tongue, rest it in the bottom of your mouth. Let your breathing open and become fuller and deeper. Breathe into and from the belly rather than the chest.

6. Keep your attention on that open space on your altar. Acknowledge—perhaps inwardly, perhaps with a nod—any thoughts or images

that come. Then let a slight breeze—a breeze of Spirit—lift them up and away. Seek that open space. Breathe it into you.

7. Invite Spirit to come, to be present upon your altar. Make this invitation aloud, in whatever way seems right to you. Be aware of this presence with all your inner and outer senses. Remember Plenty Coups's lesson of using all our resources, both inner and outer.

8. Close your eyes and allow the part of you that is Spirit to rest upon the altar too. Allow it to blend with the presence of Spirit.

▶ Let this experience be whatever it is without judgment. Know that it may change.

▶ Have a gentle timer set, so you can totally relax into the experience without worrying about time. Begin with five minutes, and then extend that time as you find it pleasurable and nourishing to do so.

▶ For me, the inner images that come are often ones of light. Spirit comes as a tender and beautiful experience of light, of warmth, of peacefulness. Sometimes it comes as a taste of nectar or honey, or perhaps as a sound almost indistinguishable, reminding me of distant chimes or fairy bells. At other times it is simply a feeling of lightness and uplifting in my body. I sense those uplifting parts of myself that are akin to Spirit—smaller yet the same—and I blend them back into the oneness. As I do this, those magical internal bells grow louder for a moment and the light grows slightly brighter, everything intensifies as though in celebration. Then all softens back to the original gentle flow, and I am bathed in the warmth of that light, and the beauty and peacefulness of those sensations.

9. When the time is up, bring yourself gently back to outer reality by opening your eyes and turning soft eyes upon the altar. Then, consciously and with much joy, bring back within yourself the awareness of that spiritual part of yourself you have just experienced.

10. Give thanks for the experience you have had, whatever it may have been. As time goes on, and you begin to feel the nourishment of Spirit you receive in this way, the gratitude will come automatically!

11. Cover your altar once again and carry the lovely sensations of Spirit consciously with you for as long as you can.

As I looked back upon the experiences, the visions, and other left-sided events of this time, I could see that many of the scattered pieces of my lineage were coming together. Chief Joseph and Plenty Coups and Grandma Rosie—Nez Percé and Apsa and Shinela—all coming together to gift me with pieces of knowledge that I could make real in my life, modeling a spiritual and social leadership that greatly inspired me. The visions were speaking to me loud and clear. A bridge of Spirit was blending and integrating within me a world where we are all one.

CHAPTER FOUR

ON MY WAY TO THE SACRED MOUNTAIN

Bear Butte was in my mind a sort of Mecca,
an ultimate questing ground.

Vision quests are an age-old human practice
for the grooming of one's spirit.

When most people hear me speak of doing three- or four-day fasting or vision quests, they immediately think that the tough part is going without food and water for those days. At first, I too used to focus more on these simple deprivations, naively thinking that the real testing and teaching would come only from my days on the mountain and what I experienced there. In looking back, however, it has become quite obvious to me that I learned hundreds of lessons in meeting the challenges that came *before* I ever even touched the ground at my vision quest sites, or received the visions given me there. Especially on the quest that stands out in my mind as the most powerful, the days I spent on the sacred mountain were a breeze compared to what it took to get me up there in the first place!

I'd known Grandma Rosie for several years by this time, but I'd had to spend much of this time in San Francisco doing my doctoral studies; she knew that with my busy schedule I could be with her only occasionally. But even when I could manage to get away from California, often her choice was not for me to be with her and her teaching, but for me to spend time under her guidance communing with Spirit, reaching toward the Great Mystery.

This frequently took the form of vision quests, where I had the opportunity to quiet myself in the natural beauty of Mother Earth and Father Sky; the first major quest was to be at Bear Butte. This lone mountain standing out from the Plains near the Black Hills of South

Dakota is a traditional fasting place for the Shinela and Lakota people. It seems to be a vortex of Earth and Spirit energy, and the recognition of this energy has long called the Native peoples of the area to it for spiritual journeys.

In my mind it was a sort of Mecca, an ultimate questing ground. It brought together the ancient spirits of Grandma Rosie's people and mine, for my Native blood on my mother's side is Teton Lakota, a branch of the Lakota nation who lived around Fort Totten, North Dakota. It was an obvious choice, for Grandma and for me, that Bear Butte would be the site of my first major vision quest under her guidance.

Unfortunately, Bear Butte is not on a reservation. It is classed as a state monument and managed as an official park. Since this designation points it out as a special place for tourists to visit, they often interrupt the spiritual practices of the Native people questing there. At present, there is also the possibility that a housing development will be built very near the foot of the mountain on land adjacent to the park. Several Native tribes are trying to buy the land, but as yet do not have enough resources to do so. (If you are interested in helping to preserve this ancient site for traditional worship, contact Tek Nikerson at the Sacred Sites Conservancy—see appendix 1, page 457.)

Back in San Francisco, waiting for my precious two weeks of vacation time, my heart longed to be with Grandma Rosie. And yet I knew the experiences I was having through my doctoral program were also an essential part of my growth and transformation. Through my studies I was being exposed to brilliant minds on the awakening edge of a whole new human consciousness—a vital balance to the ways of the past that Grandma offered. Because I was enrolled in one of the pioneering non-residential doctoral programs through which you can study what will best develop your potential, I was actually receiving credit for my learning of Medicine ways! That was a truly wonderful blending of worlds for me.

Yet, even in our separation, my connection with Grandma remained strong, for she was like a fire from which my candle had been lit. And that candle burned brightly even when we were not physically together. Her spirit seemed to stay close, making her power available to me through prayer and inner visioning. In this way she helped me with simple things, and yet profound learning came from them.

For instance, there was the time when I wanted to move from a very small studio to a wonderful, large apartment. But the landlord had told me it had probably already been rented by the first people who had looked at it. I called out for Grandmother's help, and she came to me in vision, sweeping her arm in a great energetic circle that surrounded the apartment with light. She told me to create in my mind that same kind of energy circle around the apartment I wanted, and to seal it, holding my heart and my intention at the center. Just as quickly as she had come, she was gone. I immediately did as she'd told me, and before long the phone rang. It was the landlord, saying the other people had decided against the place and it was mine! I danced around the studio in glee, sending songs of thanks to Grandma. And I have used that simple, yet profound, teaching of energy and intention many, many times since in my life—always with her inner help, expanding it to draw a thing to me, to protect something, or keep something outside my circle.

I knew our connection through time and distance was strong. Yet, I knew even then how powerful it would be to spend extended periods of time with Grandma Rosie herself. As the years have passed, I have begun to understand more fully the things I lost by not being able to live with her, often perceiving them by noting my own weaknesses in spiritual matters and teaching. By not being with her day to day and observing her life and spiritual practice, I missed this daily grounding of spiritual life. Having not had that training under the strict and watchful eye of an elder, I sometimes find myself lax in my own daily spiritual observances. Since my time on the road is so filled with intense spiritual work, sometimes I just want to stop doing everything like that and take a vacation when I'm home. However, rather than judging myself too harshly, I simply try to integrate this understanding into my life and practice.

Another thing I missed was learning Grandma Rosie's language. I would like to have learned Shinela well enough to think in it, knowing that this different language would help me to experience the world in a totally different manner. I would still like to be able to see through the "eyes" of her language.

Finally, my long-awaited vacation time came, and I began the preparations for my journey to Bear Butte. I knew that being on the mountain would be easy for me. I had already done a ten-day cleansing fast, so my body was clear and light and accustomed to no food intake. I would eat very lightly until I stopped eating again on the mountain.

The difficult part was actually getting there. Starting from California with only two weeks available, I had to make the long, tiring drive north and get the visits with other family members and friends taken care of. Then the first thing I'd need to do once I arrived on the reservation was gather together my Medicine helpers who would assist me on my vision quest both logistically and spiritually.

On a vision quest, a helper is an essential in the process of clearing and leaving behind the everyday world. This is someone who will act as a bridge between you and ordinary reality, so that you can release the outer world, knowing that essential things will be dealt with and emergency calls will be handled without you.

The next thing I'd have to do was find a vehicle big enough to transport us all from Lone Deer to Bear Butte, half a day's drive away near the Black Hills. On top of that, I had to figure on two days' drive back to California. It seemed impossible in the time I had, yet these were my only available days during the warm part of the year because my studies continued throughout the summer.

I finally managed to borrow a pickup from some of my reluctant Apsa relatives by promising them that no drunks from that "other" tribe where I was going would be allowed to drive and wreck it. Leaving my own little car behind, I headed the truck toward Lone Deer to pick up my Medicine helpers. Gossip travels fast in Indian Country, and on the way I heard that my family helpers were drunk, fighting, and probably in jail. All the Apsas seemed gleeful about that because they felt it was exactly what I deserved for going among the enemy for spiritual guidance. And the Shinelas were equally gleeful because they resented my intrusion as an outsider in their sacred ways. I felt quite alone and desperate. If in fact my helpers were drunk or in jail, things could be delayed for days or weeks, and I had only two weeks to accomplish my goal. Despair played black around the edges of my mind.

When you read stories about my mom further on, and the lessons she taught my brother and me as she raised us, you will understand some of how I developed the incredible will and intention I relied on during this time. The contemptuous energy surrounding me only stimulated my determination—no one's negativity and dysfunction were going to stop me from this quest! Crying from the hurtful energy around me, I prayed aloud as I drove along, "Great Spirit, Mother Earth, Sacred Buffalo Spirit, help your pitiful daughter whose family has fallen away from her in her spiritual quest. Help me be a model for my people rather than a victim of these circumstances. Help me to complete in a good way this quest you have called me to do. Father, Mother, as always, I dedicate this fast to serving All My Relations. Ho!" I wrapped my will around an image of me coming down Bear Butte having completed my fast, felt a deep surge of energy course through my body, and stepped on the gas for Lone Deer.

When I arrived there, the bad news was totally confirmed, and my heart just sank. But I hated the thought of everyone's derision at my difficulties and of facing failure in front of them. So I gritted my teeth, gave up on one helper who was last seen drunk a hundred miles away, and headed for the local jail to find the other one. The place reeked of urine, vomit, and stale cigarettes as I opened the door. I spoke politely to the young full-blood who came to the desk, telling him that I was going on a fast at Bear Butte, and that my spiritual helper was in his jail. A spark of interest and sympathy lighted his eyes, and he told me to go talk with the judge about paying a fine to release her.

Yippee! At last a bright light, someone helpful. Still, I worried about how many hundred dollars the fine would be, and began inward calculations of my limited funds. I drove around looking for the judge and finally found her downtown, driving her family around to get their mail and groceries. She was a heavy, big-boned woman about my age with a stern look on her face. I told her who I was, about my vision quest and the limited time I had. And then I told her that my relative and helper was in jail, gave her the complete story, and finished it with a direct plea for my helper's release.

"Well," the big judge said, slowly considering the case, "because this is a spiritual matter and because she's already been in the drunk tank for two days, I think you can pay a fine and get her out today."

I held my breath waiting for a huge fine to be pronounced, but the judge said nothing. I finally blurted out, "My funds are pretty limited, and we have a long way to go to Bear Butte. How much will I need to pay to bail her out?"

The judge again took her time considering and ponderously announced her decision: "Ten dollars. Just tell the jailer and pay him."

Although my body simply gave her a very nice nod and a "Thank you, ma'am," my heart and soul knelt in thanksgiving upon the ground! Then I swung the pickup around, and headed back to the jail.

Once again the stale, putrid smell knocked me back as I opened the door. I couldn't help grinning, and I'm sure my eyes just snapped with light when I pronounced the fine to the jailer. He couldn't resist smiling himself as I wrote out the small check and handed it to him. He ceremoniously put it in the correct drawer, closed and locked the desk, and went to release his charge.

With my attention on my own problems and the vision quest, I had not realized before that this would be a very difficult moment for my family spiritual helper—my stepmom, Ella Jay. It took me many years of going back among my people on spiritual quests to realize that this blue-eyed half-breed kid from another tribe was becoming a model of spiritual life for my entire extended family, some of whom I'd never even met. Ella Jay's Shinela family is both Christian and traditionally religious. And since the Christian church is right across the street, and the Sacred Lodge twenty-five miles away over the mountain, much more attention had fallen on the Christian side of things.

Although Ella Jay's parents were members of the society that served and protected the Sacred Lodge, they had not visited it in Benney for a blessing in a long time. Each time I returned, eagerly bent on seeing Grandma Rosie and being blessed in the Lodge, Ella Jay would gather my dad, her mother, and as many other relatives as would come, and we would all go together. I loved this because it helped me feel less alone on my quest. It was years before I realized this was probably the only time they made pilgrimages to the Sacred Lodge for blessing—unless something terrible had happened and someone was in dire need of a special prayer.

I had no anger or judgment in my heart that day when my helper walked out of her cell—I was just overjoyed. But for her it was a moment of deep challenge and chagrin. When she came out, stinking of the drunk tank, with her head and eyes very low, I hugged her and said, "Let's go." It would be several years before she would finally break the insidious hold that alcohol had come to have on her. She would later tell me how that very moment, when she had to face me bailing her out of the drunk tank to be my spiritual helper, was the turning point in her recovery. Years later I heard many stories like hers. Stories about how my simple and direct spiritual intentions had turned around someone's life. I knew that I had actually done nothing special, but it did feel wonderful to know that, even in those bleak times when my heart ached from frustration and loneliness, Spirit was moving strongly through me to serve others.

Ella Jay and I headed for the house to gather the family's camping gear. Now I understood why I had been told to bring a big pickup as my young stepsister Heta and I loaded a huge white canvas tent, a gas cook stove, big frying pans, a large wash basin, enormous bedrolls with quilts and blankets and pillows, a folding camp table, and finally a younger relative or two, along with bags of groceries from town. After one final check of their gear we headed for Benney, which was on the other side of the reservation, hoping desperately to find Grandma at home and willing to go to Bear Butte. In the Shinela way, the Medicine helper accompanies the quester, even going up on the mountain with him or her for the days of the fast.

Over years of hard experience I had come to understand that I could not just write and make an appointment with Grandma Rosie and my other relatives on the reservations. Their lives were much too immediate, and not lived by appointment books. Although I understood this, it made it extremely difficult when I was on such a tight schedule. In this case, I would have to be blessed with great synchronicity for my quest to be completed! Yet, heading over the mountain for Benney that day with the pickup loaded and ready to go, we were an excited and hopeful crew—no more school, no more jail, no more worries!

But this was still no vacation; there were many more obstacles to overcome. When we arrived at Grandma Rosie's place, she was in fact home in her little log cabin on the plain by the river. But the Sacred Lodge was nowhere in sight. My heart sank again. Now what?

Grandma let out one of her long glissading "Ahhhhhhhhhhhhhh's," and gave me a hug as we entered her little old gray log cabin. I looked around again at the familiar space: an ancient iron-spring bed in the corner, a beat-up dresser, and little else. I knew that Grandma had few needs, yet I felt sad that she was not better taken care of by those she had served so faithfully for decades.

One time Ella Jay was worried about her because she was freezing cold in the winter. When I asked about the tribe or me giving her help to get a stove, Ella Jay said that she'd received one from the tribal elders' program, but that a nephew, supposedly taking care of her, had hocked it for booze money. Most anything she had of value ended up that way, something typical of the situation with elders of all tribes in recent decades. The young often consider their teachings old-fashioned and useless and, consequently, pay little attention to their needs or their sacred ways. It seemed strange that I had come such a long way, asking for her ancient ways to touch my life and spirit when those near her ignored them. While I came in gratefulness, many of them seemed only to make her life even more difficult.

Yet, through all the challenges of her life, Grandma kept a good frame of mind. She nodded her head happily as Ella Jay reminded her of my Bear Butte plans, and turned to give me a big grin. As always, I listened with my heart to the conversation I did not understand. Her language is a very difficult one. Even my dad, who had lived with them for years, had only a smattering of words and simple expressions. Then, my heart hit bottom again when I saw clouds form on Grandma's face and her head shake, "No, no, no." I waited anxiously for E.J. to translate for me. Heta, standing beside me, could understand only some of the old language, even though she'd been raised with it. But she was always too bashful to translate even that. I poked her in the ribs and questioned her with my eyes, but she just shrugged.

Ella Jay sighed and turned her attention to me. "Grandma doesn't have the Lodge in her keeping right now," she said. "She is honored to be asked to be with you at Bear Butte, yet she wants the keeper of the Sacred Lodge to come with us too, so this fast is done exactly right for you. The present keeper, Black Hand, and her husband live in Lone Deer, so we need to go back there and try to find her." We bundled up a few of Grandma's worn dresses and her personal items, put them in the back of the pickup with the kids, and headed back over the mountain for Lone Deer.

"Here we go again, Great Spirit—slowly making progress. You, who are the source of power and goodness," I prayed silently, "help me one more time to fulfill my dream." We climbed back out of the valley, stopped at the sacred spring for blessings and pure water, and journeyed on.

Native peoples hold a deep respect for water, especially the pure water of springs. Ella Jay had taught me on prior occasions how to first cleanse myself, then to offer prayers for the waters of all life, and only then to drink for myself. As we stopped at the spring, where many prayer ribbons waved in the light breeze, I stooped, reaching my right hand into the water and bringing it all the way up the left side of my body in a cleansing gesture. Then dipping again with the left hand, bringing water up along the right side, over and down. Next, I prayed for the cleansing of all the waters on Turtle Island, offered water in the four directions for All My Relations, and only then drank of the sweet, refreshing water. This kind of respect for all elements of life, especially for those things so directly vital to us, was a cornerstone of Grandmother's teaching.

Back in Lone Deer, we drove to where Black Hand was supposed to live, but found no one there. "She doesn't live here; try on the other side of the village," we heard from neighbors, who peered curiously out of their houses. We checked two or three different locations, each time feeling less hopeful about locating her until, at last, I saw the Sacred Lodge behind a small house with faded, peeling turquoise paint.

For a long time I had wondered why the new homes built by the Bureau of Indian Affairs Housing Department on the reservations always faded and peeled after so few years. Why did everything seem to fall apart so quickly there when compared to non-reservation towns? The puzzle was solved at last when we finally got a housing director with integrity. She found that the past directors had been buying the cheapest paint possible, rather than the good paint specified in the government contract, and had then split the difference in cost between themselves and the contractor. Such practices took place more often than I could believe.

It was already past noon when Grandma and Ella Jay went inside the house to request the keeper's presence with us on my Bear Butte fast, and it seemed forever before they came out. I could feel in the air that this person was not the least bit enthused about the prospect of abandoning her personal plans for the next few days. Yet, it was part of her duty as the keeper of the Lodge to do just that. Finally, Ella Jay came out with a report: Black Hand was indeed resisting the idea, so she'd left Grandma with her. From the sounds we could hear coming out the door, Grandma was mincing no words about what the keeper's duties were.

"Why can't it just be simple? Why can't everyone be as joyful and excited as I am?" I asked Spirit when Grandma came out the door practically dragging Black Hand behind her. It seemed hours later before the pickup was re-loaded with our gang, plus Black Hand and the various young people she had negotiated to bring along, their camping gear, and a dog or two. The more people who came along, the more I had to feed, and I kept thinking about my limited funds—but also of the New Testament story of the loaves and the fishes. The two keepers, having priority as elders, got into the cab—the place of honor—with me. Among traditional Native people, elders are respected and cared for. They are allowed to go first in line and are given lighter responsibilities so that they can focus their attention on bringing forward the wisdom needed to help guide the people. In the back of the pickup, Ella Jay and the gang tucked themselves around the canvas tarp–covered camping equipment as I roared past the two-block downtown area of Lone Deer, past the old wrecked cars, and past the jail.

Many hours and a number of bathroom stops later, driving across the rolling grass-covered Plains, we saw signs on the left indicating the turnoff to Devil's Tower, which the ancestors had appropriately named the Bear-Clawed Hill—I could feel Bear Butte drawing near. Ella Jay had told me stories about how in the times long, long ago, a Great Spirit Bear had used this stump of an enormous tree as a clawing post. Over the years he had clawed lines down every side. Then the stump had petrified, and so it remained, to be renamed the Devil's Tower by white men.

My mind turned to the old days when our Native people roamed free across the fenceless Plains, and left the imprints of their spirits in the ground at these sacred sites. I thought of my own Lakota lineage, long scattered through death and "white-adoptions," in which young Indian children were adopted by white families wanting to give them "better" lives. This had happened to my Lakota grandmother, who had been orphaned at the age of four and taken to live with a white family. Thus, she lost all of her rich Native heritage, and had little to pass down to her children and grandchildren. I also thought of the wise Black Elk in his old age crying on Harney Peak—another sacred site not far away from us on this journey—for help for his shattered people. He was calling for the fulfillment of his vision of a sacred dance in which all races will come together to renew the Tree of Life—calling as I would now call on Bear Butte.

Whatever the name used for the form that in modern times is called vision quest, it is an ancient cross-cultural practice. In every religion I have studied, among all the peoples of the Earth, there is a practice of going alone into the beauty and solitude of nature to touch deeply within oneself and open to the Great Mystery. Whether it is a young Australian aborigine on walkabout, a Lakota fasting on Bear Butte, a devout Catholic getting in touch with Spirit at a retreat center, or Jesus fasting forty days in the wilderness—it is the same basic form; and it is a good one.

When we fast, we essentially refrain from taking in on the right side of our experience. This creates what might be called a vacuum in our consciousness. By our very nature, something else will come in to fill that space. If we leave behind as much as possible of our everyday, right-sided world by going away from our home, taking nothing with us, not eating food, sometimes not even drinking water, then we quite effectively cut ourselves off from the ordinary world.

What remains with us is the way we perceive that same world as it lives inside of our minds. This in itself is a profound lesson. For we learn that leaving something physically behind does not mean we are finished with it. My personal experience has been that all the concerns of my normal world follow me, and come up over and over again as I sit alone. I acknowledge them, "order" them, and let them go; as long as they are occupying my total consciousness, I put them in order to help find the basic themes, the deepest roots, of my concerns. When I get to the bottom of them, I then release them to the Great Mystery.

Often several days into the fast, sitting there in the beauty and inspiration of the wilderness, there come magical moments of quiet on my right side. And into this quiet pours the left side of my experience. The vacuum is filled with the richness of dream, vision, clairvoyance, astral travel, extraordinary perception, mystical revelation, touching the Great Mystery, and all the other left-sided events.

The fast seems to work the same way with all people. It is a brilliant tool for opening ourselves to the Great Mystery and to the Source of Life within our own being. Leaving behind our everyday world, taking ourselves into the beauty, harmony, and mystery of nature, creating the space and time within ourselves to listen deeply—all these things work beautifully to deepen our spirit.

I recently saw something almost humorous, had it not been so sad, written by a militant Native group concerning vision quest. It seems that in Colorado there is a group of young, spiritual, Earth-oriented people who have formed a group called Vision Quest—and one aspect of their teaching and sharing is assisting people on vision quests. The radical paper I read accused this group of stealing Native practices, and made the rash statement that "vision quest" is an Indian term and should not be used by white people.

This was quite humorous to me, since the words "vision quest" are themselves English. It seemed that the militant group was stealing the English words and calling them their own—quite a reversal for a group claiming to separate themselves from the larger culture. However, the sad part is that anyone—especially those who are Lakota and who carry the Sacred Pipe of White Buffalo Calf Woman—should divide themselves from others spiritually, and claim an ancient human form exclusively as their own. Spirit is the same within each of us. Personally, I am thrilled when I hear of people using this simple and beautiful form of spiritual practice. I know it is "owned" by no one but the Great Mystery, and I know those who use it will learn from it, and learn deeply.

As we approached Bear Butte, the long slant of the August sun turned the waving grass before us golden, as the magic of two-light time approached. In the far distance all around us, we could see thunderstorms and zigzag flashes of lightning. I hoped for the sake of our open-air passengers in the back that it would not rain on us.

Suddenly, ahead of us in the golden light, a brilliant rainbow filled the right half of the sky with radiant color! We were all awed into silence. Even the children were still, round-eyed with wonder. As I meditated upon this omen, I understood that I had now accomplished the right side of my task. Soon I would be able to give away these worldly concerns, and have the luxury of turning my total attention to the left side, crying for vision among the blessed spirits of this ancient fasting place.

Bear Butte, sacred mountain, my spirit is coming home at last!

FASTING—A PATHWAY TO SPIRIT

After checking with your personal health consultant and reading some of the modern literature on fasting, do a one-day fast for yourself. Do this, not as a punishment or a sacrifice, but as a joyful way to call upon another part of yourself, a way to awaken to Spirit's voice within you.

Your fast can simply be one in which you refrain from food while continuing with your daily routine. However, you might not notice much of a difference in yourself doing it this way. A much richer experience is possible if you create a ritual for yourself around your fast. Start by taking the day off. Go to a beautiful place in nature near your home. Find an inviting spot and create a sacred space for yourself, using sage as a clearing smudge for both your space and yourself. Keeping silence, spend the day in quiet meditation or centering. Such a ritual state of consciousness will add to the power of your practice.

Preparing for the One-Day Fast: Before you begin your fasting ritual, you might want to spend a few days taking an inventory of your beliefs about not eating for what may appear to be a long period of time.

1. What is your response to the following questionable statements?
  ▶ If I do not eat, I will die.
  ▶ If I miss several meals in a day, it will damage my body.

2. Note how much actual time you spend on food during normal days: its purchase, preparation, thinking about what to cook, cooking, eating, cleaning up, buying household items related to food preparation, and so on.

3. How many other roles does food play in your life besides simply nourishing your body? What gaps does it help you fill?
  ▶ Do you eat to feed yourself emotionally?
  ▶ Do you use food as a reward for completing certain unpleasant tasks?
  ▶ Do you use food to avoid thinking about or dealing with difficult issues in your life?
  ▶ Does food have a social function in your life? Is this function positive or negative?

Making an assessment of these things will help you understand ahead of time the kind of issues that may come up for you as you fast on a vision quest. *Whatever holes in your life you fill with food—or anything else you've included on your fast—will become very obvious when you begin to do without them.*

ALTERNATE FASTS

1. Try fasting from some of the other things that normally fill your days:

▶ A day of silence is a very powerful teacher. Try taking a fast from speaking. Although you can do this around others, you may find it easier at first to be more solitary. Being silent when you're around others helps you notice how much of daily chatter is either unnecessary, done from nervousness, or stated negatively.

▶ Fast from driving your car.

▶ Take a fast from city life. Spend a day totally in nature.

▶ Fast from doing things the habitual way. Totally change your daily routine beginning with getting up, bathing, and dressing. Do things out of order. Don't do old things. Try adding new things. Shake up your day.

2. Take careful note of what new places in your consciousness are opened up by experiencing various fasts. List the issues that come up around each person or experience you leave behind for a while.

3. Pay special attention in any of your fasting practices to how much your beliefs determine your reality. If you think you will suffer physical damage from fasting, there is no way you will be able to go without eating for a day without feeling bad. If you think you will starve to death in four days without food lost in the woods, know that this death is much less likely to occur if you can treat the lack of food as a fast to help open and clear you to perceive the emergency situation in a different light.

A TURNING OF ATTENTION

1. Consider the possibilities of new ways of being and doing that these reflections open up. Remind yourself that through these practices you have the ability to change your habits—your ways of being and doing in the world.

In my tradition this is called a turning of attention. Your attention—literally whatever you pay attention to—is the tool of creating your world. When it is developed it is one of the most powerful techniques for transformation that you will find. Wherever you focus your attention is where the energy of life takes you. For example, if you pay attention only to what doesn't work in your life, then you will call more of that to you. If you constantly worry about how fat you are rather than focusing on images of slimness and your essential self, you will never lose weight.

Conversely, attending to what works, to what brings you joy—focusing on what nurtures and uplifts you—will bring great rewards.

2. Begin to consider yourself as the creator of your own life, rather than simply reacting to what comes. Too often people wait for some magical happening or some savior to come and rescue them, ignorant of the fact that their inner practice is what truly initiates the change. The inner changes may then evolve to outward shifts such as finding helpers or any number of things—but not the other way around.

Don't be fooled by the confusion that reigns in the thinking of the larger culture today. It is not the physical world, but rather the powerful inner world of Spirit that is connected to all other things, which is where the action is!

3. If you have fasted before, remember that this practice is not a one-time thing. Begin a series of fasts and work up to four days. Try the ten-day "Master Cleanser" fast (see appendix 1, page 458, for further information). It consists of eleven days of "supervised" fasting on the "liquid sunshine" of fresh lemonade. You can do this fast during your regular working days if necessary; although it cleanses at a very deep level, it gives you enough energy to keep a relatively normal schedule.

4. After a fast of from four to ten days, it is very valuable to take an inventory of your inner and outer senses. Take a reading of:

▶ Your general energy level.

▶ Your feeling of clarity and flexibility in body and mind.

▶ Your state of tension or relaxation.

▶ Your willingness to release worry, anger, past concerns, and future anxieties.

▶ The openness of your heart and mind.

▶ The sensitivity of your perceptions—both physical and psychic.

Each time you fast you deepen your experience, make smoother the path to your left side, and tune yourself to Spirit more clearly and quickly. The old ones who were healers or diviners or shamans of many forms would most often fast for four days before performing a healing, a ceremony, or a divining. It seemed the quickest way for them to clear the ego self and open themselves as channels for the Divine expression. They knew that fasting in the proper spirit uplifted rather than depleted the physical body. Today, science is beginning to catch up to this old knowledge. Nutritional researchers have shown that for most of us well-fed Americans, it would take something like thirty days without food before we even began to experience the true hunger of starvation.

As I have already mentioned, I had used a "Master Cleanser" fast to clear myself before I left California to begin the journey of my first vision quest with Grandma Rosie. This made the whole experience much easier for me because not only was I clean internally in a way that would make four days without food less difficult for my body, but I was clear in other ways as well.

Proper fasting made my entire questing process easier, helping me to release tension both in my body and in my mind; to move with more flexibility and freedom; and to be more sensitive to nuances both from the outside world and from my own inner guidance. It helped me to release past and future in a way that allowed me to focus on each issue in the present moment, and having solved it, to let it go to make room in my consciousness to attend to the next moment.

As we drove the final miles to Bear Butte under an illuminating rainbow, I felt its clarity and radiance within myself as well. The light was with me, and tears of gratefulness poured down my cheeks.

THE HEART OF BLACK HAND

My form is to be the formless form: that which breaks through form into Spirit.

The focus of my learning had continually been on how to live a truly human life on Mother Earth —how to live with the Great Circle of Life, of which I am a part, in a harmonious way.

In my early spiritual questing, I often idealized "true learning" as being joyful and special. True learning, I believed, was assisted by a teacher who would lovingly draw my very best from me. While it is useful to recognize this as an ideal, my life experience has shown me that learning has many different faces. True learning has come to me many times when the instrument of my lessons—my teacher—has behaved differently from my ideal, and my heart has been greatly hurt in the process. Such a time was my pilgrimage to Bear Butte.

When we picked up Grandma Rosie and she revealed that another family was keeping the Sacred Lodge, I was somewhat disappointed since I had already formed a close relationship with Grandma. Working with a new keeper meant having to get to know someone else, going through whatever reactions they might have to my being of another tribe, and who knew what else, at a time when I simply wanted to get on with the business of the vision quest. Yet, as we drove back to Lone Deer, I began to feel excited about meeting another woman of Spirit. Grandma's acceptance and sponsorship of me would very likely help smooth any rough edges, and I realized that this was just another part of the learning and the adventure. Sometimes it is easy for me, given my rearing that emphasized "getting down to business," to neglect the realization that relationship is primary, that from a good foundation, everything else can be easily accomplished.

Nevertheless, as I sat in the back of the old blue pickup in front of Black Hand's home, visiting with kids and hearing sounds of loud arguing from the keeper's house, my heart sank. Looking past the house into the dusty backyard where the Sacred Lodge sat, I longed to go within it for the solace and strength it always provided. My thoughts turned to the Bundle, which held the Sacred Buffalo Medicine objects, wrapped in cloths and covered with a buffalo robe. Its Medicine seemed to whisper to me and call to me, yet I could not make out its words above the angry arguing, much as I strained to hear.

Arguing—that brought me back to the present moment, as Ella Jay came out to say that Black Hand was not pleased about fulfilling her duties on Bear Butte. Grandma, however, remained within, using her well-developed powers of persuasion. E.J. told me that Grandma was doing her best to get the Lodge keeper to accompany me on this quest, so that it would be formally and traditionally correct. When Grandma was involved, she wanted to do things in such a way as to call the highest energies to the quest for vision. I'm sure that in her mind, there was no question but that the keeper of the Sacred Lodge should accompany me.

I felt torn inside, sitting there thinking that the energy would be better if this reluctant woman stayed home, yet knowing my respected elder thought she should come. In my own mind it seemed that, if I had Grandma with me, I would have need for no other. I expressed this to Ella Jay, and she reminded me that in the Shinela way, the Medicine person accompanies the quester upon the mountain, staying with them the entire time, and so fasting and questing themselves. Often, a whole party would go together under the supervision of one Medicine person. And at eighty-five years old, Grandma Rosie was not in shape to be climbing steep, rocky paths, or sitting three days on a stone bed.

I knew, having participated in other tribal ways for supervising such fasts, that the Medicine person's duties include blessing each quester as they leave for their fast, staying close with them in spirit, offering formal prayers for them at regular intervals, greeting them when they return, and often counseling with them at length later concerning their experience. This way was familiar to me. But I wondered how it would be in this Shinela tradition. The thought of having an unfamiliar person, especially one with the negative energy she now seemed to have, sitting near me as I opened myself to the Great Mystery was quite distressing. My expectation in journeying such a long way to a sacred place for my quest was to have beautiful, uplifting energy to help me seek vision. After being in the busy city all those long months, I had lovely images of four quiet days alone high on the sacred mountain, communing with only my non-human and Spirit relations. Mother Earth had always been my best teacher, and I had often found such joy in her presence. I didn't realize until now that the four days of solitude were a guarantee of renewal for me, even if some great vision did not come. And this renewal I badly needed, for there would be no other such time for months and months of a busy school year.

"It looks like we're going to do it by the book," I said to myself as Grandma came outside, followed reluctantly by a younger woman dressed in the same traditional faded gingham and wide stamped-leather belt that Grandma wore. Black Hand's shiny black hair was in long braids; only an occasional silver hair glinted in the noonday sun. Wide-shouldered and husky of build, Black Hand looked very young alongside the stooped and frail elder. Although it was difficult to tell, I guessed her age to be between fifty and fifty-five years old. She acknowledged our introduction with a weak handshake, but did not look me in the eyes.

Then she went in to pack her things, and soon her grandchildren were bringing bundles of clothing and gear to be added to our pile. I realized that all the bundles would make soft seating for those riding in the open back of the pickup, and was glad for it. We climbed in, made one last stop at the trading post for more tobacco, an herb whose medicine, or unique power, is to help us become one with whatever we offer it to, and thus is considered especially useful in vision quest and other ceremonies where such oneness is paramount.

In the cab of the pickup things were quiet and strained as we started on our way. I longed for Ella Jay to be sitting with Grandma and me. Seldom did I have this much time with Grandma, and I wished for a friendly translator. I longed to hear about the old ways and the old days; of fasts she had done, visions she had seen, things she had learned. I yearned to hear from her the kind of teaching stories that Ella Jay would often tell me. "There was a Shinela boy one time . . ." she would begin, and I never knew if the story was set several years ago with one of our cousins, or back in mythical days of old when those huge familiar footlike imprints were set in stone on our hillside by a Shinela spirit warrior.

But here we were, acting again in the correct way, with the two older medicine women riding in the cab, and Ella Jay in the back. As I leaned my ear out the window, I could hear their laughter and occasional snatches of stories. I felt the loss of their joy and laughter, as well as the loss of sharing a deeper connection I had hoped to make with Grandmother. Tears welled up in my eyes, although I was not about to let them spill over in front of this hostile woman.

Then Black Hand seemed to relax a bit, and began talking, between puffs on her cigarette. "Yes, I have done this before," she said. "There was a young man who came *all the way from California* to be with me. He wanted me to take him on a vision quest at Bear Butte, so I did. He was sure a nice young man, he listened to everything I said. We stayed only a few hours, and he paid me a lot of money!" Her final statement seemed to be the most important to her, although she seemed quite proud that he had come all that way to see *her*—not thinking of herself as the servant of the Sacred Lodge, it seemed. My eyebrows raised at her prideful way of speaking. I glanced sideways, hoping to see Grandma's face, and said nothing. It was a surprise to hear Black Hand speak in such a manner, and even more shocking to see that she was willing to do this in front of Grandma. I was chagrined as she continued her story for a good portion of the drive. Grandma scowled deeply, and tucked herself in the far corner of the cab, yet said nothing.

There is often misconception among outsiders about payment for spiritual services among traditional peoples. In the old days, it was not thought of so much as payment but as a gifting cycle, an exchange of energy. If a Lodge keeper was asked by the tribe to be on duty at the Lodge twenty-four hours a day, that obviously meant he had no time to go on the hunt or do many other tasks for the support of himself and his family. It was simply common sense that he be gifted for the services he provided.

The system of gifting was likely well-established and accepted: often something like a buffalo robe was gifted for the supervision of a vision quest, in addition to the tobacco and other offerings appropriate to the occasion. Because of their close relationship and caring for each other, they had a common practice of what we now call a sliding scale. For example, a widowed grandmother with few relatives to help support her would be expected to give something less than, say, a healthy young man from a well-to-do family.

Another way of returning energy was to give something in four categories: food, clothing, housing, and ceremony. An elder crippled man might give a grouse he had snared, a small used deer hide, a buffalo horn spoon he had carefully carved, and a small bundle of sage gathered nearby. For the same service, a wealthy young woman might give an elk freshly killed and skinned by one of her brothers, a beautifully tanned pair of leggings, a buffalo hide suited for a tipi covering, and a bundle of special tobacco grown by her father. There was always a grateful exchange of goods and energies, although there was no necessity of asking for payment because the traditional exchange values were already known.

Today, many young people from other cultures come to elders for spiritual guidance and offer only tobacco in return. While the elders appreciate this traditional offering, they have often said to me, "I sure wish I could pay my bills with tobacco or eat it. That's all I'm ever offered, and I have stacks of it!" All those who come seeking gifts of support from the elders must wake up and think deeply about what they are willing to give in return to support the lives of the old ones. Often someone who would pay sixty-five dollars or seventy-five dollars an hour to consult another helping professional will offer only a seventy-five-cent bag of tobacco for hours of an elder's time. This is not right, or fair in any way.

In this experience with Black Hand, I was confident that Ella Jay, as my helper, both knew the correct gifting exchange and would take care of it for me. Besides E.J.'s beautiful spirit, these were the kinds of things that made her invaluable to me. Her knowledge and her good heart combined into a way of generosity in her dealings. As Black Hand droned on and on and on about the big payment for accompanying the California man, I was deeply grateful to have my giveaway for her part in this quest well covered. So, a few hours into the woman's monologue, I mentioned that Ella Jay was taking care of all those things for me, and I didn't speak again.

Yet, having the formal matters in hand didn't help my heart feel better. Every word she spoke not only grated against my sense of correctness, it also tore at me, rekindling the longing in my heart and spirit for elders to guide and share with me in a loving and generous manner. And it hurt my heart as well that this woman, who was supposed to be an exemplar of spiritual values, was focused on such a different level. This would become a recurring theme for me in my quest to open my spirit: seeking elders to respect and learn from, then finding them less than respectable and helpful. I looked back at our people's history—the purposeful destruction of our way of life and our values—and wondered if any of it would survive the continual pressure of the wider culture.

After many hours, each made much longer by the grinding mono-logue going on beside me, and by Grandma's brooding energy in the corner, we suddenly saw the most magnificent rainbow. Its beauty above the waving prairie grass turned golden by the late afternoon sun was stronger than the negativity beside me. Once again, my heart began to soar. My spirits lifted as this arching symbol of beauty and radiance spanned the sky before us, reminding me again that I must not get caught in pettiness and smallness of spirit. My resolve to have this be an absolutely wonderful experience returned and swelled in my chest.

At last we saw the outline of Bear Butte, a pointed sentinel on the grassy Plains with the dark outline of the Black Hills in the far distance. Soon, we arrived at the base of the sacred mountain. I was thrilled in more ways than one to get out of that little cab and onto the solid ground of Bear Butte! Sage scented the air, the children's playful tumbling eased the tension, Ella Jay's good-natured bustle in setting up camp brought my heart back to some equilibrium. I kept staring up at that butte as its pine-clad silhouette began to dominate the twilight sky.

As the head of our camp, E.J. organized the placement of tents, tables, and stoves. The kids and I unloaded bundle after bundle, helping to make everyone comfortable for four days of camping out. The scent of frying meat and potatoes filled the late afternoon air, and I walked about as they ate their dinner.

Climbing up the first gentle slopes through sage brush and twisted juniper, I lifted my eyes gradually up the miniature mountain I would climb at dawn. A well-worn trail wound around through juniper and into pine on the steepening slope to the peak. This small, upthrusting mountain seemed to have been placed here in the open prairie by the Great Spirit as though to encourage those coming east toward the Black Hills—to presage their beauty and sacredness. The Black Hills, called *Paha Sapa* by our Lakota people, have long been held sacred. Unfortunately, they were purposefully not included in any of the reservations, and consequently everyone from early gold miners to present-day tourists have been able to overrun these holy mountains.

Later in the evening, Grandma Rosie and the younger medicine woman spoke to me about the process of the fast, and encouraged me to drink and drink and drink and drink water, for at dawn Black Hand and I would climb the mountain to be without water for more than three days. I took in enormous amounts of the good, clear water there, drinking as I walked around looking up at the butte, thinking of the centuries over which our people had come here to pray. I crawled nervously into my sleeping bag, wondering about the visions to come and about how it would feel to be very, very thirsty.

My excitement kept me awake that night long after the birds had stopped their chirping and the camp settled into silence. My thoughts raced, turning apprehensively again and again to three days in the sun with no water. Although I had heard that medical doctors say one should not be without water this long—perhaps even that one cannot—I knew I had spent two days without water on a previous fast with no great challenge. While Ella Jay had told me stories of how physically difficult recent Shinela seekers had found such a vision quest, I was light, clear, toned, open, and healthy. It comforted me somewhat to remind myself that part of the difficulty others experienced very likely came from eating a huge feast, especially of meat, the evening before climbing the mountain. Over the three days of the fast, that food would putrefy in the stomach and poison the system.

I gave thanks for all the protecting knowledge I had gained in my years away from my home reservation, as well as for what had been given me at home. My learning had continually been focused on *how to live a truly human life on Mother Earth*—how to live in a harmonious way with the Great Circle of Life of which I am a part. Spirit had moved me widely in the world, and I had been given the opportunity to see the truth of Spirit's light within every tradition, as well as some loss of that light in most of them.

Daybreak came early. I jumped out of bed, dressed very simply, made a last accounting of the few things I would take with me, and was ready to go! Morning light on Bear Butte made it golden, and I longed to set foot on the trail. Since the moment I'd seen it in the distance, I'd had itchy feet to climb to the very top so that I could look out across the rolling prairie in a great circle, and give prayers to all the directions. Ella Jay was up and about, leaving the children in her large tent sleeping peacefully.

I could hear sounds from the tent where Grandma and Black Hand slept; I knew Grandma Rosie was awake, and stiff from a night on the bedroll, no doubt. I had brought a small backpacking tent for them, the only one I had. When Grandma had great difficulty crawling into it the night before, I realized how much better a taller one would have been for her—I disliked having her troubled in any way. Although she was so good-natured and easygoing I could see, as she finally made it out this morning and got herself standing, that it was very hard on her.

However, Black Hand seemed very little more flexible than Grandma, and we could hear her muttering. Grandma called out to her to get moving, but she did not appear. The sun was climbing well above the rim of sky formed by the Black Hills to our east, and I couldn't find anything to do with myself. The tension mounted in me, and I could see it in Ella Jay and Grandma too. I sidled up to Ella Jay, commented that I had thought we were leaving at first light, and asked if it was necessary for me to wait for the keeper. "Yes, it would be best," she cautioned. I thought about being on the sacred mountain for three days with Black Hand, and shook my head in dismay.

So I waited. And fidgeted. My body, heart, and my very soul longed to be on that mountain. I had thought of it for months, planned for it weeks and weeks, and now, another delay as precious moments of morning sun on the mountain slipped away. My highest and finest teachers had always taught me to experience what I was feeling, and to act from that place. In that moment it felt so right inside for me to move, to go. Yet, there was also a part of me that wanted to discipline myself to experience whatever the traditional form held for me. My patience, never my best feature, was being tested!

What seemed to me light years later, Black Hand had at last gotten up, taken her time with morning toiletries, listened to a lecture from Grandma Rosie, and with by now characteristic reluctance, motioned me to follow her up the trail. Each of us carried only our sleeping robes and a small bag of ceremonial items. I let her start ahead of me, knowing my pace would be much faster than hers, and how challenging it is for me to slow down to someone else's pace. In about two minutes, I caught up with her. We were climbing the first little rise up from the camp-ground. From here the trail evened out for several hundred yards, and then the actual climb began.

Black Hand instructed me to pick sage wherever it was abundant along the way. She said this would be used to make a fragrant and purifying ceremonial bed for me to rest on during the days of my fast. Sage is an herb which is often used in ceremony because of the cleansing properties its vibration emits when burned as smudge or simply smelled. Its particular cleansing is of the subtle energies around us, our aura, and the general atmosphere. I zigzagged among the tall sage plants, picking a small piece from each one, and offering cornmeal in gratitude for Mother Earth's abundant gifts of healing and fragrant herbs. My arms were soon full, and I caught up with the older woman again.

My body, in shape from running several miles a day, was bursting with energy. I wanted to run up that mountain and stand breathless at its top, where Ella Jay had said I would see prayer cloths from other fasters who had quested here, waving from limbs of trees. Images of my offering cloths blowing in those same breezes filled my attention, and I nearly ran over Black Hand. She had stopped on the little hill a few hundred yards from camp. I assumed she was just catching her breath, so I stepped back respectfully, and waited.

When she motioned for me to spread the bed of sage there, I was incredulous. I tried to be calm, but my open-mouthed look of shock and disbelief must have seemed almost funny. "You mean right here?" I asked in a squeaky voice. My breath would not come. I couldn't believe this. "I thought we were going up on the mountain." But she said, "This is far enough," nodding her head and motioning for me to put the sage down for my bed.

I must have seemed very dull-witted to her, because I just stood dumbfounded for a few minutes. When it finally registered that she meant it, I turned quickly to look for a good place for my bed, so she would not see the tears welling up in my eyes, or the flash of anger behind them. I had come all this way, just to sit on a little hill I didn't even consider part of the mountain? I stopped my breath so I wouldn't burst into a crying wail like an angry child. I had worked so hard. I had overcome tremendous obstacles to stand at the foot of this sacred mountain, and at its foot it seemed I would stay. My disappointment was so deep I knew it touched beyond this present moment. It reached deeply into the place where, growing up, I had been disappointed again and again by the adults around me. Oh, God, it would have been good for me to cry and wail! But I was not about to give Black Hand the satisfaction of seeing me cry.

So when I had myself in a little better control, I knelt and laid my fragrant bundle on the ground, spreading the sage out neatly, row by row, on the hard, gravelly red earth. I felt so alone—no Ella Jay to turn to here, no Grandma I trusted so deeply. So I did what I have always done; I turned to the Spirit that lives in me as in all things, the Great Spirit. In my heart I called upon the Great Mystery, and upon the Sacred Buffalo Medicine of the Lodge with whose blessing I had come here. I prayed that I might learn from these lessons no matter the outer form, that I might leave here knowing myself and Spirit better than when I came. "Don't be so prideful and self-righteous," I chided myself. "Let go of your expectations, and be awake in this moment."

The press of tears had passed. I turned my attention to the present moment and the Lodge keeper sitting on her bed of sage beside me. She reached for her medicine bundle and opened it.

The word "medicine" has many nuances of meaning, but it most commonly refers to the unique power resident in, or attributed to, each thing or being. Often each individual has a personal medicine bundle—a small bag of items that have unique and special power for them. It could contain items other people would regard as sacred; but it's also likely to contain things of significance only to the carrier. For instance, I might take a small stone from this vision quest site to remind me forever of my experience there. No one else would even know what that stone signified. Thus, for me, my found stone would have Bear Butte medicine. Tobacco has the medicine of unity; the Sacred Pipe has the medicine of oneness and holiness; and an individual might have the medicine gift of singing, or carving, or counseling.

Black Hand took out a ceremonial catlinite pipe bowl, and attached it to its long wooden stem. (All pipe carriers have their own individual ways of ceremonially moving this sacred object, which represents the Great Circle of Life. However, most often the form consists of moving the pipe—masculine stem or feminine bowl first—to symbolically connect it to one's own mind and heart, and then to acknowledge Mother Earth, Father Spirit, and all things in the Circle of Life around us.) Catlinite is an opaque terra-cotta-colored stone, more commonly known as "pipestone" since many Native ceremonial pipes are made from it. One of the few places it is found is at a quarry now called Pipestone, Minnesota, in the southwest corner of the state, a place long held sacred by Native peoples.

With very little ceremony, Black Hand filled the pipe, smoked it, and handed it to me. I watched her, wanting to learn as much as I could from the things she did for me. I watched how she held this pipe, which had its origin with White Buffalo Calf Pipe Woman, noting every detail of how she moved it. I followed the form she used when it came my turn to pray with the pipe, and handed it back to her.

Then, reaching into her medicine bundle again, Black Hand withdrew a small container. Opening it and putting it down beside her, she climbed grunting from a sitting position to kneel in front of me. "I will paint you now," she said. "Hold your head still." Ceremonial painting, whether of the face or other parts of the body, is a way to outwardly acknowledge and make real something that exists only in vision or in thought.

Black Hand began drawing a black line that circled down the side of my face, under my chin, up the other side, below my hairline, and around to join the beginning of the line. Then she told me to extend my wrists and ankles. These she circled with paint as well, telling me that these circles were indications to Spirit that I was not using my outer senses or the doingness of my hands and feet to learn these lessons—that I was fasting from the external world so that I might journey within myself and within all things to a more subtle level of communion. This would help Spirit to understand my intentions, and to feel favorably toward me. I added my own prayers, asking the Great Mystery to open me, and inviting the spirits of all things to participate in my visions.

When she finished this, Black Hand said it was time to be quiet. I turned so that I looked down off the little hill, and she did the same. It became very still, except for the chirping of the birds in the scrub pines around us. In the stillness I began an assessment of what was happening.

It seemed that there were two possibilities. First, that Spirit wanted to test my willingness to go through this form I had chosen, rather than following my instinct, as my will determined. Or, secondly, that I should pay more attention to my inner voices than to the outward form. Perhaps in some way both were true. As I looked back at the morning's events, I was glad I had waited and been respectful, although it seemed to me that Black Hand had violated even her own sacred tradition.

But who was I to know, who was I to judge? A kid, a beginner, a newcomer. Again and again I gave my judgment away to the Great Spirit and that guidance within me. Finally, an outer layer of resistance fell away, and with a sigh I settled myself more comfortably on the rocky earth, and stilled myself within.

Then Black Hand made another surprise move. I nearly hurt my neck as my head snapped around to look at her! We had been on the hill no longer than half an hour when she said abruptly and decisively, "It's time to go down now." If I had let myself, I would have dissolved into hysterical laughter at myself for thinking the tests were over! This was so unbelievable as to be totally bizarre. Things were becoming laughable—this was just too much. I looked around for coyote, the creature Native peoples think of as a trickster. I blinked my eyes and shook my head to clear it, thinking I had drifted into a bad dream. But there was Black Hand, getting to her feet.

I looked at her, totally dumbfounded. "What do you mean?" I asked incredulously—again, the look on my face must have been priceless.

"We can go down now," she said.

"But we just got up here!" I protested, thinking to myself that "up here" was an overstatement in itself.

She said again, "This is the time to go down," very emphatically and with command.

"Why?" I asked. "I came here for a three-day fast." By now the humor had faded, and my eyes must have been shooting fire as they drilled into her.

"I don't feel well," she said somewhat defensively, concluding lamely, "I have diarrhea."

Then something snapped inside of me. My own power began returning. I looked at her for a long time, my impatience, anger, and frustration slowly dying. In a soft voice I told her, "You'd better go down then, and take care of yourself. I came to this sacred mountain to fast for three days, and that is exactly what I will do." She flashed me an odd look, a strange mixture of her own frustration and a certain reluctant admiration for my tenacity. Slowly gathering her things together, she picked up her blanket and walked back down the hill into camp.

I watched her back recede until I lost sight of her below me in the junipers. It was very clear, however, when she made it into camp. Grandma's voice sounded like an angry mountain lion, echoing up to me. Ella Jay told me later that Black Hand took the incredible "chewing out" with her head bowed, and then made her way to her tent, where she stayed most of the rest of the time, although she did manage to make it up for meals. In her reprimand, Grandma had countered the diarrhea excuse by asking Black Hand if she didn't know that the purpose of such a fast as she had begun was for healing, and that she should have stayed up there to heal herself.

She reminded Black Hand that, when she had returned from taking the young Californian to such a "vision quest" on Bear Butte, the Lodge keeper had found her own son and his child had been killed in an auto wreck. Grandma warned Black Hand that if she did not stop this kind of dishonorable behavior, her whole family would be dead.

Sitting there alone in the morning sun on the hill above listening to the brokenhearted sound under the anger in Grandma's voice, I found myself crying gently, and this time it was not for me. It was for her, and for her loss, and the loss it meant for us all.

Soon, however, my attention returned to myself as I was jolted by an almost physical force. Although I had initially been very disappointed by this choice of place, the feeling now became almost unbearably strong. This was *not* my spot, *not* my place of power for visioning, and I could feel it in every cell of my body. It brought up a difficult decision for me at that point, because this was the place the keeper of the Sacred Lodge had chosen for me. Should I respect her choice or my own experience? Did she know or feel something I could not? Would Grandma Rosie be angry if I left this place?

The struggle raged inside me for an hour or so. Then I remembered the guidance of previous vision quests, which had made it clear that I would personally never have a traditional form: *"Your form is to be the formless form: that which breaks through form into Spirit."* I could see how my experiences with this elder and Lodge keeper were directly related to questions of form, and of breaking form to find the truth underneath. There was much here for me to learn.

This remembering helped me touch back into the feeling of power that had snapped within me when Black Hand first announced her decision to leave. I understood that her choice had helped free me to follow my own heart and my deepest intention. As soon as this thought came to mind, I gave thanks to her. Then I jumped up, picked up my few things, and ran almost all the way to the top.

Climbing to the highest place, I felt the exhilaration of my own energy and of the almost mischievous, childlike joy of escape from arbitrary authority that my body and deep self so loved. I found a beautiful flat stone outcropping off the trail facing east that felt exactly right to me, and again spread my robe on the wafting scent of sage. Here I would stay for three days, alone with the Great Mystery and the beauty of the mountain's life around me.

SHAKING THE FAMILY TREE

In this time of radical shifting, our generation and the generations to come are called upon to question the forms and practices that have come down to us—to find whether they have real meaning for us, or to discard them. We are doing this in many ways. For example, young people I know who have inherited wealth are questioning not only the manner in which their parents gained the money, but as well, how they used that money in the living of their lives; I see them consciously choosing to move their investments from Standard Oil and Exxon to companies and organizations working toward a sustainable future. On both reservations and every city in the nation, there are groups of Adult Children of Alcoholics recognizing that they carry those familial and emotional patterns that caused so much damage to them, and they are working to find new, nurturing, supportive ways of being. Young people of Catholic and Jewish and many other faiths are searching deep within their religions to find new meaning and guidance, rather than following the meaningless forms they were given as children. If they do not find it, they seek out other spiritual ways to fulfill that part of their lives.

THE TREE OF FAMILY PATTERNS

1. Take time to meditate on the patterns you are continuing to carry forward in your life. Think about whether these things are based on old forms or in present truth and integrity.

It would be quite useful for you to do these exercises as written journal work, so that you can reread what you have discovered and work with it over time. I suggest buying one of those beautiful little books with blank pages; or if you enjoy using a computer, create a separate file for this personal work. Set some time aside each day to reflect and write. As the days go by, you will likely find many other reflections to add to the journal.

2. To spark your meditations and assessments:

▶ List five things you do exactly the way your mother did them.

▶ List five things you do exactly the way your father did them.

▶ List five things that you do totally opposite—in rebellion against the way your mother did things.

▶ List five things that you do totally opposite—in rebellion against the way your father did things.

▶ Next, assess whether each of these patterns is in your best interests right now in your life. Both doing things as your parents did them, and doing things exactly opposite, can be very destructive ways of being.

▶ Now, list five things you do very differently from the way your parents did things—not in opposition, but from a totally new outlook.

▶ Examine these activities:

—How do they make you feel?

—How do they affect the way you look at life?

—How do they affect your relationships?

3. Examine the experiences you have had with elders other than your parents, with authority figures of all sorts, and with other traditional ways of being.

▶ When have you had experiences in which the directives of authority figures violated your sense of right action (as opposed to an ego response); for instance, have you had an experience similar to mine with Black Hand?

▶ What was your response?

▶ How would you do things differently now—if at all?

▶ Can you remember and congratulate the part of you that knew the difference between what the old form insisted upon and what your spirit knew was right for you at that moment?

▶ Is this inner knowingness related to the golden thread of connection that you renewed in the exercise in chapter 2, "Connecting to the Great Spirit Within"?

THE LAW OF SEVEN GENERATIONS

The "Law of Seven Generations" states that whatever patterns you are now living out in your life—whatever you teach your children and they learn from observing you—their own children will learn, and their children, as far into the future as seven generations. This is not only true of families but of societies as well.

Knowing the tremendous power of patterns of behavior, make an assessment of the Law of Seven Generations in your own life. Look as far back along the spreading branches of the tree of your family's behavioral patterns as you can remember.

1. If it is possible in your family dynamic, try interviewing your parents, your grandparents, and other elder relatives about their childhoods. Ask them:

▶ What were they were taught by their parents?

▶ What did they learn by watching what their parents did?

▶ What do they believe were the most important messages they received from their elders as they were growing up?

2. Take the information you discovered in "The Tree of Family Patterns" and look back along the seven generations of your family tree. Pick one of the patterns you listed and ask yourself:

▶ How long has this pattern been going on in my family?

▶ Can I spot where some of these patterns began, and why?

▶ Have I passed them along to my children? Are they being passed to my grandchildren?

▶ Has this pattern had a positive effect in all these lives—if so, how?

▶ Has this pattern had a negative effect in all these lives—if so, how?

▶ Repeat this part of the exercise with the other patterns you listed.

3. Building on these assessments, now, ask yourself:

▶ Do these patterns still have validity in my life today?

▶ If not, what would I rather do instead? What would enhance my life and bring me a sense of peace, joy, and accomplishment?

BREAKING THE PATTERNS

Once you've taken your assessment of your family's tree of patterns, it is time to begin to take action to release the unworkable parts. Writings from Native traditions and many others, including the Old and New Testaments, tell us how important each of our actions is, not only for ourselves but for All the Circle of Life. We are just now beginning to realize the wisdom of these statements.

In the Basque way, high up in the Pyrenees mountains between France and Spain, the ancestors are called upon to help carry forward only what is good, true, and beautiful. In nearly all traditions, the ancestors are those family members who have gone beyond, who have passed through the veil we call death. However, their lives and spirits continue on in that plane of existence, as does their love for us and the generations yet to come. From their different and perhaps broader perspective, they often have wisdom to offer us if only we are willing to call upon them.

Among my people, there is an understanding that those who have gone beyond have very likely had an opportunity to look back at their lives and assess the lessons. They see what did and did not work—what was good, true, and beautiful—and what was not. Out of the love they carry for the succeeding generations, these ancestor spirits add their energy to the breaking of old patterns.

Halloween—the Eve of All Souls, the fourth and last cross-quarter day of the yearly round of the Medicine Wheel—is a time when, in many cultures throughout the world, those who have gone beyond are invited back to visit with their loved ones. Recently, at Halloween, I took the opportunity to create a gathering of neighbors around a huge bonfire under the stars of my Montana home for the purpose of releasing old and unworkable traditions or patterns from our lives in the presence of our ancestor spirits.

Before we went outside in the crisp night air, we sat around talking about how many things in our lives we have brought forward from family ways and other traditions that do not serve us in the present. As the sharing continued, I gave each person a square of black cloth, some tobacco, and other objects from which to create a little offering bundle that symbolically contained all they wanted to release in order to carry forward only what is good, true, beautiful, and useful in their lives.

As we stood around the fire later, I sang a chant that calls in the ancestors, asking them to be witnesses for us and to help each of us. (The chant is recorded on my cassette, *A Gift of Song:* see appendix 3, page 473.) Individuals then came forward in their own time to throw that little bundle into the fire to symbolically release the unworkable parts of their lives, and to offer a prayer for themselves and All Our Relations.

In the weeks that followed, they reported back to me how important this ritual had been for them, and how their lives were beginning to shift toward what was more workable and beneficial.

A CEREMONY OF RELEASE

1. Create such a *Ceremony of Release* for you, for your ancestors, for the generations yet to come, and/or for your community.

2. Choose a time—Halloween and New Year's Eve are both wonderful times to do this—but there's no need to wait for them to have this ceremony. Any time you wish to hold such a ceremony is auspicious. For instance, there are three other cross-quarter days—celebrated on their eves; Candlemas on the eve of February 2; Beltane on the eve of May 1; and Lammas on the eve of August 15. There are the solstices and the equinoxes. Also, the dark of the Moon is an excellent time for releasing the old, and it occurs thirteen times a year.

3. Invite those you wish to have attend, letting them know the function of this event and describing the ceremony. This helps them meditate ahead of time so they can decide on the issues and patterns they want to release. You might also ask them to bring along any special symbolic elements they might want to burn in the fire.

4. As you gather, ask all the participants to help create a sacred space in which to do this work. Offer a prayer to the four directions, and the above, below, and the center to connect with Spirit.

5. Take time for each person to talk about past situations, traditions, family experiences, or anything else connected to what they have found unworkable in their lives. Give each person a square of black cloth, a pinch of tobacco, and random symbolic items such as stones, shells, buttons, little feathers, bits of wood, and other things they can use to represent patterns being released in case they have not brought things of their own. In addition, it's helpful to have slips of paper and pencils on hand so people can write down anything for which words are the only appropriate symbol. Lastly, give each person a string or bit of colored yarn to tie the little bundle.

6. Create a fire to burn these releasing bundles in order to transform them. This can be a bonfire outside, or a fire indoors in a fireplace or even in a heavy skillet set on a tile or trivet in the center of the gathered circle.

7. After building the fire, smudge both the participants and the fire with sage (see pages 29–30).

8. Call in the ancestors of each person to help them in this process.

9. Allow participants to come forward, one at a time, encouraging but not requiring them to say their prayers out loud, and have them throw their bundle into the fire. A good image here is for them to think of the fire as releasing and transforming all the energy formerly held in those old ways so that it can be used by the Great Spirit in new and beautiful ways.

10. Finally, have a feast of celebration around your fire!

THE PARAPHERNALIA PATH

Beware of the Paraphernalia Path in your own quest for spirituality. This path is one on which more attention is paid to the outer trappings—to the "beads and feathers"—than to the heart of the teachings. It is sometimes easy to stay at this surface level rather than attending to the deeper aspects of the tradition. There is a fine line to be walked—one that I was on myself when I was taking such careful note of the outward forms that Black Hand used. Had I not gotten beyond this level, it would have given me a very false sense of the tradition I sought to know.

THE PARAPHERNALIA PURGE

1. As you take a sober look at your own spiritual journey, are there elements of the Paraphernalia Path in it? If so, how do these manifest in your life?

2. Take a look at all the ritual objects, talismans, fetishes, plant medicines, and other things you keep in association with the tradition you wish to learn. Does each one have deep learning for you? Or does it simply invite you to stop at the surface?

3. Could you give away all these things and still have the spirit of the teachings living within you and expressing through your actions?

4. You may want to look through all your ritual objects, sorting through those things that you truly find useful on your path from those that are simply used for decoration or show. Even if you keep the latter, put them in a different place—one that helps you remember the difference.

5. Take a piece of paper and mark out four columns on it—you might want to do this in your journal:

▶ In the first column list the nine most powerful sacred objects you own.

▶ In the second column list where and/or from whom the object came to you.

▶ In the third column put down the date of the first time you used this object.

▶ In the fourth column, list the date of the last time you used this object.

6. Choose one of the sacred objects on your list, and perform a special ritual with it—one appropriate to its teachings.

▶ Record your experience and your feelings about it in your journal, along with any results.

▶ Wait three to seven days, and perform another special ritual with the same intentionality as the first, but this time without using your sacred object.

▶ Record your experience of this second ritual in your journal, and then compare it with what you wrote about the first ritual. Ask yourself:

▶ Were there any differences between the two rituals? Any difference in connectedness to Spirit? Any differences in feeling tone or my responses?

▶ Were the events in my life different after each ritual, or were they similar?

▶ What have I learned about the Paraphernalia Path from these two rituals?

▶ Will these experiences change how I think about or use sacred objects?

Your reflections on these exercises may bring you to a point similar to where I was that day sitting on the mountain with Black Hand. As I considered this and other past experiences I'd had, it became very clear to me that—no matter what the background of spiritual leaders, no matter how correctly they follow the traditional forms, or whether they used the correct paraphernalia, or how close they lived to the core of traditional practice, or how much older than me they were in years—none of these outer forms could compensate if they had not developed their integrity and deepened their spirit.

I had received a profound lesson from the heart of Black Hand—one that I would be tested on again and again.

CHAPTER SIX

RAINBOW WOMAN COMES

The bridge into a new time must be a bridge of light;
all colors, all races, All Our Relations must be included in that bridge
for the rainbow to form and to arch across the chasm.

It is less like Rainbow Woman gave me something final then,
and more as though she made a permanent connection to my center,
a path along which information continues to pass.

"Ahhhhhhhh, I'm on top of Bear Butte, at last," I sighed, catching my breath after my fast ascent. It was joyful to find myself sitting atop this place where I had longed to be for years. I began my vision quest by cleansing myself with a smudge of sage and sweet grass so that I might be a sweet and worthy companion for those whose home I was visiting.

After the smudging, I offered tobacco to unify myself with this place and its peoples of all kingdoms. Then, praying aloud, I called, "Great Spirit, rather than making this place right for me, please make me right for this place." Turning in each of the directions, I made a prayer. Then, arranging my sleeping robe under me, I quieted myself.

A hawk floated by, and I asked him with my inner voice what he had to tell me. As I did this, he caught a thermal coming up off the butte and began a startling spiral upward as though to affirm the rightness of seeing from high up in the air, as I did now from this place. Thanking him, I turned within again, softening my outer eyes and looking ahead yet focusing on nothing, so that my left-sided awareness, my inner vision was allowed to come in.

As with all my fasts, the first days were a process of realizing how much of our world we as humans are likely to carry within us as continual inner chatter, even when we leave the actual people, places, and things behind. We know that the Great Spirit lives in all things, and thus certainly within each of us, yet we must stop the mind's small chatter to touch the depths, the wisdom that lives there. I spent hour after hour in an inner cleansing, so that the way might be cleared for me to hear the great and quiet voices that speak from the deep sources within and all around. I practiced just simply noticing what came into my mind, thanking it, and releasing it, allowing it to drift away, then finding something else in its place, and repeating the cleansing process.

Although it seemed I should be uncomfortable on the hard stone I had picked as a site, I was remarkably comfortable. It created a step about three feet high behind me, which helped support my back when it became tired. And for some reason, through the entire experience, the stone continued to feel soft as a sofa—certainly a gift from Spirit. Thirst, which had been such a big issue for me before getting there, never became a problem. I felt thirsty, yet not uncomfortably so. Part of this I again credited to having my system very clean and light and not in need of large quantities of water, which it would have been had it needed to move a bulk of food through my system.

The second evening, at sunset, I had a startling experience. I was looking east out over the Plains, shifting gently from my joy in the beauty of the late summer evening to a quietness within when, abruptly, an enormously tall dark figure appeared beside me. Its energy seemed so menacing, I jumped and shrieked! Having since seen the *Star Wars* movies, I can say this energy had a "Darth Vader" feel to it. In terror, I jerked around to see what it was. Yet, when I moved, something shifted in my perspective, and there was nothing there. I sat with my heart pounding, and my mouth feeling extra dry.

But then, as I relaxed and softened my eyes I realized on that side of me, off in the distance, stood a tall pine tree, dark against the evening sky, and that it looked remarkably like this huge, frightening figure. A knowingness rose from inside me that the menacing figure had come as a melding of this huge, dark outline and of my fear, made real on the left side. But whatever had come in that moment of vision had frightened me, and my fear blocked any learning I might have received. I realized then how fear cuts us off from our loving experience as well as our openness to learning. With this understanding, I sent up my prayers again and again, calling down the light of vision.

It was just becoming twilight, the final night of my quest, the time most magical for me, when the crack between the worlds of day and night allows many mysterious things through, opening the left side between our obvious daily world and the luminous world of darkness. I leaned back against the rocks, looking out over the surrounding countryside and the lake below me; a few soft clouds flitted by high up, giving me the soothing feeling of rain.

I was very peaceful, resting there, when out of nowhere a woman appeared beside me, older than me perhaps, yet radiantly ageless. Her hair was raven black and plaited in long braids. She wore a simple white buckskin dress, and as I studied her gentle presence I was surprised that there were no beaded designs on the beautiful leather garment she wore.

She stood there quietly, looking into my soul with an almost palpable love. Just then the little clouds over the moon moved off, and as they drifted away, the moonlight shining on her dress created a flurry of rainbows, and I saw that her dress was totally covered with hundreds of tiny crystal beads. The slightest movement she made refracted prisms of soft rainbow light all around us. I was fascinated by their quiet beauty.

At the same time, upon the highest part of the mountain, I saw a trail of light begin to wind down toward me along the trail. Drumbeats began, very soft, so that I turned my ear to listen closely. As this light drew nearer, I saw that it was the ancient Grandmothers, dancing in their slow and gentle step down the mountain—each one so bright in spirit that her aura blended with the next, forming a continuous line. The White-hairs, the Wisdom Women, the lineage of light and love— dancing down, dancing down, dancing down.

They moved to the gentle beat, which seemed like the heartbeat of the sacred mountain, outside yet at the same time within and around us all—vital, echoing, reminding us of the aliveness, the spirit, of Mother Earth herself. As the ancient ones came near where I was sitting, the leader veered off and began to dance around me in a circle. As the circle closed and they continued their movement, there suddenly appeared within this outer circle another circle. The second circle was composed of young women of my age and time, some of whom I joyfully recognized. They too were shining with brilliant light, and they too were dancing. As the motion continued, the circles of women began to weave in and out of each other, swaying in and through, blending and separating.

Within those circles there came yet another one formed of seven Grandmothers—white-haired women, women who were significant to me, powerful old women. They danced close around the Rainbow Woman and me. Looking up at their beautifully lined faces, I felt the love that bonded us all. As they swirled and moved around me they began to transform as though melting or blending into other forms. They became six young women friends of mine, sisters on the medicine path—and myself, watching and yet dancing with them. Deep inside me rose a feeling of profound connection and commitment, and I knew it was part of the others' experience as well. It is so good for our spirits to dance together on this sweet and sacred Earth!

Again within that circle, three forms now spun together and danced. First, it was Grandma Rosie, Black Hand, and Ella Jay. Then it was me, and Grandma, and E.J. Then it became me and my mom and her mother, the soft-spoken Lakota woman. Again and again the circles of three changed. Again and again I swirled and blended with two women from one of the circles. We melted, becoming one, bonding in the slow, sweet spinning of ritual dance.

Often in Native tradition, there is a wonderful use of humor to clear our minds and open them to learning. And humor came while this very solemn, very slow, and very beautiful ceremony was taking place. We all heard a slight noise and looked up to see—running up the mountain with her beautiful, long, honey-colored hair streaming behind her, in skin-tight jeans and fashionable fine leather, high-heeled, knee-length boots—my friend Diana from San Francisco. Diana had almost come on this journey as my personal helper, but she just couldn't get it together in time, tending to run behind as a matter of course. So here she was, late as usual, stunningly beautiful, and graceful as a deer. She dashed into the circle, screeched to a halt beside Rainbow Woman, and stood tall, solemn, and "innocent," as though pretending she'd been here all the time.

On Diana's hand sat a beautiful white dove. Rainbow Woman looked down at me and said, "Her name is Moon Dove," and smiled at Diana in a mischievous conspiracy, then nodded. Moon Dove threw her hand into the air, and the dove flew free. Every head lifted up to watch that tiny spot of radiant white moving toward the Moon through soft fluffs of clouds, becoming finally a tiny dot that blended into Grandmother Moon.

As I brought my attention back down, the circles around me faded and disappeared, and I found myself alone again with Rainbow Woman. Once again she stood quietly for a moment, filling my senses with the beauty of her form and spirit, and then an amazing communication began.

As she "talked" to me, it was not in the form of words that came into my ears, for I didn't really hear her say anything. Her message came into me as though it were being fed through my navel, and then it spread throughout my being. I was able to interpret only a small portion of it in words. Instinctively I knew there was much more information lying dormant there for later revelation than I could understand at that moment. So the words I have put to her deep wisdom must be my own. And as the years have passed, I've consciously understood more and more of what she gave me. Looking at my experience in this present moment, *it is less like she gave me something final then, and more as though she made a permanent connection to my center, a path along which information continues to pass.*

In essence this is the message she gave me—one more commonly understood now than then:

> Mother Earth is in trouble, and thus all of us who are her children. Our Earth walk is dangerously unbalanced, and this must be corrected quickly. The thrusting, aggressive, analytic, intellectual, making-it-happen, and "fixing what Mother Earth didn't do so well" kind of energy has become dominant. It has almost buried the feminine, receptive, accepting, harmonizing, surrendering, and unifying energy. A balancing must take place in which the feminine and masculine energies within each of us, as within all things, can harmonize. In our Native way, we are not seen as fully human until we balance these two energies; we cannot make full use of ourselves and our creative gifts until we balance yin and yang, right and left brain, the active and the receptive.
>
> To be fully human is what is being required of us now on Earth. This means that more emphasis needs to be placed on being receptive rather than active; on relationship rather than on separation; on power in flow with the great forces rather than on personal dominion over others; on the dark of winter's earthy germination as well as the rapid growth of summer days; on nurturing rather than fighting; on supporting rather than destroying; and on a deep and sacred ecology that deals respectfully and harmoniously with All Our Relations rather than with isolated issues.

Rainbow Woman was speaking to me as a woman, as Earth woman, as Buffalo Woman's kin, and I was to carry this message to women in particular. She reminded me that when we choose a female body for our Earth walk, we receive with it the charge for nurturing and renewing life. We are born with more knowledge of the feminine, receptive, relational aspects of life; just as those choosing male bodies are given more of the masculine, active, analytic aspects. The challenge to each individual is to awaken and develop these inborn capacities, and then to learn those less familiar, so that masculine and feminine are truly balanced within us when we mature. This is why we are not considered fully human until we do.

Males are to develop their aspects and be the best teachers/models of them, and we women are to develop our nurturing, birthing, renewing, and relating skills; we are the ones charged with upholding those aspects upon Earth. This upholding does *not* mean that we must do it all. It does mean, however, that we must find balance within ourselves and share it in such a way that all people can develop these aspects within themselves. As mothers, we have almost total influence on the developing nervous systems, beliefs, and ways of being of our children, so what we women teach and model—who we let raise our children in nursery and pre-schools—is who our children become, man or woman.

One of the primary messages from Rainbow Woman that rings again and again in my mind and heart is this calling of women to take responsibility. Much of the women's wisdom from all cultures has been lost or neglected. Many women today have been given little if any of those mysterious teachings. As well, we have also been deeply influenced by the kind of experiences the larger world provides. Very often these experiences have set the idea in our forming minds that to have power we must "out-macho" the tough guys. Many of us have never seen, been taught, or perhaps even been aware of the power of oneness, relationship, harmony, flow, and song—the gentle and powerful feminine.

Whatever it was we lost in the past, women must now find and develop within ourselves the capacities that will balance our Earth walk. Women must become the harmonizers, the nurturers, the teachers, the models who will create a newly conscious and loving generation of two-leggeds. Like it or not, the "thumb is on us" as women to transform our world.

A common experience of many tribes of the Americas before the European invasion was the honoring of the feminine. For example, among our Lakota people there is a way of accounting for all things in the Circle of Life, an actual count: 1. Father Sun; 2. Mother Earth; 3. Sacred Plants; 4. Sacred Animals; 5. Sacred Humans; 6. Ancestors; and so on.

Yet, before that count can even begin, there are two necessary conditions. The first is the presence of *Wakan,* which I will define here as the great womb, or bowl, of chaotic aliveness and possibility, from which emerges everything that ever has been, is now, or will ever be. In my own mind it is a great starry bowl, akin to the bowl of night sky, in which each of the myriad stars is a spark of life waiting to be blown into the flame of earthly reality. It is the primary principle of all life, what I call Buffalo Woman's Womb.

The second thing that is necessary to begin creation is *Skan,* which can be likened to a bolt of lightning that strikes into the bowl, and touching one star, brings it to brilliant light of day. This is the masculine, active, procreative principle. Together, *Wakan* and *Skan* bring all life into form.

In Lakota ways, the feminine is the first cause, the primary aspect of creation, and is consequently much honored. The woman and her womb are understood to be that which is primarily necessary for the ongoing creation of human life, for the creation of the people, and so she, as well, is honored.

Among many peoples the woman is seen as the carrier of the highest law: the law of good relationship. Women, in general, and the White-haired Grandmothers especially, carry the charge of keeping relationships in good order, whether they be relationships among clan members, between tribes, or with the other kingdoms of life. Women thus create the hoop in which all life and activity can take place, for when the hoop is broken and the people are divided, life is difficult. Those choosing female bodies come to model and to teach this harmonious way of walking on Earth, so that all children grow up in active service of this principle. Even though there was much power among the warrior societies of men, the circle of White-haired Grandmothers formed a society of peace whose purpose was the upholding of the only law the Creator gave when the world was formed: *You shall be in good relationship with all things and all beings in the Circle of Life.* Those old women were often the final word in decision-making, and so held great power and respect among the people.

The feminine, nurturing, renewing qualities were developed in the men as well. Boys lived in the women's circles until the age of seven; and during that time they were taught all the skills of women, from relationship skills to sewing to cooking and the gathering of foodstuffs from Mother Earth. With that base of knowledge and understanding, they would then go to learn from the men's circles. Macho, uncaring, males of poor relationship were never praised; yet let a man ride by who cared for the elderly, took fine care of his wife and family, was a good provider, who kept the ways of Spirit, and was a loving man, then all the women would sing out praises for him, and talk to their sons about what a fine man he was, and how they hoped to be that proud of their own sons. Thus, the feminine, nurturing qualities were developed in all.

Another profound message I received from Rainbow Woman during my vision on Bear Butte was about her Rainbow Medicine. She reminded me of my "rainbow child" status—my mixed blood—and that I carry several kinds of Indian blood, as well as Scandinavian and European heritage. She also pointed out that in the United States a great majority of us are children of the rainbow, for our country is the classic melting pot of nations. The wealth and richness of life that we are fortunate to experience here on Turtle Island—the North American continent—is based not in our devastating exploitation of other countries and our frontiers, but in the model we provide of many cultures living next to each other in relative harmony. This Rainbow Medicine, this oneness among the two-legged children of Earth as well as all of her other children, is the new medicine, and the one upon which we must focus our attention. Rainbow Woman acknowledged me specifically as one who would cross between cultures, carrying messages and creating unity. And she charged each one of this generation with the same duty.

In my heart she drew a splendid picture. Beginning with this world as it is now, I was vividly shown our unworkable warring; our pollution; the devastation of forests and the ozone layer and thus our very breath; the depletion of the nurturing soil; the destruction of species after species of essential plants and animals; starving children and the homeless; the draining of precious underground aquifers; and biogenetic tampering.

Then a huge, gaping chasm was shown to me. And there, on the other side, I was shown Mother Earth as a garden renewed and flowering. I saw people dancing joyfully, and freely giving their most precious gifts; two-leggeds and all other creatures were co-existing as gentle friends; there was pure, sparkling water in which healthy children of all species were bathing and playing; and a clear, almost iridescent light radiating from everything!

Rainbow Woman pointed to the chasm lying between the two worlds, and told me that we two-leggeds must build a bridge to span the distance. I must have looked at her with despair in my eyes, for she completed the picture with an exquisite rainbow arching across this enormous gap. I then understood that *the bridge into a new time must be a bridge of light; and that all colors, all races, All Our Relations must be included in that bridge for the rainbow to form and to arch across the chasm.* No one, no aspect, can be left out or disregarded. In her words I heard the echo of White Buffalo Calf Pipe Woman's messages of oneness and unity as the only way we can move forward from this age into the future. It is the nature and responsibility of this generation to manifest this Rainbow Medicine, and thus to serve All Our Relations.

She spoke to me then of more personal things and also of my medicine name. And then, gradually, the flow into me from Rainbow Woman began to cease. We stood together, silent. A deep peace surrounded us, and I felt tears of thankfulness fill my heart and spill over. Once more, she looked directly into my eyes. Then, with her feet remaining beside me on the Earth, her body shot out across the sky in an arc that covered the heavens and formed a rainbow. Her rainbow hung in the moonlit air for a long time, then the tiny crystal beads of light that formed it began to break apart and fall like sparks from a fireworks display. Rainbow Woman was gone.

The next morning I woke and stretched my muscles (which were by now growing accustomed to nights on cold rocks). To my surprise and delight upon opening my eyes, I saw in the sky the completion of the rainbow that had begun as we neared Bear Butte several days ago. The left side—the feminine side—of the gigantic arch was now radiant in the sky! The solitude and vision aspects of my quest were also complete!

Elated and very thirsty in the sweetness of the morning light, I greeted Ella Jay, who had come for me, and we followed the trail down off the mountain. I was feeling much more like a confident woman than the confused girl who had run uphill. Upon seeing Ella Jay, my mind suddenly jumped back to the beginning of the quest. It now seemed so long ago when I left the spot assigned me by Black Hand. I knew a reprimand was still possible no matter how good I felt about what I'd done and the beauty of the vision I was given. Yet, I could see only joy in E.J.'s eyes as she came so gently to invite me down. Still, my skipping and joyful bursts of running slowed to a quiet walk as I neared the flat area upon which I had earlier sat beside Black Hand. But then, passing the place she had assigned me without any feeling of connection, I walked into camp. Grandma Rosie's radiant grin and her open arms gave me the relief of her answer. She looked as though she already knew everything that I would ever tell her about Rainbow Woman and my days on the sacred mountain.

Although I had the strongest urge to make Black Hand ride in the back and to bring Ella Jay into the cab for the return trip, I fought it and followed correct tradition, not wanting to give Black Hand even one thing with which to denigrate me or my experience. Thus I had no time during the trip to share my experience with Ella Jay and Grandma Rosie. I assumed I would have plenty of time during the next day at Lone Deer, my last day before I had to return to California. But, I was dealt one final blow because I never got that time of sharing and integration.

We had simply dropped Black Hand off when we arrived late that night in Lone Deer, so it wasn't until the next day that we heard the news: This was to be the funeral day for two of Black Hand's nephews, who had died two days before in a car wreck. Ella Jay and I looked at each other in astonishment, remembering Grandma Rosie's words to Black Hand! Much later I learned that the Sacred Lodge had soon been taken out of the keeping of Black Hand; I have not seen her since that day. As we turned our attention to the immediacy of mourning, my vision quest was left far behind in my elder and helper's minds.

Up to this time I had received two beautiful rainbows, each of which filled half the sky: the rainbow on the right symbolizing my challenges in getting to the sacred mountain, and the rainbow on the left symbolizing my going within to receive a very dramatic vision. As I drove away from Lone Deer, it became clear to me that a third rainbow was necessary for the true completion of that quest—a rainbow that arched across the entire sky, joining right and left to symbolize the integration of my experiences. What remained for me was to blend the two sides, to make Rainbow Woman's words a living reality in my daily life.

Journeying back across the country, I saw many rainbows as I processed the inner and outer events I had experienced. The most spectacular one came on the first morning back in my San Francisco apartment: a triple rainbow bridging San Francisco Bay! It was the only rainbow I had ever seen there. That spectacular display in the morning light became a symbol of the rightness for me of coming back to my ordinary life, rather than following my urge to stay with Grandma Rosie to receive her help in the integration of my vision.

More and more I realized that here, on the "front lines" of a developing new consciousness, was where the integration could take place. I realized that while Grandma Rosie would have acknowledged my experience, she would not have been quite so able to help me integrate it. And this was because she herself was a person devoted to one small group of people, one tribe—the Rainbow Medicine had not awakened in her.

So again I faced the challenge alone. Since there were few people in my daily life with whom I could share this profound experience, I had to just sit with it. I have come to understand over the years that whether or not one has a wise person with whom to process a numinous experience, one must still sit with that experience over time to truly plumb the depths of it. My rainbow vision was too enormous, too full, too important for me to just assign it a certain pat meaning and think I was complete. It required the living of my life and my own growing wisdom to find deeper and deeper meanings for myself, as well as to discover ways to share the message with others. Metaphorically, what I had been given was a conception. It would be a good while before the actual birthing of the child.

An important learning for me with this specific vision was that it became more alive and more full and more radiant as I myself became a bridge through teaching others—for a major part of this vision was specifically designed to be shared. (Some visions are very personal. They will lose power if we simply chatter about them to anyone and everyone, rather than kneading them and working them inside our own experience.)

As I recounted the story to group after group, it was as though Rainbow Woman would give me new words and enlarge my understanding of the original concepts. I could not determine if I was simply mining more and more of the nuggets from the huge vein of gold she had placed within me, or whether my contact with Rainbow Woman remained continuous. In some sense, I think both are true because the vision I was given on the sacred mountain continues to speak to me in new and deeper ways even today.

EXPLORING THE FEMININE

During this vision quest, the feminine aspect of life came to me very strongly in many ways, the most obvious of which were, first of all, my female teachers, helpers, and inner guides, and then secondly, Mother Earth herself. The challenge Rainbow Woman put before us all is to call forth the inner feminine, and as well, to know what being female means. These are not the same, yet our concepts, experience, and/or models of being "female" influence our openness to the feminine principle of nurturance and receptivity—whether we are men or women.

In many of the world's cultures, a woman's life is seen to fall into three distinct parts. For us, the embodied feminine includes: girls before the onset of menses; women in their child-bearing years; and grandmothers, women in their Moon pause years (see chapter 16, "The Mysterious Feminine").

This exercise can be as rich for men as it is for women, for it can help you get deeply in touch with your own rainbow energy. Use the questions to explore not only the natures of the women of different ages that you know personally, but also to sense where and how these feminine qualities echo within your own beingness. Examine both the inner and outer aspects of each of these three cycles.

You may want to use your journal to record your impressions so that you may reflect on them further at a later time.

1. Set aside some quiet time and space for your exploration of the feminine. Enter and bless your sacred space, perhaps offering a prayer to Mother Earth and/or the Grandmothers, asking them to bless you and to be with you and guide you in this inner journey. If you have an altar, you may want to place some special symbolic object on it; or you may simply want to leave it open and receptive to Spirit. As you sit, check to see if your body is at ease, and release any tension or discomfort with an outbreath.

2. **The Cycle of Girlhood.** Begin with your earliest memories and consider the messages you received from the women in your family and from society about being female:

▶ How were you expected to behave?

▶ Did you receive the same messages from:
Your mother?
Your father?
Your aunts and grandmothers?
Your teachers and other authority figures?
From other girls your age?

▶ If not, how did they differ?

▶ How did you feel about these messages?

▶ Were there things you wanted to do that you weren't allowed to do because "girls don't do things like that"? List them.

► Were there things about being a girl that you loved and trea-
sured? List them.

► How do you feel about these things now?

► Were there hopes and aspirations you had as a girl that you put
aside as you got older?

► Would you change any of this now?

► What would you tell a little girl of your own now about being
female?

► What do you think she would say to you in return?

3. **The Cycle of Womanhood.** Look at your models for the qualities
of the feminine. For me, these qualities are nurturing and renewing life,
receptivity, harmony and good relationship, gentle strength, and spiritual power. Feel free to add any other qualities you find important.
Surprisingly, these behaviors may be modeled not only by women, but
also by men, animals, and Mother Earth.

► **Nurturing and renewing life:**
Name the women in your life who best reflect each of these
qualities.
Name any men, animals, or natural forces that have served as
models for these qualities in your life.

► **Receptivity:**
Name the women in your life who reflect this model best.
Name any men, animals, or natural forces that have served as
models for this quality in your life.

► **Harmony and good relationship:**
Name the women in your life who reflect this model best.
Name any men, animals, or natural forces that have served as
models for these qualities in your life.

► **Gentle strength:**
Name the women in your life who reflect this model best.
Name any men, animals, or natural forces that have served as
models for this quality in your life.

► **Spiritual power:**
Name the women in your life who reflect this model best.
Name any men, animals, or natural forces that have served as
models for this quality in your life.

► Take special note of where and how you are learning these
qualities now. In your journal, write a letter of thanks to each of your
teachers.

4. **The Grandmother Cycle:** Look at your beliefs about the moon-
pause in a woman's life.

▶ What are your beliefs about aging, and about what a woman's role is expected to be in her later years?

▶ What beliefs do you hold about menopause? Where and from whom did you acquire these attitudes?

▶ From whom did you acquire these beliefs and attitudes:
Your mother, her sisters, and friends?
Your grandmother, her sisters, friends, and other elder women?
From children? Male or female?
From men? What ages? Married? Unmarried?
From society in general? In what way are these messages brought home and reinforced—at school, through the media, at work, in groups of women, in mixed groups?

▶ Are your attitudes different now than they were when you were younger? How?

5. If you have children or influence their learning in any way, what are the most important values you are teaching them about the feminine aspect? What are you teaching them about the rainbow principles?

6. What are the greatest feminine aspects you display in your unfolding path?

7. What aspects of the feminine are you connected with at this time?

8. Write a special letter of gratitude to all those who have empowered you to embody the richness of your feminine rainbow.

DRUMMING THE HEARTBEAT

A way given me in vision for how we all can manifest the feminine more fully in our lives is the way of the drum. The drum is round, a container that vibrates life: it is a feminine form that has "belonged" to women since the beginning of time. However, women have gifted the drum to men as well, so that they might use it in their growth and development.

The caring for and use of this feminine form, the drum, can be a deep practice. The drum echoes the heartbeat of Mother Earth and of all life. The development of a strong, steady heartbeat rhythm can be a part of your personal and spiritual growth. (My cassette, *Drumming the Heartbeat,* offers a model for this heartbeat and other rhythms that you can use in learning to drum as well as in meditation and ceremony. See appendix 3, page 473, for further information.)

An aspect of the drumming that is very helpful to men is that it helps raise the energy from the sexual chakra to the heart chakra, thus increasing the capacity for caring and nurturing. Although drumming can bring up powerful emotion, it should never be used as something upon which to take out anger by pounding or violent beating. If this energy comes up, use pillows or something else for your release. If you send this energy out through the drum, its vibrations fill everyone who hears it with this same energy.

A wonderful thing you can do is to get a group drum, which I call a Mother drum, one large enough for six to eight people to drum together. Excellent personal drums and Mother drums are available from my *hunka* brother, Rodney Scott of Heartbeat Drums (see appendix 1, page 455). Rodney and I share the intention of bringing the heartbeat of Mother Earth alive again for all her people through the use of the drum.

I will be using the term *hunka* from time to time as I introduce various people in my life. *Hunka* refers to a ceremony of spiritual adoption called *Hunkapi*, given to the Lakota people by White Buffalo Woman. Through it we take a person not of our blood family to be a family member. For example, relatedness through marriage is a primary *Hunkapi*. As part of any such adoption we must also recognize all the other people in the Circle of Life as our family—especially the other two-leggeds of the world.

A SIMPLE DRUMMING CEREMONY

Drums are used in a multitude of ways. One simple way to be in their presence is to gather a group together for a ceremony of heartbeat drumming. This ritual can be dedicated to Mother Earth, to peace, or to the healing of a particular person or issue.

1. Choose a drum leader—someone who has enough drumming experience to keep a good steady heartbeat going. You can use a metronome if this is difficult for all of you. Gather around a large group drum, and/or sit in a circle with your individual drums. The leader will speak a prayer of dedication for the drumming, offer cornmeal and tobacco to the drum, and then begin the heartbeat. As this beat grows strong and even, others may join in as they feel the rhythm.

One good way to make sure you join in on rhythm is to close your eyes and listen for a while. Allow the beat to sink into your body and consciousness. Then begin to tap gently on the side of your drum without making any noise, getting your arm and drumstick in perfect rhythm. When you are right on the beat, simply move up to the head of your drum and join in the heartbeat aloud with the others.

2. Imagine this heartbeat coming up from the center of the Earth and through all living things. Dedicate yourself to joining in harmony with this great heartbeat. Remember to keep your focus and intention clear because whatever you are thinking and feeling will be magnified through the drum. If you choose to drum for an hour or two, it will be a wonderful experience. In the end you will find it very difficult to let the heartbeat die because your heart will be beating with it.

3. One way to keep from being tired is to set something up ahead of time for resting sequences. The easiest way to do this is to say that at least two people need to be drumming at all times. Then others can rest at intervals. However, you will find that you need little rest if you sit in a comfortable position that allows your arm easy and balanced access to the drum head, and if you allow a gentle snap of your wrist to create the beat, rather than using your entire arm and shoulder in a tense or strident manner.

4. During this time, if it is not a silent drumming, songs that correspond to the focus of the ritual and to the set rhythm can be led by various people. If you are a practiced group, the leader can move to the center and change the beat a bit to match the songs. Whenever such a change is signaled, it is good to let the leader drum alone again until the new beat is firmly established. Then join in just as you did in the beginning.

5. To bring the session to a close, the leader will move out to the center of the big drum or into the center of the circle to catch everyone's attention. Then, the leader will count "One, two, three, four," in time with the beats. A final heavy beat will be struck by everyone together on "four."

6. It is good to take time to share feelings and experience after the drumming session. This helps integrate the experience and build group solidarity. The ceremony can end with a circle of hands and an appropriate prayer.

While the beautiful rainbow vision I was given on Bear Butte is a continuing inspiration to me, what is even more important in my life is seeing the vision of oneness and harmony, and the attitude of nurturing and good relationship become real in my life and the lives of my students. Vision quests are more certainly ways to connect with the Great Spirit, the spirit within all life. Yet we must remember that such a quest is most particularly a way to connect with your own deeper self and with your own life path. It is the embodying of Spirit and of the vision that are finally of most import to you, and to All Your Relations.

THE FLAMING ARROW

Around me I can feel them moving, yet cannot make out their forms:
only gentle hands,
sounds of wings reminding me of dry reeds brushing together on an
autumn shore,
whispered words I do not consciously understand.

Your willingness to embrace the Bear Spirit, which symbolized
your unwillingness to separate yourself from other forms of life or to
be afraid of them,
was required for this initiation upon the emerald tablet.

White Buffalo Woman was continuing to sing her spirit song to me,
asking me to learn it
so well that I too, could sing it out into the world.

Again, sitting high on a mountain, this time under the castle-like peaks above Arrow Creek on my home reservation, I sang out to the pine-clad slopes and limestone walls for vision, "Mother Earth, your daughter sits where her ancestors have sat for generations." It was a statement of purpose, of grounding in this centuries-old, vision-seeking place of the Apsa. "Father Spirit, your daughter seeks the ancient, everlasting truths of how to live a truly human life on my Mother Earth."

This was to be the final fast in the traditional series of four that I had pledged, and visions had begun appearing before I even arrived in Montana that summer of 1978. Driving up through the beautiful canyons of northeastern Utah on my way home, I became restless after so

131

many hours on the road. At an especially lovely and open crossing in a stream running beside the road, I pulled off and went down to the water to ritually cleanse myself and offer prayer as Ella Jay had taught me long ago at the spring near Benney. Splashing water on my face and arms, I felt refreshed.

As I sat there on my haunches, smelling the scents of mint and willow, I found myself swaying back and forth, swinging my head as do the great bears. It was marvelously comforting to let go and relax this way after the intense focus of driving, and I kept it up for a long time, until a trance-like state ensued. As this continued, I felt an inner calling that seemed to originate from up a little side canyon where a small brook ran sparkling in the sunlight.

Because I was wearing shorts on this warm afternoon, and moccasins suitable for running in the long grasses, it was easy to jump across the stream and dog-trot up the slight incline, moving along the sweetly singing water. The smells were wonderfully rich, the mint itself seeming to invite me onward. I ran for a mile or so to a place where the mint grew thickly along the banks of the stream in a shady area. There I lay on my belly and chewed the cool leaves like a bear cub I had once seen. Rubbing and rolling in its sweet fragrance was such a childlike joy that I lay back to rest on my fragrant bed in the sun.

Long hours of driving and the sun's warmth caught up with me, and I fell asleep. Waking to a new sound, I lazily turned my head to investigate. There, beside me on the bed of mint, lay a young Native man, his dark, sparkling eyes looking down into mine. He was so gentle, so familiar, I instinctively reached out and drew him to me. We held each other, rolling and playing in the mint. This led to making sweet love, and to a restful time afterward. I dozed and drifted contentedly, resting back on his arm. His fur felt so soft and luxurious. *"His fur!"* my brain screamed. I jerked around to look at him, but he was already lumbering away from me, a huge, soft brown bear! On the crest of the hill, he hesitated, his rich, heavy fur almost iridescent in the sun, and gazed intently into my eyes. Then, swaying his head and body in a heavy yet fluid walk, he disappeared over the hill and out of sight.

"Ohhhh, ohh," I mumbled sleepily. My own muttering brought me to full wakefulness, and I rolled into a sitting position. Rubbing my eyes, I remembered, "Oh! the bear! The young man! I thought I was awake then." The dream had been so sweet that I felt lonely on this empty bed of mint. Stretching, I got to my feet and ran with the stream down the valley back to my car. As I drove on, I pondered this dream/vision, but no meaning became clear to me, and I filed it away in memory.

Through the events of the next few days, this experience of the left side was forgotten. Home again, I visited my families, and helped Dad and Ella Jay prepare their camp for my vision quest. As we drove up Arrow Creek, childhood memories of picnic gatherings with our half-breed ranching neighbors on this creek filled my mind. I had always loved the area. One time in recent years, rather than doing a formal vision quest, I had renewed myself alone with four days of refreshing quiet along this mountain stream. I simply camped and fished and played, swimming in Arrow Creek's deep pools from which huge trout darted as I entered.

Setting up the folks' camp, we enjoyed the sound of the creek as it tumbled over the stones of a rippling fall. The box elder trees above us whirred with cicadas, whose shiny black bodies and clear, red-veined wings were occasionally visible to me if I observed very closely. Twilight came early in the depth of the canyon, and filled to overflowing by long draughts of the clear, cold water, I fell happily asleep.

In the dawning light, Dad and I climbed the long slopes up to the castle rocks, which capped the mountains. Soon he asked me to slow down, and I realized I was climbing fast, as usual, and also that I was sweating and already becoming thirsty—and the first day of my fast had only begun. So I slowed down, occasionally stopping to sit on the hillside, and looking back toward camp, listening to stories of the old days—of journeys my dad had made on horseback all across these mountains on routes I had never traveled, of hunting with his dad in times when the game was remarkably abundant. Several times we came upon large rocks, recently overturned, which he reminded me was a sure sign of bear. He kept pointing them out in a worried manner, knowing that I would be sitting alone at the top of this slope for days.

The dream/vision of the bear came back to me very strongly then, and I said, "There's no need to worry. This sign of bear is a very good sign. I was given an omen, a dream, on my way here, which I did not understand until now. It was a great bear who drew me close to him. These rocks signal his presence here, and this is for me a blessing." Dad was insistent on worrying, though, because the huge grizzlies that had bothered tourists in Yellowstone had been relocated near here, and bears especially favored the chokecherry-lined streams of these reservation mountains.

I talked with him about how what we think helps determine our reality. I asked him to remember my dream, and encouraged him to think of the great bears as my protectors. If he wanted to hold an image that would help me, I suggested he make it an image of me sitting safely on the mountain, bathed in golden rainbow light, happy as a hibernating bear, rather than an image of me being eaten by one! He relaxed and finally grinned, and we made our way up the mountain to my fasting place where, with no further worries, he left me.

Looking around for my place of power, I watched him become smaller and smaller as he went back down the mountain. I could see the camp far below, the tents and cars tiny as ants from this high vantage point. I found a rock outcropping beside a leaning pine tree with thick, full branches. With the skies threatening rain, the tree would provide shelter, and by morning it was in fact steadily dripping rain. I leaned back, warm and dry under the tree's protection, its springy branches forming a soft backrest. Snug and secure, I drifted in and out of sleep and dream.

For the rest of the day, I was drawn into a long process of inner clearing. Raindrops ran slowly down the underside of one large branch—little droplets hanging, and hanging on longer there—gathering moisture before becoming heavy enough to fall. They were like tiny mirrors, reflecting my image back to me. My total attention became absorbed by each one, until rather than seeing myself on the outside surface, I was transported *inside* one, and found myself standing in front of my mother.

The rain seemed to whisper that I was to complete now anything I'd ever wanted to say or do with my mother—as though I would never see her again. And I did. I went back over my childhood and shared our experience from my side—our joys and sorrows, the excitement and disappointments, our love and pain. I expressed things I had never told her—how much I loved her; and how much I appreciated her incredible hard work supporting us as children; how angry I was about some things, how sad about others. Anytime I stopped, the rain urged me on. When I finally finished everything there was to say, I found myself again outside the raindrop, consciously watching it fall.

My feeling of completion was remarkable, but I was not allowed to think about it long. Another small drop slid down the branch, hung there swelling, and again I was inside it. This time with my brother—clearing with him years of unspoken emotion and experience; and the drop fell. On into another raindrop, with my father—clearing, and it fell. Again with my partner—clear, fall. Another and another and another, until everyone significant in my life had stood before me during that long rainy day. With each one I felt increasingly clear, and I now felt as clear as the raindrops, and totally free. Near twilight the rain lessened, and the scents of clean grasses, pine, and wildflowers came to me sweetly on the gentle breeze—a prayer for sweetness to fill all the places inside myself that I had opened.

This experience can be seen as a shortened form of a series of techniques that the Southern Seers have used and taught for the ordering of an individual's reality. The Southern Seers are descended from an ancient Central American people, the Toltecs, and include those contemporary Native peoples who still follow their spiritual lineage, including some Yaqui and Apaches and other southern groups. Carlos Castaneda speaks of that lineage in the series of books about his teacher, Don Juan (see appendix 2, page 460).

Unless we have done significant inner work on ordering our sense of reality, most aspects of our life are scattered in memory over different times, connected with different things, and our total experience of them is very confused. It is like having a cross-filing system: by random date, by emotional feeling, by an event's significance, and by a childhood memory rather than a comprehensive system where each person or issue is filed in its own category.

For instance, take "mother" as a category. She is connected with nearly everything in our life up to age fifteen, so how can we know exactly what our experience of her has been except by sorting it out from everything else, by recapitulating our entire experience with her specifically? This kind of recapitulation (see the exercise in chapter 12, pages 252–253, for a full description of recapitulation), applied to every significant individual and issue in our life, creates a much clearer experience of each one, and becomes an *ordering of our experience*.

As the days passed, I kept thinking of the bear, wondering about him and about how he must know of a cave that would protect me from the rain. I asked his spirit to show me. That night I was escorted in dream by dark, gray, soft creatures I could not distinguish, although they had the soft fur of moles, down a long tunnel into Mother Earth. Smelling the richness of the soil, I reached out to touch its dark moistness. We went on and on, down and down, for what seemed a long time, until we came to a cave-like opening.

Standing by itself in the center of this dimly lit, cavernous room was an enormous slab of emerald, roughly oblong and slightly larger than the size of a human body. Although I knew, even before I was called forward, that this was a place of sacrifice, and that I was to die there, I had no fear—only relief. Some deep part of me knew that I had cleared everything with others in my life so this moment could be purely mine. It was my turn to clear my own life. I walked slowly forward. The polished surface of the emerald tablet shone brilliantly, as if reflecting the depths of an enormous pool.

This image of a deep pool lifted me back into a different time and place, where I had once stepped in vision through a special crystal, known to me as a door to other realities. As often happens when I step through that door, I now moved down a long tunnel, the sides of which were lined with soft gray fur, of the same elegance and richness as the dark creatures who had just guided me into the earthen cave at a different level of reality. I walked briskly down the tunnel, toward the light at the other end.

Suddenly, down beside me to my right, I noticed a tiny door that I had almost passed with my rapid strides. Some part of me knew I must choose to explore it immediately, for I would never see that same door again! So I turned abruptly, reached for its ornately carved, copper-gold handle, and opened the door. Barely large enough for me to pass through by stooping, it reminded me of the low sweat lodge doors. They humble us, bringing us close to Mother Earth, as we enter. "Humble" has nothing to do with being abject or pitiable. It comes from the same root word as *humus,* meaning "of the earth."

Humbly then, I entered this tiny door, and as I straightened up, I found myself in an enormous cavern. Its rough surfaces seemed to be made of something like dark, translucent glass, with minerals crusted over it in light patches. Looking around, I realized I was standing in a path nearly a foot deep, that felt as if it were worn into the stone by centuries of moccasined feet. The path went straight forward to a pool that filled the entire center of the cavern, and then circled it. Moving slowly forward, I turned right on the path when I came to the pool. At first, the water was dark, and I could perceive only its surface. Then light began to flash and glint within its depths, and the pool appeared bottomless. As I peered in, I could see that the sloping sides of the rock under water were highly polished emerald! The whole cave was evidently of unpolished emerald! I found myself walking, transfixed, around the pool, fascinated by its waters, which now shone emerald green. In childlike joy, I went nearly all the way around it, amazed by its shimmering brilliance.

Then I became aware of a polished area on the rim of the pool beside me, which reminded me of an otter-slide down a stream bank into the water. Starting at the path, it made an obvious dip down into the pool. Curious as an otter, I sat upon it, and found myself sliding! I tried to grab something to stop myself, but all the surfaces were polished and smooth. Down, down I went!

Surprisingly, I was able to breathe in the water. As I slid to the bottom, I found myself in an airy room where a very slim young Indian man sat on a slightly raised platform of the same emerald rock. His hair was parted in the middle and hung straight to his shoulders, where it was cut off abruptly. He wore a simple cotton shirt and pants, and a cloth band around his head. There were four straight lines painted vertically upon his forehead, symbolizing the power of a fine Northwest coast medicine man whose impeccable spirit I already knew.

Sitting cross-legged, his hands resting lightly on his thighs, he studied me silently, with eyes very deep and wise for so young a man. I could feel him assessing and weighing my spirit, holding my energy-body up as though to examine it, like a suit of clothing in the able hands of a tailor, looking for a way to balance and unify my subtler bodies. At long last, he seemed to find the solution, and without hesitation reached down beside him to each side. From two polished hollows in the stone dais, he chose a tiny, brilliantly faceted emerald with his left hand, and with his right, he picked up a small copper-gold hammer. In one smooth motion, he leaned toward me, set the emerald between my brows, the seat of the inner-seeing "third eye," and *ping!* drove it into my skull. There it remained, like a jewel in its setting, allowing light to refract through its tiny facets into my third eye. I recoiled in shock, surprised by his sudden move and startled by the green light shimmering within my head. I involuntarily touched my forehead, expecting to find an open place, but it had already sealed over, and the skin was smooth.

With a slight smile, his eyes crinkling a bit at the corners in satisfaction, he nodded, and then turned the nod into a brief but formal bow. Our time together was complete. A slight motion of his head indicated that I should go out, to his left. I arose from my cross-legged position, honored him with the same snappy, formal bow, and left him. I had walked only a few steps before I was again sliding, sliding, rapidly down, to come to a standing stop. I shook my head, and there I stood, right where I was before I sat down on the slide at the side of the pool!

For long, precious moments, I looked into the deep beauty of the pool, then began to walk slowly along the time-worn path, honoring it and the entire cavern with each carefully placed step. Too soon, I was back at the path that led to the door, and knew I must leave. Reaching into the sparkling green water, I touched it to my crown, to my third eye, my heart, and my womb center—making connection and giving thanks. Then I went out the tiny door, which disappeared into the soft gray wall when I closed it, went on out the tunnel through the crystal door, and into the light.

Since then I have been told, by an excellent gem healer, that emerald is *the healer's healer.* She gave me tiny emerald studs to wear in my ears, to balance and heal my energy, as I work in a healing way with others. Whenever I close my eyes and look with my inner eye, I am aware that all I see comes through the faceted emerald door.

I blinked my eyes to look about, and found myself again walking toward that huge emerald slab inside the mountain, under the castle rocks of my fasting place—walking so deep beneath those mountains I felt at the center of Mother Earth. This place seemed to be an initiation chamber used by high masters of the planet. Around me I could feel them moving, yet could not make out their forms. I only sensed gentle hands; heard sounds of wings reminding me of dry reeds brushing together on an autumn shore; and listened to whispered words I did not consciously understand.

I was laid upon the slab on my back with my hands crossed on my chest. Gentle fingertips closed my eyelids, and I knew in my heart rather than heard their blessing, "Rest in peace." The slab was warm, not cold as I had expected. Feeling my life energy drain from me, I consciously released my past. Death was a sweet remembering of light, a loving presence that filled everything, or more exactly, a loving presence that I recognized as myself, in union with all things.

Where I had gone there was no time. . . .

Then, after a long period of timelessness, I was back within the boundaries of time, a time when I felt myself moving, carrying my sleeping robe, sometimes stumbling in the darkness of night and dream. Again, in yet another cave, I found myself lying down, drifting into dream deeper than I had ever known, deeper than I can articulate. There, the young Bear Spirit man was bringing tiny twigs to light with moss and flint—a warming, drying fire. And again, I dropped into profound blackness.

Coming to consciousness, I opened my eyes. It seemed that I was truly awake, yet everything was black. "Maybe I *am* dead and *this* is how it feels!" I thought to myself, panicking. As I tried moving my arms, they flew up energetically, and the dark robe that had been covering my face fell off. As the light of morning fell upon me I thought with relief, "Oh, good! I'm not dead." Then I looked around to orient myself, laughing in enjoyment of the joke the dark robe had played on me.

However, I was again disoriented and startled. Because I now found myself, not under the pine tree in the rain, but in a truly cave-like area.

This place in fact was more like a hollow in a cliff wall, starting high above me and curving to the floor about ten feet back. Its shape would have offered little protection from the wind, but on that quiet morning as the Sun struggled to break its way through the clouds, streams of gold slipping through, the rain did not reach me.

I realized that this was my last day on the mountain. Lying quietly in the dawning light, I reflected on the journeys from which I had just returned. I felt a new openness in myself, a new clarity, for I had left my old self behind on the emerald tablet. The Bear Spirit must have brought me here in the night, after the cave visions. Later that day my curiosity got the best of me, and I took a few minutes to explore the immediate area. I found that I was now on the opposite side of the castle rock from my slanting tree—but not far from it. Before the afternoon was over, the sun had warmed and dried the rain-fresh grasses, so I returned to rest against the soft branches of my protecting tree. The next morning I would leave the mountain.

The sun began to drop in the west. Moving through long layers of soft clouds scattered along the horizon, it hid and appeared, and hid again. My eyes followed its light as it dropped lower and lower, its sudden appearances accompanied by streaming rays of gold. The sky turned soft pink and violet. Having been taught that much power can be gathered at this time of day by opening oneself to the light, I stood, spreading my legs and raising my arms in a receptive posture. I practiced holding them still until the last ray of light disappeared, and then, in a gesture of gathering, brought my hands together over my heart, right over left, imagining a transfer of light into my heart until it was filled.

The last ray of Sun glinted off the horizon and shot toward me, seeming to grow brighter rather than dimmer. As it approached, closer and closer to me, it became a flaming arrow. No sooner had I perceived it as an arrow than it came whistling and singing right at me, and *whomp!* pierced through my throat and pinned me to the tree.

I was frightened not only by the arrow in my throat but also by the flames, having literally been on fire before in a gasoline explosion as a child. At the age of eight, I had been set on fire by the explosion of a can of gasoline on our ranch. Fortunately, my parents were nearby, and were able to put out the fire. They drove me the long sixty-five miles to a hospital, where I was in recovery for several months. And now as I felt the flames of the Sun Arrow licking around my face, I remembered the smell of my hair burning as I ran screaming, so long ago.

Pinned there to the leaning tree, unable to move even my head, I was forced to face the flames long enough to realize that the arrow was not burning or smoking, that the flames were not truly fire, but were a radiant light flashing and streaming from the arrow. My terror turned to awe, and I watched, mesmerized by the beauty. Through the streaming light, I could see that the arrow was beaded with crystal beads, which threw rainbows of light all around. I was reminded of Rainbow Woman's beaded dress.

No sooner had the thought of Rainbow Woman crossed my mind than the "flames" began to die down and quiet into a soft glow. I could see the elegant zig-zag peyote pattern on the beads stitched around the shaft. My eyes softened for a few moments, and I became lost in study of the design. As I came to full attention again, the arrow transformed itself into a radiant warrior, who stood in front of me wearing white buckskins beaded with the same elegant design as the arrow. The moment I saw him, my heart melted with an indescribable yearning, and tears of joy streamed from my eyes.

Smiling down at me, he nodded and said, "Yes, I am *Woho'gus*, Light of the World. I am the one you have known so long in your heart, the one through whom you dedicated your young life to service of the light at thirteen years of age. No outward form contains me, yet I wear this kind of clothing as an honoring of the form in which you cry for vision. The Shinela people gave me this name long, long ago." My throat was constricted by the tears, which were both of joy and loneliness. I could only nod my head in response, but my heart sang out, "I know it's you—I have been so lonesome without you."

Our long, long history brings us a remembrance of a master who came several thousand years ago as the Dawn Star, presaging a new day for humanity. He walked on the water, healed the sick, raised the dead, and held dominion over the elements. He taught a sacred way of allowing the Light of Love of our Father, the Great Spirit, to flow unrestricted through our hearts as we walk upon our sweet Mother Earth, remembering all Their children as our family. This presence is identified by some as the Christ energy, and His transformative message is said to have been given to all our Native people directly—long before the coming of white Europeans to this land. (For more on the Dawn Star, see chapter 12, pages 238–241.)

The Dawn Star's message had long lived in my heart, yet since my young adult years I had somehow lost the awareness of it in my daily life. Until this moment of blessed reacquaintance, I had not realized the pain of my loss.

"You have seen the sister of my spirit, White Buffalo Calf Pipe Woman, as Rainbow Woman in your dream. The oneness and wholeness, the integration of all people within themselves and with all around them is the message she has long carried. It is a simple restatement of the one law that Creator gave when this world began, '*You shall be in good relationship with all things and all beings in the great Circle of Life.* *Chalíse* [pronounced *Sha lease*], your willingness to embrace the Bear Spirit, which symbolized your unwillingness to separate yourself from other forms of life or to be afraid of them, was required for this initiation upon the emerald tablet. There, you were patterned to release all the old concepts dividing you from the life around you, and you must now dance that dream awake in the world. The arrow, which represented me, struck you in the throat, that you may open your voice to fully deliver this message of oneness. I give you your name, *Chalíse*, which means 'A Chalice Overflowing with Light.' Go forth now, Chalíse. Walk this sweet Earth pouring out our Father's message for all the people on our Mother Earth."

We live in a time when few spiritual cultures remain intact. Very few people of our generation have found meaningful rituals of passage and spiritual growth to be a part of their heritage. Fortunately, that enormous aspect of ourselves—the non-material, spiritual part—cannot be easily dismissed from our experience. Even when it has not been officially invited and supported, the desire for it is still present, and "leaks" through to our consciousness.

The things of daily life that are artificial or untruthful can be put totally aside. But the truth of Spirit as the larger part of ourselves is continually there, seeking an outlet in conscious awareness. So in our everyday experience, we feel the lack of something important. There is a seeking for the unnamed wholeness that is not present for us. Even if we cannot name it as spiritual, it is still present as a gnawing little ache, an empty space never filled.

And so it is in this remarkable time of awakening, when many people are actively seeking a spiritual life, that visions and dreams and non-ordinary states are becoming the vehicle for much information and even initiation. Lacking the elders trained to offer these things to us, we have found other ways to tap into wisdom, into Source. One of our major lessons is that, although our elders can be of assistance, they are not the source of spiritual wisdom, nor the judges of it. Each person must call fervently—or, as the Sufi say, "pound relentlessly on the door of God," and awaken within themselves that golden cord of connection.

Certainly, vision questing is one of those ways of knocking on the door of Spirit. And it is not unusual for a Master of the past age to answer the call. Our histories tell us of Christ appearing to Crazy Horse; to Wovoka in gifting the Ghost Dance; to Frank Fools Crow, a highly developed Lakota elder who recently passed beyond, and to countless others. Whether through the energy of the Dawn Star or White Buffalo Woman, the truth of the message of oneness and wholeness is spoken and heard.

And because North Americans, Indian and non-Indian alike, live in a land where the spirits of the ancestors are Native, often those who appear as guides take that ancient form. More people than I can count have told me of visions and dreams of elder women or men who could only be called Native coming to them with wisdom and guidance.

A beautiful book titled *At the Pool of Wonder* by Marcia S. Lauck and Deborah Koff-Chapin recounts the remarkable visionary dreams of a non-Indian woman named Marcia Lauck. In these dreams, she is often led in deep experience and initiation by Native elders. Hers is but one published example of a phenomenon that occurs widely in the American population.

Because we are so programmed with all aspects of material reality, and so little schooled in the richness of our inner worlds, it is easy for us to dismiss our inner learnings as invalid for our outer lives. We might have had a dream that we have never been able to forget, or been given a special symbol in meditation. Often our tendency is to think of that as a one-time experience: something mysterious that flashed through, never to return. Or we may have treated it more like a TV show: "Well, that's over. Now let's see the next one." It is a mistake to believe that once we have been shown something, it is finished, and that's that. We can continue to interact with this inner experience of consciousness: asking for more clarification, enlarging the framework, and deepening the connection. Once you have made a powerful connection on the left side—use it! If you don't use what you are given, eventually the source of those gifts seems to become discouraged, and dries up.

There are many ways to bring your vision and its message into the realm of action. In fact, not doing it may bring you more pain and fear than actually finding a way to make it real in the world. I'll let Black Elk, the great seer and prophet of the Lakota people, tell you himself as his words appeared in John G. Neihardt's book, *Black Elk Speaks:*

"I was sixteen years old and more, and I had not yet done anything the Grandfathers wanted me to do, but they had been helping me. I did not know how to do what they wanted me to do.

"A terrible time began for me then, and I could not tell anybody. . . . I could hear the thunder beings calling to me: 'Behold your Grandfathers! Make haste!' I could understand the birds when they sang, and they were always saying: 'It is time! It is time!'

"Time to do what? I did not know. . . . My father and mother worried a great deal about me. . . . I could not tell them what was the matter, for then they would only think I was queerer than ever.

"When the grasses were beginning to show their tender faces again, my father and mother asked an old medicine man by the name of Black Road to come over and see what he could do for me. . . . By now I was so afraid of being afraid of everything that I told him about my vision. . . . Then he said to me: 'Nephew, I know now what the trouble is! You must do what the bay horse in your vision wanted you to do. You must . . . perform this vision for your people upon Earth. You must have the horse dance first for the people to see.' "

At that point the entire village made ready to reenact Black Elk's vision. They constructed a sacred tipi and painted it with the symbols Black Elk had seen—the sacred pipe, the daybreak star, and others. They chose four strong horses and bold young riders for each direction and painted them with the colors he had seen. They chose four beautiful maidens to carry the symbols of the four directions—essentially to bring again the gifts of White Buffalo Woman. The sacred songs Black Elk had heard were learned. The sacred hoop of the nation was constructed. And everyone came to participate.

"And as they sang, a strange thing happened," said Black Elk. ". . . Suddenly as I sat there . . . I saw my vision yonder once again—the tepee built of cloud and sewed with lightning, the flaming rainbow door and, underneath, the Six Grandfathers sitting, and all the horses thronging in their quarters [of the wheel of life]; and also there was I myself

upon my bay before the tepee. I looked about me and could see that
what we then were doing was like a shadow cast upon the Earth from
yonder vision in the heavens, so bright it was and clear. I knew the real
was yonder and the darkened dream of it was here."

The chosen participants performed the vision once, and then in the
midst of a great storm with lightning, thunder, and hail, the whole
village joined in and performed it again. At the end of the ceremony,
Black Road (the elder shaman) lit the sacred pipe, "and offered it to the
Powers of the World, sending a voice thus:

". . . Behold! I, myself, with my horse nation have done what I was
to do on Earth. To all of you I offer this pipe that my people may live!"
Then he smoked and passed the pipe. It went all over the village until
every one had smoked at least a puff.

"After the horse dance was over . . . I felt very happy," Black Elk
recalled, "for I could see that my people were all happier. Many crowded
around me and said that they or their relatives who had been feeling sick
were well again. . . . Even the horses seemed to be healthier and happier
after the dance.

"The fear that was on me so long was gone. . . . Everything seemed
good and beautiful now, and kind. . . . From that time on, I always got
up very early to see the rising of the daybreak star. People knew that I
did this, and many would get up to see it with me, and when it came
we said: 'Behold the star of understanding!' "

REENACTING YOUR VISION

One of the most powerful things that people who work actively with
their dreams have learned to do is to gather a circle of friends to act out
a particularly powerful dream or vision they have received. This kind of
sacred theater is one of the oldest of human rituals—from animal
dances painted on the walls of Ice Age caves, to the yearly round of
dances of the Katchina Spirits of the Hopi. (See discussion of Ritual
Action, page 322.)

There are several ways you might want to dramatize your vision or
dream to make it come alive and to receive—and share—its messages
and benefits, just as Black Elk's people were healed by his "horse dance."

1. Invite the members of your hoop to explore your vision. Send

each member a copy of the dream or vision you wish to reenact, so they can begin meditating on it. Ask them to bring symbolic objects to represent elements of the dream, or ritual tools and/or special clothing.

2. When everyone has arrived, smudge and bless your sacred space—which can be your living room, a beautiful place in nature, or a borrowed meeting space.

▶ The dreamer should then tell the vision aloud three times—important details will emerge with each retelling.

▶ Then gather in council and go around the circle, letting each of the participants say what the dream or vision means to them personally. However, everyone should refrain from saying what they think the vision means for the person who dreamed it.

3. And now come the choices of how to proceed:

▶ The dreamer or vision seeker chooses among the people gathered to reenact the dream/vision and guides them in the re-creation of the dream/vision.

▶ The group can send the dreamer away for a time, while they discuss what they believe to be the most important elements of the dream. And then they reenact the dream/vision. After a brief preparation, they invite the dreamer back to watch the reenactment as a spectator.

▶ After the group reenacts the dream or vision for the dreamer, they can once again gather in council and share what each of them learned from the dream/vision experience, paying special attention to what the dreamer has to say about this experience, and why this dream has come into his or her life.

Then the dreamer is sent away again, and the group discusses what the dreamer said. From this sharing they decide upon one element in the dream they want to change. Then the dreamer is invited in once again for the new dream.

▶ Another choice is for the group to perform the drama again—either the original version or the changed version, but to decide beforehand when and how to bring the dreamer into the actual reenactment.

▶ After the final reenactment, there should once again be a council in which each participant shares what living this vision has meant to them, how they would like to incorporate it actively into their lives, and offer thanks to the gifts given by the vision or dream.

Another way of leaking the power of our inner consciousness is to get caught on the detour of the Great Visions Path. This is one where we are constantly seeking the "great vision," thinking that this will change our lives, transform all our weaknesses, and heal all our ills. What is forgotten on this detour is that the integration of the vision into our lives is up to us, and in that actual practice lies the transformation. It is often easier to open ourselves to receive such a vision than to put it into practice.

I read an article in the July 1990 issue of *Common Boundary,* with Mark Matousek interviewing the visionary Catholic reformer, Matthew Fox. When asked if he had ever done a vision quest, his reply was, "No, I already have too many visions!" He had the wisdom to understand that *putting those visions into practice was the real challenge, not getting more visions.* (He has since done a vision quest to address some current issues for himself, and found it deeply meaningful.)

Remember, it's not the size or grandness of a guide or vision that is the primary point. Using anything received can bring great benefit. An ant can be as powerful a medicine helper as an eagle; a twenty-second flash of inspiration can be even more useful than a grand drama of images; a penguin can be as fine an internal guide as a white-haired Native elder. I mention the penguin in remembrance of a student who went to great lengths to receive a guide. When he received a penguin, of all things, he rejected it, wanting something grander and "more powerful." Over time, he gradually relented and called the penguin's wisdom to him. This penguin gave him enormous gifts of information, inspiration, and growth, becoming a valued and trusted inner friend.

In Native practices in the past, when a vision or numinous dream was received, it was treated with great respect. The guidance was followed—the advice was acted out in reality—and the guide was made a continuing counselor. If a woman was given a vision in which Woodpecker spoke to her telling her of ways to live an easier, more harmonious life, she would likely have kept Woodpecker as a guide for all her days, relating to woodpeckers within and around her as special friends. When a man was shown a Chickadee in his vision, he made a special bundle to commemorate this, and carried or wore it throughout his life as a talisman, calling on Chickadee's quiet power again and again. In this way, more power was added to the original gift of the vision, rather than letting it fade away in memory.

I'd like to suggest something: create a quiet space and time for yourself, and go back through your experience to find a flash of vision, a numinous dream, a magical place, a voice that seemed to speak in the back of your head, a guide you found through journeying. It could have almost any form, from an angel of light to a tiny mouse with a clown cap. You will know the one. It will be something from your inner world that affected you profoundly, even if you're not sure of the meaning of the experience.

PURSUING THE SYMBOLIC GUIDE

Let's take, for example, a turquoise butterfly that whispered to me in a numinous dream. I will never forget that image, yet try as I might, in my dream I could not hear the gently spoken words of wisdom. Rather than dismiss it or feel cheated or teased by Spirit, I relentlessly pursued this symbol. My attitude in these meditations is often this: I'm not very good at using this inner world of symbols and mysterious beings, so I ask to be told the message again, or shown it in a different way. Since I do most certainly want to receive the message, I'm willing to work and practice in that space until I know what was given. So I might do one of several things:

▶ Lie down in meditation, and call the turquoise butterfly to me, asking it to speak more loudly this time and to repeat the message.

▶ Let my imagination bring up the butterfly and imagine its story. Let myself go along with it, carefully observing where it flies and lands, what it points out to me.

▶ As I go to sleep at night, say my prayers and ask for another dream to illuminate the message brought by the butterfly.

▶ Write or tell a story using the butterfly as the main character to see what comes up from my unconscious in this way.

▶ Write a dialogue with my Spirit helper just as if I were writing a play. I put my initials in the upper left-hand margin of a page—usually in my journal—and ask politely if the butterfly (in this example) will speak with me. Often, I write down a question. Then I would write "Butterfly" in the margin of the next line, and wait receptively. I write down *anything* that pops into my mind without being concerned about how it is coming out or what it means. Then I ask or write another question—again writing down anything that comes into my awareness. Not until I have finished all the writing do I reread the dialogue and take the time to reflect on what is written there and what it means for me.

In the old Native way, I would make a medicine bundle in honor of this butterfly. In a piece of cloth, I would wrap up objects or symbols that represent this butterfly messenger. I would honor this bundle with my prayers for understanding, and offer it pollen to feed it and to call it back to me.

BRINGING THE VISION TO LIFE

1. Choose a particular inner guide you have experienced—the guide could be a momentary image, a vision, a feeling, or even a spoken word—and try one or more of the following things:

2. Dialogue with your guide. Ask for clarification of the message it brings. Ask to be given ways to begin practicing this advice in your daily life.

3. Ask to be shown another picture, to be given a feeling or told in a new way, or to receive information through any other useful modality.

4. Write a story using this guide as the main character; see what comes to you this way.

5. When you go to sleep at night, ask this guide to give you a dream that you will remember—one that will give you new insights.

6. Ask what other ways this guide might be useful to you.

7. Ask what you can do for your guide.

THE MEDICINE BUNDLE

Choose a specific inner image (guide, vision, etc.), and create a medicine bundle for it. Do this in order to symbolically make this inner image more real for you in a physical way.

1. Find some sort of object that represents this inner image. For example, if Deer is your guide, you might want to use a piece of antler or a deer skull to wrap within a deep hide cover. Or if Chickadee is your guide, and you cannot find an actual chickadee who has given away her life, then find or take a photograph of one, all the while keeping on the lookout for a fallen chickadee feather. For my rainbow vision, I might place in the bundle a piece of opal whose iridescence reminds me of the essence of the message. Use your imagination, as well as asking your inner guidance for ideas.

2. For a protective cover, find a cloth, rabbit skin, silk scarf, or a piece of soft leather that has some symbolism to connect it to your inner image.

3. As time goes on, you may want to add to this bundle new things that speak to you. You may want to add sage and sweet grass to make a clear and sweet place for the objects. Even a piece of your writing about the experience could be tucked in, if this feels important and appropriate.

4. Keep this bundle in a special place out of harm's way. You may tie a beautiful cord around it and hang it on your bedroom wall, or you may want to keep it near your altar.

5. Make a regular schedule of working with the power of this inner image through using the bundle. Once a week (or whatever schedule you can actually keep up) take the bundle down, open and smudge it with your choice of special incense, then work with it through guided imagery, prayer, or simply meditation. Continue to seek its guidance and to deepen your relationship to it.

6. You may want to offer something to symbolically "feed" it. This could be cornmeal, as a symbol of nurturing, tobacco as a symbol of connection, or pollen as a symbol of fertilization. If you choose to do this, simply sprinkle a pinch over the bundle and offer a corresponding prayer. Now and then, for the sake of neatness, you will want to clean out what you have sprinkled in; simply take it out and offer it to Mother Earth.

7. Give thanks for what you have received, and close the bundle. Put it back in its protected place.

VISION IN ACTION

Remember to make use of the gifts from your left side, even when they come in simple form.

1. This may mean taking a few minutes to really learn what an intuitive glimmer is telling you—or, it may lead to one of the more complex processes described above.

2. If you can't understand your vision immediately, write down the symbols and meanings that come to you at the time. Many times, you will look back at your notes months later, and the "aha!" will come in

a flash. Your intervening experience will have illuminated the meaning of your dream or vision.

3. Whatever practices you choose, from time to time give yourself a chance to assess any changes that have come about in your relationship with the inner image or in the inner experience itself. Sometimes a stone may turn into a butterfly, or one guide turn you over to another. Be willing to flow with what comes, and to make use of what you receive so the channels stay open!

Be active with what you have already been given, rather than waiting until the next experience "just happens." Take this powerful and effective aspect of your inner world and work with it in the ways I have suggested or in the many ways you can create yourself. There are certainly limits to this kind of work, especially when it becomes a kind of pushing or forcing. Yet, most people I work with tend to be too passive about working with such gifts from Spirit. Now is the time to begin to see yourself as active and creative in *this world of Spirit—it is not foreign to you, just unfamiliar to your conscious awareness.*

Although the images and the guides that came to me in my vision quests differed greatly from each other, the underlying theme of their messages was the same. In metaphor after metaphor, the need to recognize wholeness and to live in holiness was emphasized. The Dawn Star's reference to the one I called Rainbow Woman as White Buffalo Woman did not surprise me, for the message she brought was White Buffalo Woman's message. White Buffalo Woman was continuing to sing her spirit song to me, asking me to learn it so well that I could sing it out into the world.

What I did not know in these early years of my spiritual quest was that seeking and receiving a vision is only the beginning of the journey. Over these intervening years, it has become abundantly clear to me that the major part of the visioning process is that of living the vision. The seeds planted within me through my sacred lineages—the Sacred Buffalo Lodge, White Buffalo Calf Pipe Woman, and Dawn Star—will live and grow in me eternally. Through these quests, I was firmly grounded in the sacred. But the time had now come for me to begin to make this real for myself and All My Relations.

As I looked back over all my experiences during this time of questing, I realized that there had been a balance of light and dark, of joy and challenge, of uplifting and heartbreak on the journey. Of course, the joyful light and the bliss were easy. Yet, I came to know that learning takes one into difficulties and very tough places. It causes us to plumb the depths of ourselves so that we can come to truly know ourselves by shedding light on the unworkable and painful parts of our lives, then helps us form new and positive images to make real in our lives. Looking back, I give thanks for all the learning that I called to myself and for all those who participated in those experiences.

After these major vision quests were complete, I still needed to find my own personal meaning for those exquisite visions and experiences. I quickly learned that it was up to me to make them a real part of my life. Thus, I began the long process of being present with the visions on the path that leads to understanding. Someone once reminded me that in order to understand something, one must "stand under" it long enough to absorb what it has to give. I found myself standing under these visions as one stands under the sky, occasionally receiving the gift of clarity through the rain. Sometimes those raindrops of wisdom came through the words of a teacher; some came in sudden flashes of insight when I hadn't even been consciously thinking about the quests; and some came through interactions with friends and students whose words or questions turned

on a light in my mind, giving me new levels of meaning for the symbolism of my visions.

Seeing the gap between parts of my own life and the visions I had
been given, I began looking around for ways to bring myself more
wholeness and more ability to truly manifest in my own life the magnificent teachings I had received. I walked forward holding them in my heart
and mind. The journey had begun. The journey would continue in beauty.

PART TWO

WALKING THE RAINBOW PATH

My spirit was calling strongly for awakening and growth at this time in my life, and Grandma Rosie was not the only one who heard. At the same time that I was driving north to be with her, I was working with two master teachers in the San Francisco Bay area where I resided. Although their methods of teaching differed radically from hers, the primary lessons I was given by all three complemented and reinforced each other, teaching me that truth can be spoken in many different metaphors. One day as I was speaking about these three magnificent teachers, a student said, "Oh, how lucky you were to deserve three wonderful teachers!" I told her that perhaps that was true. But more often I felt that the Great Spirit needs to give us hard-headed ones several teachers to knock powerfully on the door of our consciousness in order to awaken us!

I now realize, as well, that many other people and things had been powerful teachers for me, starting in my childhood, and continuing well after I spent time with the three primary teachers of my late twenties. There are still teachers and guides in my life. The number of them seems limited only by my ability to recognize them and to take time to be with them.

The process of learning and awakening in Spirit is for me a continuing cycle, a spiral. I go around and around again through level after level of learning on a particular issue. If I am clear about it, then I can zip right on by. However, if I still have work to do, then I may spend a long period with that issue once again. Thus, I fully expect to be learning until I leave this body. I have an image in my mind of at last becoming clear with all my issues of this life, at which point the rapid spinning of my beingness that would be possible would literally whirl me out of my body!

In the following chapters I will tell you some stories about my teachers. While these stories may seem less intense, perhaps even less compelling than the stories of Grandma Rosie, they are no less important. These teachers grounded the gifts of my vision in reality, and so made them true in my own experience. These learnings were profound for me, and I hope I can share with you at least a scent of the fragrance they gifted me.

CHAPTER EIGHT

FIGHTING THE DRAGON

*My mother's teaching moved me to strengthen my will, to focus my
Taurian tenacity,
and to break through my limited conception of my abilities.*

"Don't let fear stop ya!"—old rodeo saying.

*The spiritual warrior takes responsibility for all that comes her way
and lives an impeccable life.*

My mom—beautifully tall, lean, strong, tough, and smart—
was capable of just about any damn thing she put her hand to: even if
this meant cutting wood and packing water up from the spring to wash
little kids' dirty diapers, while at the same time having a noon meal
cooking on the wood stove, all on a break from milking cows and
putting up hay with a team of horses. She could sew us kids beautiful
little wool coats from used overcoats, bake the best cinnamon rolls in
the world, herd cattle on a snorty horse, or whatever! She was my first
teacher, and a good one. She was primary in teaching me about the right
side of this old world—my way of saying she taught me about how to
live in this world—how to do, how to make and mend things, how to
gracefully accomplish, how to create order in my everyday world, and
how to meet challenges.

Mom, Dad, my older brother Tom, and I lived on a Montana
reservation ranch five miles from our nearest neighbor and ten miles
from the little Apsa village, so we were very much "on our own." I had
an active part in the daily work and chores that kept us self-sufficient.
Mom always grew a big garden, filled with rows of vegetables, a special
patch of the strawberries that tasted like heaven topped with Old
Bossy's thick cream, and watermelon that never had time to mature in

our short summers. We kids ran the wild hills, chokecherry-lined creeks, and aspen groves from the time we were little, and early on we began exploring the weird, blue-clay hill not far from the house. On and around that hill was a special treasure—an enormous patch of tiny, sweet, sweet, wild strawberries. Because they were our favorites, we finally talked Mom into transplanting some into the garden, and it still makes my mouth water just *thinking* about those tiny gems, warm from the summer sun.

And the cream, oh, the cream! I remember the time (as close to heaven as I have been), when my cajoling finally broke through my parents' busyness, and they consented to tighten down the cream separator. This made the cream come out so thick you had to spoon it rather than pour it from the big quart jar that caught it! That cream was divine right off the spoon, or melting on top of the coffee I drank just to use the cream. How precious those spoonfuls of cream are in the memory of my taste buds. I was sure then that everyone else had been as enchanted with the thick cream as I: it seemed inevitable that we would make it again and again. But in all my years, that was the only time. I never again found cream even close to that—until I happily discovered double-thick cream on a trip to England.

Chores and eating remind me of a major teaching I received from Mom, and of how we lived and worked. I didn't know much about dragons early on, but Mom had tackled a few. Since she knew we'd have to face our own dragons sometime down the line, she felt we might as well learn to succeed from the first. She gave us the wonderful gift—out of necessity as well as wisdom and family tradition—of participating in our own livelihoods. Whether I liked my chores of the moment or not, I did know I was making a real and necessary contribution to our lives. Mom believed in "starting 'em early"—whether it was talking to us like intelligent human beings from the time we were "hatched," or gathering eggs.

The chicken house was a few hundred yards from our house, just beyond a little creek (pronounced "crick") with a plank bridge across it. As soon as I could navigate well enough to make it back to the house with a full basket of eggs, my mom assigned me the task of gathering them. By going with her, I had come to love the adventure of finding every egg. Whether it had been hidden in a corner of the henhouse, in the nests, or sometimes even under a hen's warm breast feathers, I delighted in slipping away with her precious, recently laid prize! The hens were most lovable then, fluffy, cozy, soft, and captive. I had done this gathering time and again, and I was looking forward to being big enough to do it by myself.

Entering the chicken yard alone for the first time, however, I discovered that this was going to be more of an adventure than I had bargained for. Our rooster was big, beautiful, proud, protective of his ladies, and with his three-inch heel spurs, the cock of our walk. Almost as tall as me, he blustered around when Mom and I entered the yard, protesting loudly while keeping his distance. When I think back on his righteousness, I'm reminded of a Gary Larson cartoon that shows a farm woman who carries a basket of eggs back to her house, passing en route a rooster, who's carrying her child back to his henhouse! No matter how justified that big rooster's rage might have been, I would have felt most blessed without it. Seconds after I set foot in his chicken yard "by my little lonesome," he launched himself through the air toward me, becoming the most fearful dragon I had ever seen. As he sank his talons into my tiny chest, he crowed shrilly and beat my face and head with his enormous wings!

Not really hurt, but terrified, I didn't put up a fight—that time. Getting away was uppermost on my mind! But I had to keep enough composure to shut the gate, which kept him and his ladies inside the yard, or Mom would add to his brow-beating a few well-chosen words about how little time she had to fix what us kids messed up. The chickens had escaped a few times before, and after chasing them, cackling and flying wildly into nearby bushes, I could well understand her point of view.

Having dropped the basket in the fracas, I had little to slow me down, and ran crying and screaming back across the plank bridge to Mom in the kitchen. The sound of my screams and the look of terror in my little eyes brought her running to grab me up and find out what was wrong.

Her sympathy turned to mirth when I burst out in protest, "That rooster feawered me! He feawered me!"

She knew my speech well enough to know I meant "feathered me," and could make some intelligent guesses about what "feawered me" meant, having had some run-ins with Mr. Rooster herself. She calmed my sobs as I told the entire, horrible story, with deep emotion and tears. The response I expected after such a brutal attack was, "That's all right, honey. I'll help until you're bigger," or better, "I'll have big brother gather eggs from now on."

I felt so safe in her arms, I was sure the baby-girl would be cuddled a while. But my mom followed her "start 'em early" philosophy of childrearing, and sat me down as soon as my tears had dried. She said, matter-of-factly, "This time when you go out there, you find a big stick on the way, and you show him who's boss." When my little round face registered disbelief, she repeated her instruction, "Just get a big stick and knock him down when he comes at you. That's what I've had to do. Go on, now—we need those eggs for breakfast." Then she turned back to her work, leaving me feeling tiny, hurt, put-upon, and completely alone—along with a very yucky feeling in the pit of my stomach at the thought of stepping back into that chicken yard.

But Mom meant what she said, so I went to find a stick. She made it sound relatively easy, so I thought perhaps that stick and a few solid whacks would scare the dragon off, and I'd "have it made" from then on. Not long after stepping back into that chicken yard, I developed a deeper understanding of the older kids' expression, "That's what you get for thinking!"

That rooster—who landed on me immediately in his brow-beating attack—was not about to give up his babies (in those eggs) because of some peewee like me bouncing a few whacks off his feathers. I didn't actually get too many strikes in before he was on me, beak to beak, and again I was fighting him off bare-handed. He let me escape, and as I made it to the gate, I just knew that this time Mom would give me not only sympathy but help.

Shortly, however, I was back again with a bigger stick and several new strategies. One hope—false—was that I could outrun him, and make it from the gate into the henhouse before he got me. That hope ended with me clawed and pecked on the backside, trapped in the henhouse without a weapon, while he strutted around outside, the bold victor. I was deeply discouraged, if not downright depressed. But I had learned early to not let animals bluff or "buffalo" you—knowing that giving in to them makes it extremely difficult to ever gain control again. Well, the rooster had me buffaloed good. But although his victory was quite clear in my mind, I couldn't seem to get it clear in Mom's.

At last, in desperation, hoping he'd forgotten me, I sprinted for the basket lying in the yard, grabbed the closest stick and, with him squawking on my tail, slammed the chicken house door. Problem was, all these goings-on had stirred up the ladies, who now also squawked and flapped about, creating choking dust in the small space. This made Monsieur Le Rooster even angrier. Not only was I stealing eggs, I was traumatizing his ladies! I cracked the door and breathed the fresh air, watching that dragon strut and cluck to his harem.

At least this time I'd managed to gather the eggs, and I set the full basket beside the door. But I knew I'd never get them safely across the pen without holding him off, and the big stick was really a two-handed club, tricky to wield while carrying a delicate basket of breakfast. So, leaving the precious cargo safe behind, I stepped back into the fray, swinging wildly and continuously before he could even get close. I bounced a few solid blows off his feathered armor, and that slowed him down. We went a few more rounds, until he began to lose confidence.

In one of his few hesitations, I grabbed the eggs and made the few critical yards from henhouse to gate. I put the eggs down outside, and returned for one more glorious battle, which ended in victorious safety.

My terror turned into a kind of manic exhilaration as I scurried exalted toward the house. But then—as is so often true in life—I realized that when you break through a barrier, having met one challenge, there's always another waiting. I remembered tomorrow, and tomorrow, and tomorrow . . . stretching ahead to fill my whole life with that awful dragon.

Mom's backhanded congratulations, "See, Punkin, I told you you could do it," were not actually welcome then, given my thoughts of the future. And yet, I went out and confronted my dragon again and again, sometimes doing pretty well day after day. But then that big rooster would catch me with my guard down, my intent slack, my energy low, or my attention wavering—and we'd go at it again. If I got too cocky to carry my stick, he'd run me out to get it. My mother had found a worthy adversary for her budding little samurai. He taught me well, and I hold my own with dragons even now.

The Southern Seers understand that to live this Earthly life successfully, we must be able to handle at least two aspects of it. The first is the right side, or *tonal*, as they call it, which encompasses all of what we call "real." It includes all the things and people in our lives—the day-to-day world with its relationships and transactions—everything from tying our shoes and making a living to getting along with our spouse. It includes the wonders of rocketing to the Moon and diving among the creatures of the ocean depths. For many, this *is* life—the only aspect that is consciously recognized.

The second aspect is the left side, or *nagual*. This includes all the things in the universe that can't be knocked on or pinched—the realms of Spirit, of dream, of vision, of shadow, and of other realities separate from our normal view of the world. This is an enormous dimension of our world that is seldom known about or developed in the lives of those who do not seek a mystical or spiritual path.

My mom was unknowingly training my right side. She was teaching me to face life—not only to handle it, but to find exhilaration in its greatest challenges. Over the years, her teaching moved me to strengthen my will, to focus my Taurian tenacity positively, and to break through my limited conception of my own abilities. One of the primary values of having a command over the right side of life is that, from this foundation, one can approach the most immense, challenging, and wondrous experiences of all—those of the left side. People who cannot function well on their right side sometimes end up in our mental institutions, drifting aimlessly on the left side. Elderly people are often able to drift through time into their childhoods with precise memory for the smallest detail of a dress or an incident, yet are unable to wash themselves, recognize a friend, or remember where they are. However, if we are grounded in the right side, and can open to the infinite and beautiful left side, we become truly balanced human beings. We can then use the feminine, intuitive, non-linear, psychic, synchronistic left side of ourselves, which then increases our knowledge, our perception, and our full functioning in the world.

With such a solid grounding on the right side, my ability to take care of business became ingrained within me, even when I am open and occupied on the left. An instance of this is that I do many things while driving a car at high speed—I jot down ideas for my next workshops, floss my teeth, call vision, and go very left-sided. Yet a deep part of me is set to keep handling the right side—even while visioning—to keep driving safely.

I began driving very early, in the old automatic-shift Chevy—before I could hit the gas pedal and look over the steering wheel at the same time. I could do this because our life was spent on nearly empty dirt backroads. I drove often as I grew older. I remember clearly one time in early high school, Mom and I were driving down from Pryor Mountain, through a flat area filled with sagebrush that had grown three feet high. I had "discovered boys," and was daydreaming vividly as I drove along—about my newest love—when Mom shouted in my ear, "What in the hell are you doing?!"

I came back to my right side to find that she had let me get twenty yards off the road, through the sagebrush, before "waking me up" to a profound lesson: It is possible to go into your left side—in this case, my daydreams—and totally lose track of your body in the real world. I had difficulty believing I hadn't felt us bouncing wildly off the road and over the sage, yet there we were! It didn't take any imagination to create the picture of what would have happened three miles on down the high, curved canyon road had I done the same thing there. The necessity of being able to function well in both worlds became very clear as I realized my predilection toward the left side, my calling toward vision.

Though Mom wouldn't have used these words, she gave me the

grounding I would need to function in the world as a visionary, whose primary focus is left-sided. Through her years of hard work on the ranch and in town, she supported my life and gave it stability. In her toughness, her devotion, her generosity and wisdom, she gave me my very own dragon, and many other powerful tools. She gave me my life.

Mom also gave me another fine teacher. My brother Tom, a year and nine months older than me, was made of angel stuff—of love, hugs, and gentleness, and he was given the eyes and hands of the famous western artists Charles Russell and Frederic Remington combined. He was thrilled to see me when I arrived on the scene. Living as far as we did from any other families, he may have thought he was the only "helpless midget" in the world until I came along for company. Our family album shows pictures of us sitting in high chairs side by side, Tom grinning with his bright two-year-old charm, and me strapped in, drooling on my baby blanket. In this series of photos, he manages to contain himself for the first shot. But in the next few, he reaches over to hug and kiss me, and for the rest of the series obviously cannot be made to sit up straight and keep his hands off me! I remember fondly that he pulled me in a little red wagon; carried me around while I sucked on my blanket; and stood patiently waiting for the last few tastes of my bottle, after Mom had weaned him. He was a radiant, beautiful child.

As we grew older he filled the elder brother role well, becoming my best friend, my protector, and tutor, as well as my trainer. Loving me enough to want me to do everything as well as he did, Tom pressed me to grow and develop, most often like a little boy, as he never would play house or dolls. He wanted me strong, so he would make me pick up rocks as big as my hands could hold, and lift them straight out from my sides, to develop my "lats." Later when we fought, as all siblings sometimes do, he must have wished I was weaker. Although I was little, I was tough—and meaner than he—which alone won a few battles. As he was always a head taller and had at least a hand's reach on me, I felt that entitled me to "hit below the belt." I was definitely not made of angel stuff!

While Tom remained a gentle child, I developed a fierceness that made him sometimes say to Mom, "She's just crazy!" I remember a time when we were sitting in the old pickup, waiting and watching while Mom plowed the upper forty acres. We had been playing with things in the glove compartment to entertain ourselves, and when we finished, Tom slammed the compartment door, with my little fingers still in it!

The pain burnt intensely, and he felt so bad. He kept apologizing and trying to hold my hand.

I insisted that he had done it on purpose, and when he saw my anger flare, he jumped out of the truck and ran toward Mom. I, too, jumped out, still raging, and picked up a good-sized rock. By the time I heaved it, he was a long distance away, yet to my surprise and chagrin, *kerchunk!* It hit him right in the back of the head. Down he went, and I felt terrible—partly because I had hurt him purposefully, when I knew in my heart he had hurt me by accident, and partly because I knew Mom would extract some heavy dues for my orneriness. She would shame me for my behavior, and that hurt me more than I think a spanking would have.

Whether experiencing me as crazy or not, still Tom continues to teach me. One summer not long ago we were breaking horses to ride. He would work with one just until it understood the saddle and wasn't too interested in bucking, and then he'd turn it over to me for the miles and miles of riding important for them at that stage. When we rode those colts, they would start out snorty and spooky and unsure of the monster on their backs, and after the many miles of a good workout, "they would have had their mind on something else," as Tom would say.

One day he gave me a little black quarterhorse stallion to work, and he rode along with me, on a beautiful gray Arabian stud. We eased them into a run "to shake a few of the kinks out," and raced along. Even though Tom had warned me, I let my black get too close to his gray, and in fine stallion style, the gray jumped my horse and started a fight! Getting them separated definitely taught me to heed Tom's warnings.

We rode on then, out east of the ranch for several miles along a small stream, into the low piñon-covered hills, and on up a mile or so until we rested on the high red hill that towered just above our ranch corrals. It was a long way down, and the horses were nervous with the height, but we coaxed them right up to the rim, so we could relax and survey the country below. Being so close to that high precipice, on a partially broken colt, made me pretty nervous myself, for my control of the black was not all that I had wished. The rim dropped straight down about three feet, then became a talus slope of a thousand yards of slippery shale rock.

And what does my brother, the trainer, do but surprise both his horse and me by spurring the gray hard in the belly! The little stallion's instinct jumped him forward, off that three-foot rimrock, and my heart sank! I watched them fly, expecting to see a helluva cloud of red dust rise from their tumbling death, but the gray instinctively sat down on his hindquarters, front feet stiffly braced, and slid gracefully down. They were already halfway down the hill to the corrals when it dawned on me that I either had to follow suit, or ride my tired ass all those miles back around.

In a moment of supreme indecision, I cussed Tom for all he was worth. But I was not about to ride around or to be outdone, so shouting an old rodeo hand's saying—"Don't let fear stop ya!"—I kicked my black over the edge. My heart jumped into my mouth as the little stud slid and sat, as Tom's horse had. But I thoroughly enjoyed the wild ride down to Tom who watched, waiting and grinning, near the corral. Although we're not able to spend much time together now that I am busy on the road and seldom get to visit his ranch, I continue to appreciate Tom as my teacher.

This kind of teaching is the finest I have experienced. It's a style practiced in the shamanic tradition—one works with an apprentice on skills through practice, practice, practice. Then the learner is put into a situation where the only path is to abandon control and make powerful use of those skills. Even though I'm an experienced horsewoman, I would never have jumped any horse off that cliff without my brother's example and the urging of all those weary, extra miles.

In addition to those aspects of modeling and practice, there was also the "kinesthetic" learning that had been generated. My body, the instrument through which I live this Earthly life, then knew something that my mind, my fears, my reasoning could no longer deny. This intense method is designed to quell students' inevitable questioning of their abilities—held even after long practice. It also makes use of the principle that patterns are deeply embedded in the nervous system by intensity of emotion.

Tom also initiated me into the wonders of the left side, through his amazing artistic and imaginative abilities. As an artist he was a genius. Even as a small boy, he created out of his imagination wonderful drawings and carvings. When I was still in the primitive, stick-figure stage of artistry, he took a little piece of two-by-four and carved the most exquisite deer, complete with delicate antlers!

His imagination created a great part of our daily play, too. We had our own miniature ranch on the cool side of the house in the summertime. He bought the most realistic horses he could find to match the size of our ranch. Then he made tiny, beautiful saddles for them by hand, carving the saddle-tree himself, and using fine goat hide to lay each piece of leather just like a real saddle. He even added minute, carved wooden stirrups. Mom would help us by crocheting tiny cinches, to make the saddles complete. We divided our "pastures" with stick and string fences, made little gates that opened and closed, and kept our fields "planted and harvested" with the miniature John Deere working farm implements that were our special treasures. Sometimes we tired of the ranch life we knew so well, and became gauchos on the pampas of Argentina swirling our bolas; or we became nomadic herders on the small, sturdy horses of mountainous Tibet. As my constant companion and playmate, Tom supported my imaginative left side in a hard-working everyday world, where daydreaming was never valued.

My dad taught me right-sided lessons as well in the early years of my childhood before my folks divorced. He and I were quite similar and got along doing most anything. In the first years of my childhood, we had no electricity, carried our own water from a nearby spring, farmed with a team of horses, and often went to town in a horse-drawn buggy. I helped with all aspects of farming and ranching, from gathering cattle on horseback to branding them, from plowing with a two-horse team to putting up hay with an old-fashioned lift-arm stacker, from building to fencing, to conducting veterinary procedures and learning the rudiments of mechanics by being his pint-sized assistant on cars, trucks, and tractors.

Since we lived far from any sizeable town, we did most of our own work on everything. Together, the family built additions on the old log house, hunted wild game, irrigated fields, bred horses, and castrated pigs. By the time my folks divorced, and I left the ranch to go to school in town around the age of eleven, I was pretty darn good at designing, building, making, repairing, handling, and taking care of most anything.

But the most powerful contribution Dad made to my life, and his most valuable gift, was not these right-sided things. It was his introducing me to Grandma Rosie and the lineage she carried. In this way, he influenced a huge portion of my left-side development, my spiritual life.

The simple teachings from my childhood, given by this family I chose, have been invaluable lessons, preparing me in a way I did not then understand, for my work in teaching others. Until I lived around young people who had been raised with silver spoons and who had few right-sided skills, I did not know how many strengths my folks had given me. With their grounding in the world, I could stand solid and clear in my double Taurus nature, and move from there into the realm of spirit.

Our families of origin give us the basic patterns and beliefs by which we continue to live our lives—unless we consciously intervene and change them. In every family I know, there is a mix of very positive and powerful things, but also many that are negative and unworkable.

In my family, much attention and positive feedback was given in the area of "doing" and accomplishment. Much of our feeling of worth was based on how well or how much we accomplished. To not take care of business, to neglect the right side of the world, was tantamount to sin.

Our inner worlds were a different matter. Feelings and emotions did not receive much attention in my family. We were intensely busy on the ranch making a living, and neither of my parents had been raised with any experience of honoring the emotional side of life. Too often, an exchange meant something very "heavy" was happening, so such exchanges of feelings were seldom a part of our lives.

As I grew up and experienced different ways of being, I realized that feelings are vitally important, and our lives are dull and somewhat numb and ungrounded if we shut down those aspects of ourselves. So naturally, tremendous accomplishment in the world is easy for me. Yet, clear communication, open emotional experience, and intimate relationship are more difficult.

Through my studies of human learning, it has become clear to me that as newborns we are like blank books. Only the form, title, size, and general character of the book are already there. The words that will make up the heart of the book are yet to be written. It remains to be seen if the pages of this human book will be neatly written, smeared, or torn out to use for paper airplanes. The writing is done by our experience, especially our early experience in the family, which we might say determines the chapter titles.

We then spend the rest of our lives filling in the story along these established thematic lines. Unless we make a conscious assessment of our early programming, and take the challenge of transforming those habits and beliefs that we've come to find lacking in usefulness, we will simply go around and around with level after level of those original chapter themes, whether they be accomplishment or intimacy, dysfunction, or victimization.

I highly recommend that all of us undertake personal growth work to help us become who we truly are meant to be, rather than remaining merely who our early programming has set us up to be. Since it is usually too complex to complete this kind of healing by oneself, we might need to find this growth work through self-help groups; any of the twelve-step programs begun by Alcoholics Anonymous (which include Adult Children of Alcoholics, AlaTeen, Overeaters Anonymous, and many others) now available in every city in the United States; through workshops focused on specific areas of growth; or through long-term group or individual therapy.

The life of a spiritual warrior is a challenging and very rewarding one. One of its basic choices is to engage life fully—to make full use of both the beauties and the challenges we bring to ourselves in order to gain wisdom and find our true selves. *Thus, the spiritual warrior takes responsibility for all that comes her way, and lives an impeccable life.* To begin with, this means that we must be willing to *see,* to be willing to look both at the obvious aspects of our lives, and deeper, below the surfaces of life—and to do so without denial or acting like victims. Based in our understanding that we call all our lessons to us in order to learn, we work to become aware of the influences of our past and to clear them, as well as to face new experiences with openness, responsibility, and curiosity. One of our primary questions when faced with either an opportunity or a challenge is, "What is the lesson here? How can I make the best use of this to learn for myself and to serve All My Relations?" For instance, having the opportunity to teach a class in something you know well may turn out to be a lesson in human relations as much as a lesson in teaching.

Once we are truly willing to see, then we are confronted with many choices. "How do I make the best use of this particular talent I was given? Do I want to do the hard work required to clear this old, unworkable pattern, or am I willing to let it continue to drain my power away? Choosing to work on it, what is the best way to begin? How can I learn well the lesson I have called to me in this form?"

Aware that we learn from each and every experience, the spiritual warrior is willing to choose. Whatever she chooses will lead her to new experience, and give her feedback upon which she can base her next choice. This means that the warrior, once perceiving a choice, will not only choose, but *act.*

ASSESSING THE OUTER (RIGHT-SIDED) WORLD

Let's take a look at your right side to help you begin to see yourself more fully. We'll look at how you experience yourself, and how you learned the patterns you have, as a means of giving you more choices and new possible actions.

To begin with, to deepen your knowledge of who you are right now, you might want to reflect on these questions:

1. What are the roots of your right side? What messages did you receive on doing, and on "taking care of business"?

2. What were you told you could expect from the world?

3. How were you taught to deal with challenges and difficulties?

4. What would your life be like if your right side ran everything? What would you miss or long for?

5. Which qualities of the right side do you need to develop more fully?

6. Which qualities from the left side would help you balance the right-sided ones you may know more about now? For example, if you have learned to focus on accomplishment, would some form of quiet centering or meditation help balance your life? Or, if you were taught to rely on yourself, might you complement that by learning to work with others cooperatively?

THE INHERITANCE SUITCASE

Looking back at my family and what I gained from them has been very useful to me. In order for you to make such an assessment, I suggest doing an exercise I call "The Inheritance Suitcase." It is based on the knowledge that you inherit many different kinds of things from your family, which might be thought of as a suitcase you carry around, often without examination. I suggest that you examine what is in that suitcase so that you may deal with it more impeccably.

1. Take out your journal or two separate pages of paper and create a column each for:

▶ Those things you learned from your family that seem *workable and useful* in your life,

▶ Those things that seem *unworkable and detrimental.*

These lists will likely be comprised of attitudes and family aphorisms, such as "Keep a stiff upper lip"; beliefs and decisions about "the way it is and will always be": ways of being and doing, patterns of living, and family rules, such as "Don't ever discuss family emotional problems with anyone else."

2. Begin these columns by going back into your childhood; most of the patterns and ways of being you inherited were set there. For example:

Workable:	Unworkable:
1. Meet your challenges with courage.	1. Push hard to get ahead— never let up.
2. Be willing to try new things.	2. Never show how you feel.
3. Be self-reliant and responsible.	3. Never let anyone else get the upper hand.

3. If it's difficult to really see your own life this way, ask your friends or spouse to help get you started. A counselor or therapist can also be helpful here, if you have one. Others you trust can give important input from a perspective different from yours. They may see patterns that you do not, or may feel that some really stink that you thought worked just great!

4. Take plenty of time to think about these things as you list them. Make sure you put them under the category of how they affect *you*, not what usefulness your parents thought they would have. For example, if Mom thought it made sense never to cry because it didn't seem to help anything, that would have been positive to her. Yet, if you have found that repressing sadness or any other emotion has been negative or dysfunctional for you, put that attitude in column number two.

5. Set a time frame of one week to uncover the major things you want to add to the list. But also keep it in the back of your mind as the weeks go by. Notice what works for you and what does not—in family, at work, at play, in your inner world as well as outer, in happy times and times of conflict or upset. Have the courage to observe yourself fully without judgment.

6. Once you feel the list is relatively complete, sit down with it and study your assessment.

▶ Congratulate yourself on the things that work for you. Really take in and affirm these things. Sometimes, this might be just one aspect of a family pattern. For example, if your dad was a workaholic and never knew when to quit, that might have been negative overall; yet out of that you might have learned how to accomplish things in a good way. Recognize these positive attributes as aspects upon which you can build.

▶ Now look at the unworkable column. Acknowledge the emotional feelings that come up—from panic to pain to hopelessness. These feelings are an important beginning step. When you stop numbing yourself and avoiding these issues, the old feelings associated with their inception will very likely arise.

▶ Here again, it's good to have someone to share these feelings with. Someone who can simply be present, thus making a safe space for you to experience what is coming up.

7. Come back to the list again and divide it into two parts:

▶ Things you can shift yourself.

▶ Things with which you will need help.

8. In the first part you might want to put things like "My family followed a rigid schedule." You could work with this by varying your own rigid schedule, and by practicing flexibility and spontaneity. You may choose to act a different way.

9. In the second part you would include such things as, "I learned to feel that inside I am a bad (dumb, incapable, etc.) person." These deep issues are the ones where we all need help. If you choose to get that help, then private therapy, support groups, or groups for dysfunctional or alcoholic family issues would all provide a good place for you to go. It is an especially important decision to take action in this aspect of your life.

10. The two most important things to remember here are:

▶ To assess yourself with courage and integrity.

▶ To know it is possible to change what you do not wish to keep, although it will take time, discipline, and the help of those around you. The warrior *sees* and *chooses,* then *acts.*

I bless you in this process, and I know that as you grow and heal yourself, the world around you will be healed as well.

These days it seems very popular to look at our families of origin and examine the unworkable patterns we learned there. However, I think that in these reviews we must realize that each and every one of us in each family was doing the very best we could at the time.

I firmly believe that we chose, long before we were born, the group of people who will become our family; that we chose each other in order to learn the lessons that are important for each of us in *this* lifetime. So, it is crucial to work with what we were given, and to truly learn from the challenges we created for ourselves, rather than simply covering them up or denying them. In addition, it seems vital for us to be grateful for the good energy given by our family members, and to be thankful for the positive things each one contributed.

Here, I wish to give thanks to each member of my family for all that they have contributed to my life!

CHAPTER NINE

A CHALICE OVERFLOWING WITH LIGHT

Names can be profoundly useful in calling forth aspects of ourselves
out of the realm of spirit and mystery.

Knowing that each person, like each snowflake, is absolutely unique,
our people allowed the Great Spirit
to help them attune to the name that would match
the essence of the child,
thus helping, as the name was called out and spoken
again and again,
to bring forth the child's true nature and gifts.

Always, it is a process of seeking the truth within you, and expressing
it in the world.

Chalíse. "What a beautiful and unusual name," I thought, as I ran it over my tongue again and again, *"Chalíse. Chalíse. Chalíse."* This new name, given me in vision by the Dawn Star on my last quest, called to mind all my other names, and caused me to meditate on the traditional ways of naming. Over the years of my lifetime I have been given many names, some from the right side and some from the left side.

When I was born I was given the name "Emaline," in a political move to please my father's side of the family. My older brother Tom had been named for my mom's brother, and this resulted in his being largely ignored by the relatives on Dad's side—the ones who lived nearby. It was hoped that "Emaline" would create a different response, and, in fact, I was showered with gifts, treated with pride, and cooed over. But there was a catch: My brother, standing there beside me, was still ignored. This was hurtful to all, and eventually made my parents so angry that they refused to call me by my given name. That name was forgotten long before I'd learned to say it. So what to call me? My brother, thrilled to have another little person in his life, called me "Bebe," because he couldn't say baby. And that became my name. I was called Bebe, which eventually evolved into Bebes (pronounced "Bébz"), and that is how I knew myself.

When I went off the reservation to a formal, public school, I was enrolled by my given name, which came as a surprise. Soon, however, everyone learned my "real" name, and I remained Bebes. This strange duplicity lasted throughout my college years, the given name hanging on like a cobweb growing dustier with the years. When I realized that names can be legally changed and chose to do so, the judge was glad to grant the order once he understood that my formal name was never used.

Many of my relatives called me by a Native name, meaning "Wild Mountain Rose"—an old family name—which fit me well because of my love for the sweet-scented pink blossoms that filled the creek bottom every spring. And my maternal grandmother's name was Rose. After my parents divorced and we went away to school, that name also became a memory—but it has secretly remained a favorite.

Having several names seemed perfectly normal to me. Traditionally, children were given a name at birth, and over the years many others as well. These names were an important part of a person's growth, in that they gave formal recognition to various aspects of one's personality, various states of personal growth and development, and various functions within the tribe. In our northern tribes, a baby was often given its first name by whatever the mother observed when she re-emerged from the birthing lodge. A story is told that in olden times, one of our Apsa women came out of her birthing lodge in the spring, near the swollen Yellowstone River. Upstream many buffalo had died in crossing, and one bull was floating by, all puffed up and distended. His bloated penis was what drew her attention, and she dutifully named her son, "Bull's Penis."

During puberty initiations, young people were given an adult spiritual name. Membership in some clubs or societies often brought another name, sometimes a secret one used only at those gatherings. An important social or emotional event might call forth another name, or a powerful vision quest might give another. All these names added power and continuing recognition to the event or life stage at which they were given, and thus emphasized the varied aspects within each person.

In some Southwestern Pueblo cultures, each baby at birth was simply called something like "He Comes" or "She Comes," until the time of christening. Several weeks after the child's birth, on a "secret" day (well known to the mother), a group of the village's old women would come to the door at dawn, and "surprise" the family by asking to have the child. (That the entire family, including the child, were dressed up for the occasion would indicate that the cat was out of the bag, but no one took notice.)

The crones then took the child out into the dawning light of day, and performed a rite that in other traditions might be called baptism. The eldest grandmother held the child up toward the Sun, and spoke a prayer something like: "Father Spirit, Mother Earth, Powers of all the Directions, we come acknowledging this new life as belonging to you, this child's true parents. We ask that anything this new person has received since conception, that does not truly belong to her, be lifted and released, so that this new life may be purely her own. We commit ourselves to be family and helpers to this child whom you have given into our care, in ways both material and spiritual. We dedicate her life to All Our Relations."

The child would then be lowered into the old one's arms. Quietly cradling her, this wise woman would listen intently for the name. When that absolutely unique name had been gifted by Mother Earth and Father Spirit, the old one led her group of wisdom women back to the family's door, and presented the baby to them, announcing, "Here is 'Wind That Blows Softly Through the Grasses,' " or whatever name had come. The baby's family then gave a welcoming party, and shared the new name with everyone who came, so they might greet her correctly. This name would never be given to any other newborn, so that its energy vibration, by which she was called, would be hers and hers alone.

The old ones knew that the vibrations we create with our voices, as well as the more subtle ones created with our thoughts, have a profound effect in determining what happens in our lives. Thus their namings, as well as their songs, chants, and dance rhythms, were a fine science. Knowing that each person, like each snowflake, is absolutely unique, they allowed the Great Spirit to help them attune to the name that would match the essence of the child. As the name was called out and spoken again and again, this helped to bring forth the child's true nature and gifts. This wise, lovely way had obviously, and unfortunately, been lost to my family by the time I was born. Yet in calling me Wild Mountain Rose or Girl of the Wild Roses, they honored the practice of giving a second name in childhood, in this case an honored family name, belonging to a relative who had gone beyond.

Again at puberty, when children were traditionally taken through rites to initiate them into the spiritual life of their people, they were given a new name. Sometimes this name was received in vision by the young person herself, sometimes it was given by the Great Mystery through the elders, and sometimes it was given because it had been earned by the young person's conduct during her first thirteen or so years.

In the latter case, whenever children were behaving badly, they were reminded by their elders that they might later receive a puberty name reflecting their conduct, and this helped them remember that *at each moment* they were creating their future life. A girl who had continued throwing temper tantrums until thirteen might be named Screeching Owl, or Grouchy Badger Woman. Another one, of more generous nature, or always singing, might be called Gift of the Wind, or Sweet Song of the Lark. Since at this time the baby name was left behind, and one was thereafter called by this new name through much of one's adult life, it paid to put forward one's best gifts!

Few people I know of, during the years of my rearing, were still being formally initiated and given adult names. It seemed I had done my own initiation into adult spiritual life when I pledged at thirteen, in the sunshine of a spring day, to serve the Light and All My Relations. Yet no true adult name came to me then. I had to wait until many years later when I was gifted one in vision, without any conscious asking.

This happened when I left an academic post in Minnesota, and journeyed toward California in the early seventies, looking for a new, more fulfilling, healing way of work and service. This journey would take me into the world of vision; give me Grandma Rosie and other masterful teachers in California; and would lead to my formal vision quests and to my awakening of the spiritual lineages within me. Traveling through the November snows of North Dakota, I thought back on what I had left behind, what I had completed, what I had learned. My family had always encouraged me to continue my education, to use the good mind I had been given, and to develop my gifts through study and schooling. I had done this, but was not satisfied. Although by appearances my outer life was very successful, an incomplete inner life pushed me toward new horizons.

In leaving Minnesota, I released my job security, my wide circle of friends in both academic and other milieus, my home, and a relationship of long standing. I sold most of my possessions, stored a few, loaded the rest in a small station wagon, and headed west. Although this was very scary at one level, it felt absolutely right and completely necessary at many other, deeper levels. I knew that to stay in my "good job" would be spiritual suicide, although it seemed to be one of success. I knew I needed to find out more about myself and learn the healing ways that were not part of my present way of working in the world. Driving along, I felt light, clear, and hopeful.

On my way west, I stopped to visit my family in Montana, and traveled on to spend a night with my Lakota grandmother, Rose, in central Wyoming. Traveling on down through Wyoming the next day, heading south before turning west toward California, I was flooded with light: bright sun shone through my car windows, and rainbow light reflected off the snow which stretched unbroken for miles in every direction. Traveling on wintry back roads all the way, I seldom saw another car. My perception of the entire day was simply light—snow white, crystal rainbow light.

Finally arriving in Colorado, at the home of my friends Pam and Jerri, I sat gratefully sipping a cup of tea at their round dining table. "This is a very magical house," said Pam, inviting me to "look around." After sitting for eight hours in the car, walking around felt wonderful. I entered the lovely "fireplace room," where there was a hearth in the northwest corner. Along the east wall were a stereo and low bookcases. The open floor was comfortably carpeted. Sliding glass doors opened out southwest to a beautiful mountain view, and on the south wall near them was an old bureau. The room was cozy and uncluttered, and I walked forward to look out at the view, then turned my attention to an array of candles on the bureau.

Although I would not have known to describe this so then, at that moment my left side opened (the aspect of myself that is non-linear, non-rational, and receptive to spiritual images) and I was moved by an irresistible force. Arranging the candles in the form of a spire, I lit them, then stepped back a few paces and knelt down in the waning light of dusk.

As my knee hit the floor, I was flying, high above the Earth, a spotted eagle surveying the land below. I could see my wings, feel the breath feathers of my chest ripple in the wind. I circled and spiralled on thermals and long winds above green meadows and mountain forests, above flowing streams that shone in the late afternoon sun. My heart sang with love for the land below, and for this high, soaring flight. Then, as suddenly as it had begun, the vision vanished, and I found myself kneeling in the dark of the fireplace room. The mystery of twilight had taken me in vision! I was startled, and immediately told Pam and Jerri of this magical happening, which I did not fully understand.

I stayed a few weeks in the wonderful company of these nurturing women, and explored a feminine, artistic, visionary side of myself I had never known. Although the eagle I had become was not specifically a Native American image, such images were what poured into my mind— as though that mystical eagle had flown me into the crack between the worlds of day and night, opening a new door, a floodgate for information that had dwelt unconsciously within my spirit. The eagle flies highest of any known Earthly creature, lifting above storms to heights of sixty thousand feet or more, closest to the Above One, Father Spirit, yet nesting at home upon Mother Earth. Thus the eagle represents our inborn ability to lift ourselves to Father Spirit, to bring that inspiration back into our daily, Earthly lives.

This and other symbols that barraged me were from my Native past, as well as from seemingly ancient sources. The clearing accomplished in the brilliance of that snowy, light-filled journey, had opened the way within me for vision, and for the beginning of a life of Spirit. Medicine Eagle had spoken for the first time, although my new name had not yet been formally given. I knew I had been called back to the ancient medicine ways. That the great Medicine Wheel—the symbolic wheel that contains all of life's experiences and possibilities (see chapter 14, page 281)—would become mine to turn, I did not yet know.

On Bear Butte, during the vision of my fast, Rainbow Woman had stood beside me just before she arced herself across the sky as a rainbow, and said, "I am to gift you with a very formal name. It consists of many words, and each of those words has power and meaning for you. Some of that meaning I will share with you now, and some will come to you through your own life path." She held out her right hand, full of tiny stars and sparkles of every color, saying, "Your name is 'Daughter of the Rainbow, of the Morning Star Clan, Whose Helpers Are the Sun and the Moon, and Whose Medicine Is the Eagle.' " With those words, she swept her arm in an arc over my head, and formed there a rainbow.

Again, knowledge seemed to pass between us without words, along the golden umbilicus.

As I meditated upon the words of the name she had given me, I recalled that the traditional form in which I was questing was Shinela, that of the Morning Star clan; Morning Star and Dawn Star are names for the same being, and this aspect of the name was my connection to that lineage of light from so long, long ago.

It took longer for me to understand the roles of the Sun and Moon as my helpers. Through years of acting as the rainbow child, standing between many worlds, I began to see that part of the meaning for the Sun/Moon symbols lay precisely in my connection to, and balancing of, many polarities: white/Indian, masculine/feminine, academic/experiential, business/art, physical/emotional, material/spiritual, old ways/new times. This came consciously to me as I practiced gathering power on evenings of the full moon. I would stand facing south at sunset, letting Grandmother Moon shine upon my left cheek, and Grandfather Sun upon my right, just as in my ceremonial face paint. My formal face painting consists of seven iridescent arcs across my forehead or nose, a golden star at my third eye, a blue moon on my left cheek, a yellow sun on my right cheek, and a flying eagle symbolized by a line in the cleft of my chin. (A photo of this face painting appears in Joan Halifax's book, *Shamanic Voices.*)

This literal standing under my name ("understanding" comes, my teachers say, by standing under something long enough) helped catalyze my awareness of existing between so many opposites. I had often regarded this as a handicap, a negative aspect of my life, because so much conflict was played out between those parts. What I learned was that these seeming opposites were in fact complements, and very powerful.

Another situation through which I learned about the dual nature of my life was when I became involved with Scott, who was born almost exactly 180 degrees from me on the astrological chart: April–November. We experienced conflict, opposition, and intense aggravation through our differences. Shortly after leaving that relationship, I began to spend time with my spiritually adopted *hunka* sister Norma, whose birthdate is also in that November opposition to mine. But what we did with our diverse energies stood in remarkable contrast to my former relationship. Norma and I shared wonderfully. She filled in areas where I lacked knowledge, and I did the same for her. As complements, rather than opposites, we became a formidable pair.

From these kinds of experiences, I continue to learn that my polar opposites can be fantastic allies! I see not only by the sun, but in moonlight as well; I hold the fortune of lineages from both white and

Indian worlds. My masculine and feminine sides are each being developed. I can see both points of view, both sides of many arguments, and thus have the opportunity to unite those polarities in a wholeness, a literal healing.

"And Whose Medicine Is the Eagle." That part of my name was very familiar since I had become an eagle in that first, unbidden Colorado vision. *Eagle medicine is about flying high and seeing far, picking up the light in the east and carrying it across the sky to create a new day. It is often seen as the medicine of the visionary—the one who sees from the universal perspective—as well as the medicine of one who travels carrying the light of knowledge.* The name I was to be called was, "Little Sister of the Eagle Who Walks the Medicine Way," yet it was quickly shortened to "Medicine Eagle."

I did not understand until years later how fully these names would describe my experience. As I completed my California apprenticeships in the late seventies and began teaching on the road, Medicine Eagle became not just a name, but a calling. It was a calling to travel across the land, carrying the light of the teachings I received to many who yearned for such teaching and guidance. The eagle described my inner learning, as well as this strong, active movement in my outer life. Flying out of the east of the medicine wheel—the eagle's aerie—was exactly where I experienced myself: in my quest for new knowledge; in illuminations dawning with increasing regularity; and in the focus of my studies on the powerful use of awareness, the eagle eye. At that time, from my friend Lynn Crow Spreads His Wings, I received eagle feathers that I carry to this day.

The Bear Butte vision quest, when I formally accepted my adult name Medicine Eagle, coincided with a time when my baby name, Bebes, was becoming uncomfortable. I had always loved that name—I knew no one else named that—yet it didn't feel right anymore, to me or my close friends. So I opened myself to receive the new first name that would be right. Inwardly, I heard a special name, but did not make it public. Then, one day, when seven wonderful women friends and I were gathered, we began talking about what my new name was to be. Each woman gave her ideas, from serious to extremely funny ones, and we had a great time. At the end of an hour or so, they had not come up with anything that "clicked" for us. So I told them the name that I had known within myself for months, but had thought of as perhaps a middle name. When I said, "Brooke," they all literally screamed: "That's it! That's it! That's perfect!" Those seven beauties helped confirm to me on the right side a name given on the left.

Not long afterward I was christened "Brooke," while standing in a clear mountain stream under two symbolic trees: one a live green pine, and its complement, an aged, silver-gray, dead one. For my part, I then dedicated myself to work that would help restore the clarity, purity, and beauty of the waters on the whole of Turtle Island before I leave this life.

Reviewing all these names and experiences brought me back to my consideration of the newest one, *Chalíse*. As each of my past names had sent me on a specific life path, I knew this name, which I rolled again and again on my tongue, would do the same. More aware this time—after feeling the power "Medicine Eagle" had had in my life—I looked consciously at the name and what it might mean, how I might live its pattern in the world. The first and most obvious thing I saw is that a chalice is a very feminine form. Unlike the high-flying eagle, it sits in one place—receptive, welling with light, and pouring it out to others. It reminded me of something I had taught my students: If we call the light to ourselves, yet stop it there, a shadow is created outside us. If we call the light to not only fill us, but then as well to shine through us to others, there is no shadow—the gifting circle of the light is continued.

Not long ago, a new friend gave me an additional inspiration about the name, Chalíse. I had always imaged a light that overflowed, welling from within. In talking about our common work, this man said, "Some of us right now are building pillars of light that hold up the sky." When he said that, my left side opened, and I was given a beautiful vision of myself as chalice, standing with open arms, willing to receive, and actively calling down the light of Father Spirit. That light literally poured from above to fill the vessel, thus creating a pillar to the sky, a pillar *to hold up the sky*. With that vision I understood the importance of standing in an *actively* receptive mode; of calling the light both from within and from Father Spirit; of the nurturing and renewing of life made possible in this receptive, feminine mode.

I began to see how assertive, how masculine and yang, I had needed to be to live on the road the way I'd been doing—constantly dealing with new experiences and people, and continuing to pour out new information. This had been quite easy for me, as my natural gifts were of strong, powerful, outward movement. Yet, what became more and more obvious was that I had not developed the ability to be still, to stand in one place, to receive.

For many years on the road I hadn't even kept a home. Since I was never there, it made more sense to live in my car and make great circles around the country, following the flowers north in the spring, and the golden leaves south in the fall. Add to this that, in my family, I'm what is called a "hero child"—a helper, a doer, a fixer, a controller. By very old patterning, it is easier for me to be active and to give than it is to be still and receive. I knew this new name would challenge me to develop another aspect of myself, one that would not necessarily be easy for me.

Thus some of the lessons of "Chalíse" began to manifest as changes in my life. As I look back over the several years since that naming, I see its effect on me and on my life-style. I have now lived in my own home for most of these years—paying much more attention to developing the feminine aspects of myself; teaching about women's mysteries in my outward work; and noticing old dysfunctional family patterns making themselves obvious for transformation.

At present, I am in the process of creating a home base and retreat center for myself, to which others can be invited for retreat and learning on the land. These have been wonderful, and yet at times, difficult changes for me because they have pressed me in all the areas of my life that remain personally challenging. In my astrological signs, I came into the world this time with high development in Aquarius, which represents universal love and new consciousness. The part I am being challenged to learn about and develop, however, is how to make this larger love and consciousness real in day-to-day life, real in intimate personal relationships, real at home as well as on the road. This process is a continuing one in my life, and one for which I have sought outside help.

These different names have brought forth and developed aspects of myself over decades, keeping my experience fluid and full of growth and new awareness. Each time I am called Brooke, or Medicine Eagle, or Chalíse, I am called again to gifts I am to give the world: restoring the purity of the waters, bringing Spirit down to weave into our Earth walk, and building a pillar of light to hold up the sky.

And so it is that names can be profoundly useful in calling forth aspects of ourselves from the left side—out of the realm of Spirit and mystery. Many people I am in contact with—whether they were San Francisco flower children, or ardent vision questers, or people building new lives for themselves after divorce or major life changes—are looking for a name that speaks of who they truly are. They want to be called something that is meaningful to them now and expressive of their uniqueness and their special gifts—not of their father's name or what thousands of mothers thought sounded cute when they were born. Sometimes this name-seeking actually takes the form of reclaiming their given name and its meaning, when they have been called a diminutive of it as a nickname for all their lives.

THE NAMES YOU CARRY

First, let's look at the name you now carry and its meaning in your life:

1. If you have not already done so, look up your given names in the books of children's names that give their meaning and cultural derivation, or in the back of some dictionaries. Knowing, for example, that Estelle means starlight, in addition to being your maiden aunt's name, might give a whole new light to your name and your attitude toward it.

2. Spend some time considering this name you have carried. Truly assess it and its connection with you, past and present.

▶ Does it fit you?

▶ Did it fit you as a child, but not now? Or is it a name that felt too big or formal as a child, and you have now grown into it?

▶ You might even want to check with a numerologist about that aspect of the name's vibration.

3. Interview parents, relatives, and friends on their sense of this name.

4. Look inside as well, and bring to light the names you might have called yourself, without ever telling anyone else. They may have been child names or fanciful names or fun names, yet they certainly have meaning for you, and deserve some focus.

THE SEARCH FOR YOUR TRUE NAME

If you find that none of your present names suit you or feel right, then you may quite automatically embark on the wonderful process of finding the true name for your current being. This is a very useful process, because it means that you must pay attention not only to who you really are, but to who you are becoming, the new person that the right name might help call forth. This process can be quite useful even if you only use it for some aspect of yourself that is developing in your awareness.

1. Review the history of your current name.
- ▶ What is not right about it?
- ▶ What hints does that give you about a new name?

2. Although this cannot be the determining factor, it's always fun to ask your friends what names they think fit you, how they call you in their own mind. Often around my friends and students, a name for someone will arise in my mind and literally block out the given name. I was very embarrassed about using the "wrong" name for some people, until I began to realize that these names were very fitting for them, and they enjoyed being called by them. Between many friends and me there are special names, perhaps some which no one else calls them. For instance, Peggy has become Ariel, Sandy is Mera Bianca, and Greg is John Paul.

3. If several names come to you as possibilities, check their vibration through numerology.

4. Sometimes a name may be changed only a little, and be just right. The first name Marilyn might become Merilee and express a completely new aspect of personality. The middle name Grace, which has a wonderful energy the person wants to keep, might become a last name Gracen.

5. Notice what qualities you want to bring forth or acknowledge in yourself. Look up the name or names for those qualities.

6. Pay attention to the left side as you stalk your new name. Often you will hear something inwardly that will be a name you have never heard before, as happened to me with Chalíse. Or ask to be given your true name in dreams.

7. Try out new names by saying them aloud, and by saying them while looking in your eyes in a mirror. You might even introduce yourself to a passing stranger you visit on a bus with one of these new names, and see how it sounds to actually use it.

8. *If you are one of those who is serious about changing your name, don't rush the process, just be attentive and in process.* Most people who have gone through very appropriate name changes found that it took several years for them to plumb their experience. When the name is right, it will have the feeling of rightness deep in your gut, and will strike your friends the same way. Besides, you may find, after all the searching, that the name you have now is just perfect!

9. When you have found your true name, you may want to do a small ceremony (described in the next exercise), where you share with friends and relatives the process of this transformation in your life, and make official announcement of the name you will use and wish to be called. Jane may become Dawn Maria, Cathy may claim Catherine, N. Everett might become David, or a Native man whose anglicized last name is now Beaumont may return to his tribal name of Bull Mountain.

10. Be prepared for all kinds of reactions, especially from close friends and family who will find it difficult to change. Gently, but firmly, disregard the old name, and continue to call yourself by the new one. Some people may never change; for instance, part of my family still calls me "Bebes," which is fine with me although not very current. Others may protest loudly, and then change if you give them no resistance. My boyfriend at the time when I took the name of Brooke swore vehemently that he would never be able to call me anything but "Bebes." Yet, within a week, he was calling me Brooke without thinking, because it was so right for me.

A CEREMONY FOR TAKING YOUR NEW NAME

This simple ceremony can have a very profound effect, in that it openly expresses and makes public a very meaningful inner experience. For convenience, I will address you as the ceremonial leader. However, if you are the one being named, assign someone else this role.

1. When you are first asked to do a naming ceremony, it is of primary importance to sit down with the person and council with them about this process. The naming ceremony has a powerful impact and should not be undertaken lightly. It should certainly not be used for a passing nickname or a name that has no integrity for the person. Within a few moments' conversation, you can usually determine the person's readiness and the integrity of the name. I would have some serious questions about names like Crystal Iris Rainbow Fallen Rock or Madonna Marilyn Manning. If you feel the choice of names is inappropriate, say so. If you feel the process of finding a truthful name is not complete, suggest continuing the process to completion, then returning.

2. When the name and the energy feel right, determine together the time, place, and guests who are to witness the ceremony. Ask the one being named (hereafter referred to simply as the named) to dress in clothing appropriate to or symbolic of the new name.

3. Begin with smudging yourself and the named. Then announce to the group the intention of this gathering, and perhaps speak briefly about the power of names to call forth aspects of ourselves.

4. Ask the named to speak about her previous name. Have her contemplate this ahead of time as preparation for the ceremony. She

should speak of its origin, its meaning for her, how she will continue to hold that part of herself, and perhaps even how it came to feel inappropriate for this phase of her life. Then ask the named to make a tobacco and cornmeal offering to her old name and to the part of herself it represents. It is important that no part of us, even though not primary at present, be disowned or disrespected. The named should complete this offering with an appropriate prayer of gratitude for all that came from that name and the time when it was primary.

5. The named—again, having prepared—will speak about the new name: telling a brief story of the search for it, how it came to be chosen, its meaning, and so on. Her final statement in this part of the ceremony can be something like: "I now choose to be called _____."

6. You as leader can then say a prayer, asking Spirit to bless this person and this new phase of her life, calling forward appropriate attributes and energies that the named has revealed during her statements.

Then declare: "I name you _____," and say something like, "May you carry this name in beauty." Ask the witnesses to then speak her name to her aloud together; this serves the function of "setting" it in her mind and their minds as real.

7. Taking red paint (an old lipstick will do if you have no red ochre/earth pigment), put a dot of red on her throat and on her crown chakras to symbolize the circle of All Our Relations—and more specifically the circle of all the aspects within her.

This ends the formal ceremony. Gifts appropriate to the new name can be given—I like to give a simple rendering of the name in calligraphy on a strong white background that can stand on an altar or desk. Feasting and celebrating is a special way to complete the ceremony.

Attending to our names is one, and only one, of the ways we can pay attention to what is true for us. But it is an extremely powerful one. Paying attention to our names—whether they are used day to day or only on ceremonial occasions, whether they are nicknames or given names, whether they are the same as others' names or totally unique—can be a powerful focus of attention. If you choose to become involved in this process, you will learn much about yourself and how to truly be yourself in the world, which is the primary aspect of our spiritual growth. *Always, it is a process of seeking the truth within you, and expressing it in the world.*

My names have given me many gifts of growth and awareness, and I expect the learnings from them to continue long into the future. They have come to me in the midst of other great changes in my life, and yet as I look back at them, I see how much they have helped me make real those aspects of myself that lay dormant and undeveloped. Whenever I hear "Medicine Eagle," it calls me to remember the power of the vision given me by White Buffalo Woman on Bear Butte, and of the helpers I have been given to carry it into the world. When I hear "Chalíse," it fills me with the love and power of the Dawn Star, standing in my vision pointing, as did White Buffalo Woman, to wholeness, and to holiness for our world.

CHAPTER TEN

AN OLD SAMURAI MOVES ME

Movement is life.

Awareness not only hones our perception, it actually improves our functioning.

He was teaching us to be fully present, fully aware, fully functioning, and, hopefully, fully human.

"Indian! . . . Indian! I said move your *left* leg, not your right!" shouted the man at the front of the room, who looked rather like Einstein with his white hair standing out from the sides of his head. It was Israeli body-work genius Moshé Feldenkrais (Moshé is the way the French girls pronounced his name and he seemed to get a kick out of it, so rather than the traditional Moishe, we called him Moshé). We were just getting to know each other.

In all my years of teaching I had always tried hard to learn everyone's name correctly. But in a cavalier manner, Moshé called us by whatever name first struck him, whether complimentary or not. And the name often stuck, for he would use it during the next four years of intense work together as we participated in his first major training class, held in San Francisco. In the first few days of our training, Fred, a student of scientific bent, got into a heated debate with Moshé about whether "cause and effect" have anything to do with anything. Fred contended that cause and effect were just exactly that, while Moshé, the old physicist, deprecatingly insisted that Fred was assuming more than he knew. Thereafter, Fred was known as "Cause and Effect," and it reminded us of the lesson in presumption Moshé had taught us that day.

In his continuing process of helping us to functionally integrate our entire nervous system, Moshé made a lesson from calling me "Indian," as well. He teased me about not walking with my feet Indian style: aligned straight forward and back, which seems quite pigeon-toed compared to the average person's walk today. Most of us have a tendency to walk "duck-footed" (toes out, heels in), which puts tremendous, unnecessary pressure on our knees—the weakest link in the human frame. Moshé knew a lot about knees because his entire healing way had grown out of his own healing work on an old, severe injury to both of his knees. As a young man, he had badly damaged them in a soccer accident. This had left the supporting tendons and ligaments very weak, so his knees were likely to puff up with water at the slightest misstep.

After years of suffering, Moshé was finally forced to see a Navy physician while he worked on the unsteady decks of submarines during World War II in England. The doctor's diagnosis was that Moshé was in desperate need of a knee operation. Just a day or so before going into the hospital, Moshé asked the M.D. what the chances were of his knees fully recovering. When the surgeon told him that there was about a fifty-fifty chance of his knees being fully functional—or completely paralyzed—Moshé told him, in his wonderfully direct and not so polite way, where to put his operation.

Declaring, "I'm sure I can do better than that!" Moshé went off to find out about knees and how they worked, and perhaps how to heal them. In the process, he learned not only about knees, but also about the total human anatomy and brain, and the functioning of the nervous system in learning, child development, animal behavior, creativity, health, and much more. From his in-depth study of how we function physically as human beings, he developed a remarkable new healing way, which over the years has proved helpful for everyone from multiple dysfunctional babies to the finest ballerinas and athletes. Through his own development and teachings, he would bring to light the idea of awareness as a powerful principle of physics. Out of this came the use of mental focus and imagery in the development of motor skills, which has become integrated into our society, and is more evident today through its successful use by our professional athletes.

Early in my life, my right leg was badly burned in a gasoline explosion on the ranch. Although it remained scarred, its function returned through the help of my physicians and my own persistent exercise. Mom would sagely advise me, "You can't be babied and just lie in bed. Move around and do whatever you can to help." For six weeks, I scooted about on the floor with my stiff leg extended before me. Finally, in a vividly memorable moment, I pulled myself up on a chair and attempted to walk, and this time it worked! I shouted to Mom in the other room, "I can walk! I can walk!" After several years, my leg seemed to return to normal, but I had no idea how deeply the patterning of tension and trauma remained imprinted.

When Moshé teased me about my walk, he was pointing out to me that I walked duck-footed, especially on my right leg. This is how I later would think of it, but at the time what he did with me were gentle movements of my foot, leg, hip, back, and neck, which allowed me to inwardly perceive the difference between my ability to use my right and left legs, and how the pattern of tension established by the accident still affected my whole body. I began to see how, in the emotional and physical trauma of the injury, I had pulled my right leg up and heel inward in a natural gesture of protection. Although the leg had healed, no longer needing that protection, the pattern had been set, deeply.

Because I had grown accustomed to an extreme position while first healing, the less extreme position I now used seemed correct and natural. Yet, it was still a long way from normal carriage. Unaware of the difference, I had no thought to change it, let alone any effective way to make that change. Through his gentle touch and movements, Moshé enabled me to become aware of these old patterns. In his wisdom, he not only showed me other, more healthful possibilities, but also understood that my burgeoning awareness would continue the process of my return to a natural and full functioning.

Moshé reminded us again and again that awareness is the first step in any learning process, and the most important one, for without it there is not even a thought of changing. With it, the whole system begins naturally to search for new ways of being. He taught us that *the entire process of learning is becoming aware of finer and finer differences,* and thus used the *principle of differentiation* in all his work.

That work consisted of two main things. First, he developed a method he called "Functional Integration," in which he used hands-on movement of the body, and the connection through his own integrated body, to teach the student, who was usually lying on a low, wide table similar to a massage table. For Moshé, Functional Integration meant that each and every part of the body, a person's entire being, is to function in concert with all the other parts.

For instance, in order to turn our head we must release the muscles on one side of the neck while simultaneously tightening them on the other side; or in order to lift something, we can use the large muscles of the thighs to assist our arm and back muscles. I discovered that if I unconsciously hold tension in my right hip rather than freeing it to move with the other hip when I'm running, I make it more difficult for myself to accomplish the conditioning I intend.

The second basic principle of Moshé's work was "Awareness Through Movement." It developed out of his desire to work with more than one person at a time. He soon found that he could have large groups of students follow his verbal instructions and find improvement and better functioning through small, gentle movements—without his actually having to touch them.

In my work with Moshé, not only did my foot and leg shift to a straighter position, but my back stopped hurting where tension had pulled my hip and ribs into a painful curve. My head became more upright, and my breathing fuller. I had taken the first steps in a personal functional integration that would lead eventually to a similar healing ability with others. Feldenkrais's training was a gentle, persistent process of making us more and more aware, more and more functional, so that we might then pass this possibility of higher functioning on to others.

Another part of Moshé's teaching on differentiation became very central to my own learning process. He reminded us of the principle of sensitivity in physics: In order for a person to feel the difference in something, there has to be $1/40$ difference in weight or pressure. Let me give you some examples. Let's say you are carrying a forty-pound backpack of bricks, each brick weighing a pound. I would have to take out just one of those bricks, or add one more ($1/40$ the total weight), in order for you to feel the difference in the weight of your backpack. By the same token, if you were holding an oat straw in your lips and a little fly landed upon it, you would be able to tell the difference. It takes only a tiny use of effort to hold up the straw compared to the bricks, and thus you can sense minute differences. So it follows that if you want to be sensitive to small changes, you use very little effort. If I would like to feel a muscle twitch in your arm, I cannot have twenty pounds of pressure leaning on you; I will want to touch you very gently with my fingertips so that I can feel the minute changes.

Continuing on this line of thought, then, when we want to notice the finer and finer differentiations that comprise the learning process, we must approach our subject with gentle yet keen awareness rather than force. If I want to learn to pick out various grades of sandpaper without looking, I use my fingertips rather than a rough, grasping hand. If I want to learn the difference between a mountain chickadee and a blackcap chickadee, I sit quietly and note the minute differences in their coloring. If I want to teach my body how to be more flexible, I pay exquisite attention to each small movement, gently stretching my limits rather than forcing and pulling myself into soreness. If I want to change the way I relate to my partner, I begin to be fully aware of my current patterns and sensitive to exactly how I do them. When I know the way I act now, I can choose to try small changes and move myself toward a better relationship in a gentle manner.

Moshé spoke of this as the *principle of ease,* and urged us in our learning to focus on finding easier and easier ways rather than on muscling our way through things. If I'm learning how to use a new hand saw and it wants to bend as I push it, then rather than pushing harder and using more muscle to try to get through the board, I soften up, lighten my touch, feel the way the saw wants to move, breathe, and pay attention to getting the movement of my arm straight with the cut. As I get all the small things lined out, then I can use more pressure and the saw will "behave."

In moving the bodies of our own students, he urged us to "dance with them" in gentle awareness of where they could change, rather than pushing them around. He taught us to be centered and relaxed enough that we could become one with them, and so know in a different and more complete way what was happening with them. In all our lessons, Moshé would continually remind us to find an easier, and a still easier way. When we had found an easy way, we suddenly realized we knew how to do it!

This gentle, wakeful way of working with ourselves and with the people we touched in Functional Integration lessons reminded me of White Buffalo Calf Pipe Woman's message about the need for a truly feminine way of approaching our world. This way is one where respectfully attending to things replaces forcing them, nurturing and becoming aware replace controlling and damaging, harmony and coming into oneness replace separation. It seems that Moshé's concept of Functional Integration had seeped into the depths of my consciousness, and that I had begun to apply it not only to my body, but to my working relationships with my larger world. I realized how similar his message was to the one brought by White Buffalo Woman in her teaching that, *"All of earthly life is one unit, and we must learn to function in harmony with All Our Relations in order to remain on Mother Earth."*

As a boy of fourteen, Moshé had walked out of Russia in an enormous caravan of Jews, leaving what had been their homeland, to eventually arrive in Israel. One of his contributions to his new country was to develop what might be termed a martial art. Warring was constant between the Israelis and their neighbors, and many young people were drafted into the armed services, to be sent into battle with pitifully few skills. As this occurred primarily because there was little time to train them, Moshé invented a method to speed their training, which would save many from being sent unprepared into hand-to-hand combat.

Like much of what he gifted the world, Moshé's method of self-defense was unique. He used the natural, defensive reactions of someone under attack, and turned these around into powerful, offensive moves. Not having years to change the soldiers' instinctive responses, Feldenkrais found ways of extending those initial, protective movements of withdrawal—continuing them into effective attack techniques. Once again, his principle of finding the easy way worked exquisitely; rather than fighting the natural response, he taught them to be in harmony with it and then to extend it in the way they wished.

Later, when he was reading physics at the Sorbonne, he visited one of Japan's finest judo masters, who had heard of Moshé's work in Israel. Wanting to introduce judo into the Western world, he offered to teach Moshé so that he might in turn teach many others. A remarkable bargain was struck, and Moshé eventually started the Judo Club of France, from which the martial art spread into the Western world. An excellent student, he took the art beyond its simplistic self-defense aspects, into a science of human life functioning, to become what I think of as a true samurai—a noble warrior. Moshé's teachings fit right into my rainbow lineage—being taught a profound physical discipline by an old Israeli samurai!

An attempt to share Moshé Feldenkrais's remarkable, comprehensive work in these few pages would be futile, even laughable, as he spent four years giving us the mere basics. Instead, see appendix 4, pages 480–482, for the extensive references available on his life and work. Meanwhile, I will continue with the story of our personal contact. As has frequently been the case in my life, studying with Moshé—one of my most powerful and rewarding experiences—was one of those unplanned, synchronistic events.

Another had been when I received in the mail a beautiful, gold-embossed letter from a college I didn't know existed, to which I certainly hadn't applied, and which offered me a full-tuition, full-room-and-board, four-year scholarship. Having then a total of fifty dollars in my savings for college, I joyously accepted the University of Denver Centennial Scholar's Program offer!

My studies with Moshé began at the time I was participating in an innovative Ph.D. program in the San Francisco area, with special emphasis on the body as a focus for healing—especially emotional/psychological healing. Credit was given me for my pursuit of shamanic ritual healing, for aikido lessons, and for courses with Stanley Keleman, whose neo-bioenergetics were profoundly stimulating to his clients and students.

I was like a kid in a candy store, the whole new area of transformative therapy in front of me, an open door. Yet my sight was limited—I had not heard of Moshé, so I was not impressed by his name when my advisor, Tom Hanna, suggested I take his training program. Tom explained that he was bringing this internationally known Israeli "genius" to the United States under the auspices of the institute, for the first full training program Feldenkrais had ever done. And that this was a remarkable opportunity, available to me as an enrolled student for even less money than others would pay.

Without much further thought, I said, "OK, Tom, sign me up!" During the first days of the program, I noticed that other students were in awe of Moshé, and very nervous around him. But to me, he was just another, wonderful grandfather. In the Native way, all elder men are addressed as grandfather, and related to with affection and respect. This was how I felt about him, and I was aware, despite his occasional shouting and upsets, of the love with which he gave his gifts. Through some extracurricular activities we participated in together, I grew quite close to his senior assistant, and frequently spent time with her. Many of these lunches and dinners included Moshé as well, and I found him to be the singularly most entertaining and enlightening companion I had ever met. Moshé always had a wonderful teaching story about any topic.

If the subject of lions came up, he would ask us why lions roared just before they attacked their prey. It was a good question, because one would think that such an obvious announcement would scare off their prey. "No," Moshé pointed out, "what happens is this: The roar causes the gazelle to draw in its breath and listen attentively. Then, before it can gather its energy to run, it must let out that breath, and draw another. In that added second, the lion is upon his prey and pulls it down." *Many of his lessons to us were about our breathing: how our breath has been literally taken away by habitual tension generated from trauma and cultural patterns of restriction, robbing us of the very deep inspiration that gives us life, feeds our brain and nervous system, and fires our muscles.* His gentle "Awareness Through Movement" lessons helped us become aware of our own habitual tension and unnecessary auxiliary movements, such as sticking one's tongue out and squinting when concentrating—totally needless movements, of which most people have many. As we progressed in this awareness, more ease, grace, and full function became possible in our lives.

From early childhood, I have had especially loving relationships with animals, and Moshé knew many animal stories. One of my favorites came from the question, "How does a cat actually catch a bird, when feathers are made to repel the cat's claws?" We would guess that the feathers are really soft and not protective, that the cat's claws would penetrate them even if they form a sort of shield. Again, no. What happens is, the cat stalks as close as possible to the bird, who is sitting or walking on the ground. Then he rushes the bird, who throws his wings open to fly. This is what makes him vulnerable, because every bird has a fine line down his breast and chest where there are no feathers! As the bird's wings pull back, this line opens, and the cat's well-aimed middle claw sinks through it into the heart. Moshé dramatically concluded that sometimes the cat pulls the entire heart out of the bird! Since then I have examined every bird I have had access to, and every one has that unprotected line on its breast.

During the first year of our training, the movements to increase our awareness under Moshé's instruction were minimal and not very taxing, yet I found myself coming home in the late afternoon quite exhausted. Those of us who had the same experience speculated that, though the outer movements were minor, the inner movement was enormous, and so we required extra rest. We were learning to be deeply aware of ourselves and our experience, and honored this mental and physical call to rest. My way of doing this was to come home and, unless I had appointments later, take off my watch. Then I practiced attending to my own inner clock concerning when to sleep, wake, eat, read, write, or study. Sometimes I came home, undressed, and went directly to bed, sleeping until I awoke, whether it was at 8:00 P.M. or 2:00 A.M. Then I would arise and continue my day. Often I found myself awake in the sweet and quiet hours after midnight, before the city awoke again.

My experience of this "non-schedule" was very interesting to me, because I knew that many mystics suggest that four hours of sleep is the most a person should have at one time. More sleep than this stiffens and "deadens" the body. In addition, our practice of sleeping six to ten hours at a stretch, and staying awake for the remainder, creates an artificial boundary between night and day. It becomes too easy for us to think of sleep as a *non-ordinary* state in which we are unconscious—a state that has no relationship to our "real" life during the day.

While I was asleep one night, this concept became more real to me. I had been living in a studio apartment I loved, which overlooked Dolores Park and the Bay Bridge. However, I felt an inward calling to live with other people—to spend more time in relationship. My friend Lori and I decided to become housemates, and to find a place where she could have a golden retriever puppy again, since she had recently lost her old one.

About a week later, while practicing my odd sleeping schedule, I woke in the middle of the night to a strange noise near me. Opening my eyes and looking around the room, I jumped when I saw, curled up a few feet from my left ear, a soft, fluffy, beautiful golden retriever puppy! My mouth flew open, and then I looked around to see how he'd gotten in. My apartment was on the second floor, and the closed door chain was visible in the streetlight. I didn't think he could have flown in my open window! So I gave up on the rational pursuit, and turned back to the puppy, whose soft eyes raised to look at me, although he did not lift his head. I reached out to touch that dark gold fur, to pet this new presence in my life, but before my hand touched him, he seemed to melt and run like a golden river, down off the head of my pull-out sofabed. Again, I was stunned!

I lay back down on my bed and decided that I *must* be dreaming. Yet I was fully awake. As I reached this startling realization, I heard another noise from the place where the puppy disappeared. Turning to look, I saw four tiny paws sinking their razor-sharp claws into the sheet, and two tiny kittens climbed up onto the bed. They meowed softly and tottered right toward me. Crazy about kittens, I was thrilled when they crawled up onto my chest and curled up to sleep. I crossed my arms so I could rest a hand on each one to feel its soft purring, and went to sleep myself. In the morning, they were not there.

When Lori and I looked at the apartment on the hill overlooking both the Noe and Castro valleys, which we chose as our home, the young men living there showed us a momma cat, and five babies they hoped to give away. We were immediately taken with them, and each of us chose a kitten. I did not at that time think about the lucid dream, yet when we moved in, and the kitties first climbed on my bed, I remembered them. I named them Heta ("Loving Child" in Shinela, after my stepsister) and Nochita ("Little Night Girl" in Spanish). We never did get the puppy.

I now call any two cats raised together from the same litter "a dreaming pair." Heta and Nochita were to come to me many times after that, in lucid dreams. They always slept with me, and seemed to miss me terribly when I went away: so they would simply astral project and sleep with me! By Halloween that year they had done this many times; and I began to think about how our myths are often grounded in some truth, which time has obscured. I wondered about the myth of cats being on witch's brooms, as they sailed across the sky in Halloween images.

One afternoon as my dreaming pair hopped gracefully up on my bed and spoke in their almost chirping cat-talk to me, I told them that I had them figured out. "I know you can astral project, and I want you to teach me how." They then climbed right up on my body and did a very un-catlike thing. Heta laid herself across my heart area, with her front legs hanging along my right side, and her back legs hanging over my left side. Nochita did the same on my solar plexus, except that she was facing the opposite way, with her head on my right. Then they seemed to "seal" themselves down against me tightly, and began to purr. I closed my eyes and relaxed to enjoy this experience.

At first, their purring was its usual soft humming. But then I realized it was quickly becoming louder and louder. It was not a deafening sound so much as an enormous vibration, like waves rocking me. Then, going into a trance-like state, I found myself out of my body, my consciousness flying high over the city. I journeyed on the left side to do healing work on two friends in distant cities, and returned. When I came to consciousness in my body and stirred, Heta and Nochita got up and casually walked into the kitchen for a drink of milk.

This left-sided experience was a thrill and joy to me. The integration of my nervous system that Moshé was accomplishing went far beyond my physical body, and helped me integrate the totality of my reality. No longer were day and night, sleeping and dreaming, left-sided and right-sided, two different things—opposites; I began to understand them as simply two aspects of the one reality that was me. The old samurai was moving me in ways I had never guessed.

Moshé dealt with many aspects of our individual and societal experience. This brilliant teacher spoke to us often of how in our modern times, humans have been able to protect themselves physically from many dangers, and so can survive without being aware and fully functioning. He helped us understand that just because we have our eyes open does not mean we are truly, wakefully perceiving. Often we walk about in a sort of trance in which we are quite unaware of what is happening around and within us—with our perception and our sensitivity extremely limited. He taught us that *awareness not only hones our*

perception, it actually improves our functioning.

This reminded me of the early days of my father's Apsa people, when the great enemy Blackfeet nation extended hundreds of miles to the north and west, and the enormous Lakota/Cheyenne confederacy threatened on the east. At any moment of any day, a neighboring war party might be waiting in ambush or slipping up to steal one's horses, children, or wife. A person owned only what he could take care of and protect. This kind of danger kept my people fully awake and aware at all times—even a slight or momentary inattentiveness could cost one's life, family, and/or property. Moshé was not advocating warring or violence; he was simply pointing out that modern people are now being challenged to find means and motivation for becoming fully aware.

We occasionally asked Moshé why, with his background and other abilities, he decided to teach in this way, through the body. He reminded us first of all, that *movement is life,* and explained in detail how the nervous system is already in movement even as we *think* of doing something, before any outward movement is evident. He often had us imagine movements to perfection before attempting them outwardly—a surprisingly effective way to improve our functioning. And, secondly, he used the metaphor, "If you want to get somewhere, why not go down the broad avenue?" By this he meant that a good 90 percent of the information coming into the brain at any moment is triggered by the body's minute movements in space; thus it makes sense to get into the brain through the motor cortex—the broad avenue of movement.

Over the years I have come to understand how closely connected many of Moshé's methods are to my Native people's way of teaching—using physical metaphor; deepened perception, awareness, and focused attention; plus powerful teaching stories as primary teaching methods. An example from one of the Southern Traditions—of which I've already spoken—is the working with the differentiation between the three *attentions:* 1. First Attention—the body, which was the beginning place in Moshé's work, as well; 2. Second Attention—which could be focused externally or internally to meditate upon a chosen thing; and 3. Third Attention—holiness, which we can develop sufficiently for us to hold the entire circle of life in awareness. Something else that reminds me of White Buffalo Woman's teachings is Moshé's idea of "dancing" with the person with whom you are doing hands-on work—coming into harmony and unity, and letting knowledge and understanding flow between you without words.

The component of Moshé's work that involved action and physical metaphor I developed into what I came to call "ritual performance" (see chapter 14). It is my belief that by turning a simple activity into a ritual for growth we can achieve powerful transformative change for ourselves and others. For example, we have many bridges to cross in our lives—some actual, some metaphorical. Let's say Joan wants to leave New York and create a new life in San Francisco. Rather than sitting in a counseling office talking about it, a more effective way of enabling her to move across this emotional bridge in her life would be to take her for a walk to find an actual bridge. On the journey, I would ask her to mentally connect the end of the bridge on which she's now standing to her life here in New York and then to connect the other end of the bridge to the life she will find in San Francisco. Having made that conscious hook-up, I would now have her physically walk across the actual bridge, thinking about her move to San Francisco. Asking her to take this idea and make it real in her physical body will create a strong imprint in her brain and nervous system—a much stronger one than the idea alone would have had. This kind of physical metaphor and its imprint on the brain can then be expanded to other actions. For Joan this would mean the activity of actually packing and moving to her new home, with all its attendant issues and emotions.

Because our consciousness is a unified field of awareness, when our brains know something, it can be expressed in many different ways. Feldenkrais used to tell us that if you know how to write, then you can make words not only with your dominant hand, but also with your other hand, or with chalk held in your mouth or the crook of your elbow. It's not just your dominant hand that knows something—your whole self knows via the pathways you have set up in your brain through learning. Thus, acting something out through your body physically "sets" that brain pattern, and it then becomes much easier to manifest in other ways in your world.

The deeper part of ourselves, which determines much of what we accomplish, speaks in simple but profound metaphors, and the body is an especially fine voice and tool to access these inner messages. Another metaphor might concern the leaps we occasionally need to take in our lives. Take Alan, for example. He wants to change from his life of outside employment, to earning his living from his favorite hobby, carving decoys. But he is frightened of the enormous leap this entails. Nothing could be more useful to him than to go outside and take a leap off something, connecting where he stands to his present situation, and where he lands to his new vocation. If he is a normal adult, he may find that he has not leaped off anything very high for years; his ankles are stiff, his body fearful. I would first have him jump off a curb or small rock, then increase the height to the seat of a picnic table. When he becomes comfortable with each of these steps, and his body is ready, I would ask him to jump off the picnic table itself, or even higher. He will find the ground solid under him, and his ability to take leaps growing daily. This kind of bodily metaphor will give him an enormous boost in his capacity to take the metaphorical leap in his life.

A small group of us used this understanding of action and metaphor to gift Moshé with a humorous and beautiful ritual performance at his apartment in Tel Aviv not long before he passed away. He was bedridden and restless, unable to speak except in a limited manner, and everyone around him tiptoed and whispered. I could tell that it was very aggravating to him. We decided that this great man needed something more magnificent than that for his last days, and set about creating it. Valentine's Day was the last day we could see him, so we planned the event for that day.

We gathered simple costumes, a guitar, and a few props, and trooped merrily into his room. His family and assistants didn't know what to think, but he seemed delighted to see us again. My adopted *hunka* sister Ginger began the performance by entering his room as the angel Gabriel, attired in a white hotel sheet and an aluminum foil halo. She carried a little book of his good deeds, and told Moshé that he could not yet go to heaven because he had not done all the good he intended to do. He had not taught enough others his remarkable healing work. He had not begun a new enlightened type of judo dojo. There were several countries in the world he hadn't yet touched with his work. He hadn't had the love of his life, which he had so longed for.

At which moment I jumped into the room, dressed in red long johns, aluminum horns, and a long red tail ending in an aluminum foil heart. I carried a three-pronged foil trident, around which was twined a red rose. Moshé immediately cried out (some of his few words that day), "My teacher!" He had always said, "The devil with conventional ways of thinking!" and now he was acknowledging this renegade part of himself. His Israeli family and friends who were gathering around had their hands over their mouths in shock. But this broke us all up into gales of laughter, and Moshé beamed like a child.

When I regained my composure, I growled and snarled and shouted at him, poking him with the trident, "Moshé Feldenkrais, you cannot go to hell either, for you have not done nearly all the dastardly deeds of which you are capable. You are one of the finest judo masters, and you have not yet mangled anyone with your skills. You have not cursed your ignorant students nearly as much as they deserve. You could charge the poor souls who are so in need of your work an enormous amount of money and you don't. And you have not been rowdy and raucous enough, or laid enough women!"

Here I made suggestive movements with my hips, and again had to stop, to keep myself from laughing. The family was very taken aback, all the more so when Moshé excitedly managed to say, "I did masturbate the other day, though." Then we all laughed and laughed. What a wonderful, irreverent, humorous, and *alive* old man this was!

Now Scott jumped through the curtain, dressed as a genie, and announced that, since Moshé could not go to heaven or to hell, he must *live*. He must not only live, but must realize his unavowed dreams (something he had many times admonished us to do)—he must find that true love, he must lecture to all the physicians and healers in the world, and he must act on the stage, becoming the character actor he'd always wanted to be. Much to our delight during his lectures, he'd acted out character after character, with perfect mannerisms and bodily actions. Scott gave him a ten-year contract for the Broadway stage, saying he must get up and get healthy so he could begin. Here, Moshé said hopefully, "I took five steps the other day." And Scott said, "Just twenty more and you can be at center stage."

Moshé had always felt his work was worthy of a Nobel prize, and so did we. With great pomp and circumstance, we awarded him not one, but two! The first Nobel was in physics, for his introduction of awareness as a physical principle. The second was the Peace prize for his contributions to integration and oneness, which had brought peace to so many individual lives and would eventually contribute to true peace on Mother Earth. These two documents and the stage contract were carefully hung beside his bed. Then we played guitar and sang for a long time; I remember some of the songs—"Climb Every Mountain," and "When You Wish Upon a Star." But when the old samurai's sparkling eyes began to droop, we knew it was time for our farewell. We each hugged him and wished him Godspeed. I was never to see him again.

Sometimes I miss Moshé's stories and the joy of his presence, yet my primary experience is that his teaching lives within me and shines out through all that I do. His elemental principles are active in my daily life and my sharing with students. One such daily life incident came about when I went home to visit my brother Tom on the ranch that Mom, he, and I had developed off the reservation after Tom graduated from high school. It had been years since we first started working the ranch together during my summer vacations from college. Then, we had no equipment, and no money to buy any, so we did all the work by hand. I will never forget stacking sixty-pound bales of hay by muscle alone— throwing them up one tier and up another, and another, stacking them high and tight in the old way. I was incredibly strong by the end of that summer, and my biceps so heavily muscled that I could not wear women's blouses.

After I left the ranching business to Tom in the early seventies, and went full time into the healing work that called me, my brother would often tease me about my fancy ways, saying I had become weak and lazy. One day when I was home for a short visit, not long after studying with Moshé, he asked me, "Well, are you too weak to throw some bales around? If not, come and help me stack some hay!" It probably would have been smart to say, "I'm too much of a weakling," and to stay in the cool house on that hot July day. But I was not about to let him get away with that remark. I took the bait, grabbed some heavy leather gloves and a long-sleeved shirt to keep the hay from tearing up my arms, and headed for the field. All the way out I was muttering to myself that I probably *was* pretty weak, and would wish I had not said yes. I have always been well toned, but as I secretly checked, there was very little bicep evident that day.

Climbing up on the stack, I thought, "The worst that can happen is that I will get really behind, and have to listen to him tease me while he waits with the loads. But at least it will save him from having to crawl up and down off the stack to arrange the bales once he dumps them." He brought in the first load, and I did just fine, although it took me a little while to remember the jigsaw pattern of correct stacking. But then I began to realize that every time I finished, I was waiting for him to come in with a new load. Somehow, it didn't seem as difficult as I had remembered.

During my few minutes of waiting each time, I began to speculate on the power I seemed to have even though I had very little muscle. Then, a light bulb popped on in my head, and I heard Moshé say, *"When your entire body is integrated, all muscles working together in unison and balance, and when you are not doing any extra work through auxiliary movement, you will find ease in what you do."* Now I could see that the principle of ease he had spoken of so many times had become real and present in my life. I said quietly, "Thanks, Moshé," and grinned at Tom with a bored expression about his "hard" work, flexing my lithe arms for him.

Another time I experienced Moshé's teaching deep within me was when I got into real trouble on a high-challenge ropes course where I was helping lead groups at camp in Oklahoma. I had been up on a fifty-foot platform all day, supervising an experience called the "zip line," where people are hooked securely to a rolling apparatus on a line several hundred yards long. They then jump off the high platform, and go zipping down the line to another pole at the other end. Lastly, they slide back down to a low place in the center where they are taken off on a metal ladder, which is propped against the line after they come to a stop.

Another staff member came to relieve me during a lull in the late afternoon, and we confessed how scary it was to us every time we hooked someone to that harness, knowing if anything went wrong he or she would very likely die. Then we did the usual double-check on my equipment, and I leaped off the platform. As soon as I was airborne, I saw that the metal ladder had inadvertently been left leaning against the line. I was about to crash into it face-on at a tremendous speed! The ladder assistants stood between me and the ladder, looking up to watch me. I started screaming at them about the ladder behind them, but they couldn't understand me. In any case they would never have had time to make it to the ladder and move it in my few seconds of descent. It was obvious that I was going to hit it. The others who saw what was happening watched in horror, but they could never have gotten to that ladder in time either.

My mind was racing and no answers came. But my body knew what to do. In perfect timing, I arched my whole body back a little, then just before the collision point, I swung myself up so my legs were straight in front of me, like a martial artist jumping through the air to deliver a kick. That was how my body felt, and I flashed back to Moshé's talking about how powerful a force we can have when we're totally aligned against something—for example, the fingers have to be exactly aligned to punch them through a board, as martial artists demonstrate, or the bones will snap. *WHAM!* I hit the ladder with my feet. The impact swung my body and head around in a complete circle and banged my shoulder into the back side of the ladder, which brought me to a grinding halt. That smarted a bit, but I was amazed: Everything else felt fine—I had sustained no injuries!

When the ladder assistants and supervisor, with much chagrin, had unhooked me and helped me down, we talked about how fortunate the company was that this had not happened to one of the participants in the training. They would very likely have just thrown their arms up in front of their face, and the impact would have snapped both arms and caused severe injury to their head and neck. When I stepped onto solid ground and looked back up at that bent ladder, there was a prayer of thanksgiving again, for an old samurai whose teachings were alive in my body.

On the surface, we were being trained to become certified Felden-krais instructors in order to do healing work with our own students. Yet, Moshé would remind us that he was teaching us much more than "pushing bodies around." He was teaching us to be fully present, fully aware, fully functioning, and, hopefully, fully human. A strong emphasis was made on our own uniqueness. He reminded us that if we didn't develop and offer our own special gifts to the world, we were just being "a gray blip on the evolution of humanity." Because each of us is unique and has a gift to give that no one else brings to life, it is of primary importance to be aware of our uniqueness and develop it.

"Think of what you hated about yourself in high school," he would say. "That is likely a strong hint of the greatest gift you have to give." I thought of my hooked nose and my untamed reservation ways, com-pared to the nice girls in my small town school, and laughed, not yet fully realizing that these pointed to the very gifts of Native knowledge I would begin to share within a few years' time. One way he spoke of this, even when referring to the way we would teach the body work, was to say that we would each have "our own handwriting." If we copied him exactly, it would not belong to us, it would be only a poor imitation.

In the years since then, my work *has* taken its own, unique direc-tion, although many of my Feldenkrais fellows feel that I have aban-doned "the work" when I perform ceremonies to work with the critical mass of humans, seeking to align us all toward harmonious, integrated functioning. I laugh and tell them that I am still doing Moshé's work, but this time my client for Functional Integration is rather large—Mother Earth herself! My own handwriting, my own uniqueness, is to perceive globally, to see the larger picture, through the power of my rainbow medicine. Although I still love to do individual integration work, and know that healing change for the world begins with the individual, I cannot neglect the larger Circle of Life and the charge to work for All My Relations, which stems from Creator's law: You shall be in good relationship with [yourself,] each other, and all things.

Not long ago, out of the blue, a very wise person came up to me, and said, "You know, White Buffalo Woman has many special workers in the world in our times, and Moshé Feldenkrais was certainly one of them!" A higher compliment I could not pay him.

When we are fully functioning, we humans will be awake to a much greater portion of the total experience possible to us in life. Mystics, seers, and sensitives often tell us that we perceive only a small portion of what lies before us—that we see only what we have been trained to see. A large part of the practice of becoming a woman of wisdom in the way of seers is to break through the artificial boundaries we have allowed to form around us, to break through into a larger field of perception, into true seeing.

Such well-documented bio-energetic phenomena as auras and energy meridians seem very mysterious to our untrained eyes, and yet have been documented by people in the Far East for at least five thousand years. Using the dreamer (or, the dream-body self in lucid dreaming) has been a practice of native peoples around the globe for all of history—since it was recorded on cave walls, and likely before that. The "primitive mind" was much more finely tuned to All Our Relations, and could journey in ceremony back through time, experiencing and commuting with every form of life along the phylogenetic continuum. But now, having given the limits defining "what is real" over to science, we have limited ourselves to things we can touch and feel, to a very small part of the "right side" of experience.

However, our body is a primary part of us as we live in human form. Too often this part of ourself is neglected. We attempt to become spiritual by leaving our body behind, by numbing it, or disregarding it, and then turning our total attention to our mind, emotions, psyche, or spirit. *It is clear to me that we must bring our bodies along, and that our challenge as Earthly beings is to bring enlightenment to our full and total being, to embody Spirit fully.* Moshé's focus on awareness and on the body helped bring the light of consciousness into each cell of our bodies, and to very effectively bring our fully integrated self into the process of personal growth and spiritual work.

BEING THE BODY

Here are a few simple Awareness Through Movement exercises as Moshé might have shared them with us. It's always helpful to have partners to lead us through these exercises because they often notice things about our instinctive patterns of movements that we might miss through familiarity. And once we've done the exercises, we can return the favor for these partners.

However, we can also do this for ourselves by making a tape and using each part of the exercises as a script—leaving enough time between each point to do what the directions suggest. When you're ready to do the exercises, just play the tape—loud enough so you don't have to strain to hear, but not so loud it interferes with your concentration.

AWARENESS THROUGH MOVEMENT: TENSION CHECK

1. Sit comfortably wherever you may be.
2. Tighten your right hand and hold it tense.
3. With your right hand still tense, direct your attention to:

▶ Your right forearm. How does the tenseness in your hand affect it?

▶ Your right shoulder. How does it feel?

▶ Your neck. Is there any tension or strain there?

▶ Your ribs and your breathing. Does what you're doing with your hand affect how and where you are breathing? Is it coming shallowly from your chest or deeply and gently from your belly?

4. Now, try tensing different parts of your face:

▶ Tense your forehead. How does this make you feel?

▶ Tense your mouth. What's your emotional response?

▶ Tense your eyes. How does this affect your vision? How does it affect your emotional response to what you see?

▶ Tense your jaw. How does the rest of your body respond to this? How do your emotions respond to tension in your jaw?

5. Stand up and begin walking around the room in a relaxed manner. As you walk, try tensing your right hand again.

▶ Is your tense hand affecting the entire way you walk? Check this by releasing the tension for a moment and walking around the room, paying attention to how you carry your body and how it feels.

▶ Now tense your right hand again and continue walking. Is there a difference? How do you feel it? Where do you feel it?

▶ Try this with your left hand. Is there a difference?

▶ Keep walking around the room and try tensing other parts of your body—both large and small—as you move. Each time you tense a body part, take an inventory and see how this affects other parts—and the whole body as well.

▶ What happens when you tighten your jaw?

▶ Try holding your stomach in. How does this affect your stomach muscles? Your back? Your rib cage? Your breathing? Your whole carriage?

▶ Try tensing something small, like a finger or a toe. Does it have a similar effect?

5. Notice how much your awareness of yourself is building. Can you sense more fully, now that you are an integrated being, rather than each little part being separate from the other?

AWARENESS THROUGH MOVEMENT: NOTICING HABITUAL PATTERNS

1. Fold your hands, interlacing your fingers.
2. Note which thumb is on top.
3. Now try interlacing your fingers with the other thumb on top.
4. Notice how odd this feels to your hands.
5. Check how this different interlacing feels:
▶ In your shoulder.
▶ In your neck.
▶ In your rib cage.
6. Does it feel as though your entire body is accustomed to your habitual way of folding your hands—not just your thumbs, or hands?
▶ Is your awareness of yourself changed in any way? How does this feel?
▶ Is your response to your surroundings changed in any way?
▶ Would you like to keep folding your hands this new way every now and then?
7. List five other patterns of movement that are not necessary, only habitual.

For instance, cross your legs. Which leg is on top? Repeat number six again with your leg. Or, which shoe do you put on first? What happens when you reverse this? Now pay attention to your body, and your movements through the day—what other habitual patterns do you come up with?
▶ How do they affect your entire way of being?
▶ Can you do these things in a different way and open up your consciousness a bit?
8. Perhaps you might like to try a slightly longer experiment. Which side of the bed do you sleep on? Try switching sides for a night. Are your sleep patterns affected? How do you feel when you get up? Are you disoriented? Does this add an interesting freshness to your day? Are your dreams affected? How? If you've switched sides with a partner,

compare notes in the morning. Would you like to try this again from time to time?

AWARENESS THROUGH MOVEMENT: MOVING BLINDFOLDED

When you have a half hour or an hour of free time, stand in the center of a familiar room and blindfold yourself. This is a good time to use the tape you've made of these exercises; otherwise, your partner can talk you through it. If there are two of you, after the blindfolding, have your partner spin you around gently several times so you have to reorient yourself to the space.

1. Find a comfortable chair and sit quietly for a few moments. Become aware of what you notice when you cannot use your eyes.

2. You may find yourself reaching out to touch things with your fingertips, which is quite a natural response.

3. Also notice that you are beginning to use your sense of hearing more fully.

4. Now stand up again and begin to move around the room slowly—feeling your way if need be. Try moving from object to object in the room just by your bodily memory of how far apart they are.

5. Become aware of your breathing as you move. Are you holding your breath? Why? Are you tense or nervous? If so, stop where you are, relax your body, and take three deep breaths. Then, breathing gently and fully, continue your exploration. Any time you feel yourself holding your breath again, stop and repeat the breathing exercise.

6. Become aware of how much you can perceive through your feet. In fact, you might want to try this entire adventure in sensory awareness wearing only socks, or even barefoot. Do remember to move slowly and gently so as not to stub your toes.

▶ Do you notice the change from a hardwood or tiled floor to a carpeted floor?

▶ Can you feel a difference in the warmth where your family pet may have been lying?

▶ What else do you notice through your feet?

▶ Are you more aware of exactly where the floor creaks?

7. If you're feeling more confident now, try moving through various rooms in your house—paying special attention with your nose. Can you tell when you're in the kitchen, the bathroom, the study? Flare your

nostrils and allow them to gather as much information as possible.

8. Now that you've covered the house, sit down again, and go back over your experience. What senses have awakened that are normally asleep? What awarenesses can you take back into your world of seeing?

9. Take off the blindfold and retrace some of your journey through the different rooms. Can you use your sense of smell, your feeling through your feet, to add to your awareness, even now that you can also use your eyes?

10. Are there other ways you can begin to wake up and hone parts of your awareness that have been sleeping? If you are a therapist, could you be daring enough to blindfold yourself during a session to heighten your awareness of other than visual cues? Close your eyes for a moment before you cross a street, and perceive the cues you receive about when to cross safely. Open your eyes and check what your other senses perceived.

Moshé spoke to us often about how much of our brain and our awareness lay dormant. He pointed out how tremendously human beings can develop and grow when they focus on a specific talent—such as being a fine musician, athlete, or craftsperson—but how little we use the full range of our potential. He reminded us that the more awareness we develop, the more differentiations we make in any area, the more our intelligence increases, and the more fully human we become.

AWARENESS THROUGH MOVEMENT: BREATHING

1. Pick up a rather heavy object. Are you holding your breath? See if you can breathe fully while lifting it.

2. Do some very delicate movement or task, such as threading a needle. Does your breathing change as you concentrate? If you pay attention to your breathing, does it return to normal? If so, can you still do the delicate task?

3. Have your exercise partner speak to you in an angry voice. Notice your breathing. Has it almost stopped? How does your body feel? Do you sense tension anywhere?

4. Listen for the farthest sound that you can hear. Can you identify the sound? What has happened to your breathing while you were listening? How does your body feel?

5. Now, sit or stand quietly and comfortably. Take a deep breath

by inhaling through the nose and guiding the breath down to your belly, filling it like a balloon. Now, let the breath expand up to fill your chest. Exhale by allowing your stomach muscles to push the air up out of your mouth. Repeat this two more times. Now, breathe naturally and gently—from the belly. How does this make you feel? Interview your various body parts.

6. Begin noticing other things that seem to keep you from taking full, deep breaths. We need this kind of deep, relaxed breathing in order to feed our brain, organs, nervous system, and muscles. Many cultures around the world believe the breath is the very essence of life—that with each inbreath we nourish ourselves with pure energy, and with every outbreath we cleanse the body of impurities.

Anything that unnecessarily changes our breathing from this fullness can activate our awareness. We can use these signals to alert us to less healthful patterns of movement and emotional response. And with practice, we can begin to choose differently.

AWARENESS THROUGH MOVEMENT: REALITY SHIFTS

Shamans down through the ages have used many different techniques to help their apprentices move through the boundaries of ordinary reality. Some involve complex ritual, some involve extraordinary stressing of the body, and some involve hallucinogenic plants. Yet there are also simple ways to move through these boundaries. The shifting of our normal patterns, our rigid forms, is certainly one, although because it is not such a shattering intervention, it takes a much longer time to dislodge our normal way of seeing. In our human experience, it seems to be time to open up the windows and begin to enjoy the perception of a much larger, more interesting reality. We can use these techniques to begin to pay attention in experiences other than our normal day-to-day patterns.

Our patterns of sleep are one of the easiest routines to shift.

1. Begin by taking a nap or two sometime during the day. If you work where you're allowed a fifteen-minute break in the morning and afternoon, get up and take a drink of water, sit back down, rest your head, and allow yourself to release everything in the outer world. Take time to rest and visit that sweet, dark, soft and starry realm where all possibility lies. Tell yourself you will be "gone" for ten minutes, and wake up refreshed. It may take some time before you can drop away

immediately, yet just the practice of releasing the outer world will begin the process of inviting another part of your experience to come forward. Nature abhors a vacuum, and will fill your consciousness if you empty yourself receptively.

2. At lunch break, rather than eating a big meal or going outside, take the time to again invite yourself to that inward open space where time and space are unlimited. Eat a healthy snack and lie down for a good half-hour nap. For many years, a close friend of mine would lie down on the wooden benches in the lunch room and take a wonderful nap while his buddies played cards.

3. In the evening, allow yourself to follow your body's direction in your sleep patterns, if possible. If you live alone, or without children, this is quite easy. For others, it is more challenging, but certainly possible in small ways. Establish quiet times and places for yourself.

4. It's not so much the length of the naps or sleep time, but the difference in your patterns, and the integration of the sleeping experience as a part of your ordinary world that's so important.

5. As you find yourself awake at different times of night, notice the difference in the feeling quality of the experience. Sometimes just being awake at three o'clock in the morning in the unusual quiet of a large city is an extraordinary experience! Or walking in the quiet of a misty hillside dawn can open new levels of seeing.

6. Try going to your public library and looking up the many references on lucid dreaming—the practice of learning to be consciously aware in your dreams. You might like to add some of the suggested practices to your experiment. However you approach this, move toward a honing and opening of your perception, your experience. Don't hold rigidly to having a certain kind of pre-ordained lucid dream. Something very different might occur.

For example, one day a student of mine was walking in the rocky hills of northern Arizona, when suddenly a strange, phoenixlike creature of the left side emerged from the ground and confronted her. Although she was walking the hills in our consensus reality, she was also in an altered state of consciousness! She ran screaming away, and yet returned again and again to the same place, where this being would once again appear. Finally, her curiosity called her to get to know this very extraordinary "guide," and it proved to be a wonderfully helpful companion. Allow yourself to open to Mystery without expectation or strings attached! It will enrich your world, no matter what happens.

While you're in the library you might also want to look through the wonderful books on working with your more ordinary dreams in other ways—drawing them, dialoguing with them, writing about them, and doing gestalt work with them. These techniques are also superb openers to the mysteries of the left side. In fact, written dreamwork exercises are much more accessible and less demanding (or threatening) than lucid techniques may be for beginners. Written techniques also help anchor visions in the waking world so they can be worked with further in the process of self-development. Most good dream books describe such techniques. One of the very best is Patricia Garfield's *Creative Dreaming*. She gives a complete rundown on the range of approaches to dreamwork, including shamanic and Senoi techniques. All these tools are wonderful ways to explore and become aware of your larger consciousness.

One of the primary things Moshé proclaimed he wanted to teach us was *how to learn.* He helped us understand that *awareness is the key in all learning processes.* Only when we become aware of the differences in things or ways of being, do we give ourselves the opportunity for deeper knowledge and for choice. Moshé's work with me touched not only my body but my whole consciousness; he helped me understand myself as an integrated being. Parts of myself that had been scattered in my consciousness now came together in the Awareness Through Movement exercises. His techniques were invaluable for me in approaching and learning with ease and awareness from both the left- and right-sided experiences I had outside of class. It became clear to me that this inner wholeness and functional harmony was a part of the wholeness of which White Buffalo Woman spoke. This approach to myself, then, could be extended into a way of harmony, wholeness, and holiness with All My Relations.

CHAPTER ELEVEN

THE HEAVIEST SWORD AND THE SHARPEST RAZOR

You are all magnificent, and trying to be okay.

Knowing us to be loving and magnificent beings with intelligent and compassionate gifts to give,
he wished to set our Ultimate Selves free in the world.

"You're going to see a Being channeled from another dimension?" I asked my roommate Lori, with incredulity and a little sarcasm, when she told me of her imminent visit with a being named "Dr. Kaskafayet." As is probably obvious to you—because of the flourishing of such channels today—this was many years ago, in the mid-seventies. Few people had heard of such beings then, and most of the few who had thought the whole subject strange and questionable. Certainly, it was not popular in the wider culture as it is today. Then, the only published material, new on the market, was the Seth work, channeled through medium Jane Roberts (see appendix 2, page 465). I had found Roberts's work fascinating, extraordinary, useful, and mind-expanding.

Now, Lori's friend, Howard, the medium for Kaskafayet's messages, had invited a group of close acquaintances to the first public "appearance" of Dr. Kaskafayet, and Lori was going. "It sounds pretty weird to me!" I warned her. Though it was clear to me that just because a being comes from another dimension and has no body doesn't necessarily mean that being has wisdom, I was still anxious to hear her report.

"Wow!" Lori said upon returning. "It was really different from what I expected. I thought it would be airy-fairy, mystical stuff, but he really confronted everyone present about their emotional experience—or more correctly, their lack of it."

This was to be Kaskafayet's hallmark—no funny business about where he came from, or what the other dimensions are like—but intensely confrontive, present-moment, personal, emotional work. If you raised your hand in his presence, you potentially asked for the most challenging half hour of your life. His basic message was framed as a question to us: "If you cannot be yourselves enough even to experience the truth of your own emotions, how can you expect to express the true depth and beauty of who you are?" His method of teaching was to *be* in his *own* emotional experience in regarding *our* lack of emotional integrity, and to press us hard and relentlessly to uncover, and to fully experience with self-love and acceptance, what we were feeling inside ourselves.

Many of us found this remarkably difficult. At first we had no idea what he was talking about because we had no conception of how buried our emotions were. To almost any question he was asked, Kaskafayet's response was, "What is your emotional experience right now?" I, for one, didn't even know I had emotional experiences. My family, like those of most of my friends, had suppressed and negated our emotional life. This was a matter of generational learning, and I had probably never met anyone whose emotional integrity was intact, let alone experienced this myself. Emotion to me meant an outburst of something painful or violent, and as such occupied a low ranking on my list of priorities for enlightenment. At that time I had not even considered such emotional work for myself, nor had I become aware of the dysfunctional patterns that lived within me. The Adult Children of Alcoholics twelve-step program, which would later offer me so much, had not yet even come into my awareness.

Yet this powerful being continued to insist that emotions are one of the first steps, not merely to "enlightenment" (a mystical quality to which he didn't pretend) but to integrated, functional daily living and decision-making. And, though my baser self hated to admit it, some deeper part of me knew him to be exactly right. I came into his presence again and again, almost panicky on this unfamiliar ground.

Sometimes this approach felt disastrous to me: the straight "A" student, the valedictorian, the Phi Beta Kappa scholar, the good girl, the one with the right answers for so long. This was not an intellectual or physical task at which I could excel, it was a task of uncovering layers of conditioning, hurt, and fear. As a child I had been told that my irrational anger made me a crazy person—that it was unacceptable behavior—for which I became ashamed. How could I possibly now confront all that buried emotion?

In Kaskafayet's class I would purposely sit behind a tall person, hoping not to be seen and confronted, hoping to learn by just being there. But Kaskafayet pressed me, and called me out of my hiding. In the beginning I would raise my hand when he asked a question, thinking I knew the answer, or had at least a good guess. But my fine intellect was not the issue at hand: I was completely chagrined when he responded in an angry and emphatic tone, "Medicine Eagle, sit down until you are in your emotional experience!"

He talked about humans having been created with a full circle of emotions, all the way from hopelessness, depression, sadness, fear, hostility, anger, hatred, and excitement, to bliss. We have come to think of some emotions as bad and some good, some acceptable and some not. These are our strange judgments of what Creator has given us to use. But Kaskafayet described all of these feelings as simply vibrational states given us through which to communicate our experience. Why not take a moment right now to feel for yourself the remarkably different "vibrations" of the various emotions. Try running through sadness, fear, anger, hatred, excitement, bliss.

Kaskafayet would talk with us about emotional states, saying: "*Sadness* is what humans naturally experience when there is loss in their life. It doesn't matter whether they lose their best friend or their abusive husband, sadness is still the emotion that arises. *Anger* is an inner statement that someone has stepped on your toes. *Excitement* is your way of revving up for intense activity. And *fear* is useful to awaken people when they might go half-asleep into a life-threatening situation. What humans have done is to become afraid of fear, to label it bad, to resist it, and thus to magnify it beyond all truthful proportion. Tears are held back because 'we shouldn't be sad,' and anger is suppressed until, like a kettle of boiling water, it explodes in violence. If you could but—without judgment—experience what you feel, each emotion would pass quickly, its message having been received and acknowledged."

When we first tried what we thought he suggested, we simply blurted out our feelings, splashing them all over anyone close by. "No," he admonished. "That's not it. I didn't say you had to express everything and dump it on everyone else. I simply said you must truly and fully experience your emotion. Others will get the message!"

I finally came to realize what he meant when I was able to remember my old white-haired grandmother. She never once screamed at us or beat us if one of us kids did something wrong. She simply whipped her head around and looked down at the offender, with her black eyes snapping anger and her nostrils flared. In that moment we knew exactly what she felt—her silent message was clear—and at times we understood from the mere jerk of her body. Obviously, a person's experience can be known without a verbal outpouring.

Kaskafayet continued our lessons, teaching that even when we try to hide it, others deeply feel our experience—that we are naturally tuned to each other in this way. The problem is that we have a cultural agreement to act dumb and mute, to not acknowledge what is happening to us, and to pretend that we feel only the emotions we label as "nice." This suppression not only numbs and deadens us, it throws us out of our integrity. This makes it difficult for us to know what our own experience is and thus to be guided by it. It also deprives others of the only feedback they can ever have.

If a spoiled child is never given the signal that his behavior is displeasing, he will never have the choice of changing. As we all know, it is easy to become habituated to our own way of doing things, and to be unaware of our effect on others. If your roommate is not told immediately that something she does makes you unhappy, the situation will deteriorate without her consciously knowing what is happening.

One of our profound functions is to be a mirror for others, giving them truthful, accurate feedback about our own feeling experience of what they do, stated not in terms of right or wrong, good or bad, but simply as what we feel. For example, it is really possible for us to tell someone, "I feel really sad when you refuse to hug your little boy after he has hurt himself"; or, "I feel very angry when you abuse that dog"; or, "I feel excited and thrilled when I see you perform so beautifully!" It is as important for others to know those things as it is for us to tell a friend that his zipper is down!

In my personal work during this time, I came to realize that I had not cried since I was a little kid. My family, wanting to save me—and themselves—from pain, would say, "Don't cry, honey. It doesn't do any good." And so I suppressed twenty-five years of tears. When I finally opened that door, tears ran down my face for days. It was not noisy boo-hooing, and I had no conscious awareness of the cause of my sadness—the tears simply ran, and an aching vibration hummed in my chest. Yet, it felt good to me.

Master Kaskafayet had reminded us that when we are resisting a certain emotion in ourselves, we will have difficulty facing it in other persons. On the other hand, if we are comfortable with an emotion, then the expression of it in our presence will not be a threat. So Katherine, one of my good friends, would encourage my tears, saying, "Your face looks so soft and beautiful after you cry. It's so much better than looking hard and stiff when you try to hold it back. Keep it up!" Then she would go on about her own business.

Both reactions—of denial or encouragement—were played out dramatically one time when I had a deadline—to mail some packages— during the time of my running tears. I sat in my car outside the UPS office where I could see a long line inside, dreading to go in there with tears streaming down my face. "But," I thought, "if I had just heard that my mother died, and I still had this errand to do, I would feel OK about crying in there!" With that rationale in mind, I went in and stood in line. People immediately divided themselves into two groups: the first met my eyes and nodded with empathy; the second became very uncomfortable, with extreme cases leaving the line to go outside!

Kaskafayet taught us to notice that when we resist an emotion, it's likely to be the one almost constantly present in us. If you are suppressing your anger, doesn't everything make you angry? If you are holding back tears, doesn't every upset make you want to cry? And certainly, if you are holding back your own tears, aren't you likely to join in if someone else is crying their eyes out? He counseled us again and again to love ourselves and trust ourselves enough to experience our emotions fully. This emotional work was very challenging to me, and yet I knew deeply that it was exactly what I needed to learn. I stuck with it, even though there were many moments of discouragement.

In the first few months our group was together, Kaskafayet developed our concepts of *loving intention,* impressing on us that to give truthful feedback is the most loving thing we could do for others. In *all* our experience—including anger and all the other emotions our limited minds think of as negative—there is a gem of truth in our response, which the other person deserves to know. But, rather than blurting out what might be three years of history we carried about an issue, Kaskafayet suggested that we look within ourselves to find the loving message at its core, and deliver that. If someone is behaving horribly, for instance, we have two basic choices: to ignore it, or to share our experience of it.

We have been culturally conditioned to look the other way—to not embarrass our friends by catching them at their worst behavior—and have been trained to call this "love." Dr. Kaskafayet took issue with this definition and way of loving, asserting that the most loving thing we can do is to let others know how we feel in the presence of their behavior—to give them an accurate mirror. This is akin to seeing your best friend go out the door with a glob of spinach in her teeth, and to just let it go to avoid embarrassing her—not the most loving thing to do! As Kaskafayet kept reminding us again and again, loving and caring about each other is the most basic part of our human nature.

At first, when we all tried to love each other by sharing our emotional experience, some of us spilled out deep wells of old hurts without ever getting down to the loving intention. And some of us used it as an excuse to browbeat others with our own self-righteousness. Not a very successful beginning—on the surface. But Kaskafayet urged us to keep working on it, no matter what the risks, assuring us we would do less harm by going overboard than by suppressing the truth, which was, in any case, somehow discernable underneath all along.

One of my struggles with this process became a great teaching for me. During this time, I was also in the Feldenkrais training. One of our assignments—while Moshé was away—was to try with many, many people, a few of the simple things he had shown us. We were to explain to them that we were practicing and needed their help. One day, after a comment to my roommate that I just wasn't doing enough practicing, she asked why I never worked on her, because she would really love it. I hemmed and hawed a while, saying that I would have to do that sometime, and slunk off to my room. I knew something felt bad to me about working on her, but I couldn't immediately pinpoint it. I sat in my room with Kaskafayet's voice in my head, feeling that I must be honest with her, and trying desperately to get my loving intention straight.

Still unable to frame my experience in very loving terms, I nevertheless went to her room and told her what was on my mind. "I need to tell you the truth," I said, "and it may not make you feel very good. The reason I don't want to work on you is that I can't stand to touch your body. You're mushy and untoned, and it would just feel gross to me."

Her reaction was just what I imagined. She was first shocked, and then hurt and angry. Finally, she burst out crying, and told me to get out of her room. I walked slowly back into my room, my thoughts in a muddle. "This time it didn't work. I told the truth, and it crushed her." I, too, felt crushed. There was nothing else to say; I could not deny the truth of what I had said. So I just picked up a book and lost myself in it. Time dragged on. I could hear her crying, and then silence.

About half an hour later, Lori came into my room with a smile on her tear-streaked face. She said, "You know, I was raised in a family that pampered me and never taught me to condition my body, or to move joyfully. I have always known my body was total mush and out of condition. And I have feared all my life that someone would say to me the exact words you just said. But you said it. Now my dread is over, and I'm OK!"

I grabbed and hugged her, and we danced around my room. When our energy calmed down, she asked me to help her find ways to begin the conditioning and strengthening that she really deeply desired, but had always avoided. We set to work on this together, in a new loving harmony. I rolled my eyes up to the sky and said quietly, "Master Kaskafayet, you were so right."

A group of seven women, involved with me in Kaskafayet's teachings, gathered occasionally to visit, relax, and share what we were feeling and learning. We developed a wonderful form that we called *transformed gossip* around Kaskafayet's idea of *loving intention.* We noticed when we were together that we loved to talk about everyone *else* in the group, and we were especially vindictive about some particular people whose behavior we didn't like.

One of our favorite subjects was Lon. He was incredibly self-righteous about the teachings, telling everyone how wrong they were, and acting as though he "had it all together." Having spent time around a very high master at one time, he now evidently considered himself enlightened. But he treated his girlfriend and most women like dirt, and we women thought he was the lowest of the low. The men, however, thought he was special.

One day, after everyone in our circle had complained bitterly about Lon, someone asked, "What is the loving intention behind all this? Is there something we have to say to Lon? If we just gossip behind his back, it doesn't help him change a bit, and it doesn't become us to be so backhanded." So we spent the afternoon helping each other get down to the one-liner that was the essence of our feeling for him—the message that might help him see himself more as others saw him, so that he could quit embarrassing himself and everyone in our circle of friends with his self-righteousness and arrogance. Then we each pledged—in our own way and in our own timing during the following week—to tell him what our experience of him was. I have always wondered what it was like to have seven powerful, clear women call him on his act. It definitely influenced his behavior.

Transformed gossip became one of our best tools for finding our loving intention. This practice of expressing my emotional truths was hard work for me, but the tool of uncovering my loving intention made it very much easier. Expressing my feelings felt much more natural when in harmony with the basic loving nature which is our true self.

Soon after our formal gatherings had begun, Dr. Kaskafayet told those of us who had stayed around to call him "Master Kaskafayet." He admitted he had called himself a "doctor" because, "You believe anything a doctor has to say!" We knew that he was right on that score. Again and again he caught us in our habitual ways of thinking, and called us on our lack of truthfulness. But then, sometime after this, he one day casually revealed—to a new attendee who asked in a sarcastic manner about Kaskafayet's past lives—that his name was actually "Frank Kaskafayetski," and that he had been a Polish street sweeper in Detroit during his last lifetime. From that day forward he asked us to call him "Frank." We old-timers got an enormous laugh out of that one, and began to call him Frank. We had come to understand that it did not matter where he came from or who he was; the fact was that he served us magnificently, and we would call him whatever he desired.

Master Kaskafayet's intentions were beautifully spelled out in something he wrote for the trainings we organized:

> *The purpose of the Kaskafayet training is to illuminate your relationship with your Ultimate Self, and to discover the compassionate intention behind your every action, thereby releasing your ability to manifest your true intentions in the world.*

Although his work with us was focused at a very personal level, it soon became apparent that his love for the Earth, and all things upon Her, was a strong motivation for his work with individuals. Knowing us all to be loving, magnificent beings with intelligent and compassionate gifts to give, he wished to help us discover our Ultimate Selves and to set them free in the world. He knew our deep intention was for our world to work.

Increasingly I felt the same underlying theme of "oneness with the Great Spirit and all things" emerging—although Frank seldom uttered a "spiritual" word. Creator's laws were again being spoken, by an unusual being who referred to himself only as self-realized—able to be his true self in every moment. Yet he thought of himself, too, as only a student, because his goal, as ours, was God-realization: a state in which we know and experience ourselves to be one with all and everything at every moment. Again and again, White Buffalo Woman and Dawn Star's words about a holy way of living with All Our Relations came to me. They helped me realize that this work, too, was a gift of spirit, a gift that was helping me learn to make real in my everyday life the visions which had been given me. They were helping me to understand that holiness is not just about a separate part of life labeled spiritual, but about being whole within myself, and with All My Relations, at all times.

At a certain time in the beginning of each session, our group was called to order. Then the door was locked so there would be no further coming and going during the channeling. Howard sat in a meditative pose, relaxed, cracked his neck a few times, and became very still. In a few minutes, his countenance changed subtly but distinctly, he cleared his throat, and Kaskafayet began to speak. Howard often likened the sensation of channeling to sitting in the backseat of your car and letting someone else drive, while you relaxed. He gradually came to understand that even the emotions "Frank" expressed were Howard's *own* experience. They were simply being used with a power and integrity he could not ordinarily express.

We soon found the locked door had a further function, beyond preventing interruptions. When the going got rough, many people wanted to get up and leave to avoid their experience. Even some of those not being worked with at the time often found the tension and emotion too much, and asked to go to the bathroom or anything, just to get away. This was not permitted. We made sure that people were informed the doors would be locked, and they would be asked to stay for the entire channeling. If anyone "broke out" despite the rule, they were not allowed to come back. I remember one haughty young man who first came when the seminars were held on the second floor of the building. He started asking snotty questions immediately, and Kaskafayet pinned him down like a verbal judo master. Very shortly he got up and tried to leave, cussing Frank and throwing a crying tantrum. He was not allowed to leave, and the frying pan got hotter. Kaskafayet would not let him off the hook or turn his attention elsewhere. The man finally decided that the fire would be better than this sizzling frying pan, and jumped off the balcony—landing safely in some shrubbery below. He felt persecuted. But the rest of us felt very sorry about his inability to use this incredible teaching he was given.

Years later, when I was given a scholarship to EST—the training seminars founded by Werner Erhard—I attended what others thought a very intense session. But it was all "ho-hum" to me after being in a locked room with Kaskafayet! Those of us who recognized that we were gaining something there that we'd not found anywhere else, stayed on, even though the hot seat was burning hot. Perhaps our tenacity came from the fact that Frank had told us he would remain with us for only a year. This was because, if he stayed longer, we'd begin to depend on him rather than on our own experience, or we'd try to turn him into a guru, which he certainly did not wish. This knowledge of his imminent leaving helped me to move through my inner struggles. It also enabled me to stick with it when the going got rough, and to stay in close touch with this remarkable teacher.

In occasional relaxed moments with long-time students, Master

Kaskafayet shared with us his past lives. During his last life, he had actually been a Sufi master, highly developed in his *siddhis,* or "powers." He could move through time and space, perceive more deeply than we think of as normal, and perform such "shamanic" magic as changing himself into a deer to wander the meadows near his home at twilight. For him, becoming a deer was not the difficult part. What was harder was becoming human again. He told us that in deer consciousness there is no desire to be human, and he could easily have lost himself there. Other highly developed shamans have told me the same thing—that smart-aleck novices try to change their forms before they've learned how to maintain the conscious focus necessary to return to human form. "We lose a lot of young apprentices that way!" they say.

Frank told us this in explaining why he wanted to return into human consciousness, from the plane where he now experienced himself. With great sadness in his voice, he conveyed that though he had been a high Sufi master, with great skills and powers, the tragedy of that life was the one thing he had never accomplished. He had never been able to "give away" his knowledge to his students, so that they might become greater than he. In this way he had failed, and his longing to truly teach what he knew was what had drawn him back.

Many times those who interacted with him seemed to go away crushed and broken. However, if they took to heart what he had drawn forth for them, their growth and changes were rapid and enormous. We asked him why he was so harsh, and his reply was, "You think I am crushing you, devastating you. In truth I am crushing who you think you are, so that the beauty of who you truly are can emerge." He called this *ruthless compassion,* and helped us to understand that the truth, rather than the experience of being coddled and mollified, would in fact set us free; and that what we usually think of as love is not love at all. Being nice is not being loving, unless it is in absolute integrity with what we feel at the moment—it is just a cultural conditioning for socially acceptable behavior. What is truly loving is to be truthful—to stop treating the other person like a weak, fragile doll whom the truth may damage. That kind of treatment is the most deprecating thing we can do to another, reinforcing their self-image as small, weak, and incapable. Kaskafayet said, *"You are all magnificent, and trying to be okay."*

I began to understand through him the idea of the wrathful teacher, as expressed in Tibetan tradition. Some of our teachers do best by bringing us along slowly, gently, tenderly, sweetly—our empathic teachers. Yet, for our full development, others are required who have the ruthless compassion Kaskafayet demonstrated. Sometimes a teacher has the talent to be both, at appropriate times, but more often there are two.

For example, Don Juan and Don Genaro in Carlos Castaneda's books: one empathizes with and cajoles Carlos, while the other pushes him relentlessly beyond his presumed limits.

Kaskafayet's ruthless compassion reminded me of Tibetan paintings I had seen—of the goddess Kali with her necklaces of human skulls, dancing on screaming human bodies—a representation of the destruction of the Lower Self so that the Higher Self may emerge. The more I experienced Kaskafayet, with all his harshness, the more I felt him to be the most loving presence I had ever experienced; not the easiest to be around, or the most fun, but the most loving. I still feel that he carried the "heaviest sword" of any being, human or otherwise, I have ever experienced.

But if he carried a heavy sword, his "partner," Terra, carried the sharpest razor. She could "cut your head off in a split second and laugh while the blood ran." We privately called her "Terror" to each other. Terra had been the first one to contact Howard. He'd been lying on the couch in his San Francisco apartment, his arm hanging over the edge, attempting to write a folk song, when something began to move his hand. He jerked his arm in astonishment at the strange sensation! But when he began to write again, someone else had control of his arm. Again he stopped. But finally it became less frightening to give in. In this first contact and thereafter, Terra "used his arm" to write notes to him. She introduced herself, and shared such fascinating insights that Howard lay spellbound for hours.

I remember one concept with which they worked for days; *souls love to love.* She drilled him again and again until he grasped that our basic nature, our true essence, is love, and that we truly love to love. He said he didn't bother to shave for days on end, he was so entranced with their "conversation." She slowly began to introduce him to the ideas that Frank would later expand, working with him for several months by himself. One day, she asked him to sit in a meditative posture so her "partner" could speak with him. Much to his surprise, his vocal cords instead of his arm were borrowed this time: Dr. Kaskafayet began to speak!

Eventually, Terra receded into the background, as Kaskafayet asked Howard to begin sharing his information with others through small group meetings. However, she still came through on occasion, especially when questions of relationship, partnership, and sexuality came up. She never entered the room until the group was divided into men on one side and women on the other. She used this physical division to point out differences between the experiences of men and women, which became graphically apparent through this seating arrangement.

She talked with us about the fact that women were like a *separate race, gifted with knowledge of all aspects of relationship, and that our task was to model, to share, and teach this to men.* She pointed out to us that, when women gathered, we talked about "who did what, when, where, and to whom": about *relationship.* One entire side of the room would nod its head in unison. Then she turned to the men, asking them if they knew anything about relationship, or whether they had been at the mercy of women all their lives in that regard. We looked across at the men, and whether they were twenty-one or sixty-one, they looked like little, lost boys, shaking their heads, "No, no, we don't know. We haven't a clue. We have been lost since the beginning. We don't have a clue." But while she pointed out their ignorance and stupidity, she also consoled them by explaining, "You came that way," and was not so tough on them.

However, we women were in for some stronger lessons. One feminist complained that women have no power, are so often used by men, and are second-class citizens. Terra tore into her for her weak, victimized manner, and gave us one of her most vivid metaphors. Women had always been smarter, more gifted, and more capable, she said, and if things were now bad for us, it was our own fault. She went on to remind us that women have the most influence on their growing boys and what kind of men they become.

"Besides," she asked, "what do men always want from you? What can they not get anywhere else?" Though we had some idea what she was aiming at, no one spoke. "Sex, you idiots! Female, genital sex," she shrilled at us. "It isn't to be had anywhere else, and it has an incredible power. If you didn't just give it away all the time, without any requirements of the men you give it to, you might have some power in your lives—you might influence men with what you supposedly know about good relationship. You have the shoe stores, and men want shoes! Now shape up and do something with your simpering, bootstrap lives!" She departed in disgust at us, leaving behind a room tittering and reeling. Although her teachings were very intense and totally challenging to my old mind-set, there was also something that felt completely right and truthful about what she shared with us. Whenever I was in her presence I simply tried to keep breathing and stay open to the learning that was available there. I knew that my system would filter her teachings, keeping what worked for me and discarding what did not.

As Frank returned, he would shake his head at Terra's intensity, which was even greater than his own, and begin to talk with us about relationship from a different aspect—one that has been a great gift for me. "We are born as totally loving beings," he would say again and again. "And we spend much of our lives *suffering for others*—using unworkable ways to say 'I love you.' " By reminding us of our basic loving nature, he took away any blame we might give ourselves for our "bad" behavior.

"Why do you hold back your truth?" he would ask. "Why do you learn to repress yourself and be totally out of your integrity? Because you have been taught that if you are truthful, passionate, willing to feel, and to *say* what you feel, in every moment, that you will hurt and damage others. What then would a loving person do? She would hold back her truth, her passion, her integrity *out of love for the other person*—not out of stupidity or meanness, but out of love. She would suffer for them in an unworkable attempt to say, 'I love you.' The Buddha talked about it, and we are living it every day.

"I know that you all want to truly love each other, to express the deepest truth of yourselves. And the way to do that is to recognize that suffering for others doesn't work." He gave us a law to use in our struggles in relationship: *If it doesn't work for you, then it doesn't work for them.* Since we are in fact one with each other, it is crazy to think that something that causes us great suffering would truly work for another. How often do we hear married couples, who should obviously be apart, say, "We're staying together for the kids' sake." If you have been a child of parents who do not care for each other any longer, who expressed this either as a mere lack of connection or in violence, you know that the best thing for you would have been for them to separate, so that you could have a modeling of something besides pain. "I can't leave her—it would just kill her," you sometimes hear a boyfriend say, although he no longer wants to be in a relationship. He doesn't understand that he is depriving this woman of the chance to find someone in her life who truly can love her, who wants to be with her. These are simple examples of a simple truth: *Suffering comes out of unworkable attempts to care, from a place outside of integrity.*

Another guideline Kaskafayet gave us has been one of the most helpful—and the most challenging—for me to apply in my own life: *"If it's not totally yes, it's absolutely no."* In response to any question, request, or decision, we have a whole range of possible answers, from "no," to "maybe," to "yeah, I guess," to "OK, I know I should," to "YES!! Of course, no question!" Master Kaskafayet pointed out that all the answers from "no" all the way up to "YES!" constitute an absolute "no." Unless we are totally experiencing a "YES," we should always answer "no."

Think about this in your own life! How often do you abide by that intuitive guideline? How many more "no's" would there be in your life, if you took on the challenge of living this? His explanation was that, if you gave a positive first response, and then changed your mind, it might be said, "You don't keep your commitments. You said you would, and I want you to keep your word!" But did you ever hear anyone accused of that when they change their answer from "No" to "Yes"? Very seldom does anyone say, "Your word isn't any good. I was counting on you not to help me!"

Let's take, for example, a situation in which a good friend has asked you to help her move to a new apartment. Inside, you know the truth for you is a "no" answer. Check into your heart and see what keeps you from saying yes. Perhaps you have all sorts of considerations—for example, "That day is my kid's birthday; My bad back is acting up; I hate moving boxes; You never help me when I ask." Saying "no" gives you time to really look at these concerns. Maybe you find your child is going to the circus with friends on his birthday, so you'd be happy to help—now say "yes." On the other hand, perhaps you just despise moving boxes, and that won't change. You could suggest some other possibilities to the person, or pay your strong young nephew who wants to make a few bucks to help her. "No" is still the answer, but it is not without compassion.

I challenge you to try this powerful tool in your life. It requires that you begin to truly experience your own feeling experience. Without that, you will answer "yes" by rote, thinking you mean it, and then wonder why you suddenly dislike your favorite old aunt, who has always needed your help. Begin to rely on your own experience, and live the life of a warrior—seeing the truth of your experience and living from the heart of it.

Frank left us, just as he had said he would, after about a year. Before going, he asked us what we thought would happen to this close-knit group in the coming years. My partner Lalo, one of those whose energy had helped keep our group together, spoke up and shared a dream of us all being together in a community, working together to serve the world.

Kaskafayet responded to this with characteristic bluntness, "Pooh, no! You will be scattered across the world, each using your experience to do work that is uniquely your own, while modeling a way of living that works for others. You have never been separate, and you never will be separate from this group—your Ultimate Selves will be loving and supporting, and a deep knowing will exist among you. Many of you have been together since your lifetimes in the Egyptian Mystery Schools. Down through time you have been masters, teachers, and high priestesses who held great mystical knowledge and power. You have withheld this knowledge until now for two reasons: (1) Humanity has not until now been developed enough to hold and use this knowledge well; and (2) You sometimes wanted the power and the glory for yourselves. Your task in this time is to take this mystical tradition you carry, and give it away to everyone! Humanity is ready; it is time. The intensity of the energy now focused on Earth—for its transformation into a new and glorious future—means that every step you take will be magnified. I send you forth. Use yourselves well."

When Frank left us, all of us longed for his wise council. Some eventually turned to people who were beginning to channel other entities. The counselor to whom I turned was quite different. She was a lovely, white-haired woman who had for fifty years of her life been in "direct conversation with God." Aunt Josie not only talked to God, she talked back! She was crystal clear that we all have within us the ability to touch the Great Spirit and "channel" that infinite wisdom through writing, or through another personality or entity, or whatever way suited our purposes and personality. She reminded me, in her own clear and direct way, of Creator's law concerning our oneness with all things.

What Frank had been about was further illuminated by a later teaching benefactor who helped me understand, from the Central American Southern Seer's view, what had been accomplished. Although each human being has many points of power in his or her repertoire, often in the wider culture people get stuck using only the first two: thinking and emotion, running back and forth between restricting rationality and unresolved emotion.

In focusing on emotional freedom and integrity of being, Kaskafayet helped open our spirits to the other points, including will and dreaming, which are readily available when we withdraw our power from wasteful preoccupation with only thinking and emotion. When we are free to experience the whole wheel of the heart given us by Creator, and to have our truthful feeling experience complement our mental capacities, then we have a greater chance to open our spirits—to become more of who we truly are.

Master Kaskafayet's teachings are a strong part of my daily practice still, not because he was a strange, channeled being, but because they work in my life. When something doesn't feel right in my home situation, I remember Frank's teachings and realize that it's not working for others in my household either. That makes it easier for me to sit down and talk about what is happening. When I must decide on a schedule nearly a year ahead of time, where there is no rational way to make choices, I reach inside myself to my gut feelings and check each possibility with the "yes/no" principle.

In addition to these simple things, Kaskafayet gave me a great start on the challenging work with my emotions, a process which continually becomes more primary in my life as years go by. The learning I gained from Frank and Terra on how to relate to myself and to my world in a good way seems a vital part of learning the lesson that is before me—and all of us—about how to live in good relationship. More and more I understand that this kind of emotional work, as well as other things that lead me toward an experience of unity and harmony, is absolutely essential if we are to continue to live on Earth and make our way into a new age.

THE ABSOLUTE YES!

The most profound beginning exercise I could give you is the one I discussed above: the Absolute Yes! As I said before, I give you the loving challenge to practice this in your life. Learn to say "no" when your inner experience is anything other than an excited and definite "yes!" You will find this to be more difficult than it may seem at first, and yet it will transform your experience very deeply if you continue to practice it.

1. List five recent situations in which you have said "yes" when you meant "no." Note the results of those experiences in your journal.

2. List five situations of major importance in deciding the pathway of your life when you said "yes" although you meant "no." Note the results in your journal as well.

3. Each day for the next seven days, use the form below to assess five situations in which you are challenged to make a conscious choice.

▶ Pay exquisite attention to your inner process as you make your decisions. Notice the habitual ways you tend to respond. Assess whether or not your habitual response represents your true feeling. If it doesn't, then try something different this time.

▶ Pay attention to the inner "hooks" or beliefs that trip you up most often. Do you think you "should" help others? Do you think you must please others in order to be okay? Examine these "hooks" with care, so that you begin to know the patterns that create the lack of integrity to your true self. This will help you to challenge them.

Situation	Answer	Hook	Consequence
EXAMPLE:			
Mom asked me to stop for groceries.	Yes	Guilt	I was very angry when I got there, and she felt very bad.

THE INTEGRITY OF FEELING

One fun way to practice following your true feelings is to go on what I call an "adventure quest." You need no one else to help you, and may discover that you really enjoy it. This exercise will call on your true feelings moment to moment without any planned result, and will take you on all sorts of fascinating expeditions! Your only goals are having fun; practicing responses in integrity with your feelings; and seeing what interesting and delightful experiences you gain.

1. Find a free afternoon and dress in a simple way that will be appropriate in many situations. Take a little backpack if you wish, to extend the range of what is possible for you to do. For example, a pair of sneakers would be useful if you end up hiking, and a nice jacket to put on over your jeans would be helpful if you end up in a fancy restaurant.

2. Take a moment to bring up within yourself a feeling of excitement and anticipation at the interesting and delightful experiences you might find on this journey.

3. Step out your door and check your feelings: Do I take the car or the bike? Do I take the bike or walk? It obviously doesn't matter what you choose since you have no specific goal in mind. Just let yourself do what you feel like doing. If it seems hard to figure out, just do one. Don't take a lot of time or get into intellectual discussions with yourself. You don't need to make it feel difficult.

4. At the first corner, and each succeeding one, ask yourself, Left or Right? Keep an attitude of fun, rather than putting pressure on yourself.

5. You come to a roadside cafe, or a library, or a store. Ask yourself, shall I stop and go in, or keep going?

6. Realize that, wherever you are, you have choices about which part of the multitude of things to pay attention to. Do you watch the sky for birds, or do you watch the ground for arrowheads? In a store, do you look at the merchandise or watch the people? In a restaurant, do you sit quietly observing, or do you engage in conversation with someone at a neighboring table?

7. Notice how many points of choice you have, and use each little one to practice feeling your own experience.

8. Pay attention to when your adventure feels finished. One day, you may have an experience in the first twenty minutes that gives you a feeling of completion. Another day you may wander for hours.

9. Upon returning from your adventure, take note of whether following your inner experience seemed to get easier over time. Remember as clearly as possible how you felt when you did this, so that you can use that experience to help you in daily situations that have more pressure and intensity.

I have something Master Kaskafayet gave us not long before he stopped directly communicating with us. Printed on fine gray paper in beautiful calligraphy, it expresses to us in a special way who Master Kaskafayet was and continues to be, for I sense him standing next to my spirit, in total support, at every moment I look within:

My intention is to contribute the most workable, viable, and creative suggestion I can to the world in general and to anyone who wants to listen in particular. My view of reality may possibly illuminate your view of reality, and if so, I will be happy in the act of giving what I have learned through my experience.

My observation is and has been that every time I am confronted with the experience of moving forward, I am inclined to resist and avoid becoming more of what I already am. My experience has demonstrated to me that every time I am confronted with moving forward, I am also confronted with allowing someone else to stay where they are. It has been in discovering more and more workable ways to reconcile the illusion of conflict in this dilemma that has contributed the most to my own conscious evolution. To be more direct, my experience is that the source of suffering is in the ways we suffer for other people in an unworkable attempt to say I love you.

Therefore it would seem that if we are all to become as great and magnificent as we truly are beneath our costumes, then the secret must lie in the ability not just to become great yourself, but rather to become so great that you inspire others to reveal their own greatness to themselves, to you, and to humanity. We are all magnificent and trying to be okay.

I am not here to be great, but rather to reveal your own magnificence to yourself. I choose to give and to serve because I receive the most value from giving. For me, love is what I have left when I give what I have away.

> *In my eternal compassion,*
> *Master Kaskafayet*

From the distance of almost fifteen years, I look back on my time with Master Kaskafayet as some of the most useful learning I ever received. His, and Howard's, unwillingness to hang around and play guru—his emphasis always being on our magnificence rather than his—stand him in a very high place in my experience, while some other popular channeled beings seem very shallow.

Woven into my experience of Master Kaskafayet were the teachings I received from Grandma Rosie and her spiritual wisdom, and my studies with the old samurai, Moshé Feldenkrais, with his deeply integrating movement awareness. Now I see that the call to transform myself, which had led to my vision quests, was also calling to me the teachers who could help me integrate these visions into daily life. Although they were not all Native teachers, they were magnificent in their own ways, and helped me extend the principles of the Native teachings into my life and work. I am indeed grateful for the masterful quality of the teachers I have been gifted through Great Spirit's grace.

Although all of us are grateful for the fine teachers who come into our lives in different ways, it is more difficult to recognize and appreciate the subtle range of teachers who are more consistently with all of us. These teachers sometimes take the form of a smiling child, a beautiful sunset, a crabby old lady at the supermarket, a dominating boss, a garden, or an angel whispering in our ear. Spectacular, big-name, or major teachers are not necessary to develop our potential to the fullest; we call them to us only as they are needed. As I worked with each of my teachers, I prayed for my own special mastery, and that I, in turn, might give my learning away to those I would touch.

CHAPTER TWELVE

A NORTHERN FACE, A SOUTHERN HEART

Anything that is not serving All Our Relations in a high and useful
way is not worthy of attention or energy
from a warrior woman. It is a leakage of power.

Those elders you speak of may not have recognized those blue eyes,
but they have been praying for you for a long time.

The amount of presence I bring to any situation is directly
proportional to the amount I receive from it.

Dawn Boy, the one called by seers and prophets Younger Brother, is a thin man and a young man, with hair all curls and gold. I did not at first perceive him as a teacher for me. My prejudice in medicine teachers had been toward older, and certainly darker, Native people. This one, it turned out, had Sioux blood from way back stirring in his Caucasian veins, and a mission as big as Crazy Horse's. I would see him again and again standing on the edge of my circles, wild-eyed and untamed, watching and listening—not so much to the outer messages I shared, but to some strange inner whisperings that only he seemed to detect behind my words. I was to learn that he was listening to my spirit and sending me power; speaking, moving, shifting; and moving others.

He first came to me after I had left the San Francisco Bay area and had been teaching on the road for several years. He found me in quiet places, and slipped up like a coyote to let drop a strange message or a rough question. Although he spoke English, I did not often understand his meaning—his words carried a different intent from what I had come to accept as normal. I was confused by what he had to say, uncomfortable with his disheveled clothes and the unkempt hair surrounding his piercing, sky blue eyes. In what seemed to me very strange moments, he would throw his head back and laugh a raucous cackle. In fact, Cackling Crow was his humorous name for himself. I didn't know what to make of him. Yet he found his way through my prejudices, and became a spiritual benefactor the likes of which I had never known before. A "spiritual benefactor" is how many southern tribes refer to their primary spiritual elder.

One of the main elements in our relationship was his supreme aggravation for my not doing more than I was already doing, seeing more clearly than I did, manifesting Spirit more in the world, bringing women to Spirit through their Moon times, working with my renegade spiritual family much more closely. He was like a return of karma to me, because I, too, often focus on people's potential, more than attending to what is actually happening right now. Besides seeing their potential, I press them to actually manifest that ideal. However, I seldom had anyone to point out my own shortcomings and my fuller potential.

Dawn Boy's sight, his perception of my experience as well as of the world and Spirit's movement in it, continue to be deeper, broader, more universal, more fully left- and right-sided, and much more powerful than anything I have ever experienced. Of course, it doesn't please me to be found lacking, yet I've managed to stay in relatively constant contact with this source of uneasiness and growth and the mysterious unknown for many years now. The amount of intent he holds for the forward movement of Spirit in our daily world continues to astound and inspire me.

One of my most profound experiences early in my apprenticeship with Younger Brother was when we spent a New Year's weekend in Oklahoma retreating together, and he put my entire world back together in a different and more solid manner. I was carrying much pain and confusion in my heart because of my frequent estrangement from various elders. And it all began to surface as he spoke about individuals among them with whom he had contact. Demanding that I get a pen and a large piece of paper, he began to have me place myself and others in a circle on the sheet by talking about the burning line of Spirit moving in the world, and which people were dancing on that fiery edge.

Then he did a classic medicine wheel meditation, in which it became obvious I was centered in an amazingly rich world, and in close relationship with a majority of the Native teachers on the obvious edge of a new way of sharing with the larger world. Up to this time, I had felt very small and alone and isolated. Suddenly, my world was rich and full.

Now I stood in good relation to my world. To my sniffling about not being recognized or coddled by any of my elders, and my resentment at their outright rejection of my half-breed status and knowledge, he said something that changed my world, because I understood it to be deeply truthful: *Those elders you speak of may have not recognized those blue eyes, but they have been praying for you for a long time.* They have been praying for all these rainbow children spoken of in the prophecies.

"Let me remind you of your history," he counseled. He went on to explain that in the late 1800s, in the midst of the devastation of the Native peoples that was then happening, Crazy Horse, Wovoka (the Ghost Dance Prophet), and other powerful spiritual men were bringing through a similar message of salvation for the Indian people and their children of generations to come: *First, peace must be made with the oppressors, and second, the non-Indian people were to be given the deep knowledge of the Indian people. Without these two things happening, there would be no hope for either of the peoples. The non-Indians needed to begin to live the philosophy and harmony of the native, land-based way. And all must come into harmony, or no one's children would have a world to live in.*

Part of the vision of this criss-crossing of knowledge and culture were the *métis,* the mixed-bloods, the half-breeds who naturally became a bridge between these peoples. In recent years, many non-Indian people find a Native path to be their true calling and vocation. The key concept of this way of salvation seems to be oneness, unity, harmony, peaceful togetherness: good relationship among all.

North America—Turtle Island—is a feminine place; it is a mother turtle who holds this part of the world on her back. The feminine way of harmony and good relationship with the greater Circle of Life has been more prominent in the hearts and ways of the Native peoples than in Europeans and others who colonized this land; the way of this Earth has spoken itself through those who have come to be Native here over the centuries. And this way will speak again. Long, long ago the elders spoke of the spirit of the land itself being born again in the children of the oppressors.

When the white Europeans came with their aggressive yang ways to conquer and possess and hold title to this land, they swept over the land like wind over the soft grasses that cover the plains. For a long time that harsh wind has held sway. Yet, just as grass eventually pushes its way through even concrete, growing wherever it is not carefully weeded, the more feminine cultures of the Native peoples are beginning to grow through very many cracks in the concrete. The gentler forms cannot be held down forever; there is a turning of the cycle in all natural things.

But there is also a deeper story, a story that spans centuries of time in the Americas. Several thousand years ago, the being we call Elder Brother came from Asia into Polynesia and on into Central America. Instead of taking a small boat across the coves from the enormous craft that plied the waters even then, He simply walked upon the surface of the water onto the land. He wore a long white robe with black crosses at the hem, and had blue-green eyes that changed like the color of the ocean. When asked His name, He replied only, "Call me what you will." Able to heal the sick and raise the dead, He held dominion, as well, over all Earth's elements. He taught that miracles are natural when we allow the love and light of the Great Spirit and Mother Earth to shine forth unrestricted from our hearts—a way of love and good relationship, of the family of humankind prospering together.

This master spread these teachings in a spiral of light to all the peoples of the Americas, and each of them named Him differently. In their own languages, many of them named Him Lord: *Quetzalcoatl,* Lord of Wind and Water, in Central America; *Ce Atl,* Lord High One, in other southern languages (which became Sealth or Seattle as He journeyed among the people of the Northwest Coast). Other Northwestern tribes around Puget Sound continued to call Him *Tla Acoma,* as He had been named in South America, and gave that name to what we now know as Mt. Rainier. This was eventually anglicized to Tacoma.

The name *Dawn Star,* by which He is generally known among many tribes, came to Him as the people watched Him go out each morning with His chosen apprentices to pray in the dawning light under the morning star. It took on deeper significance as they began to understand that He himself was the dawning light of a whole new day, a whole new time on Earth. He carried the Christ light to peoples of the Americas. It has long been said of him in the oral tradition: "He is the first fruit of the awakened ones. The miracles He performed so naturally so long ago, we in this time will come to do even more powerfully as we are able to channel the love and light of Spirit and Mother Earth through our hearts unrestricted." The Shinelas named Him *Wohogus,* Light of the World, and adopted the Dawn Star emblem as their central symbol, becoming the People of the Morning Star.

He touched each people, in turn, as He moved across all the land. During the time He spent with a people, He would find twelve among them whom he felt could carry his teachings after he left, and worked intensely with them. Fanning out from the Sun centers of the central Americas, the master walked and the message spread. Through His teaching there was formed upon this continent, for one shining moment in time, a confederacy of love and light—a unity of all people with each other and with all children of Mother Earth and Father Spirit. Trade and artistry flourished as the people used their time for creation rather than for destruction and warring. Life prospered for all. The cities of that time shone golden and pure; clear water coursed in small streams through them; beautiful flowers grew abundantly; exquisite birds sang in the blossoming trees; and agriculture was developed to astounding levels.

When the Dawn Star left the people, He called a great gathering of people at golden Tula, the city in Central America that was the epicenter of His teachings. He stood high on one of the temples, looking out over the throng that stretched farther than the eye could see. Even miles away they could hear Him as He counseled, saying such words as: *"If you keep together this Flowersong—this flowering family of love and light that you have begun with me upon these continents, you will experience a golden time that makes even this time of peace and bounty look pitiful by comparison."*

Yet, being a seer, He was painfully aware that the people might take another road, and he spoke to them of that, telling them in so many words: *"If, however, you should choose not to continue in love and cooperation, if you should forget that each of you, and all things, are your family, if separation and warring come to be a way of life again, then you will fall so hard and so far that standing here in the beauty of this day, you cannot perceive how dark and devastated will be the children of your children. Choose well. Remember that you are one with all things and all beings. Be a happy family."*

History shows us that people of the Americas chose the latter path at their crossroads of choice, and so, among the people of these continents, warring and fighting and vying for territory became the rule. When the white Europeans came, the Native peoples of the Americas, rather than being an allied and unified family confronting the people who came in boats and asking them to either learn the ways of harmony or get back on their boats, were instead fighting and warring among themselves.

For an in-depth look at the kind of disharmony, pillaging, destruction, and disease brought by one such group of boats, read Kirkpatrick Sale's well-researched book on Christopher Columbus, *Conquest of Paradise* (New York: Knopf, 1990); *The Crown of Columbus* by Louise Erdich and Michael Dorris (New York: Harper Collins, 1991); and *The*

Devastation of the Indies by Bartolomé de Las Casas, trans. Herma Briffault (New York: Seabury, 1974).

The Native peoples aligned with separate groups of the immigrants and their powerful guns, and eventually those guns spoke the death knell of a whole way of life for the people of Turtle Island. The prophecy was fulfilled. The genocide of the Native peoples, the dishonoring of the sacred, the wiping out of the enormous buffalo herds, and the subsequent two-edged gifts of the conquerors—white sugar, coffee, alcohol, smallpox, TB, and reservations—could not have been imagined in the golden days of the Dawn Star's time.

So the different peoples, both Native and non-Native, all joined in this great disharmony, this continental war, and thus became one people in need of regaining peace and a sense of the sacred, a way of harmony with All Our Relations. Out of the Dawn Star's Christ light, the new prophecies called for peace, unity, sharing, and working together toward a new world, for the children of all. Of course this has been very difficult to realize. Centuries of fighting, parochialism, and prejudice among all peoples have had to be purged. A melting pot had to produce a tasty soup; and out of strange bedfellows a new generation of unity will be born.

"And you are part of that story," said my benefactor, Dawn Boy. "The Dawn Star's disciples among every tribe were highly developed shamans who practiced the 'white' magic of healing and wholeness and who passed their lineage down through time. The Southern Seers, beginning with the ancient Toltecs of Central America, carried it the most strongly, as do some Apaches and Yaquis today. Even my name, 'Dawn Boy,' comes from that lineage. Your northern tribes continued over centuries to send a young person of highly developed spirit to the temples of Central America for apprenticeship and initiation. An elder went with them, and they walked the long way south. *You are an active participant in a story that involves all of humankind. The spirit of oneness and unity for which you stand is what will build the Rainbow Bridge into the future. You can become increasingly active as an architect of that bridge.*" He had placed me not only in my present time and contemporaries, but into deep history. He opened my understanding of my place in each. He had given me new heart to smile at the small aggravations I experience because of individual elders' perceptions of me. Dawn Boy had given me back my heart, and reordered my world.

He ended this part of his teaching by reminding me of another painful part of this historical process. The Native people of Turtle Island obviously had the message of the Christ, the Dawn Star; they knew and cherished it. Yet, when the Spaniards and others came to these continents to colonize them and make the land their own, they came with priests who were to make sure that the Indian people had the word of Christ. And the newcomers set about creating converts to this "new word" being brought among them.

Many Native people recognized the Dawn Star's message in their words, and understood that these new people had heard it as well. Yet, the Natives were not believed when they shared their knowledge. It was much more convenient for the colonizing Spanish to destroy every evidence of the Dawn Star's light, and call Natives heathen and impure, in need of subjugation and conversion. The Christian message of love and light and forgiveness on the one hand, contrasted with the destruction of the sacred ways and the culture of the people on the other hand were, to say the very least, confusing for the native people. They soon came to hate these oppressors who had no intention of recognizing their spiritual ways or the value of their culture. The Native people's high priests and priestesses—their white shamans—were killed on sight. Anyone in the mystical lineages had to hide themselves away or at least become totally secretive about their sacred knowledge.

The Christians had succeeded in giving Christ a bad name among the Native people. And the outcome of that, even today, is that when they turned their backs on Christianity, they also turned away from the truth and light of the Dawn Star, the Christ energy of the Americas. This has caused spiritual devastation for the peoples because, by not identifying with the great light who helped establish the foundation for these centuries of growth and change toward oneness, they cut themselves off from incredible spiritual power.

The Native peoples had their own names for this great teacher and for his message; they need not use the names others used. *It is vital for us to remember these teachings that have been passed down for centuries through the lines of light, whose flowering and radiant harmonies lie at the source of all the songs. This rainbow medicine must spread among all the peoples, so that we re-member, and become of one body again.*

"*You have a northern face, but a southern heart,*" said Cackling Crow, with one of his familiar chortles. He found this quite funny— probably another one of what he called his "Indian jokes" that I seldom found humor in. Becoming serious again, he said to me, "You have a northern face: your people are a mixed group of northern peoples, and you stand in the north, looking south. Yet your deepest lineage is the line of light from the Dawn Star in the south. You are like the chosen ones of old who walked to Palenque and Tulum for their highest initiations, and returned as 'twisted hairs' after many years, singing 'Flowersong' among all the peoples on the way. Your heart is connected to the Dawn Star and the golden southern lines of light that came down from him. A part of your mission is to reconnect the southern lines with the northern ones, to teach the people to keep the baby when the bathwater is thrown out. Your song, as well, is Flowersong! It is time to sing it out powerfully and beautifully!"

During many of my early interactions with this strange person, I understood little of what he was saying to me. In one of our initial meetings, after dark outside one of my teaching circles, I asked him to reiterate the main point of his rambling talk. I did not know what his confusing words meant, and he seemed far away in another reality, his eyes distant and veiled. In that moment he turned and opened his very bright eyes toward me, and spoke his message in a clear voice that I will never forget: "The most important thing is that plants love us." I had not recognized until then that he was a plant shaman. Later I was to learn that he had turned to plants as friends, in the same way that as a child I had turned to animals. Between him and the plant world, there was an indefinable and strong bond of understanding and Spirit.

As a central part of his teachings, Cackling Crow spoke of the friendship between plants and the two-leggeds—even though our culture has been so devastating and deprecating to them. He spoke of tobacco, whose sacred medicine gift is one of unifying and bringing together all peoples. Yet, we humans have turned to using it for our own gratification, to numb and ease ourselves, ignoring the disharmonies within us and in our relationships. When I asked him about tobacco giving people cancer, Younger Brother snorted, "It's mostly the chemicals sprayed on the plants that have that effect, but it's a wonder that tobacco has not dealt even more harshly with the people who made a sacrilege of it. Tobacco loves us, or a lot more of us would be dead from its misuse."

Under this influence, I began to look more at the healing ways that involved plants—herbal remedies, wildcrafting (gathering wild plants from nature to create herbal formulas), and especially the practices that use flower essences in oral remedies and aromatherapy. It seems that the plants have in their makeup many patterns of integration that we do not have innately. Through ingesting some of the plants' energetic essences, we give our bodies a model of new integration we can then use to build new patterns, helping ourselves to heal—on emotional, psychological, and spiritual, as well as physical, levels. These gentle modes of healing are clearly the way of the future—of unity with a healing agent—a way superior to the cutting and separation that now characterize our medical practices.

Dawn Boy spoke often, too, of his friend *Peyote,* sometimes called *mescalito*—the plant around which the Native American Church formed. "Peyote is one of the Dawn Star's plant archangels," he would tell me. "The work of re-unifying the people done by that simple cactus has been more powerful than anything any human has done."

I remembered how in the Native American Church, when you bow your head and step through the door of the Sacred Lodge, you acknowledge everyone there as your family, whether from an old enemy tribe, whether you have never met, and even if you don't like them. As a result of this remembering of the Dawn Star's laws, Native American Church people have family all across the land, in almost every tribe. The lines of differing tribes, cultures, and ways of living are erased in that brother-sisterhood of Spirit. Indeed, peyote is continuing to do the work of a saint.

Dawn Boy introduced me to peyote as a plant medicine that would help to open my left side. In Native American Church meetings, he helped me touch the side of vision and other realities, while at the same time asking me to keep my right-sided attention strong so that I did not simply get lost on the left. He said too many people use plant medicine frivolously and dangerously, to simply "get drunk and pass out," rather than using the expanded perception they offer to do the work of Spirit. Peyote's medicine includes other things as well. Those who use it ceremonially often experience physical, emotional, and mental healings. Research shows that Native American Church people are healthier, tend to have regular work and stay with it, and have good family lives without the problem of alcohol. Given these facts, it is almost inconceivable to me that in some states rulings are presently being made to outlaw this powerful plant medicine's use. Peyote's power is that of spiritual action. Its model is for us to move into spiritual action ourselves, to serve the growth of Spirit and unity among the peoples of Earth by our work in the world.

Another of Dawn Boy's powerful teachings came in relation to the world of the insect people. As most people do, I often thought of them as a nuisance—although I never killed spiders, and tried to warn mosquitoes when I'd had enough. One day, while riding down a country road with me, Dawn Boy suddenly found that a bee had blown into his facial hair. I laughed at the predicament, and he lectured me sternly. "That is a message from my benefactor. He speaks to me through the insect world. Don't ever laugh like that again!" I was quite taken aback.

Shortly after this, on one of his quick visits, he tossed me a ring that he had picked up in New Mexico on his way through there. I accepted it and didn't take time to examine it until he left, except to note that it had some kind of weird insect on it. When I looked more closely at it, I found a tag on the back that read "$14," and the ring to be a very strange piece. Mounted on a flat piece of silver was a spiderlike figure, whose body was set with turquoise and coral, making it look a little like an ant. It did fit my finger, but the flat silver piece cut into me, making it very uncomfortable. It was not something I would normally choose to wear, so I was in a quandary. Since every gesture Dawn Boy made held the potential for enormous meaning, I didn't want to disregard this gift, no matter how odd. I put it in a lovely little stoneware bowl on my dresser, which held other small and precious items.

At this time, many things were in flux and change in my life, and one day I was lying in my cabin, on my buffalo robe, attempting to make sense of my experience. My Native American Tarot deck was nearby. Tarot cards are decks of cards used for divining and augury, and are the forerunner of common playing card decks (see appendix 1, page 458). This one is not as well developed as a traditional Tarot deck, but its Native images are useful to stimulate the subconscious. I casually picked up my deck, shuffled through the cards, and drew one. The card was titled "The Stars," and its image was a background of multicolored stars. However, on a web that joined these stars was an enormous spider, who took up most of the space. The message was from the Pima Indian people of the Southwest, and it told the story of the beginning of time. Creator had made the people, but there was no light. The people appealed to Creator for help, and he sent them Grandmother Spider, who helped them fashion a hide shield and throw it into the sky, where it hung as the Sun. Yet, there was still half their day that was not well lighted, so they asked Grandmother's assistance again. This time she wove an iridescent web between Heaven and Earth. Then Creator spewed water over it, and in each place where a droplet hung, a star was formed, and lighted the night for the people. Grandmother Spider's medicine is the weaving together of Heaven and Earth to create enlightenment.

"That's it!" I shouted. "The spider ring makes sense now!" And I dashed to the little bowl to retrieve it. I had been looking for a deeper level of meaning in my overall work, including the Feldenkrais practice.

Now, a new phrase came to mind for that awakening, which was at the core of much that I did: *Embodying Spirit*. "My work is about bringing Spirit alive and awake within us, here on Earth," I thought to myself. "That's in essence what Younger Brother has been talking with me about." Piecing all this together made me very happy, and I spontaneously made a little meditation place, leaning the card of The Stars against a turquoise stoneware chalice that had been given me, in honor of my name, Chalíse. I placed the ring in front of the card, close to a small beautifully flowering tree-like plant. Then I fell asleep on the floor near them, covered with the buffalo robe, and slept soundly.

Sometime around dawn I was awakened by some noise I could not hear once I awoke. Lying there, stretching and coming to full wakefulness, I suddenly remembered the ring and the card, and I turned my head to look at them. And there, with her web woven around and among all four things—the ring, the card, the chalice, and the flowering tree— was an enormous spider, literally bouncing on her web like a trampoline. Her vigorous movement made the tiniest humming noise, and I knew that her dance had awakened me. Once I saw her, she quieted and sat proudly on her creation, an incredible confirmation of my thoughts and Younger Brother's teachings.

I was living in the South at the time, in summer a place of abundant insects. They paraded by the light I kept on at night to observe them. Every single day of that entire season, a new insect appeared—tiny bugs, beetles, flying ants, and moths. All came crawling and flitting through my light for close examination. The beetle's bright colors, the iridescent wings of the tiny fliers, and the intricate, elegant, yet subtle patterns of the moths astounded me and fed my senses. One day, the queen of all the insect family came, looking as though she were dressed for a royal ball. This moth's tiny head and mantle were brilliant white, sparkling under the light like diamonds in the snow. On the collar of what seemed an elegant, full-length cape was a design that looked like poured cranberry juice, deep red at the collar and running into gently faded pinks down the back. The trim on the very bottom was the same sparkling white. Her delicate beauty seemed unreal; I thought of an angel as she stayed and stayed for my enjoyment. The snow queen had come in the summer to grace her family gathering. Her king turned out to be a shiny red and black beetle, the most powerful and beautiful of all the others.

Dawn Boy often questioned me on how much attention I had available to pay. "What will you buy with your attention today, Medicine Eagle?" he would laugh raucously. And I began to understand how truly he spoke: Whatever I paid attention to was what I got. *The amount of presence I brought to any situation was directly proportional to the amount I could receive from it.* I had begun to pay a lot of attention to the insect world. In so doing, I began to see more and more varieties, and began a collection of a certain blue-green iridescent kind of beetle that I found dead on rare occasions. I found a small glass case just for them. The first I found looked like a scarab beetle, its deep green shell outlined in gold, a shimmering deep blue with lighter green underside. Then came one that looked more like an enormous ant. The last one had enormous long legs, the most powerful figure of the three. Just for fun, I added to the case a little box of matches I had found, with that same iridescent design.

When I showed them to Younger Brother, he cackled madly, and asked if I knew who I had in there. I just shook my head, and waited for his explanation. "That's me," he said, pointing to the matches. "And that's my spiritual benefactor, who I call the Apache Kid. And that one's *his* benefactor [whom I had heard called the Nickel Man because he posed as a beggar]. And this one is *his* benefactor, a numinous figure in our lineage's history. You've captured us all." And he went into gales of laughter.

As usual, I didn't know quite what to think about this explanation of his, but I stored it for my left-sided experience to illuminate more fully. Soon I began to understand. On those rare instances when I saw them, the blue/green insects' appearances would signal me. They would draw my attention to something specific, or let me know when my spiritual benefactor was likely to drop in. They always puzzled me by their sudden disappearance, although they seemed to move very slowly. It became clear with repeated experience that they were messengers from that southern lineage of light that descended from the Dawn Star.

Now came one of the richest experiences of my adult life. My friend Jim had taken me on my first real vacation—days and days on the coast of Quintana Roo, a part of the Yucatan area in the panhandle of Mexico near the city of Cancun. We went exploring and swimming in the turquoise waters. Near where we were staying was the ancient Mayan ruin of Tulum, and I loved being among its beautiful stone buildings, perched high on a cliff above the rolling white lace of the aquamarine surf.

On our final day there, I knew I wanted to spend some time with an older Mayan man who was one of the guides. Someone had told me he would give me the "real" story of this place which fascinated me so much. Although I knew little about their culture and history, I thought I remembered that the Mayan civilization followed after that of the Toltecs, and thus must have had access to the Dawn Star lineage. I wanted to talk with him about my assignment to carry the southern teachings to my people in the North.

For the moment, the old man was talking with someone else, so I rested my arms on a partially tumbled wall and waited. Beside me, my friend Jim said, "Look!" There, among the crumbled stones, was a tiny beetle about the size of my little fingernail—iridescent turquoise blue— throwing light around him in a radiant halo several feet wide. I was entranced by the beauty and warmth of that light, and felt immediately in my heart that the Dawn Star himself was calling to me, awakening me in some new way.

Soon the beetle flew away into the morning light, and I had little time to contemplate the experience as my attention returned to the old man, who was just then free. He introduced himself as Juan. He spoke as we walked, and pointed out the significance to his Maya people of this ceremonial site. On a small central building at Tulum, there is an image of a king on his throne—*Kulkulkan,* the Father God. Below him was a representation of Mother Earth, and between them a figure, upside down almost as though birthing, with one hand outstretched toward the Father and the other toward the Mother. This is *Itsa Ma,* the descending god, the one sent from the Father to awaken light and love upon Mother Earth. On each side of the doors beneath *Itsa Ma* are red imprints of his healing hands, dedicated to All Our Relations.

Juan took us behind the buildings, out of general earshot, and sat with us, quietly overlooking the lacey surf. I spoke to him briefly of my intention to reawaken our northern peoples to their connection with the southern lineages; it was a different generation of twisted hairs who could fly here, rather than walk, from the North, yet I felt myself in that same tradition of those who had come to the Sun temples of the South for their learning and initiations.

He thought for a long time. Then, with his shining eyes looking directly into mine, he broke the silence: "In our language the Dawn Star, Jesus, is called *Itsa Ma.* He and Joseph of Arimathea came to be with us and to initiate this site when *Itsa Ma* was thirteen. His energy is still powerfully present here in this place, which is dedicated to Him." I returned Juan's loving gaze, telling him of the beautiful insect who signaled these things a few short minutes ago. My spirit had found another home, and from it I sent gratitude to Dawn Boy far in the North.

The women of these lineages had begun to signal me through the insect world as well. These southern lineages are said in our history to be spiritually descended from the Dawn Star's shaman lines, through the Toltecs, and Sonoran peoples such as the Yaquis and Apaches. I felt strongly connected on the left side with the men of this southern line, but little had come to me from the women. So one day in meditation, I put out a call for the Apache Kid's *nagual* woman, his left-sided spiritual partner, to make herself known to me. And she did, in the blink of an eye! Before me, glaring in an intense, "What do *you* want?" kind of way, was the presence of a heavy, dark woman. She had shining black hair with copper highlights, chopped off at her shoulders, which were enormous. In her body I sensed no fatness although she was very rotund—what spoke there was an immense strength. Her rather flat face indicated perhaps a Yaqui lineage; her simple black peasant dress the same. She was a relatively young woman and very powerful.

Her glaring presence said to me without words, "The women of our line are strong, courageous, fierce, and willing to serve in the highest way. Do not waste time asking us silly questions, or calling us when you want only to stare out of curiosity." With that she was gone, and only the remembered shiny black color of her hair, with its copper iridescent highlights, bespeaking her essence, remained in my mind. I was taken aback by her fierceness, when I had hoped for a friendly visit. Yet I appreciated her message: Mother Earth and all her children are in great danger from mankind's foolish ways. *Anything that is not serving All Our Relations in a high and useful way, is not worthy of attention or energy from a warrior woman. It is a leakage of power.*

Needless to say, I did not soon call her again. But I began to be signaled by numerous shiny black insects with iridescent copper wings—bringing messages from the female line of the Southern Seers. One of the first times this happened I was in New Mexico, and had stopped at the adobe home of some friends outside of Santa Fe. On this breezy day, Caer was outside hanging up clothes and I stood nearby talking with her. I had just gotten off the phone with someone I had hoped to settle with in this area, and my hopes for that relationship and new home had been shattered. The egg of my dreams was broken before it could hatch.

As Caer walked back and forth along the hard, dry ground under the clothesline, I noticed that several times she almost stepped on a beautiful, turquoise bird's egg, and I cautioned her, "Watch out, you're about to step on your little egg." "What egg?" was her reply, and I knew the egg had been meant for me. Just then a very large insect, which looked like a flying ant, landed beside the turquoise egg, her body shining black and her wings iridescent copper. She climbed up on the lovely little egg, and allowed me to pick her up with it. I knew it was a message from the line of powerful southern women that my egg of dream had been replaced; something even more beautiful was to come. I held the egg in the air and the ant-woman flew away to the southwest, leaving my heart grateful behind her.

A numinous dream I had about this time came from the same left-sided place of the Southern Seers. In the dream, I was standing in line at a discount store. Several women were in front of me, and I was thumbing through the glamor and sensationalist magazines as I stood there, rather bored. It was the turn of the little old lady in a scarf right in front of me. As she stepped forward with her few purchases, I was amazed to notice how tiny she was. She had to reach up to place her items and her money on the counter, and she was having a difficult time, fumbling with her change purse and gloves. She took her gloves off and I stared at her hands: they were covered with something almost like fur. I looked at her face, mostly hidden behind the scarf. Her pointed face was covered with that same kind of fuzz, and it struck me, "She isn't human. No wonder she's been having such a dreadful time with this 'foreign' money. I think she's an insect!" Her shiny black eyes glanced up at me as though she knew that I knew, and before I could say anything, she grabbed her little package and scurried out the door.

Hurrying through my purchases, I came running out of the store to catch up with her. I was conscious enough in the dream to realize that she held great power for me. I wanted to talk with her, so I ran to catch her. She allowed me to come up beside her before she stopped. I asked, "Insect Grandmother, what message do you have for me?"

With that she flung off her coat and scarf, as though relieved not to be pretending any longer, opened her wings and flew off, saying, "Follow me."

We were in a parklike area of beautiful grass, under well-trimmed evergreen trees. A path wound through this park and on toward a hill that rose behind it. Sometimes I would lose her in the trees, but I always caught up just in time to see which way she went. At last, I glimpsed her at the hill, crawling into an opening in its steep side. I knew I was to follow, yet when I reached the opening I saw it was only big enough for her. However, by stretching my arms and wiggling I finally managed to push my way inside. When I stood up I saw I was in a cave that seemed to be an enormous crystal geode. Inch-thick and larger spikes of quartz crystal comprised the entire cave. Insect Grandmother stood again on her back legs and indicated other beetles scurrying around the room. Making each word clear, distinct, and emphatic, Grandmother said, "This is a communications room. My people use these crystals to communicate with each other over very long distances."

As she said this, the scene faded, and I awoke, quite clear that I had experienced her and her message in a very real way. She was telling me that there are even more direct ways of using the crystals for communication than the technologies we have invented. And that room of spires was certainly more beautiful than any broadcasting station I have visited! Still to this day, occasionally her soft brown face and gentle eyes are sometimes in the corner of my eye as I look around at a slight noise, or see a soft shadow in the woods.

The Southern Seers' lineages teach us that in order to free ourselves of energy leaks, and thus to gain the energy and attention to open our left side, we must bring order to the confusion of our past experience, clear our past history, and choose our experience in the present moment—the moment of power. When we examine our experience, the present moment is in reality the only time we can act. We cannot act yesterday. We cannot act tomorrow. We can act only in the present. Thus, it is important to bring our full attention and power to every moment as it arises. When we have cleared our past issues as they affect us now, and are not worrying about the future, we have the attention to focus on what we can actually do **now.**

Because human beings live much of their lives caught in old habits and patterns, it is of utmost importance to the spiritual warrior to make sure those patterns are useful and workable: that the "sleep" of habitual behavior is disturbed and we are awakened. In our modern world, for example, this kind of deep work is experienced in therapy by adult children of alcoholics and dysfunctional families. They are helped to see that the patterns set in their childhood are still active. They are then taught how to identify these patterns in their everyday experience, and how to discover new ways of being that are much healthier and happier. At best, many experience a releasing of past history.

Dawn Boy sprang a powerful tool on me unexpectedly one day—in his usual pattern. We were making a simple offering of tobacco, and I watched as he broke a cigarette into four parts and offered them to the Four Quadrants. Something in me must have jerked at the use of a cigarette, for he turned to me and said, "I don't like your attitude about tobacco!"

I was surprised, and stammered something about not knowing what he meant. He looked at me with disgust, and said, "I will teach you how to figure it out." And he taught me the Recapitulation exercise you will find on page 252, and instructed me to continue it for five minutes a night for a hundred nights.

As I began this practice of gathering all my memories around tobacco, starting with the earliest one I could retrieve each night, I went further and further back. I found myself remembering very early child-hood—being in my dad's arms while he had a cigarette hanging out of his mouth. As I inventoried my childhood, I realized that the majority of my experiences with tobacco were of what I call the "dirty ashtray" kind—the messiness, the awful smell, the nauseated feeling I'd get when my mom asked me to light her a cigarette while she was driving in our old lighter-less car. I began to sweep those childhood years into my hand in just a few seconds, understanding that my attitude toward tobacco in those years had been a very bad one.

As I followed the string of memories into my older years, I recalled starting to understand tobacco as sacred. As I saw myself watching the filling and smoking of the sacred pipe, seeing offerings being made, rolling tobacco in corn husks for the beginning prayer-cigarette at peyote meetings, and learning about tobacco's medicine of unity and oneness, I could see how a different attitude had begun to form in me. I kept sweeping all those memories up in my hand, and now had a "ball" there that seemed very real and substantial. I had pulled out of all my myriad past memories all those related to tobacco, and I'd ordered them chronologically. "Get every one of those wispy memories, every trail of smoke, every ash," Dawn Boy would urge me in his guise as Cackling Crow, teasing me about my "dirty ashtrays" attitude.

At the end of the hundred days, he instructed me to hold that ball of memories in my left hand while I assessed my attitude toward tobacco. And I knew exactly what attitude held the balance in my mind and heart, and I knew exactly how it had come about. The heavy imprint of the dirty ashtrays of my childhood had continued to hold sway over the attitude of sacredness I had learned in later years! Even though, by now, I wasn't surprised by this, I was still chagrined. No wonder Dawn Boy hadn't liked my attitude.

"Now that you have that full string of memories gathered into a solid ball," said Dawn Boy, "now that you know what your experience has been and how it has formed your attitude, I want you to wind up and throw that ball far away from yourself. Then make the act of a warrior, and choose what your attitude toward tobacco will be. Cast away past history and choose in this moment of power." And I did. I threw that ball far away from me, and chose an attitude of reverence toward this very sacred plant. The recapitulation was complete.

Later, Dawn Boy took me by surprise in a situation of intense mystery, and challenged me again: "I don't like your attitude about the unknown." Once more I was taken aback, but I immediately began a recapitulation of my experience of the unknown. What came out in the long run was that although I'd had many amazing, wonder-filled, light-filled experiences of angelic beings and loving guides who came to me from the unknown, my primary experience of the unknown had also originated in my very early childhood.

The predominant unknown came when my daily routine erupted in some sort of family craziness and disharmony. And this was the attitude I still carried—that pattern of deep imbalance and fear set so long ago. As I did the recapitulation exercise for a hundred nights, I inventoried my experience of the unknown. Stringing the memories together chronologically, I rolled them all in one ball, assessed my total attitude, and then threw away my past history in favor of choosing my attitude in the moment. I now carry an open and curious attitude toward the unknown, allowing much more room in my life for what is unusual, extraordinary, and mysterious.

"Much better," Cackling Crow agreed.

RECAPITULATION

1. Choose an issue in your life that is of concern to you at the moment. It could be a thing, such as tobacco; a person—mothers and fathers are great to begin with; an emotion, such as loss; or an old pattern, such as greediness. Then follow Dawn Boy's instructions to me.

2. Beginning tonight, take five minutes before you go to sleep and go back in your mind to the very earliest memory you have of the issue you've chosen to work with.

3. Spend the next few minutes coming forward in time from that point, identifying each memory connected to this issue, and "gathering them" in your left hand.

4. Go to sleep.

5. Do this for one hundred consecutive nights!

6. You may find, as I did, that you will slip up a night or two here and there. Don't let that discourage you. Build your will by keeping up the process until your total is a hundred nights.

7. Each night go back as far as you can, to the earliest memory, and begin there, coming forward. It is very likely that this stimulation of your attention will help you remember further and further back. So always begin with the earliest memory and come forward. You will gradually collapse years of experience into a few short minutes.

8. As you go through the process, sweep your left hand through the air, gathering each memory and closing it into a fist, as though you were making it into a solid ball. Gather these memories and string them together like beads—get them in hand. This physical aspect of the process is one of the most powerful parts and helps make it real in this daily physical world, not just in your inner world.

9. When you have finished the hundred nights, hold that imaginary ball in your hand and assess your current attitude toward your issue. Take a sincere look at your attitude and exactly how it came to be.

10. Next, take that full string of memories that you have gathered into a solid ball in your left hand and put it in your right hand. Heft that ball of memories in your right hand—get the feel of it, the weight of it. I sometimes use a rock to signify my ball of memories.

11. And now, throw that ball of memories as far away from you as you can possibly hurl it! Release it completely.

12. After you've thrown away the old patterns surrounding the issue you've been working on, take some time to carefully choose your new attitude, one that will empower you and open your experience rather than limit and debilitate you.

13. Although this was not a part of what my benefactor Dawn Boy suggested, I often create a ceremony to mark this turning point. I announce my new attitude to the world, perhaps even creating a talisman of some kind to commemorate this moment. You may do this also, if it works for you.

The Southern Seers often spend years in recapitulation, working with every person in their life as well as every belief, issue, and concern. This not only clears personal history, it also builds an incredible will, as you will find when you begin this seemingly simple practice.

This exercise points to the power of our attention. Whatever we attend to fully, we can gain mastery in. This one technique—recapitulation—if practiced exactly, can transform your life, enhance your personal power, and build a wide pathway to your left side.

Again and again, in myriad ways, Dawn Boy dropped into my life, and then mysteriously disappeared. Each time he cross-examined me on my expenditures of attention and energy. Was I being wasteful? Was I leaking power? "Are you leaving space for the Unknown, the Great Mystery to enter—or are you all booked up?" he asked one day, cackling. "Are you paying attention to the movement of Spirit in the world? Are you aligning with your own renegade spiritual hoop to empower all our teachings?" (This is how he referred to me and many other non-traditional Native teachers on the circuit. He felt we should be working together to increase the power of our work.)

What was I offering women of spiritual intent? Did I know what was happening in the Christ-inspired cactus plant churches of South America? with Don Eduardo and others? Did I know that in Brazil there was an enormous movement of faith healing? Why did it receive no attention from the American media, which was itself continuing to focus on what pig's heart or plastic tubing could be transplanted into what American body? Was Peyote moving me into spiritual action, and through me, moving others? Did I remember myself as one with the lines of light from ancient times? Was I, too, singing the Flowersong of the southern lineages?

These probing questions continue to expand my awareness of the possibilities for my own work in alignment with Spirit. To this day, Dawn Boy's left-sided presence continues to open me to the Great Mystery moving in my life. His knowledge of healthful birthing practices and women's ways are a continual amazement to me, and a blossoming part of my teaching. His displays of power and intelligence, and the unrolling of his spirit in the world, are a guiding force in the life of my spirit and in my sharing with others.

I would like to share with you a Flowersong expressed in his words to me:

PSALM TO MOTHER

Sing to mother!
   Shout and raise up your voices to the sky!
All peoples, turn your hearts to your salvation.
   See mother's womb give birth to peace;
Her groans and pains a wedding song
   Of mankind to the holy spirit bride.

Sing to mother, all the earth!
The island peoples and coastland peoples
Netting her bounty of fish
Even as her saints have netted men
In her spirit oceans.

Honor to mother; rejoice all the earth!
Peoples of the valleys and of the plains;
Bounties of grain and fruit, nuts and flocks;
A feast in all seasons comes upon man
like flowers on the steps of spring.

With rains brought in on mother's winds
Seeds produce bounty like her very breasts.
Mankind's spirit grows in her earth
Mankind's dances flower on her harmonies
Mankind's dreams fall from her skies.
Rejoice and celebrate—jubilation!
All peoples near to far, great to small.
Mother's blessings surround us all!

Sing, sing to Mother!

CHAPTER THIRTEEN

A CRYSTAL AMONG THEM

"You're a crystal healer; don't you know that?"
Mad Bear asked gruffly.

Our challenge is not to get lost in objects outside ourselves, but to use
them as reminders to explore and expand our knowledge of what
Spirit gave us that we may not yet have developed.

Crystals have been coming to me for a long time. My old friend Lalo and I bought one of the first large ones I ever used for healing and shamanic work when we journeyed through the Southwest, stopping in Taos to shop. It was a very clear piece about four by one by two inches. When we arrived home, I set to work with it, although I had very little knowledge of the use of crystals. Lalo's back was hurting him, and I felt it would be good to hold the large crystal in my hand while I worked with him, using some of Feldenkrais's gentle movements. It fit perfectly into my right hand. After working this way for a while, I had a strong urge to touch my forefinger to each of two different moles or discolorations on his back. When I did this, a tiny blue lightning flash cracked and rippled between the two, and I almost dropped the crystal in surprise. He said, "Did you just pop my back? Something feels different!"

That powerful experience led me to learn something further about crystals. They have the capacity to gather light and pulse it out as pieso-electric energy, which is electricity generated in response to pressure. My interest was primarily in using them to magnify the energy in ceremonial circles, but I respected them greatly beyond their utility (although it was clear to me that I consciously knew very little about them).

I had heard from my friend Dhyani Ywahoo, a Cherokee teacher and healer, about how her traditional grandparents had trained her in their way, and I thought how fortunate she was to have someone pass those wonderful teachings on to her. She told us that when she was tiny she was given her own crystal and told that it was a conscious being. It was her friend, and she could grow to know its voice if she listened carefully. Her crystal became one of her favorite companions; she carried it with her daily. Then one day, it was missing, gone, nowhere to be found. She searched and searched, and finally went sadly to her grandparents. They said (knowing from observation that she was ready for the test), "We have hidden it in the woods. You will be able to find it, because it is lonesome for you, and will be calling out to you. Since you know its voice, it will be easy for you." And she did find it by following its voice. What a joy it would have been to learn these things as a child!

The next crystal I received was a beautiful one from a man whose friends described him as the most peaceful man they knew. I met him only briefly at a gathering about wild animals in film, where he represented Greenpeace and that organization's efforts at saving many species from extinction. Michael handed the crystal to me, saying simply, "I know this is yours."

And I loved it. Its squat little being sat jauntily like a frog ready to hop, and the sunlight created rainbow after rainbow in refractions through its faulting. Much to my surprise, the moment I thought of it as a little frog, I could hear its happy, chirping, froglike voice—like tree frogs chorusing. Little Frog was the first crystal whose voice I heard, and it led me to some new experiences with other crystals I already carried. Lalo had finally given me that first, big clear crystal he had bought with me in Taos—realizing, like Michael, that it belonged with me. I used it on the altar I created in all my group ceremonies, but never actively.

One day, not long after hearing Little Frog's voice, I picked up that big crystal, which was absolutely clear—except for one, tiny, flat rectangular faulting inside. I studied and studied the little door within it, and suddenly I was pulled through that door, and out in vision through a tunnel—a soft moleskin-gray lined tunnel—with brilliant light shining at the end. In meditation after meditation since, I have used this door to travel through the tunnel to the left side, to receive teachings and information.

One day as I sat near the big crystal, I heard its voice. Or rather, it was like not-hearing its voice—it was much like the enormous, echoing silence of a deep canyon as you stand on the rim; a "whoooooooooooaoooo" sound of open air and open space—the sound of an open door, of something that is not there! I was joyful at hearing another voice from the stone people; my inner ear was improving. From then on, the "Door" took an active role. I passed it around our circles so each person could *see* the door, and then led them in meditation through that door and into the shamanic experience of leaving behind their body—and all they recognized as their daily selves—to experience the eternal, wise part of themselves. Many people "walked" through that door into incredible journeys.

These few, remarkable experiences of *hearing* were precious to me, yet when I spent an evening in Tucson, Arizona, with one of the finest modern Native American healers, Mad Bear Anderson, I was aware how little I knew. Mad Bear had heard a lot about me, yet when I came in, he took one look at my blue eyes and started to run me through the standard questions the old ones ask—to check my "Native credentials." He had expected me to be making a presentation that would give him time to "check me out." But I had come in tired from teaching an intense two-day workshop. In fact, I had come because I thought he was going to be talking.

Sitting beside me in his Hawaiian flowered shirt, he cocked his head and glared at me, until I answered his questions. I did okay at first, it seemed, until he asked me, "What kind of a healer are you?" Stumbling over my words, I said I did not experience myself as a healer, but as a teacher, a map-maker. This aggravated him and he raised his voice, waving away my lame explanations with an impatient gesture. "What kind of healer are you?"

I was tired, I didn't feel like being grilled, I didn't have anything to say, and shook my head in a gesture of resignation. He said again, forcefully, "What kind of healer are you? Do you heal with tobacco, with cedar, with prayer, with crystals, by laying on your hands or what?" Ah, now there was something that might satisfy him—laying on of hands. I said that I did in fact do a kind of body work where I worked on people with my hands—perhaps that's what he meant.

This did not mollify him, it only seemed to aggravate him more. He fairly burst out, "You're a *crystal* healer. Don't you know that?" Taken aback, I explained that I certainly didn't experience myself that way; or that I didn't understand what he meant, as my Northern Plains people had not used crystals in any ceremony I had seen, and I certainly hadn't been trained in their use. Disgusted, he turned to share with the general group some stories of the powerful healing crystal he wore on a thong around his neck. Just before leaving, Mad Bear looked at me carefully once more, and said, "A small healing crystal will be coming your way soon. Use it well."

Not long after that my friend, Susan Savell, called me from New York, breathless. "I just saw an enormous healing crystal, and I know it's yours!" she cried. I had no idea exactly what "an enormous healing crystal" meant to her, and so I didn't know quite what to think about it and asked her to tell me more. She said that she and her friend Meredith had been driving near Meredith's home in Maine. They stopped along the road at a gem and lapidary shop that occupied part of an old building, and went in. Meredith had an extensive knowledge of stones and crystals, and Susan was interested in their healing qualities; they both looked forward to stepping through an unknown door to the stone people.

Even with their interest and knowledge, they were young and naive compared to the old man sitting behind the counter. As they visited with him, asking him questions, picking up and commenting on many things, he told them that he had loved stones, particularly crystals, all his life, and that he had been in the business for fifty years. Like many of the old-timers who know and love the crystal people, he was amused by the last decade's sudden rush of "new-age" interest, especially when these neophytes acted like they, or perhaps some new guru, had discovered or even invented crystals and the knowledge of their medicine powers. He enjoyed reminiscing with these deeply interested, gracious women, for in his out-of-the-way spot he had few visitors to spend long hours with, talking knowledgeably of crystals.

As Susan and Meredith were leaving, the old man said, "Before you go I want to show you some things. Over the years I have kept and displayed for others' enjoyment, as well as my own, some of the finest of the crystals that have come through my hands." He took them to an old glass case, the finely grained beauty of its wood shining through the dust. As he opened the case with a key from around his neck, the two women scanned its four shelves. One thing *only* stood out among the many wonderful pieces there.

He showed them this one, and that one, until finally, unable to keep quiet any longer, they asked to see the large, amazingly clear quartz crystal that had caught their attention, and which occupied the middle thirteen inches of the top shelf. He grinned, as though he had been teasing them by showing them the other beautiful, rare objects first— almost testing them. Proudly, he reached in with both hands to cup the double quartz terminations, saying, "This is my favorite," and lifted the marvelous crystal out of the case. Lying on its side on a counter in front of them, the most prominent thing about the crystal—what jumped out toward them from its clear depths—were the Arabic-looking letters, some separate, and several blended together in a sort of script.

"How did they get in there?!" Susan and Meredith asked at once.

"Look at it," he gestured, an open invitation to examine it more closely. Meredith picked it up and turned it around. The letters looked like they might have been carved into the back of this long, spear-like gem. They were not! They were inside, seemingly about two-thirds of the way through. When she turned it point-up and stood it up, the mysterious writing looked Chinese! It seemed meant to stand in this position—a spire, a stela, expressing to all who would *look* a certain, ancient message. At the very bottom, contained mostly within the termination, there was a miniature ice field, blown over by small, swirling clouds of tiny snow crystals, and above, the silvery mountain peaks of the inner fault structure. And always, the mystical letters, calling one's attention, again and again.

"Wow!" Susan exclaimed. "We know someone who would love this. Her rainbow medicine is a way of wholeness, of making whole and holy, of the healing brought by oneness. These tiny rainbows that glint from within remind me of her!" Both of them joined in an excited chatter. He let them play with that idea until they settled down a bit, and then said to them gently, "It's not for sale. None of the things in this case are."

"Oh, yes, you had said so," Meredith replied, a little embarrassed. "We just got so excited we forgot," Susan said apologetically. "But we're going to tell Brooke about this anyway."

"Yes, I hope you do," the fine old man replied. "She will enjoy hearing about it."

Susan called me as soon as they got home that weekend, and I could sense by their excitement that this crystal was something special. "Let's see if Spirit says it belongs to me," I said. "This is evidently a project that will take time. Stay in touch with me about it if you visit there again."

Meredith was in school in Boston, and Susan busy with a double career as a minister and musician in New York City, so they were able to go to Meredith's country home only on school vacations and infrequent family visits. Each time, however, they went back to visit the old man. One day when the two young women walked in, there, instead of the old man, were two older women, lilac-haired, and seeming unsure of themselves.

"Hi!" Meredith and Susan greeted them, happy to be in this magical place again. "You've been here before?" one of the women queried. "Yes, we have often visited with the gentleman who owns this place. He's always been here before. Where is Mr. Carlson?" The women were very solemn. The taller one said formally, "I'm his wife, Mrs. Carlson, and I'm taking care of his shop. He's gone. He died suddenly a few weeks ago."

"Oh, I'm very sorry," the young women gasped, and asked how it had happened. In sharing with them the details, Mrs. Carlson revealed that she knew nothing about his work or the crystals. She had been a typical wife of that day, staying home with their family and seldom venturing into "the business," as she called it. Meredith and Susan had fun regaling the older women with crystal stories and bits of information about their uses, especially in healing. Mrs. Carlson and her friend were round-eyed with wonder—they had never heard of such things! "That's why we would like to buy this crystal for our friend, Brooke," they said, pointing to the crystal sword. "She works with that sort of thing."

On the mention of selling, the older woman shook her head. "Those in that special case are his treasures—or were his treasures. And I don't think I should sell them now, even though he is gone. I haven't had time to think of what to do with all this," she said.

Meredith and Susan could see in her eyes how loving this old couple were after so many years, and assured her that they understood. "When you've had time to think it over, if you ever decide to let someone take it for healing work, please let us know. Call us anytime." Having received some helpful information from the younger women about the burden of her husband's material things, Mrs. Carlson looked a little relieved. She promised that if she ever sold the big crystal, Brooke could surely have it. They left reassured, and surprised me with a phone call, informing me about the new status of the crystal.

Several more months passed swiftly, then Susan called again, very excited. "Mrs. Carlson wrote us a note and told us we could get the big crystal for you! She said she decided that those things should all go to someone who would enjoy them as much as Mr. Carlson had, and she wanted Brooke to have this for her work. Yippee!" Susan was blissful. And though I still did not share her experience because I had not yet seen this "remarkable" crystal, I was really pleased, and asked when they would pick it up. "When we get up there next time—I'm not sure when that will be," was her reply.

When I hadn't heard from them for another month, I began to wonder. Then, late one afternoon, Susan called. "We almost lost it!" she exclaimed, and proceeded to tell me the whole, fascinating story of their trip to buy my crystal. Meredith was in school and stressed with end-of-term papers and studying. Susan had been busy with her ministry

and her music—practicing, and playing the New York clubs at the end
of her working day. They knew Mrs. Carlson was a woman of her word,
and since they were very busy, they kept putting off going all the way
to Maine. They didn't feel the need to call: they knew she had promised.

But at the fatigued end of a long drive, as they debated whether to
go that evening or get up and go the next morning after resting,
something pulled them to get their business done before going to visit
the family. They drove to the shop, and as they walked through the
door, Mrs. Carlson was just about to lock up. She had recognized them
getting out of their car, and this customarily formal woman embraced
them, heaving an enormous sigh and exclaiming again and again, "I'm
so glad you're here! I'm so glad you're here."

"What is it, Mrs. Carlson?" they asked, noticing her obvious agitation. "What's happened?"

"Tomorrow morning at nine A.M., when the shop opens, I would
have sold your crystal! I hadn't heard from you, and I couldn't be sure
you were coming. Oh! I'm so *enormously* relieved that you came tonight.
Thank you, thank you. I would have felt dreadful had you come after
I sold it to that persistent young man."

"Tell us all about it," said Meredith and Susan, as Mrs. Carlson
immediately began to write out the sales slip. The wonderful old woman
told them the story—about a young man who had come through town
and stopped in the shop two weeks before. He was a pleasant and
knowledgeable young fellow, and she had enjoyed talking with him.

"Up until the time he saw the crystal sword, that is," she said,
shaking her head.

He was most persistent about buying it. He had stayed in the shop
and persisted, hoping to wear her down. But no, she had promised it to
someone else, and that was that. The young fellow left, saying he would
come back. And he did! Within a few days he was back, saying he'd
booked a motel to stay a while. He had arrived on Monday, and having
nothing much else to do, had spent most of his week in her shop,
frequently urging her to sell the crystal, saying that these other people
were obviously not interested since they hadn't responded in so many
weeks.

This was Friday night; as he had to leave the next morning, Mrs.
Carlson had finally relented. "I'm closing the shop, you must realize,"
she told the ladies. "Yet you know, the only reason I did relent was
because he was buying it for an Indian person to use in medicine ways
as well. It was not for him. He, like you, wanted to buy it for someone
else to use in a good way. He, like you two, was very sure it was right
for his teacher, a man named Chuck Storm."

Meredith and Susan just grinned, and thanked her for keeping her promise to them. "We knew in our hearts that this was for Brooke, and she will get it." Everyone was visibly relieved. The older woman's silver hair glinted lilac in the sun's last rays. "Now I've finished his work," she said, and wished them farewell.

Many more months passed before I was to hold that crystal sword in my arms. We didn't feel right about sending the crystal through the U.S. mail or UPS. Besides, they wanted to be in its presence themselves for a while. Susan and Meredith knew we should pass the crystal with ceremony, eye to eye. They were, of course, right, and I knew I'd be in New England that next summer. "It will rest safe on my altar," Susan said, and I knew it would.

When I finally arrived in New York, with my sister Ginger in her little Honda car, it was wonderful to see Susan and to meet Meredith, who had come down from Boston for the occasion. We went to concerts and had a great time on the town. We reserved Sunday for the ceremony, and all looked forward to it as the big event of the visit. Excitement rippling the air, we stepped into Susan's bedroom, where she had laid the crystal sword out beside a huge cluster of amethyst: Susan said they'd realized that the crystal sword's absence would leave such a hole in the energy there that they'd tried to replace it with the large amethyst.

"Ahhhhhh!" Ginger and I drew in our breath in unison, amazed when we saw it! The double-terminated quartz was truly magnificent, and looked even larger than I had imagined. With Ginger sitting between us in front of the crystal beauty, Susan began the ceremony. After smudging us and the crystals, she began to speak about how wonderful her experience had been while in the presence of the crystal. Her life had begun to move very rapidly; everything had intensified. She laughed, and admitted that if she hadn't already promised it to me, she would have kept it herself—we could all easily understand that.

Then she took it in her arms for one last time, asked blessings on all of us, and handed it to Ginger, as the intermediary. Ginger flushed as its weight pulled her arms down more than she'd anticipated, and took a few moments getting accustomed to handling it. She expressed her honor at being in this place in the gifting cycle, and said a beautiful prayer. Then she handed it to me—the crystal sword had come home.

Most of what I shared was appreciation, and I spoke a prayer whose original form had come from avatar Meher Baba, a remarkable East Indian guru whose work I had been reading. *"Grandfather Great Spirit, I come to you not asking for anything, but with open arms to receive your blessings."* The crystal coming to me was a confirmation of that trusting relationship with Spirit. I wanted to express that attitude of receptive gratitude again.

The ceremony over, my crystal packed carefully away in a cosmetic travel-case I had brought, we went out to dinner to celebrate before we left town. We would leave directly from there, so we put our suitcases in the car, and parked it in front of the restaurant. I had a moment's hesitation, as we got out of the car and locked it, about leaving things in a car on a New York street, but couldn't think what else to do. Susan and Meredith arrived, pulling my attention away, and we left the car.

If you've ever lived in New York, you already know the rest of the story. When we came out, the window had been broken and the car robbed. I could hardly believe it—although we didn't have much with us, there were some precious things in those few bags. Then I remembered the crystal! Had I been foolish enough to lose something that precious before I'd even had a chance to experience it?

I looked deep in the darkened backseat, and only one thing was left—the little cosmetic case, tucked safely down behind the seat. I grabbed it and checked—the crystal was safe! As I'd prayed to come with open arms to receive Spirit's gifts—this enormous, magnifying crystal—now my arms were certainly bare and open, except for the crystal sword they cradled.

On the way home, freezing in the windowless car, Ginger and I looked at each other, into the backseat at the crystal, and said, almost in unison, "Do you think we should throw it out? Maybe it's more than we bargained for!" Then we laughed and laughed, knowing that we magnified every action, thought, and belief that we expressed or experienced in the presence of this sword of light.

The big crystal traveled with me, shining its clearing light and its magnification on all those who came in contact with it. I taught simple evening workshops to help students clarify what they wanted, and then asked them to make a prayer through the crystal sword to Spirit, for whatever they needed and wanted. The latter part took only a few minutes; the beginning of the night was spent in getting *absolutely* clear about how and what to ask because, as I told them from my experience, *"You will get what you ask for:* be very clear when you ask, that you are ready for it."

My own words seemed like an echo of those words I had heard years before when I entered the Sacred Buffalo Lodge: "You stand in front of truth; the truth will return to you." It was gratifying to get postcards long after such workshops, which in essence said, "You were right; I got it!"—usually followed by either, "Thank you so much for your help," or "Next time I'll know better!"

I often remembered Mad Bear Anderson's telling me "a small healing crystal" would come my way soon. Since this was the one that had come, I assumed it was the one he meant, and as I carried its seven pounds through airport after airport, and miles and miles across the country until my medicine bag marked deep lines in my shoulders, I sent up a thought to Mad Bear: "If this is a little crystal, I hope you have to carry a big one in your medicine bag!" Mad Bear left this Earth not long after that, a loss for us all, especially those who could have benefited from his great knowledge and healing ability.

Crystals have increasingly swarmed into my life, sometimes by the dozens, tiny ones gifted to me at gatherings and seminars. My challenge with each of them is to use it well, or to pass each on to someone else with whom it really *belongs*. I appreciate the crystal experts who assign a different energy and usefulness to each different kind of stone—but working with crystals in such an applied manner has never become a calling for me.

This has puzzled me, because of what Mad Bear had said. I considered him very wise, if a bit gruff, and handled his information to me as if it were a gem to be polished. I mulled it over and over in my mind, "Crystal healer, crystal healer," always carrying the image of those who used crystals in external healings.

I kept my ears open about crystals, and learned one fascinating fact: crystals have a similar energy pattern to water, and since each person is made up largely of water, the energy of the human body is crystalline, as well. In a flash, I put this information together with that from Mad Bear, and came to understand that *it is not the crystal stones themselves with which I am a healer—it is my own crystalline nature.* And I remembered experiences—some very painful—that this way of seeing myself would explain.

In the presence of Sand Crabs and the Sacred Lodge, my awareness and innocence had magnified and catalyzed something hidden or ignored. It had brought his debauchery to the front for all to see its effects, and lost him the keeping of the Lodge. And Black Hand, too, had made a clear display of who she was and what her deep intention was, and thus had felt the heavy consequences of her actions magnified. Perhaps my own crystal energy had added to the powers held by the Sacred Lodge and Grandma Rosie.

Another incident came to mind, too, where another elder had been shown—through his actions in a difficult situation involving me—to be a very deep and committed spiritual person. Anger generated among reservation families by the earlier incidents involving the Sacred Lodge fueled the fire of my being from an enemy tribe; there was animosity toward me in certain circles because of my involvement with their most sacred place. Some of these people began to put pressure on Strongly Bears the Spirit, the new Lodge keeper, not to allow me, or anyone else they didn't like, to be blessed in the Lodge. The support money that enabled this keeper to feed his family while being at the Lodge every day to help the people and care for the Sacred Bundle now came from the government Bureau of Indian Affairs. In the old days, people would have supported him directly, but things had changed to dependency on BIA money. The people who were angry with me had power and influence in the BIA system, and they had threatened to cut off Strongly Bears the Spirit from financial support. It was shocking to this fine man that anyone would stoop to such dirty politics—it hurt his heart. Yet he stood firm in his conviction, and said, "This Lodge is in my keeping. Spirit chooses those who come to this lodge. Truth judges them, not me. This is the way it has always been. You cannot tell me who will enter this Lodge, Spirit will."

They did cut off his support, and his family suffered. But he would not give in to spiritual blackmail. The people who knew and loved him for his strong spirit, and who supported the true function of the Lodge, gathered around him and helped him through that time. I did not learn of this until I came home for a visit one time, and went to the Lodge to be blessed.

Strongly Bears the Spirit asked me and my family to come outside with him to talk first, and he kindly but firmly asked me about the accusations against me. I answered as truly and clearly as I could. When we had finished, he sat for a long while deliberating within himself, and then he took me to the Sacred Lodge for a blessing. I know that I again magnified and catalyzed a situation in my heart and mind in which this beautiful man's spirit shone like a light for his people. He stood in the face not only of ridicule, but of his family's going hungry, and did what Spirit asked him to do. I was sorry for the pain that had been caused, but very proud of this fine man who stood his ground when the going got rough. I was profoundly grateful.

More and more, I began to see myself as a crystal among my students and my elders. That crystalline energy not only pressed me to grow by leaps and bounds, it catalyzed and magnified the key issues in people's lives around me, too, without any conscious effort on my part. I began to understand that I am the crystal, and the healing simply takes place. I would not have chosen this quality—it has put me in situations of extreme stress, when I would rather have been nurtured and taught gently. And it has made it so for others, too, as one woman recently put it beautifully in a letter: "Sometimes I am happy to have found you and

I adopt you as a model for my Higher Self. But many other times my
life would be much more convenient without you!"

Once I was asked to speak at a Crystal Congress that my old friend Lalo
and others were putting on, where a wide variety of points of view
concerning crystals and their usefulness was represented—scientists, jew-
elers, healers, and others all come together. I was asked to represent a
Native point of view about crystals during the opening talks. So in preparation, I asked the crystals what they would like to have me express for
them.

They replied that two things were of utmost importance. First, people
must know that crystals are torn away from their natural home and from
their cluster families so that we might have them. Many of the means used
to mine them are violent and shattering. Thus, when a crystal comes to us,
it is vitally important that we do a healing ceremony, to ease the distress
of the crystal. And that we do a ceremony of adoption as well, so the
crystal is once more part of a family.

Secondly, remembering that these crystals have made enormous sacrifice in order for us to have them, we must pledge that we will use them
in service of All Our Relations. Too often, the crystals reminded me, people
have them for show, or to be groovy, or to simply decorate themselves with
"jewels." The crystals objected mightily to this kind of use—after all they
have gone through, and considering what they are capable of.

Our elders tell us that when Earth was first formed, the primary
"building material" was crystal formed in struts, around which all other
materials could then gather. This makes total sense to me: when I think of
taking what is non-material, the ethers, if you will, and making of them a
solid mass, crystal seems the obvious form that would result. Thus crystal
is ancient, carrying the wisdom of the ages of Earth within its experience,
and very powerful in its light-gathering abilities. Certain crystals are
thought to have been used in Atlantis and other highly developed civilizations to record information.

I am told that there are sixteen specific crystal skulls that were imprinted with information by sages in the East, or perhaps these too go all
the way back to Atlantis. While each crystal skull carries within itself
enormous quantities of powerful information, if all sixteen can ever be
peacefully gathered in one circle, another incredible level of knowledge
will be released. However, because of selfishness, conflict, and disbelief,
this has not happened—the wishes of the crystals are not being honored.

NURTURING OUR CRYSTALS

If you possess crystals, or other stones and gems, choose one to begin working with.

1. Take the crystal or stone in your hand, or lie down with it resting upon your heart, and let it take you back to its place of origin, into the sweet Earth where it was very likely connected in cluster.

Imagine yourself taking it away from that cluster with gentleness and gratitude, wrapping it in something soft and beautiful like deerskin, silk or red velvet. Crystals seem to love such materials, and I would suggest wrapping each of your crystals in something like this when storing and carrying them.

Leave a gift of gratefulness and nurturing for its family. This can be done in your meditation, and is also excellent to do in reality. If you are near where the crystal came from, go there to offer tobacco and corn-meal. If not, stand outside on the land and simply offer it to Mother Earth and the crystal people within the Earth.

2. Return your attention to the crystal you are holding.

Now focus your awareness totally on the crystal, first simply feeling it as it touches your body.

▶ What impressions do you receive?

▶ What sense of its function and usefulness do you receive?

▶ Is it for healing? Does it contain stored information? Is it a magnifier of energy?

▶ Will it clean the vibrations of things it rests among?

When you have opened to your crystal as much as you can in this fashion, ask it what would help it heal the wound of its breaking from its crystal family, what would make it feel good.

▶ In this process I have been told such things as: "Put me in the Earth for four days. Put a pack of mud on my damaged end. Put me with other crystals overnight. Bathe me in salt water for cleansing."

▶ Whether or not you receive exact instructions, follow your intuition. From a very loving place, do something for your crystal that feels to you to be healing and nurturing for it.

3. Create a simple ceremony in which you welcome this crystal as a beloved member of your family.

Talk about how you will use the crystal.

Renew your pledge to continue using it in a good way, a way that serves the circle of Earth's family.

4. If there are crystals for which you have no immediate use, wrap them in sage and bury them in the ground. This acts as a cleansing, and also renews them, giving them much more comfort than being thrown in a drawer somewhere and forgotten.

CLEANING YOUR CRYSTAL

There are many ways to clean your crystals, including the following:

1. Bury your crystals in the ground, wrapped in fragrant herbs, such as sage, for one to four days.

2. Soak them in a saline solution of sea salt and water from one to four days. I prefer to leave them outside in the light of Father Sun and Grandmother Moon during this process.

3. Rest them in a protected place on the Earth where they will receive the light—again for one to four days.

4. Use the cleaning sound of Tibetan bells or other gongs or bells used for sacred purposes. Continue the sounding until your perception is that the crystal is clear, whether this takes five minutes or an hour.

5. You can also use your intention and your breath. Hold a single crystal in front of you in both hands. With the intention and image of clarity in your mind, bring the crystal to your heart, drawing in your breath at the same time. Then expel your breath explosively over the crystal as you bring it in front of you again. Do this three times.

6. The mineral, labradorite, is purported to have clearing properties that act on other crystals when it touches them. You can try this as well.

FILLING YOUR CRYSTAL WITH INTENTION

You can program an intention into your crystal and have its electrical energy continually pulsing out that intention. For instance, you could program it for something general like "global peace," or for something personal like "healing my family" or "healing my broken leg." You can also set a one-time intention into your crystal, such as "keep me safe on this trip." Set the crystal for whatever energy you want to have steadily supported and magnified in the world.

1. Use any one of the clearing techniques above, or any others that work for you.

2. Perform clearing step five above, and on the third out-breath speak aloud your intention while you also symbolically image the intention in your mind.

Increase your awareness of your crystals and of how you care for them. Let this lesson carry over to other objects you possess. Respecting the life of Spirit in each and every thing is vital to a way of life that will carry us into the future. So begin to think of yourself as being in partnership with, rather than in possession of, peoples from other kingdoms of life.

Begin to own yourself as crystalline energy. Remember your crystals' qualities of clarity and magnification of energy, and their ability to gather light and send it on to others. Know that you possess a similar structure, and begin to accept yourself as having similar energies and abilities, so that rather than using things outside yourself to "gain power," you develop within yourself the miraculous abilities given you by Creator.

The lesson of crystals is a lesson for us all in owning and developing the abilities we possess within ourselves. It echoes the teaching of White Buffalo Calf Pipe Woman as she urges us to claim our own holiness, to awaken the limitless Spirit that lives within each of us, just as it lives in the stone people and in All Our Relations. Sometimes I think we have invented such things as computers with their amazing abilities in order to remind ourselves that our brain is an even finer tool. Our challenge is to not get lost in objects outside ourselves, but to use them as reminders to explore and expand our knowledge of what Spirit gave us that we may not yet have developed. We can then begin to see ourselves as the hologram I believe we are. Not only the challenges, but the joys and powers of life, can be owned in a good way, as we come to know this greater oneness and unity of all life.

I have told you of Grandma Rosie's firm stand about speaking her own Native tongue rather than English. Her humorous exclamation as the huge truck whizzed past scaring both of us was the first time she'd ever broken her rule. The last time came as her final words to me.

It was Christmas time and a new decade was about to arrive. I had come to Feathered Pipe Ranch in Montana to celebrate with a group gathered there the beginning hours of the 1980s. My plan was to go see Grandma Rosie and my family before I went back to California. When I talked with Ella Jay the day after Christmas, she told me she had heard that Grandma had been very sick and had died. Although this grieved me deeply, I knew that she had not been well for over a year, and that this passage from an old and debilitated body into Spirit was likely a welcome change for her. I decided to go there anyway, to be with the family at this time and to touch Grandma Rosie's spirit.

When I arrived, I found everyone delighted: Grandma had not died! It was only a rumor. So I went to see her every day I was there. She was propped up in a big bed, with a high fever ravaging her, and her breath coming in gasps and wheezes. I would simply sit by her and hold her hand, giving her the best, most loving, most nourishing energy I could offer, and praying that she might receive what she needed.

On the last day I was there, before driving the long snowy 150 miles to catch my plane, I went to see Grandma. This time she opened her eyes and brought them to clear focus on me. With a slight smile, she squeezed my hand and said in astoundingly clear English, "I'm very tired. I'm going to sleep now, and you must carry on." I kissed her soft, brown cheek, told her I loved her and that I wished her a beautiful rest, and left. When I got to the airport, I called back to Lone Deer. Grandma Rosie had passed to the Beyond World shortly after I had left her. Her personal medicine bundle was to be buried with her.

As the big airplane lifted off the ground, I sat in my seat looking down over the country she had loved, and gently cried, for myself and what I had lost. Yet I cried as well for the beauty of my time with this wonderful woman, this shining light. I remembered that she was sometimes called Stands Near the Fire, and I heard her whisper in my ear, "I am now called Stands Near the Fire of God. And I, too, now stand under the medicine rainbow."

She had gone home to the Light, and had transmitted to me a lineage of wisdom that I was to carry forward. I understood that, as much as we will miss the old ones, the transfer of power to the rainbow children had begun. It was time for me, and for all my generation, to stand at the helm, to carry the vision, to speak the wisdom, and to be a model for the people.

PART THREE

DANCING UNDER THE TEACHING SHAWL

Standing on the hill of my knowing, I looked around me. Grandma Rosie, Moshé, Master Kaskafayet—all gone, disappearing like the flowers of spring turning to fruit in the autumn—leaving me standing there with a full and precious bundle on my back and a gourd dipper at my belt. I knew there were those somewhere on the plains below me who were hungry for the fruit I carried, and thirsty for the water of Spirit that I had been given. I looked up to the stars above me, and there, bright in the night sky, was the Great Drinking Gourd—the Big Dipper—which represents the pouring of spiritual water to the people. Around it soft clouds began to gather, which soon formed an image of White Buffalo Woman's hand on the dipper. She tipped it to pour out the water of Spirit to the thirsty as the Dawn Star stood guard. I realized that my calling is to open to that pure, clear flow; transform myself with it; and pour it generously out to others.

I remembered the Dawn Star's images to me at the temple in Tulum (see chapter 12). He showed me how he as elder brother would now hold the shield and Buffalo Woman would shoot forth her arrows of beauty into the world. He said, "Buffalo Woman is Earth Woman, Buffalo Woman is you. Stand in her law and shoot forth her arrows into the world."

And I knew that he meant for me to carry the ways of holiness I had been given through her name. An age had already passed in which the elder brother, the god, the lord, the eagle, had been prominent through the Christ light. Now an age had begun where elder sister, the goddess, the shell, the chalice would step forward. Time had come for the balancing of masculine with feminine.

I was reminded of something Dawn Boy had told me as he read the Bible "the Indian way." He spoke of a passage where God says to us, "When all the dark shamans have turned to the light, then Spirit Man/Dawn Star will marry Earth Woman/Buffalo Woman, and a new time of abundance and light will be upon the Earth." I understood this marriage to mean a spiritual marriage of the two sides of our consciousness, in which a fine balance would be found. The old Native saying, "Walk in balance," would finally be true for us on Earth.

Looking down again from the stars to the dim lights of the plains below, I knew that I could stumble and fall, spilling my precious bundle of fruit and gourd of water upon the ground. I knew also that I could hold my head up, moving down with ease and grace, awake and open to sharing. As best as I am able, I have chosen the second path: accepting the shawl of a teacher, dancing with that as my way of life.

The giving away of what I had received lay before me. But now I had to face the problem that I tend to be a perfectionist, especially in regard to myself. Up to this time I'd always felt that I must "get it all together" before I could presume to teach anyone else anything. Then one evening, some friends and I were sitting in conversation with Werner Erhard, the founder of EST and the FORUM growth seminars. Werner had always been someone whose thinking stimulated my own in a deep way.

This night he was talking about his personal experience of learning being like a rubber band. As each of us seeks and receives learning, we stretch our rubber band. We stretch and stretch as we receive more and more. But then there comes a point where the rubber band has stretched to its maximum and must spring back. Werner spoke of this as the point at which we must give away what we have learned to someone else in order to integrate what we know and to open the way for more learning. He emphasized the importance of sharing our knowledge with others as we move along the path of growth.

This was very important for me. That evening Werner struck a telling blow to my perfectionist concept, helping me understand that if I teach only what I know and have experienced, then I am congruent as a teacher at any time. He reminded us that although there are always many areas in which we have more learning to do, we also always have many things that others do not. Those are the important things to share wherever we can. I began to think about simple things like the ability to tie one's shoes. If we all waited until we were quite enlightened to begin teaching, little children would never learn how to tie their shoes. By the same token, there were many people out there who had not been able to receive the teachings I had been fortunate enough to experience, and they were hungry for them. It began to feel very selfish of me, rather than righteous, to keep these things to myself.

This began a process in which I started assessing what things I knew well enough to offer to others, and also what things I was exploring myself that others could join me in. In the past I had been a teacher at many *levels—grade school through college—and yet there had always been a set curriculum. Dancing my life with the shawl of a spiritual teacher was more challenging and enlightening for me, because it required assessing not only what I knew well enough to share, but what I believed others might find useful. I remembered the teaching ways of my Native people, where everyone is considered a teacher to anyone else who doesn't have their skill, whether child or adult. Each person takes responsibility for giving away what they know for the edification of all the people. Thus, everyone is a student at times and a teacher at times, for we each have unique experience and learning to share, as well as many things to learn.*

And so, in both small and large ways, private and public, I accepted the mantle of teacher and began the giveaway of what I knew. I had expected the mantle to be a burden. Instead, it turned out to be light, light as a rainbow. I began weaving the visions and the wisdom into the fabric of my life, which took me on the road to share with students all across the land. I understood that, as I am one with Spirit, then all things are included in my circle, and the road became my home.

As an Earthkeeper, teacher, singer, visionary, and celebration leader, I have walked a healing way, developing a unique blend of teaching methodologies—both traditional and modern. On my path I use ceremony; chanting and ritual honoring Mother Earth, Father Spirit, and All Our Relations; the sharing of ancient and Native voices of wisdom; as well as my own visions on the achievement of harmony with the environment, on human wholeness, and on the balance needed between masculine and feminine energies and power. I have acted as a guide along the way, synthesizing healing, personal growth, spiritual traditions, physical embodiment, and ritual celebration—encouraging others to draw upon their own resources of strength and power, helping them to understand their unique task in transforming Earth and moving her toward balance. Much of my work focuses on the extraordinary abilities keyed within all human beings that will awaken as we come into true oneness with each other and all things.

CHAPTER FOURTEEN

AROUND THE RAINBOW WHEEL

Rainbow medicine
represents the need for all of us on Earth to work together
in building this bridge of light to a time of peace and
abundance for all.

By the late seventies I had been given enormous amounts of information through vision—some of it obviously personal, and yet a large percentage of it literally directed through me to others. I had gone crying for vision—calling aloud in prayer—with the warrior's words: "Not for myself alone do I ask this, but for All My Relations," and I had certainly been answered. Yet the means by which I was to share those visions and sing the song of my heart were not clear to me. Then I made a phone call that turned out to be very important in my life and work.

I had heard of Joan Halifax and of her work in researching shamanism and medical anthropology. She was at Esalen on the California coast, and I telephoned her there to visit with her about my experience, and to learn more about her and what she was doing. After we had spoken for only a few minutes about my background and visions, Joan said in her characteristically direct way, "Why aren't you sharing this with other people? These things need to be heard! People are crying for this kind of spirit and information." When I responded that I didn't know exactly how to find an audience of interested people, she invited me to come and speak to her group.

I did that, sharing some of the visions and techniques from my experience and growth. Most importantly, Joan and I became friends: not social friends so much as spiritual companions—two women of like intent. She invited me to teach with her in several settings, saying that she tended to be rather "heady" and needed someone to get the students into action on the land. From these beginnings, I was invited by students to do work in their respective geographical areas. My circling movement of teaching across the country had begun. I went where I was called, and the spiral grew rapidly.

The students who were coming to me were a mixed group of people: some interested in medicine ways, some with deep spiritual intent, and some with a simple desire to grow and transform themselves into more healthful beings. I taught from a rainbow of teachings I had been given, and began to see that a central theme of what I was able to do with my students was to help them "embody Spirit"—to come fully alive and truly awake in their bodies and spirits in their daily lives. My spirit seemed to do incredible work with their spirits even on the few occasions when I was not personally feeling very inspired. I taught workshops and seminars, and gave lectures at conferences, traveling to city after city, wherever I was called. Even though it was difficult to teach effectively about Mother Earth and the Circle of Life while standing in a stuffy hotel room in a city, I did my best, knowing that this was where the awakening needed to come.

During this time in my teaching, I would often choose one theme, develop it into a powerful two-day workshop, and teach it in ten cities across the United States and Canada. One series was titled "The Body of a Warrior." There I used techniques including Feldenkrais work to awaken participants to a fuller sensing through their bodies and thus to create an awakening of their spirits. Another time I taught "Heyoka, the Fourth Great Power," using the Lakota principle of the coyote teaching and humor to help students awaken in a new way. Laughter is one of the great universal powers because it functions as a total clearing of our minds, thus opening our nervous systems to receive new learning.

My next workshop, "That We May Walk Fittingly," focused on making ourselves right for the world in ecological and other ways, rather than trying to change the world to fit us. Next, we gathered for "Sacred Voices: Sacred Sounds," to explore the magic and power of music in many forms. In "Deepening Your Relationship with Power," we worked with creating our own power objects, and the idea of casting aside unnecessary objects in order to find the true power within us. "The Looks-Within-Place" provided an opportunity for participants to learn about quieting themselves and listening to Spirit.

In many different ways, we expressed and explored White Buffalo Woman's view of sacred ecology—which includes a much deeper look at harmony than simply the physical, since it also includes the spiritual, the holy. We did this through "Dancing Buffalo Woman's Dream" and in "The Call of the Drinking Gourd" (the Big Dipper). In "Spirit of Beauty, Spirit of Peace," we dealt with walking a path of beauty, harmony, and peace in our lives—yet another form of sacred ecology. In "Walk in Balance," we continued this exploration with more Feldenkrais body work included.

Another time we explored "Earth Woman, Woman of Light," a teaching for women from Rainbow Woman's vision about the feminine calling to carry a new way of life on Earth. In "Listening to the Ancient Voices," we opened ourselves to spiritual guidance, which included the Dawn Star's voice. In "Flowersong: Walking in the Dawn Star's Light," I gave participants a view of the flowering of humanity spoken of in the Dawn Star's teachings.

During this time, I also led journeys to sacred places. "Singing the Sacred" enabled our group to sing sacred songs at many special sites in the Southwest; and "Gateway to the Gods" took us to enchanting Peru and its sacred places.

As always seems to be true, my teachings came from what I had recently been learning myself. From this continual process of learning and growing in my own inner and outer worlds, I loved to explore these maps of consciousness discovered through my own journeying with those who came to see me. Often, what my students reported was that what I shared with them was something they had already known somewhere deep inside, yet they had never been able to express it or bring it to the point of consciousness so they could grasp it in daily practice. Spirit seemed to be using me to express archetypal experience and to deepen others' grasp of it. Yet I wanted to deepen myself as well, and this led me to seek out master teachers wherever I could find them.

One of the themes that ran through all of my work was that of rainbow medicine—of the need for all of us on Earth to work together in building this bridge of light to a time of peace and abundance for all. Being a métis, a half-breed, put me in a familiar position in all this new learning and growth. Around me in that swirl of teachers and leaders, I began to notice other mixed bloods as well as full-blood Native elders, teaching and sharing wherever they were called. I opened myself to their knowledge and their spirit as I stood beside them.

During this time, a man named Sun Bear contacted me. He told me of his vision of awakening the neglected ancient medicine wheels in the consciousness of this new wave of seekers by creating actual stone wheels upon Mother Earth wherever he might be called. He was putting together the first Medicine Wheel Gathering at Mt. Rainier in Washington State, and invited me to teach there. Although Sun Bear was of mixed Chippewa heritage, he, like me, had been instructed by elders of other tribes. He even carried a sacred pipe given him by the Shinelas.

Some of what Sun Bear was doing in dancing awake the medicine wheels carried strong echoes of the animal dances that the Shinelas had done in the old days on the years when the Sun Dance was not held. (The Sun Dance is a great ritual of rebirth, held in the hottest part of the summer in which the focus is on the power of the Sun—the light/Father Spirit—to renew all of life. Dancers usually dance for four days in the Sun without food, water, or shade. It is a very intense ceremony, and much is sacrificed to renew life for all the people.)

The animal dances, which (according to my family) had not been held since my great-grandmother's time, were an honoring of all the life-forms of the Great Wheel—the Great Circle of Life containing all things.

"Medicine wheel" is the name given to large circles of stones found on the ground in many places in North America. These circles had been used in ceremonial ways by early Native peoples. As well as representing the whole Wheel of Life on Earth, they were often aligned with certain other stones or geographic features to indicate solstices and other planetary and astrological events.

The term "medicine wheel" also refers simply to the full Circle of Life as represented on the stone wheel. Different tribes and cultures have varied ways of dividing the Wheel of Life into its various aspects. However, in the medicine wheel I use, Earthly life and its aspects are divided into the four quadrants of the cardinal directions.

The **east** represents the dawning and illumination of morning light, and thus our awakenings, awareness, and "aha's!" In the circle of the year, the east denotes Spring and green shoots of plants showing above the ground. Birth and childhood are here. East is symbolized by the golden eagle, who is said to fly into the dawning to pick up the light of the sun and carry it across the land for the enlightenment of all. It implies the high

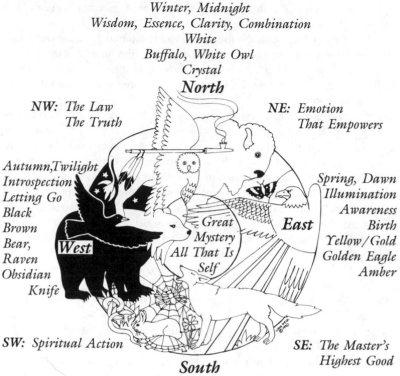

Winter, Midnight
Wisdom, Essence, Clarity, Combination
White
Buffalo, White Owl
Crystal
North

NW: *The Law*
The Truth

NE: *Emotion*
That Empowers

Autumn, Twilight
Introspection
Letting Go
Black
Brown
Bear,
Raven
Obsidian
Knife

West

*Great
Mystery
All That Is
Self*

East

Spring, Dawn
Illumination
Awareness
Birth
Yellow/Gold
Golden Eagle
Amber

SW: *Spiritual Action*

SE: *The Master's
Highest Good*

South
Summer, Midday
Heartfulness, Action, Growth
Red or Green
Coyote, Mouse
Catlinite, Pipestone

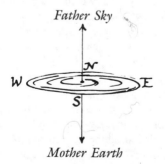

Father Sky

W — N — E
S

Mother Earth

flying and far seeing of the visionary and prophet. Its color is the golden yellow light of morning.

The **south** then holds the place midday in the twenty-four-hour cycle, and represents midsummer in the yearly cycle—the times of most intense heat and active growing. The green of thriving plants and the most active part of our own human nature is represented here. It is a place not only of external warmth, but of the warmth of our hearts; the openness to learning and growth of youth; the laughter that warms our lives and opens our minds. It is the place of trust and innocence, as well as of the trickery of coyote, who in many Native systems symbolizes the one who learns and teaches through trickery, most often tricking himself. Coyote represents the spinning confusion that takes us out of our fixed certainties and thus opens us up to new learning. South also represents the active time of adult learning and productivity. Red is its color, although in reference to some things the green of growth can also be used to represent the south. Sometimes mouse is seen to symbolize the south with her ability to see closely and to organize very actively. As the waters run from north to south, so we stand in our lives looking to the south, where our destiny lies.

In the **west** we find twilight and autumn. We call this the *Looks Within Place*, for the sun is going down, and we stop our active work to come to a more contemplative time—a time to go within. In the cycles of our lives, it would be going home from work at the end of the day and also retirement. In this two-light time, the crack between day and night allows us to touch into other realities, develop our intuition, and go into the "shaman's time." Autumn brings the time of harvest, when we gather not only the external fruits, but the internal fruits or lessons of our experience. Then, just as the leaves fall, we can let go the unnecessary past and clear out our lives and consciousness. This is the place of obsidian, the black volcanic stone that makes the finest surgical/cutting knife known to humankind. It, too, symbolizes the act of cutting and clearing away that which we no longer need—cleaning our wounds so that true healing can begin. Raven, crow, vulture, and the other carrion birds, who clean up that which is no longer needed, belong here. The black bear with his knowledge of going within for hibernation symbolizes the west, and black is its color.

The white of snow and winter lie in the **north.** It is a time of seeds lying still within the ground in germination, and thus a deeply internal time of beingness rather than one of doing. It is the quiet of midnight, which balances the activity of midday. Crystals rest here, symbolizing the clarity that comes when we release all that is non-essential and get down to the root of things, the essence. As in the west we harvest the facts and information of the cycle, in the north we distill those facts into wisdom: here sit the law and the truth underlying all things. The white-haired ones, the elders with their full life experience, are placed here on the wheel. White Buffalo Woman in her wisdom stands in the north, as well as the snowy owl, who moves gracefully and silently through the darkness of night.

Whether it is a day, a year, a project, a lifetime, or any other human cycle, it is represented on the medicine wheel. We travel around and around the wheel in our Earth walk, and if we remember to spend as much time in the releasing and quieting quadrants as in the sprouting and doing quadrants, we find a balanced way.

AROUND THE MEDICINE WHEEL

This ritual honors the Wheel of Life by focusing attention on the Four Directions—actually the four quadrants. It is important to focus on an entire quadrant of the wheel rather than just the single direction. For instance, the eastern quadrant includes all the area from the NE to the SE, the southern quadrant or direction includes everything from the SE to the SW. Honoring the four quadrants—plus the axis of Father Spirit and Mother Earth, which creates not just a circle, but a round, all-inclusive sphere—allows us to have some sense of the totality of all life.

This honoring can be done anywhere because, in spiritual terms, the center of the wheel is where you stand at the moment, within your own heart. You may choose to stand on a high point and look to the horizon in each direction. You may create a small symbolic wheel with objects representing the four directions—with two at center for the axis of Mother/Father. Or you can construct a full medicine wheel such as Sun Bear lays out in his *Medicine Wheel Earth Astrology*. If the wheel is large enough, you can stand at the center to do this ritual; if not, stand near it. At a large wheel, acknowledge the space of a "door" or "gate" next to each direction stone. I customarily stand at the eastern gate, and ask for permission to enter. When I feel that positive signal, I enter and stand at the center.

The ritual is begun by cleansing myself with a smudge, and then cleansing each stone or symbol. If I am out of doors, in nature, I will simply offer the cleansing smudge in a symbolic circle. If other people are participating, they can then be smudged as well, usually by you or someone standing at the entrance to the wheel.

In honoring and invoking each of six directions—the four quadrants plus Father Sky and Mother Earth—you may simply offer a prayer, or additionally, tobacco or cornmeal, whatever is appropriate to your purpose. One way to do this is to stand next to the symbol of the direction and make offering there. Another way is to hold your hand toward that direction and acknowledge it that way. You may begin where it feels appropriate and continue through all four directions. The main thing is to consciously choose a pattern by feeling what is appropriate for the specific occasion. Below, I offer you a simple example of what might be done. As you spend more time in awareness of the directions, you will find that the powers of each direction reveal themselves to you in special ways that you can then use as you do this ritual.

HONORING THE SIX DIRECTIONS

1. Facing the east or touching the east stone: "Oh, spirits of the eastern quadrant, bring your holy powers to us and our circle this day. We stand giving thanks for our lives and for your presence in them. Come, illumination and morning light. Come, dawning and springtime—awakening and awareness. Come, golden eagle, and bring the light of the Dawn Star to us all. Be with us this day that we may be reborn with new eyes as a child."

2. Facing or touching south: "Oh, spirits and powers of the southern quadrant. We give thanks for you in our lives this day. Come into our circle that we might know you more fully within ourselves. Come, innocence and trust—open our hearts that they might be warm and generous. Come, teach us good relationship with all things. Come, red warmth of midday, of summer. Come, green of growing plants and healing. Be with us coyote and teach us your lessons."

3. Facing or touching west: "Ho, Look-Within-Place and great ones who live in the west. Hear our call for your wisdom this good day. Come within our hearts and our circle that we may experience your wisdom more fully. Teach us of the importance of quieting ourselves in the sunsets of our lives. Help us to still ourselves so that we may hear the great voices within the introspective silence. Teach us to reap well the lessons in autumn and to share the harvest. Great bear, give us your wisdom of healing herbs and of going into the cave of silence. Crow and raven, help us to release and clear what we no longer need in our lives."

4. Facing or touching north: "Great ones of the north, hear us as we stand calling for your wisdom. Honor us with your presence as we walk a sacred way around the wheel. Let the crystal clarity of winter snows bring us purity within and without. White Buffalo, turn the lessons we have learned and the knowledge we have gained into wisdom and abundance through deep contemplation of simply being. Help us to know the truth as we are willing to come to stillness and not-doing. Bring us bright dreams in the dark and starry night. Bring us visions during the long winters of our lives. Snowy Owl, protectress of the night, teach us to fly with quiet grace and opened eyes through the dark times of our lives. Give us the deep truths within us that may then be born into the light of day as we circle again to the east."

5. Kneeling to touch the Earth: "Oh, sweet Mother Earth, you are our true mother, and we come to you with humbleness and honoring in our hearts. You give us the food we eat, the clothing we wear, the houses that protect us from storms, the air we breathe, the water we drink. And not only that, you give us the very cells of this Earth suit—the bodies we wear. Thank you for cradling us in your arms and nurturing us with your abundance. Teach us to give in the same way. Make us like you, sweet Mother Earth."

6. Looking or reaching toward the sky: "Great Spirit, hear us as we honor you not only outside ourselves in each part of your creation, but inside ourselves as well. Thank you for the light of your holy days, and help us awaken the light of Spirit within us. For light and air and sky, for our lives, we thank you. We thank you for our lives [repeat four times]. Ho!"

Excellent songs to use in this ritual are the "Medicine Wheel Song," recorded on my cassette *Singing Joy to the Earth,* and "Circle Round the Wheel" on the *Vision Speaking* album. These or other songs may be used at the beginning, end, or throughout your ritual.

You may then leave the circle by the west door, giving thanks and acknowledgment as you pass through. If you are leaving the area or place, you may choose to leave the medicine wheel you have made as an honoring of the Earth there, so that others may use it. Or it may be appropriate to leave the area just as you found it by putting each stone or object back exactly where you found it.

I had the opportunity, during these years of teaching in great circles on the road, to spend time around elders from many tribes and to learn from them. While in Albuquerque, New Mexico, in the mid eighties, I sought out a fine teacher and healer named Bear Heart Williams, a Muskogee Creek, who had touched many tribes and their healing ways through his function as road man for the Native American Church. Attending church with him on the Navajo Reservation, I had a chance to deepen my acquaintance with peyote, one of the most powerful plant medicines. Peyote's energy helped me open my left side, become more conscious of the movement of Spirit across the face of the Native tribes of this land, and hone my intention to serve the rainbow circle through spiritual action.

Beginning in the early sixties, it became more and more clear that young Americans were aware of being starved for the active presence of Spirit in their lives. Many of their churches and religious traditions had become rigid forms without spiritual aliveness. So they reached out for the ways of the people native to this land, touching the Earth and plant medicines in their searching. These plant medicines and the depth of spirit of the ancient Native ways awakened among the young seekers a spiritual fire that began in California and raged across this land.

The spirits of the young were parched and thirsty, and they called for the water of Spirit to soothe them and give them life. And so, those Native and metis teachers who stood under the stars of the Great Drinking Gourd were called into teaching and sharing, to pour out water to all who would drink. I, like many others, was called by the thirst of their spirits to give what water I could to quench the burning fire. And I, as well, learned and grew from our spirits' mutual intention.

In one of my experiences during a Native American Church ceremony, Peyote showed himself to me on the left side in a very humorous way—he became the Wile E. Coyote who always gets in trouble in the "Road Runner" cartoons, dancing and laughing and teasing me about my seriousness. He danced closer and closer to me, and as he did so, his left eye took on a luminous quality that called my attention. As I focused on his eye, which grew larger and larger as he approached, I began to see another scene through it. The luminosity of his eye transferred itself to a softly radiant light behind two figures emerging from the distance. To my surprise, the two figures coming closer were Dawn Star and

White Buffalo Woman, walking in balance and unison. Upon later reflection, this helped me to see how Peyote is carrying the principles they gave us, and making them real in the world.

In the early eighties, when I was new on the rainbow wheel of teaching, I spoke to a Native American Congress at the University of Colorado in Boulder, where I then lived. After my talk, several young Indian women invited me to come to a stone-people lodge with them.

This rite, more commonly called the sweat lodge, *inipi,* or purification lodge, is a very basic rite, often done for ritual cleansing and purification at the beginning of much more complex ceremonies. This intense ritual of steam and radiant heat, produced by pouring water over heated rocks, in a small willow and hide enclosure can be very profound in its physical, emotional, mental, and spiritual effects. It often opens the left side quite powerfully, as well as connecting participants in a real way with Mother Earth by means of its dark, womblike structure. It is one of the rites that White Buffalo Calf Pipe Woman blessed as holy when she came long, long ago.

My friends had asked a man I had not yet met, Wallace Black Elk, to conduct the purification ceremony. He and his half-side—his wife and partner Grace Spotted Elk—came out from Denver to spend the day with us. I was excited to meet them because Wallace came from the same group of Lakota people as my grandmother—the Teton Sioux. Although I felt good teaching in all I had received directly from Spirit, and all that I had synthesized from the lessons of my early teachers, I still longed to ground myself even more deeply in the lineages of my blood lines.

This sweat lodge ceremony began my acquaintance with a very simple man of enormous vision—I felt him to be an uncle of mine. Yet with my blue eyes I was not easily recognizable to him, and it hurt my heart to experience some of Grace's well-known hostility toward those she perceived to be non-Indian. Nevertheless, that stone-people lodge was powerful. All through it Wallace kept calling me "The One Who Is Awake"; but I was so dense I didn't realize he meant me, until one of the other young women pointed it out. Over the years, I would continue to see and learn from Wallace as we taught together again and again on the circuit. His courage, depth of vision, dedication to truth, and simplicity continue to be elegant models for me.

So from California to New York, from Mt. Rainier to the Shenandoah Valley of Virginia, we answered the cry for spiritual water. Young white people of serious spiritual intent were finding Spirit alive and well in themselves through the Native teachings, which have traditionally emphasized the awakening and grooming of Spirit within each person, rather than needing a priest or someone else to make that bridge. When I stood back to look at the larger picture, the cultural cross-fertilization was quite astounding, not only across the lines that had divided Indians from whites, but across and among the tribes as well.

However, some Native people were very angry at the crossing of these lines. They felt that the white oppressors had taken everything away from them in a material sense, and that they were now trying to rob them of their spiritual ways as well. This was easy to understand in a logical sense. But on the side of Spirit, it made no sense at all. Some militant groups seemed to want to hang onto Spirit as though they owned it—to keep "it" safe by containing it. My teaching had always been that Spirit is strengthened for all of us the more we share it. Trying to hold on to it like a possession only limits, deadens, and destroys it. Still, all of us teachers who shared with those students across cultural and racial boundaries, those of us who stepped across the old lines, felt tremendous pressure from such groups, especially from the older men from various tribes who were paid to form a "council of elders" to denounce the rainbow teachings. For me, in contrast, these teachings fulfilled the Dawn Star's and White Buffalo Woman's ancient call to oneness and harmony.

To add to the problem, all such limiting interpretations and lobbying efforts were complicated by the naiveté and plain ignorance of some of those who sponsored and worked with Native and métis teachers. For instance, they would call us by traditional names that few of us claimed. Again and again, I'd talk with my groups about the fact that I am not a traditional medicine woman; and yet, again and again I would find, in something they had written, references to me as a "medicine woman." Then, the name of one of my elders—which, traditionally, is something one does not talk about—was specifically mentioned in a book after I had been promised the right to edit such things out. The bad feeling and complaints this disrespect engendered continue to this very day. The person editing the book was evidently rushed for time and had no idea of the serious implications for me in violating that Native "rule." Another time, I was speaking about the kind of dance step used in Sun Dance, and someone misunderstood and publicized that I taught traditional Sun Dance. She obviously had no understanding of what an actual

Sun Dance ceremony is, or of the depth of knowledge and experience needed for leading (teaching) it.

Another instance involved a young German man, who wanted very much to take traditional Indian ways to Germany. He publicized a Sun Dance that would be held there. Without even knowing me or contacting me, he made a huge poster indicating that I would be part of the Native group putting on the Sun Dance. This was not only ignorance, but total lack of responsibility and integrity on his part. Yet, my unwitting association with this unauthorized event led to my condemnation by many tribal elders.

Though most often unintentional, such seemingly exploitative uses of Native culture have made it exceedingly difficult, not only for me but for other Native teachers who were sharing with the rainbow circle of students. Sun Bear's medicine wheel gatherings have been picketed by groups from AIM (the American Indian Movement). Other teachers were condemned in letters by those councils of elders who had never met them or experienced their work, and an "Indian Hit List" was circulated, warning that cross-cultural teachers would suffer dire consequences.

These, and many other things, were to me stunning examples of just the kind of fighting and separation the prophecies had urged us to forsake in order to pursue unity and a new time of harmony among All Our Relations. Many who proudly exhibited the sacred pipe that White Buffalo Woman urged us to carry and use in our pursuit of oneness nevertheless practiced aggression and violence against others of the family of two-leggeds whom they judged to be outside their particular circle. Thus, while they carried Buffalo Woman's form in their hands, they did not carry her song in their hearts. It is obvious that the war councils still have not found their proper place in peace.

And yet, despite all the dissension, Spirit has been moving forward powerfully in manifesting the dream of peace that has been set deep within all of us.

As recounted in *The Gift of the Sacred Pipe*, by Vera Louise Drysdale, when the mysterious holy one, White Buffalo Calf Pipe Woman, came to our Lakota people and gave the Sacred Pipe, she spoke to them—and now to all of us—in this way:

With this pipe you will, during the winters to come, send your voices to *Wakan-Tanka,* the Great Spirit, who is your Father and Grandfather. . . . With this sacred pipe you will walk upon the Earth: for the Earth is your Grandmother and Mother, and She is sacred. Every step that is taken upon Her should be as a prayer. . . . all things of the universe are joined to you who smoke the pipe. When you pray with this pipe, you pray for and with everything. . . . Every dawn is a holy event, and every day is holy, for the light comes from your Father *Wakan-Tanka.* You must always remember that the two-leggeds and all other peoples who stand upon this Earth are sacred and should be treated as such. . . . [This pipe] will take you to the end. Remember, in me there are four ages. I am leaving now, but I shall look back upon you in every age, and at the end I shall return.

Our Elder Sister, White Buffalo Woman, is presently "calling in her accounts," as a representative of Creator, whose only given law at the beginning of the world was that we should be in good relationship with all beings and all things. We are each being called into account for living—or not living—this law that White Buffalo Calf Pipe Woman expressed with her words. Her call is the ultimate call of the feminine: to nurture and care for all things, for the whole of our universal family. This feminine energy within women, men, and all things is being called forth to rebalance a world that has forgotten or ignored this most basic and essential principle for the renewing of life. It represents for us, in profoundly simple form, an answer to our problems on Earth at this time. They are problems of relationship: relationship between peoples, races, tribes; relationship between two-leggeds and the other peoples of Earth; even relationships among family members and friends. We have forgotten the message she and all other holy ones have brought us, which reminds us that whatever we do to any other creature or thing, we do to ourselves.

And surely what we want for ourselves is caring, nurturing, health, freedom from harm and repression, and a developing expression of the highest and best within us. The basis of such a life is *love,* that wonderful glue that binds the universe together and allows its creative expression. This way of the heart was modeled for us during the Age of the

Eight-pointed Star, the Piscean Age, by our Elder Brother, Dawn Star, who showed us in human form the miraculous power of letting the light of love from our Father *Wakan-Tanka,* the Great Spirit, flow unrestricted through our hearts.

This is the lesson we are being asked to carry as we graduate into the Aquarian Age, the time of the Nine-pointed Star, the age of making the golden dream come true right here and now on Mother Earth. We are being asked to use this love now in our lives to create a truly beautiful, harmonious, abundant, and peaceful time on Earth. Can we two-leggeds pass the test of time and graduate with the rest of the class? How will our accounts with White Buffalo Woman tally?

And when we truly live that oneness the Sacred Pipe represents, miraculous things will come about. As we take down barriers and fences, we will awaken to our ability to communicate fully with each other and all things through infinite time and space, without need for telephones, electrical devices, even computers, and other such "primitive" tools. We will be at one with each other, as well as with the ultimate source of limitless energy, and thus will have no need to tear our Mother's face and pollute in order to get what we require for life. One of the great "Indian jokes" is that the present civilization has been tearing up the Earth for the materials to build and fuel its ponderous space ships, when Native shamans have been traveling to the moon and back in their dream bodies for eons! Mother and Father may be attempting to discourage these cumbersome and primitive craft by the problems recently experienced in the space program—a hint to try something more ecologically workable.

Yes, very clear messages all around us are calling for ways and means to follow White Buffalo Woman's reminders of Creator's Law. Our Elder Sister's message of oneness, love, prayer, good relationship, and holding all things sacred point us to the deepest ways of the shaman and medicine person. These, through and beyond all forms, are what will be taken into the final accounting of this passing Age. Will we carry with us her Sacred Pipe and the oneness it represents, and move into a new age? Or will we be left behind?

WALKING THE WHEEL OF RELATEDNESS

Sit down quietly with each of the peoples of Earth, each of the kingdoms (two-leggeds, four-leggeds, wingeds, finned ones and swimmers, creepie-crawlies and scaly ones, green growing ones, crystals and the mineral kingdom, etc.) and use White Buffalo Woman's eyes, her reminder of Creator's one law, to take your own accounting. Why not spend a week of your meditation time to accomplish this inventory, working with one kingdom a day.

MONDAY: TWO-LEGGEDS

Begin with yourself, which is where your attitude toward others begins:

1. Do you know yourself as sacred? Or do you mistreat yourself with an unhealthy life and abusive relationships?

2. Do you nurture and care for your spirit as well as your body?

3. Do you seek harmony and peace within yourself?

4. Do you treat each day as holy and special?

5. How does this extend to other two-leggeds? Repeat questions one through four with:

▶ Your family?
▶ Your friends?
▶ Your business or school associates?
▶ Other races?
▶ Other religions?
▶ Your community?
▶ Your country?
▶ The two-leggeds of other nations?

TUESDAY: FOUR-LEGGEDS

1. Do you know your family pet(s) as sacred beings?

2. Do you nurture and care for them as well as you do for yourself or other family members? Do you perhaps treat them better than you do yourself? If so, ask yourself how this came about.

3. Do you seek harmony and peace with the four-leggeds you know well?

4. How does this extend to the other four-leggeds of this world—both domestic and wild? Do you know all four-leggeds as sacred beings?

5. Do you believe humans owe a special debt of care to those peoples who have allowed themselves to serve us through domestication?

► Does what you eat and the clothing, jewelry, and cosmetics you wear and use reflect a love and respect for the four-leggeds?

► Or do you encourage the devastation of factory farming and the abuse of animals in scientific research, product testing, and fur trapping?

(An outstanding video to help sensitize you in this area is "Prescription for Survival." It was filmed at the "Dreaming the New Dream Symposium," by Dr. Michael Klaper; see also John Robbins's book and video, *Diet for a New America,* which inspired Dr. Klaper. Consult appendix 2, page 463, for more information.)

6. Are you aware of the destructive impact of environmental changes on the four-leggeds and other peoples of Mother Earth? Do you help by conserving water and electricity; by recycling trash, old clothes, and furniture; by keeping your car engine tuned up to avoid even worse emissions; by avoiding buying items of or in plastic; by recycling or cutting down on your use of other petroleum products?

► Do you know how many four-leggeds and the peoples of other kingdoms are on the endangered species list?

► Do you know which ones and why?

► Do you know how the cutting down of the world's rain forests is affecting the many peoples who live within them as well as us?

► Do you eat fast-food hamburgers and contribute to the destruction of the rain forests?

► How do you feel about big game hunting?

WEDNESDAY: WINGEDS

1. Do you consider all wingeds as sacred beings; not just the most grand, or beautiful, or sweetest singing, but the little brown wrens and pigeons of our cities, the raucous starlings and jays, the crows and vultures—the cleansers of Mother Earth? Did you know that Benjamin Franklin proposed the wild turkey as our national bird?

2. How do you feel about caged birds? Do you know how they are caught, and how they are treated during transportation, and in pet shops?

3. Have you considered the cruel practices involved in the factory farming of chickens?

4. Have you considered what the pollution of our waters, especially oil spills, is doing to the lives of the wingeds of the waters?

5. Do you know how the loss of woods, prairies, and open croplands is seriously affecting the migratory wingeds? On the other hand, did you know that nations such as the Soviet Union and the United States are beginning to cooperate on protecting the migratory routes of

such wingeds as snow geese, who know no political boundaries? Are there other things we can do to protect them?

6. If you live in city or country, do you consider the survival of wingeds in the hard winter months? Do you leave them birdseed and suet? Do you remember to renew the supplies regularly?

THURSDAY: FINNED ONES AND SWIMMERS

1. Do you consider all finned ones and swimmers as sacred beings; again, not just the most grand, or beautiful, or tasty, but all the life of Mother Earth's waters—from snails and eels to the endangered alewives of our polluted Great Lakes?

2. Do you practice water conservation techniques in your own household? Do you use non-poisonous and non-polluting cleaning products? If you work in industry, are you focused on inventive means of avoiding wasteful and polluting practices?

3. When you are enjoying our wilderness areas, our seas and seashores, and our national parks, are you very respectful of Mother Earth and all her many children? Do you clean up after yourself and take out everything you brought in with you? Do you avoid dumping garbage or gasoline or oil overboard when you're boating?

4. Are you concerned not only with the welfare of our whale and dolphin relations, but also with the less well-known finned ones and swimmers of our planet's distant seas, shrinking wetlands, ponds, rivers, and streams? Are you encouraging the protection of spawning grounds?

5. Are you encouraging the acquisition of such areas for nature preserves? Are you aware of new moves by wealthier countries to buy up some of the heavy debt load of many Third World countries in exchange for their setting aside lands for the preservation of wildlife and endangered habitats? What can you do to help?

6. How do you feel about factory fishing practices and game fishing?

7. Do you teach your children respectful ways with the many peoples of Mother Earth and good conservation practices at home and away?

FRIDAY: CREEPIE-CRAWLIES, SCALY ONES

1. Do you consider all creepie-crawlies and scaly ones as sacred beings—ants, earthworms, slugs, spiders, gnats, mosquitoes, cockroaches, beetles, snakes, lizards, alligators, frogs, toads?

2. If you are repulsed by any of the insect peoples, why not take time to consider their function in the great dance of interrelatedness? What is it each of these peoples do, how, and why? What teachings do they

offer for your own life? For instance, the much-maligned cockroach is one of the greatest survivors of all the kingdoms.

3. Remember my stories of the beetle grandmother and the other shimmering beetles (page 245) who brought me messages from the left side? Are there peoples of this kingdom who have been spirit guides for you? If not, why not summon one as a teacher? Without preconceived notions, be very aware of who comes to you and how. For instance, don't shoo away the fly that lands on your finger. Watch how she washes her face so thoroughly. Enjoy the iridescent beauty of her wings. Think of her function as a cleaner of the Earth, every bit as powerful as the jackal or vulture.

4. Are you aware that our honeybees, who are irreplaceable in agriculture as crop pollinators, are seriously endangered by a plague of viruses and infestations—as well as by the spread of the fierce African bees that have now reached our southern borders?

5. What is your attitude toward snakes? Try using the recapitulation exercise on pages 252–253 to trace back your feelings toward them. Did you know that in the mythology of nearly all the two-leggeds of our planet, snakes and serpents are thought to be carriers of the deep wisdom of Mother Earth? The two serpents twining up the healing staff of the Greek god Hermes, the messenger of the gods, represent the blending of the two worlds, the marriage of the right side and the left side.

6. Do you wear or use products made from the beautiful skins of endangered crocodiles, alligators, or snakes? Did you know that many of these skins can still be legally bought and sold in the United States, and that in a number of countries these wild peoples are still hunted for the skin trade?

SATURDAY: THE GREEN GROWING ONES

1. Do you treat plants as live, conscious beings, given by Mother Earth and Father Spirit? Do you ever talk to your houseplants? Do you ask them if their living conditions are right, and then observe them carefully for several days for an answer?

2. Are you aware of the contribution made by many fine plants that are often called weeds—their soil-renewing, edible, and medicinal aspects? For instance, take those dandelions you spend so much time trying to gouge out of your lawns and gardens. The tender new leaves of the dandelion make splendid salads, every bit as tasty as arugula. They have long been eaten by many two-leggeds around the world as a spring tonic after the dearth of fresh foods in winter. Roasted and ground, the

roots make a coffee substitute. Medicinally, herbal healers through the centuries have recommended using dandelion root tea as a blood purifier, and in skin, kidney, liver, and spleen ailments (see Jethro Kloss's herbal classic, *Back to Eden*).

3. Are you aware of the many herbal healing formulas available in your health food store? Have you read any of the many books on herbal lore—from medieval times to the present—now available in bookstores?

4. Do you support organic farming and your own health by purchasing organically grown produce?

5. What kinds of fertilizers and pesticides do you use? Are these chemicals that will damage the life-giving soil of Mother Earth, and thus eventually all other forms of life?

6. Did you have a favorite tree when you were growing up? Do you have one now? Have you ever simply placed your hands around the trunk of a living tree and felt the deep Earth energy running through it—felt it sway and dance to the music of the wind? Have you considered asking for a guide from these magnificent wise ones?

7. Are you using recycled paper products? Are you cutting down on your use of paper products and/or finding reusable items made of natural fibers to replace them—such as cotton diapers, handkerchiefs, and kitchen towels?

8. As you plant your flowers and garden seeds, you may want to take a few moments to offer tobacco and cornmeal to them, to their plant devas, and to Mother Earth. The tobacco offering can be a prayer of connection and oneness, to help you keep in communication with the plants and to learn from them. As always, the cornmeal is an offering of nurturing and caring. During the time of their growing, take time to be with them quietly to observe, to listen, to appreciate. (See bibliography for the *Perelandra* books by Machaelle Small Wright.) And certainly, at harvest time, a thanksgiving and celebration is called for. Find a way to offer a giveaway for the abundance you have received.

▶ Did you know that non-hybrid seeds, which grow plants that will produce their own seeds, are becoming dangerously scarce? This is because a large percentage of well-known seed companies have been bought up by chemical companies, who are patenting their hybrids and thus may have a monopoly on plants and seeds.

▶ Look around your local area for small seed companies—such as the Talavaya Seed Company in Santa Cruz, N.M., or Abundant Life Seeds in Port Townsend, Wash. (see appendix 1, pages 455–456)—who sell seeds that have developed a generational tolerance for your climate

variations and are not hybrid—and thus will reproduce their own seeds
year after year.

▶ Talk to older gardeners in your neighborhood to search for old
seeds they may have stored. Grow them out and share them with
neighbors, and through seeds exchanges such as the Seeds Savers Exchange in Decorah, Iowa (see appendix 1, page 456).

▶ Have you investigated using landscape plants from your own
bioregion? They grow very well and don't need nearly as much care or
excess watering.

▶ Have you looked into the new lawn grasses that also require very
little water and need to be mowed much less?

▶ Talk to your local nurseries, and search out state and local
"natural plant" societies who specialize in such things. Read about and
find your local Permaculture group—they will be very knowledgeable
about all planting, growing, and Earth-nurturing possibilities (see appendix 1, page 456). An excellent book you may want to read is Bill
Mollison's *Permaculture: A Practical Guide for a Sustainable Future* (see
appendix 2, page 463).

I also recommend the workshops of Susan Weed, Machaelle Small
Wright, and Pam Montgomery to add to your learning.

SUNDAY: MOTHER EARTH AND THE MINERAL KINGDOM

1. How do you think about the soil of Earth? Is it simply dirt to
you, or do you recognize it as the foundation of life, rich and precious?

2. Remember that the word "humble" comes from the same root as
"humus," and means "close to the Earth or soil." In the Bible it is said
that the humble will inherit the Earth. Are you in the kind of relationship with the soil that gives you the right to that inheritance?

3. Can you begin to reframe your attitude toward the land you own
as a piece of the rich and precious foundation of life, a part of your true
Mother Earth to be cared for in a good way for the generations to come,
rather than as property—a thing you own and can do with as you
please? The Hopi and the Aboriginal peoples of Australia see themselves
as caretakers of the Earth, but this is an honor and a duty that belongs
to us all. Won't you become an Earthkeeper as well?

4. How have you treated your crystals and gems and other stone
people? Are they simply your possessions, or do you treat them as
partners in your growth and healing? (See chapter 13, "A Crystal
Among Them," page 257, for more information on the care and healing
of your crystals and stone people.)

5. Do you know that *Tunkashila,* the Lakota word interpreted as "Grandfather," "Great Spirit," has something to do with the "Great Stone One," perhaps referring to the Earth's stone self, which is the grandparent of us all and carries the wisdom of all time?

I had consciously stepped on the swirling rainbow wheel with many others, all of us learning and growing and developing our spirits through mutual intention. Beginning in the east of the medicine wheel, I had awakened to the need to grow and transform myself, which then led me to powerful awakenings and rebirth. My work with Grandma Rosie, with Moshé, with Kaskafayet, with Dawn Boy, and others had opened and illuminated me not only in spiritual ways, but in mental, physical, and emotional ways as well. My name, Medicine Eagle, came at this time, as a further confirmation of the eastern aspect of my work: I became like the spotted eagle who carries the Dawn Star's light across the land.

Thus, as my heart swelled and opened with new knowledge and spirit, I began working in the south of my wheel—actively teaching, sharing, and establishing good relationship all across the land. I was received by warm-hearted people everywhere, and together we walked toward growth and healing for ourselves and All Our Relations. Here too began the challenges to good relationship posed by those who felt it was wrong to share these ways of oneness.

In time, this brought me to the west of my own wheel, to a period where I could sit back a bit and examine the lessons I was learning, as well as harvest the gifts that had been given so far. The name Chalíse began to manifest its feminine, receptive, quieting form in my life. This time in the west of my medicine wheel allowed me to take a sabbatical from the intensity of constant life on the road teaching. It gave me a chance to catch my breath and to assess myself and the situation. During my time in the east and south, I had little time for reflection. I acted based on my gut-level experience and kept moving.

In the autumn of my wheel, I began to spend more time in the mountains. I found a home in the Montana wilderness as my own retreat place and began to call my students to Eagle Song camps for their own retreat and deepening. This book began then, and provided an important way for me to reflect on my experiences and to integrate them in a much deeper way. Although I still felt very young—a beginner—I realized that I was becoming an elder in the vocation I had chosen. It became obvious that there were few women teachers like me on the road at the time I began, and that I had gained a status that at the same time honored and embarrassed me. So I undertook the work of clearing and resolving within myself the parts of me that engaged any disharmonies I found in my world.

Now I find myself moving toward the north of my rainbow wheel, working to turn the experience and knowledge I have gained into wisdom—the continual process of seeking the truth for our lives as human beings. I spend many winter days skiing across meadows of snow that glimmer like diamonds in the sun, touching into the larger life of Mother Earth and Father Spirit around me. The snowy mountain behind my home reminds me of a great buffalo with ice caked on her hump, standing quiet in the crystal winter. Inside myself I feel the germination of old seeds and new awakenings.

AROUND YOUR PERSONAL MEDICINE WHEEL

Using the medicine wheel pattern on page 285, or drawing your own on another sheet of paper, begin to think about your own life in terms of the wheel. You can work with a segment of it, or with your whole life. Refresh your memory of the meanings of the quadrants by rereading pages 287–289. Although it is not absolute that you will follow this pattern in all aspects of your life, you may find illumination from considering it in this way.

1. You may feel that you have skipped over a segment of the wheel. This is quite possible. If so, consider whether spending time in the parts you skipped would have added depth, joy, understanding, or energy to your process of unfolding. For example, if you jumped from the challenges of one relationship (south) right into the bright excitement of another relationship (east), might you have enriched your experience and the next relationship by spending time in:

▶ The west, assessing the lessons you learned and developing your intuition?

▶ The north, gaining some wisdom from your lessons, before you began another relationship?

2. Just knowing where you are in your cycle around the medicine wheel can be a powerful tool. It can help you to accept the process you are in—a good beginning for working through it.

▶ Many people find it very difficult to be in a state of quiet, not doing much, perhaps between jobs, not having answers for the many questions in their mind, not being able to make plans, experiencing the void—a classic visit to the north of their wheel. Instead of using this time to go into the quiet, into the darkness, to plumb the depths of their experience and gain wisdom, they spend the whole time fretting that they are not having the same experience they had in the east or south. But the north has rich lessons for us, we must try not to waste such an opportunity for growth. Being where you are and using the powers of that quadrant to the fullest can move you beautifully along your path, integrating each aspect as you go.

3. Have you experienced your life as "flat" and rather dead, maybe spinning around but not really getting anywhere? Perhaps you need to spend some time working with the Mother Earth/Father Spirit axis, filling out the flatness so that you have a ball that will roll. Remember that this axis is central: it lives within you and the center of your heart.

▶ Start by grounding yourself in Mother Earth; coming into more harmony with the fullness of all life around you may serve you at this point.

▶ Then, take time to develop your connection with Spirit—this may also serve you greatly.

4. Wherever you find yourself on the wheel, begin to work specifically with the time of day it represents.

▶ Let's say you sense yourself in the east, yet very little illumination seems to be coming into your life—the darkness still hangs over you. Then make a practice of going out in the early morning at the time of the Dawn Star and praying for illumination, for awakening. Ask that the growing light of day begin to live inside of you. Call all the aspects of the east to you.

▶ For the south, midday would be a strong time of learning; for the west, sunset; for the north, midnight. Always remember to ask for the help of not only that time of day, but all the great cycles and guides who are the teachers of that aspect—seasons, animals, colors, etc.

5. Another powerful thing to do, while you are in a certain quadrant, is notice what special animals, trees, guides of any kind come to you with help. In this way you begin the process of creating your own unique wheel, and your own special understanding of it, in addition to the general one.

Although I have added many new dimensions to my teaching over the years, I continue to do some portion of my teaching through an international circuit of growth centers, private sponsors, and large conference gatherings. This gives me an opportunity to touch many people and to invite them to a deeper level of healing work and growth within themselves, as well as with me and other teachers whom they seek out. So I continue my circling around the rainbow wheel, a wheel that consists not only of the teachings of oneness and harmony, but is made up as well of people of all colors and backgrounds who have honored me with their presence at my teaching.

CHAPTER FIFTEEN

HEALING THROUGH RITUAL ACTION

I discovered how important it is to work with and through the physical body
in the transformation of people's lives.

This simple, yet profound way of becoming more whole
is something you can use easily in your everyday life.

"Leap!!" I hollered. And he leaped off the ledge, symbolically leaping off the bridge of an old job into a new way of life. He hit the ground lightly, and running free, moved joyfully into the next phase of his life easily and gracefully.

I had been working with Alan, a student who was struggling very hard in his life with a change he wanted very much to make, yet could not because he was so frightened. He had been making a good living as an accountant, a profession his poor family had urged him to take up for security and for the well-being of his children. He had been doing accounting for years, but had recently begun to realize that he hated going to work. He found that he not only disliked being in an enclosed office, he actually disliked the work with figures.

Alan's heart longed to pursue what up to now had been his hobby: sculpting wood. Everyone around him encouraged him, because he was a fabulous artist with old pieces of wood. At the same time he was frightened by the past messages living within him: messages of scarcity, the difficulty of making money as an artist, the lack of solid financial and social grounding in such a craft. Feeling that they had no real value, he gave away his beautiful art works to friends who liked them. However, one of these friends had taken his work to an art dealer who became very excited about the sculpture, knowing he could sell this work for a great deal of money. Even hearing this, Alan hesitated to take the leap. He had been in counseling about it, had gotten high encouragement from friends, had become very clear that sculpting was his true work, and yet could not find it in himself to actually quit his job and make the change.

When we began to work together, Alan had done most of the homework he needed to do. He had become clear about what he desired, and he knew exactly what he needed to do. He just couldn't do it. I immediately began working with him in the out-of-doors, having him jump off of curbs and rocks. In the beginning, even this small distance was uncomfortable for him. He realized that he had sat so long in an office, and done so little movement, that his ankles were stiff. I asked him to practice jumping and hopping off such things during the week until I would see him again, increasing the height as he felt he could. When we met again, I assigned him higher things to leap from, teaching him how to land on the balls of his feet (rather than flat-footed), to flex his knees, and to use his thigh muscles for the rebound. During this time, I introduced him to the idea that the movement he wanted to make in his life was a metaphorical leap, and that he must get ready to make it.

The leaps got easier, and he was soon gracefully jumping from wooden tables in the park, and some of the huge boulders we found there. He was even enjoying it! In the meantime, I had found a ledge nearby, taller than his height and several feet higher than anything he'd jumped off yet. With much gravity, I took him to this ledge. I told him that the ledge represented the leap he knew he wanted to take, and that this was the time to do it. I gave it more emotional weight, suggesting that if he could not make this leap (knowing perfectly well that he could), he was to go home, go back to his accounting, and stop wasting my time and his, daydreaming about an artist's life.

He looked at me sharply, as though to check my seriousness.

I kept a very stern face, and said, "This is it. You can do this easily. It's now or never." I knew this pressure was a good move on my part because he was totally capable of the leap. It would test him, but he would pass the test.

I had him stand on the ledge and acknowledge that it represented his old life of accounting. Then I asked him to look down and connect to the Earth below as the artist's life that was awaiting him. I suggested he flex his knees and relax himself with four deep breaths, then jump.

Watching Alan, it was clear to me that this was truly more than just a physical leap for him. A whole life pattern of conservatism, self-doubt, and fear showed on his face. Standing near him, I stared into his eyes with an intense gaze, sending him love and courage from my heart. Then I yelled, "Leap!!"

And he leaped.

During the next week, Alan gave notice at his job, and turned his attention to his craft. Not long after, he realized that it was important for him to live in the country where he could have both continuing outdoor exercise and the inspirational beauty of Earth around him. Today, he is a successful artist, well known for the beauty he expresses through wood. His success, however, is less important to him than the courage he found to live the way of his heart.

As my understanding and experience have grown, I have found more and more ways to apply my knowledge of the importance of working with and through the physical body in the transformation of people's lives. I began to do what I call ritual performance, or healing through ritual action focused through the physical body.

It is clear to me that in healing we must pay attention to our bodies, not only physically, but in other dimensions as well. As long as we are in human form, whatever we do manifests itself through our physical bodies. We can think about something all day and work on it in our minds for weeks. But the final test is whether we can put that knowledge into action in our lives. We are beginning to understand that our nervous system carries imprinted patterns that determine much of our behavior. While therapies that simply talk about one's behavior are useful, I have seen them given tremendous impact by engaging the physical side of our nature.

Moshé Feldenkrais reminded us again and again that "movement is thinking"; that the brain functions through the movement of the physical body. In his healing work he considered the body to be "the broad avenue," meaning that enormous amounts of information are fed into the brain through movement, and that one may as well use that broad pathway for transforming consciousness. In my studies of Neurolinguistic Programming, I found that they too emphasized that the physical or kinesthetic component is a primary part of all decision making: We all move into our kinesthetic sense for a final check before we make a final decision to act. Called NLP for short, this method of personal growth and transformation uses what might best be termed a hypnotic way of working, in which verbal metaphors are used to transform nervous system patterning. When the developers of this approach, Richard Bandler and John Grinder, became acquainted with Moshé and his work, they referred to it as physical NLP, meaning that the same kind of transformations and patterns were effected, but through different aspects of the person's functioning. For further information, see Bandler and Grinder's *Frogs into Princes,* and Leslie Cameron-Bandler's *Know How,* and other works by these authors, listed in appendix 2, page 464.

So I began to use the "broad highway," remembering Moshé's very humorous talks about life not being lived sitting on one's behind, so sitting on one's behind in a therapy session was not the way to learn to live. Students came to me wanting to begin new lives in many forms. Sometimes it was moving from New York to California. Sometimes it was moving out of a marriage and living alone for the first time in decades. Often they felt they didn't know how to do this—they couldn't walk across that bridge.

I would take them out for a walk while we talked over their situation. We'd finish our walk at a nearby bridge. There, I would tell them the side of the bridge on which we were standing represented the life they now had, and the other side was the new life or home they envisioned. Then I would have them walk very purposefully across the bridge and shout a "whoop" of celebration when they arrived. Time and again this seemed to program their nervous systems in such a fashion that they were effectively able to cross the bridge in their life path.

A personal living example of this came in my own life when my companion and I were having difficulty giving each other freedom— letting each person fly free and be an individual without restriction. So I purchased two white doves. Each of us held one of them for a long time, making it our own and expressing the kind of experience of life we wanted to have. Then we handed our doves to each other, so we each held the other's dove. After giving that dove our best and highest energy, we cast them into the air and let them fly free. This made a tremendous difference in our relationship.

Do you get the idea? This way of working is a very simple idea, but quite profound in its effectiveness. These ritual actions seem to touch the core of our transformative ability—wherever we feel that may reside within each of us.

During this kind of work, I found many situations in which to use an aspect of ritual healing I jokingly called the "spaghetti" theory. In order to explain it, let's do an exercise I call "Having Your Cake and Eating It, Too!" (If you want to experience this now, you will need to have someone read it to you.) This exercise is used to work with an issue where you think, "I can't have my cake and eat it, too." In other words, a situation in which you feel you can have only one of two desirable things—and you believe that having one automatically eliminates having the other.

HAVING YOUR CAKE AND EATING IT, TOO!

1. Look at your life and find a "catch-22" issue. It could be as simple as a desire to eat all you want and still lose weight. It might revolve around some old concept like "You can't do what you want to do in life, and still make a good living." In my case, I once experienced that I couldn't have a good home life and travel on the road teaching. A friend who is a talented vocalist felt she could not pursue a singing career, which often meant appearances in night clubs, in combination with her life as a minister. You probably will find more than one such issue if you look closely.

2. When you have this issue in mind, sit down and get comfortable with your hands resting on your knees. Leave your left hand resting and lift up your right hand, holding it in a cupped manner as though you are going to receive something, because I'm going to have you put some things in it in your imagination. We'll call this right hand the "having your cake" side of this issue. The other side will be eating that wonderful cake, and we will work with it later.

3. In your imagination put all the things I will suggest below in your right hand, kneading and working them together as you would a ball of dough. (Remember these are only things connected with the first side of the issue, "having your cake." They can be something already true or something you want, or something negative or positive; just make sure to include everything you can possibly think of.)

Into your right hand put:

▶ All the people who are connected with this side of things—individuals and groups.

▶ All the things and objects associated with this issue—from wedding rings to beach balls to Rolls-Royce sedans or childhood toys.

▶ All the physical places related to this desire—your honeymoon cabin, the school you wish to attend, your old room, a vacation home you'd like in the Bahamas, or the room you got locked in when you were "bad."

4. Put all these things in your right hand and lift them gently up and down, feeling the growing weight of them. Make it as real for yourself as you can. Continue by adding:

► Any thoughts you have about this side of the issue—any ideas, expectations, or fears.

► All the images that arise from these thoughts—whether fantasies, memories, or present sight.

► Any tastes and smells associated with your issue—Mom's apple pie, the exhaust of city buses, a memory-filled perfume, old wallpaper, a fresh spring morning.

► All the sounds that arise from your issue—the gurgle of a mountain stream or the noise of rush-hour traffic, the crackle of a wood fire, and all the voices—your dad when he was angry, a lullaby sung by your favorite aunt, your counselor admonishing you, things you say inside your head.

5. Now, add to the growing collection in your right hand all your feelings ever associated with this:

► Emotional feelings—the sadness of loss, the pain of hurt, rage and anger, bliss.

► Kinesthetic/movement feelings—the swaying of a train, running free in a meadow, hammering nails, pushing a baby carriage, water streaming past you as you swim.

► Physical feelings—the heat of a midsummer afternoon, the pain of a broken arm, hugging someone, sore muscles from rowing a canoe, being sick and throwing up, taking a warm bubble bath.

6. Last of all, add all of your beliefs around the issue, any judgments, and certainly any decisions you have made—such as "I sure won't trust anyone that way again," "I never cry in public," or "Everything I eat makes me fat."

Run quickly through the contents of your right hand and the previous list again. Add in anything else that pops into your mind connected with having your cake.

7. Spend a moment or two continuing to knead all these things in your right hand into a big, weighty ball. Now, rest this hand, let it rest on your knee again, and forget this side for a while.

8. Lift your left hand, and go through the list once again—only this time for the "eating your cake" side, the other side of the issue. Keep lifting and lowering your hand as though you're weighing this load, and keep rolling and kneading it into one ball that gets denser and denser.

9. When you have completed this full list of associated things, and you've made your quick review, rest your left hand holding that ball.

10. Lift up the right hand and its ball again—weighing it and remembering quickly all that is there. Have you got it? All of it? Then keep it up there.

11. Now, lift your left hand, with its ball of associations—weighing and remembering them.

12. Now, without hesitation or thinking, bring your hands together in one enormous CLAP! mashing all these things together.

13. Know that you *can* have your cake and eat it too! Know that this technique has helped you to have both of these things you desire, in ways that you had never guessed. The results will surprise and delight you.

I call this the "spaghetti" theory because this process essentially asks you to pull out each of the "strands" of your nervous system which is connected to one side or the other of the issue at hand—the spaghetti. You end up with a big plate of spaghetti in each hand. When you mash them together, they become totally intertwined and there is no way you will ever untangle them. The technique combines the deepest and most powerful essence of the two sides. And in performing this "ritual action," you have taken two separate units, circles, or hoops in your divided consciousness, and meshed them into one through this "collapsing hoops" technique, which seems to reprogram your nervous system to come up with all kinds of new ways to combine these things in reality. Although these new things may be very simple, they're usually totally surprising because you had the categories so separate in your mind, you would never have thought of them.

These revelations may occur to you over time or happen immediately. For instance, when my friend Susan did this with "minister" on one hand, and "popular singer" on the other, she got an immediate answer. When her eyes stopped spinning, she looked up and said, "Ritual Performance! That's it. Ritual Performance." She could now see a way of performing that would be a ritual for growth, or joy, or making peace in the world, done in a beautiful setting where it could be a part of her spiritual teaching rather than separate from it. She and I made this image real by performing what we called "Ritual Performance for Peace" at a theater in Boston, where we sang and talked and taught our audience all that we deeply felt around the issue of world peace. Susan Savell still does ritual performance at the Peace Church she founded in Portland, Maine. This allows her to carry her spirituality and the things she wants to share into her musical offerings.

Not only did Susan find a wonderful resolution for herself, she also helped me name this aspect of my work. For me, ritual performance has now come to mean the kind of healing work in which a physical action adds power and depth to the inner work being done. In the "Having Your Cake and Eating It, Too!" exercise, it was important for you to get your hands in the air, to feel the weight of the imaginary ball on each side, and to actually have the experience of putting them together so powerfully. Remember, when you are doing this work with yourself or others, that this physical component is essential—it cannot all be done in just the imagination.

There was a somewhat humorous instance in one of my classes when a good-looking young man had been very fervently doing the process. He lifted and massaged and weighed what he had in each hand with care and relish. However, as soon as he clapped his hands forcefully together, his eyes opened in alarm and he blurted, "Oh, no!" Then he got very quiet and embarrassed.

Although I did not ask what had happened, I had a clear image of his suddenly realizing that his wife and his girlfriend were going to get together sometime very soon, and there was going to be big trouble. I would guess he made some major choices right at that moment! So know that the work is very powerful because you have used your body to help program your nervous system to help create a transformation.

Another important aspect of a ritual healing performance is the stimulation of intense emotion. Each experience we have metaphorically reams a small groove in our nervous system. Everything is recorded there. However, when we have an experience of intense emotion, the groove is dug very deeply. Take, for example, the fear and pain generated by a bad car accident in which you were struck by a black car coming straight at you on a bridge. You can bet that for years afterward, you will have a panic reaction whenever you meet a black car on a bridge. It may even recur when you see any black car, or go across a bridge.

This kind of response happens with powerful positive emotions as well. In our growth work, we often come face to face with these deep grooves. Very likely our sculptor friend, Alan, had some very deep grooves around security and making sure there was always enough to eat. Perhaps he had gone hungry as a child. Or perhaps his parents had, and they passed their fears on to their children. These deep grooves of habit and set ways are often the most difficult ones to challenge in a purely psychological fashion.

Thus, in your ritual performance work, it is essential to create some emotional charge, which may be equal in intensity to the original experience, in order for it to work. Attempting to trade a child one jelly bean for a candy bar will likely meet a refusal. But offering an enormous ice cream cone of his favorite flavor might get the job done. I used somewhat artificial means to achieve this with Alan. Although the ledge was very real and quite high, the pressing need to do it *now* was my own invention. Yet it connected to the reality within him in such a way that it brought up real and intense emotion, and carried the day.

I saw this happen again and again as I participated in taking groups through high-challenge ropes courses. Such courses consist of many individual elements designed to challenge a person's abilities, especially through balance, height, and very physical modes. There are beautifully designed mechanisms to insure safety without the participants' being able to sense that directly. People may be asked to walk a pole thirty feet in the air. But, although they are attached to a safety line connected to the back of the harness they're wearing, it doesn't feel safe. There is nothing to hang on to. We used this challenge and intensity to good ends.

For example, a woman came to us who had problems with a mother-in-law who was constantly critical of her every move. This threw her completely off balance, which left her feeling constantly confused and frustrated, and made her life miserable day to day. She was almost ready to leave her marriage, since this woman lived close to their home. So just as she found her balance in a very precarious place on one of the high beams, one of my colleagues shouted up at her, "What do you think about your mother-in-law now?"

It was amazing to see her weave and wobble and almost fall. Yet in that intense situation, there was no way she wanted to fall—even though she would have been caught within a foot or two by her safety rope. Her body screamed for her to get in balance, to not fall and be hurt, even though her mind knew she was safe. She soon managed to take command and bring herself back to exquisite balance. Then she continued her walk across that long beam, all the while dealing with us saying the kinds of things her husband's mother would say: "Can't you cook even the simplest thing right? Don't you know how to do something as easy as mend a torn shirt? Why is the house never really straightened up?" She had done the powerful work of hooking up her nervous system in a way that balance meant more to her than her mother-in-law's taunts. She went home to save her marriage, knowing she now had the strength to ask her mother-in-law to leave when she got too overbearing.

On another element of the course called the "Burma Bridge," we helped people move more easily to their goals through especially shaky times. This infamous fifty-foot-high bridge—used for actual crossings in many remote places where there is no lumber or steel or equipment with which to build a proper bridge—was made of three cables: one to walk on and one beside each elbow for steadying yourself. If you panic, you can make it a very taxing, bouncy, jerky, uncomfortable passage. But once you are able to relax and find a different kind of balance, the trip might even be called enjoyable. We helped people experience the power of metaphor in their lives, and the walk across the bridge imprinted their nervous systems with the ability to deal with crises calmly.

One of our more intense elements was called the "zip line." Participants came to this at the end of a long series of elements including the crawl up a slanting log to the high beam, the walk across the Burma Bridge, and then climbing another fifteen feet up a pole to a small platform, sixty-five feet above a small lake. At this point people were transferred to another safety setup that allowed them to leap off the platform holding on to a small bar, and be carried along, zipping wildly three hundred yards down across the lake and onto a low area where they slowed down and were taken off the line.

The zip line was both a fun and an exhilarating experience to say the least, but the initial journey was very difficult to take. Of course, we used this with any kind of leap they needed to take in their lives, any leap into the unknown that is so much a part of human life if we are living fully. In truth, we face the unknown each new moment. But how we face that aspect of life makes a very big difference. This element helped people understand that, although in some major leaps of life they would certainly have excitement and intense anticipation, as well as a lot of adrenaline pumping during the jump, they had the choice of going forward rather than getting stuck where they were. I've come to believe that it was the emotional intensity of these high-rope elements that made the powerful new positive grooves in the patterning of their nervous systems.

This reminds me of my friend Tom Brown, the well-known tracker and survival teacher (see Appendix for information on Tom's many books and his wonderful Tracker School). Tom learned something valuable from his Lipan Apache teacher, Stalking Wolf—a method eventually used by all good teachers. Stalking Wolf taught in the coyote way—not through giving his students a cookbook recipe they could follow, but through creating situations in which they had to find out for themselves the ingredients and the combination to make that recipe, to learn a complex skill.

Let me give you a classic example of creating a ritual healing situation that helps a student learn what is necessary. I was in New Mexico doing a ritual performance workshop, where Ginger was saying to Paul, "You know, I think the biggest challenge in my life is that I've always been so nice. I'm always trying to help others out, always paying attention to everyone's needs but my own. I've had a hard time paying attention to what I need and taking care of myself."

While I was pondering what I would do for a ritual if I were her partner, Paul did a wonderful thing. He had her lie down, get comfortable with closed eyes, and bring up images of other people needing things, wanting things, asking for her help, telling her he needed help in figuring out his life. When she seemed totally absorbed in this, he reached down with both hands and covered her nose and mouth so she could not breathe. Naturally, it didn't take her long to reach out and push him away to get what she needed!

You may have a question about programming in fear here. Had Paul made her struggle and fight to the point that she was afraid she would not ever get a breath, fear might have come in. However, he let her get a breath the instant her startled response pushed his arms away. Paul had done beautiful work in two specific ways: He had not only brought emotional life and death intensity to the ritual, he had caused her to respond in a way that programmed her to go for what she needed before taking care of everyone else. It was a powerful lesson for her.

At some camps, sections of the ropes course were very close to the ground; these tested people's balance and revealed their patterns without added height as a factor. They were especially useful for teaching new patterns of movement because an instructor could stand right near where the person was working. Balance beams, swinging logs to cross, a series of stumps to jump on, a swinging net to climb, and other elements were included. We found this course especially useful for watching how people metaphorically revealed the overall patterns of their lives in a challenging physical situation. We could watch their approaches to problems and challenges, and help each person strengthen and transform their patterns before confronting the high elements.

On a log beam two feet from the ground, Linda would start prematurely, before she got her balance. Janine wanted to walk with her head leading rather than her pelvis, and fell forward constantly. Frank, on the other hand, did the reverse—he leaned backward as though head shy, yet led with his crotch. This constantly caused him to fall backward. Jess and Ramona were afraid to begin, seeming frozen in time. In talking with each of these people, we found these very things to be unworkable patterns in their daily lives as well. Linda had the habit of "going off

half-cocked"; Janine tried to deal with everything in her life intellectu-
ally; Frank would become sexually involved, yet never achieve real
closeness and intimacy; Jess and Ramona were frozen in very old,
unworkable jobs and habits. Helping these people simply learn how to
cross that low beam with ease and grace was remarkably helpful in their
larger lives. In our instructions for working the course, we helped them
translate their learning about balance and forward movement into daily
life.

Something you might run into working with yourself or others is
a tendency to want to figure out each of the steps leading to what you
want rather than just going directly for what you want with the ritual
action. The idea is to get clear on a simple metaphor and do it physically,
not talk about it for hours. This was the case with Marilyn, a woman
who wanted very much to work with children through performance and
drama. Her partner in the exercise seemed to be having a very difficult
time finding a physical action to help her. Marilyn was going on and on
about how she wanted to work with children, but that required a
teaching degree, and she didn't have the money to leave her job and go
to school, and on and on. She had her partner thinking about metaphors
for making money.

I stopped them, and asked them to go back to the original idea—her
wanting to work with children through performance. I reminded her
that she might go through this trauma and drama, graduate from school
(which would likely change her mind about how to work with children
anyway), go to work in a grade school, and find out she hated it. She
was a performer, not an institutional teacher!

So I set her a more immediate task. "I want you to go out and gather
up some kids in the neighborhood or from your close friends. Within
two weeks of today, I want you to do a performance for them. If you
like it, perhaps you will do more of it. If you get good at it, people will
begin to hear about it and bring their children. You don't need a degree.
Just do it, try it, perform an action instead of creating a hopeless
situation in your head."

To her partner I gave the task of getting back in touch with Marilyn,
to make sure she did it, and to help her assess the results of her
performance with the children. Marilyn got very excited, and I'm sure
she learned a tremendous amount from that literal ritual performance.

I think you're getting the idea about making up these ritual healing actions for yourself and others. One of the most wonderful things about this kind of transformational work is that you can do it for yourself, mutually with friends, with children, or in your professional counseling work. It will be a welcome change for you counselors who have felt you needed to sit around in your office all day! You may run into many kinds of situations where determining a physical action seems difficult. Let me give you a few more examples from my work to stimulate your imagination.

Patrice had difficulty keeping projects going, i.e. "keeping the ball rolling." She would start something, then hesitate, stop, try something a little different, hesitate, stop, get discouraged and quit. I had her do something very simple. I bought her a small ball, one that was easy to roll around in her hands. During our whole session as we talked of her challenges, I had her roll that ball continuously around in one hand or both. At first I had to remind her and remind her, yet by the time our session was up, she was doing quite well on her own. I had her take the ball with her to continue to practice.

Kenny could not let go of things. He clung to his past, to his anxieties, to memories, even to things he didn't especially like. He was like a pit bull terrier whose jaws locked on anything he bit into. For this kind of person, we created a "let-go bar," a simple iron or wooden rod the right size for gripping, suspended above the ground several feet higher than most people could reach. We had Kenny get in mind something he wanted to release from his life, yet was having special difficulty doing. We then had him put this issue "on the bar," using the iron rod to symbolize what he was clinging to. Then we boosted him up so that he could hang on tight, just as he did in his life. Of course, he got tired very quickly. But we encouraged him to hang on—the opposite of what people usually suggested to this tenacious/stubborn person. "Don't let go. Don't give up," we shouted. "You can do it. Hang on. Use your muscles. Keep it up." Finally, there came a moment when he could no longer hang on. With much relief he let go, releasing his grip on that unworkable part of his life.

Joanne was a mother who never had a life of her own. She was constantly doing things for her children and never creating what she wanted in her own life. But now her kids were old enough for her to actually have the free time to do something for herself. Yet she couldn't seem to get started. Old habits were stronger than her motivation, although she talked about it constantly. She was the kind of person who responded strongly to being told she couldn't do anything. So, when we began working together, I told her I didn't think she had the strength, the intention, the guts, or anything else it took to live her own life, and that she might as well forget it. This really got her going—she became more and more insistent. So I found two adjoining rooms and put her in one, telling her to think of that room as her life as it was at the present. Standing in the doorway, I had her look into the room behind me and put there everything she could possibly want in this new life she talked about. She told me again all the things she was thinking of, and I had her elaborate upon them until the room behind me had become very desirable. Then I stationed myself in the doorframe, holding on for dear life, and told her she'd have to have the courage to come through me to get what she wanted. She couldn't just wimp around jabbering anymore. "And I'm incredibly strong and tough," I cautioned her.

Well, she began by doing exactly what she does in her life. She whined and cajoled and flirted and tried to talk her way through. That didn't work, so she got petulant and gave me feeble little pushes that would hopefully not insult or hurt me. All the while I kept giving her a hard time about her lack of power and intention until, finally, she stood facing me across the room with a fiery passion in her eye. Then she made a run at me that I could not resist, and burst into the new room. Finding herself there, and me laughing on the floor, she burst into tears of relief and joy.

It can sometimes be difficult to find physical symbols for a grand concept or a dream a person hopes to attain. In other situations, some people think of themselves as unable to have anything they want unless someone else does it for them. In these and other situations, I often use something like a pillow or towel to symbolize what they want.

Marie was an older woman who thought of herself as feeble, and "over the hill." Yet she wanted something new in her life very badly. I had her work with a very strong young man who held the pillow of her "dream" and would not let her have it. I had instructed him to let her get close to getting it—just enough to keep her interested and willing—but not to let her have it without some real effort on her part. She piddled around for a while as he teased her with it. Then something shifted inside her, and she turned into a tiger. She grabbed hold of him—and that pillow—then wrestled him to the ground, and although he held on quite tight, managed to take the pillow away from him. They were both panting and laughing when she finally jerked the pillow free, and stalked proudly around the room with her eyes shining. Her back was straight, her gait was fluid—no more was she a feeble little old grandmother!

Kate and Dean were having trouble creating a peaceful household together. There always seemed to be dissention, aggravation, and upset. Among many other things, I taught them a simple song where one sang the harmony to the other's melody—a peaceful, gentle, relaxing river song with a swirling waltz rhythm entitled "Peace of the River." (It is recorded on my *For My People* cassette, see appendix 3, page 473.) I asked them to sing this together whenever they needed to work together, or when things seemed to be degenerating into arguments or aggravation. They learned to love the song and the feeling it generated within them, and began to use it a great deal to help their relationship. Dean said that, just for fun, he would occasionally bow to Kate and then waltz her around the room.

I remember another young woman who had been really excited about her job when she first got it. Sharon loved the actual work, as well as the service her company provided. Before long, however, she found she'd taken on too much and it had become a burden. It was no longer exciting or fun. She expressed a longing to get back to the joy of it, while getting some of the weight off her back. When her workshop partner could think of nothing to do, I had a sudden insight. "Come over here and back up to this chair," I asked. She did so, and I climbed onto the chair and onto her back piggy-back. "I'm the burden of your job," I said, giving her little kicks like I would a pony I was riding. "I'm the heavy part. I'm the part you don't like. I'm the part you want to let go of." All the while, Sharon was carrying me around the room, and all the while she was muttering, just as she did about her job, "I don't like carrying this weight. I don't want to do this. I don't think this is fair. You should walk yourself. Blab blab blab blab blab."

Finally, I realized she would probably carry me all night, so I challenged her, "Why don't you put the burden down then?" It was like I had suggested something she'd never thought of. She stopped in mid-stride and considered this new approach deeply. I was amazed at how long it took her to come to the decision that she could in fact put me down. So she began to shake me, and pull on my arms. Not making it easy for her, I finally slid down her back and yet still clung with my arms around her so she was not free. She kept struggling, until she realized what she really wanted and asked for it.

"This is not it either," she said. "I don't just want to let go of it all. I want to have fun with it."

So I brought the ritual action to a positive conclusion. Taking her hand, I led us skipping around the room, jumping over other participants, and having a great time until we fell down laughing. My actions were very simple, yet they helped her bridge a gap in her experience and create a much happier working life for herself. (This material and much more is contained in my cassette, *Healing through Ritual Action;* see appendix 3, page 474.)

Of course, this chapter will not be complete for you until you have taken some healing action for yourself. You may have already thought of some things you are excited about trying. Here are some reminders of how to create a healing for yourself through ritual action.

TAKING RITUAL ACTION

1. It is easier and certainly more fun in the beginning to work with someone else, sharing healing action work. This person can help you decide what you need to work on, and will perhaps come up with a more interesting symbolic action, while opening up many possibilities for action that an individual could not do alone.

2. Spend some quiet time choosing an issue that is important for you to work on at the present time. Finding physical actions to symbolize some things may be easier than others, so as you begin, choose one to practice on that doesn't give you too much trouble.

▶ Remember to stick with the primary thing you want. Don't assume you know some of the steps toward it, and then try to work on creating them instead of focusing on the primary thing. Work on the real issue with the trust that the needed steps will unfold through the creative process. Often you will find that there is just one little gap in your consciousness that needs to be bridged; from there it may be easy sailing for a while.

▶ Pick a core issue. Get down to the root of things. For example, rather than "I need five hundred dollars to get me through this month," how about working with "I'm willing to have abundance in my life." Rather than saying, "I need to know where to find packing boxes," deal with the fact that you need the courage to actually make that move to California.

▶ Be sure it's something in your own life you are choosing, not something you're trying to force someone else to do. Rather than "I want Jim to love me," you might want to aim for "I want to know how to be in good relationship with my partner." Own your responsibility.

3. Come up with a symbolic physical action that represents the issue you've chosen.

▶ Whenever possible, use the "coyote principle," which suggests that the action should press students into "doing it themselves." Remember my ride on Sharon's back until she had to shake me down?

Then there was Paul holding Ginger's nose, and Joanne needing to push through that door to get what she desired!

▶ Create as much emotional charge as possible, so that this new action will create the deepest groove possible in your patterning. Remember the example on pages 314–315 of trading a huge ice cream cone instead of a jelly bean for someone's candy bar? The positive charge on this symbolic action needs to be close to the charge on the groove or habit now present.

▶ Whenever possible, end your action very positively, even if there are difficult parts within it. Laughter, fun, joy, peacefulness, celebration, and other good feelings are wonderful in combination with new ways of being.

▶ In creating your symbolic action, remember to touch into all the sensory experiences. Use sound and singing; your senses of taste and of smell; your sense of touch as well as motion.

▶ If two people are involved in working through an issue, get them doing something symbolic together. Making an apple pie together and eating it might be used with a couple who had trouble enjoying the process of nurturing each other.

▶ If a specific symbol is difficult to find, use one that's generic to the process of working through the chosen issue. Remember my examples of using a pillow, another room, a let-go bar, etc.

▶ If you are a therapist or counselor, create situations for clients in which they clearly reveal their everyday patterns, both to you and to themselves. Recall how much we could learn by simply having someone walk along a two-foot-high beam. This can help you both in diagnosis and in helping someone face their real issues.

▶ Use what is around you, or go find what you need. Features of the room you're in may work, or you may need to go find a ledge or bridge a good distance away. Do what is necessary to find or create what is needed for that next step—it will be well worth it.

Perhaps it is wise to offer you a reminder here about the difference between pressing limits in a useful way, and doing something stupid, foolhardy, or excessively dangerous. Each step you or any other person might take should be a small increment that can be accomplished with a little effort—even though the person may feel somewhat unsure. Remember that Alan's leaping from the high ledge was the *final* act in a process of weeks of work that built up to this powerful moment, and also by that point he was clearly ready and prepared to do it.

4. Be sure to connect this symbolic action to the necessary inward change. You may do this through metaphor, guided imagery, talking directly with the person, etc.

5. If you are working through an issue of your own, be sure to do the symbolic action! Get your body moving. Make it a powerful experience for body, mind, and spirit.

6. Look for the changes you want in your life after trying a ritual performance. If one thing doesn't work or doesn't seem to be the right one, try doing something else. You will learn from each step what is missing and thus what needs to be added in the next one.

Grow and learn through ritual action. Find more and more of yourself. Become more whole—and have a wonderful time doing and *being* it! This simple, yet profound way of becoming more whole is something you can use easily in your everyday life. Whenever you go downstairs or down a hill, you can use that action to work on "getting to the bottom of something" in your life. Going upstairs or up a hill can be a symbolic action for "getting on top of something" in your life. Have fun with it. Teach it to your children and your friends. Make it a part of your movement in the world.

Using this technique of healing through ritual action with individuals became a real joy for me in my work and continues to be a part of my teaching. It helped me to see why ritual and ceremony had been such powerful tools of medicine people down through time. For example, when a young girl is given a ritual celebration at her first blood, she is often asked to perform many womanly tasks—such as making certain kinds of ceremonial foods, putting up her hair in the adult style, doing certain Moon rituals—that help set the patterns within her of a woman in that society.

Because I could see the applicability and importance of ritual action in group situations, I began expanding the technique into larger and larger rituals. It seemed to me that when the Lakota long ago danced the young Black Elk's rainbow vision in a great ritual reenactment, they were using this principle. Taking something from the level of idea, fantasy, vision, or dream, and acting it out through a physical metaphor, makes it real in the world of our daily lives. An old way of saying this is that "it was set in the ground," which I believe meant making it real in a grounded and earthly way. Remember the illustration of our unified consciousness (chapter 10, page 198) in which Moshé Feldenkrais demonstrated our ability to write with any part of our body. When we know something in one way—which he saw as a physical metaphor—we can know it in many other ways. Thus, acting something out through our body in the physical world sets that new, more productive brain pattern, which then makes it easier to manifest in other ways. Our ritual action work as individuals and in groups also seems to imprint the consciousness of Mother Earth in a way that can then manifest in the world on a larger scale at a later time.

This way of thinking led me toward a powerful phase of my work during which involving my students in larger ritual and ceremony became central.

THE MYSTERIOUS FEMININE

"Follow your Grandmother Moon. Her illuminating cycles will
transform your spirit
as you awaken to them moving within your own body."

"Follow your Grandmother Moon," I was told. And thus I began a process of learning about the feminine mystery teachings—a process that continues to deepen with every Moon cycle.

The feminine mystery teachings have been lost to several generations of women in many native cultures, and to many more generations in most European traditions. The puritanical attitudes of the missionary school teachers who had power over our Native elders often caused them to turn their faces away from the issues of the feminine, especially as they related to women's menses. Now this women's wisdom is coming back into our consciousness from the few remaining elders who carry it, from our inner questing, and from our practice of the teachings themselves. It has tremendous import for not only our spiritual practice, but also for our general health and physical well-being.

Let me take you around and around the cycle of Grandmother Moon, so that you may begin to know her as she lives within you. Ideally, we begin with Grandmother at her brightest and most open: the full Moon. This is a time of outward activity and high energy. If you sleep where the moonlight touches you, you will often find yourself quite wide-eyed until very late on these magnificent, luminous nights. It is a joy to walk outside where there are no artificial lights, so that you can actually see how bright Grandmother's light makes the world at this time. Magic seems to touch everything as the silver light shimmers upon it.

Then Grandmother begins to cover her face, and gently to withdraw. This is the *waning Moon,* growing smaller and smaller in the night sky. In our Moon practice, we women as well can begin to withdraw into a quieter and quieter place, becoming less outward and social. We move toward an inward place that has more to do with "being" than "doing." As the dark of the Moon comes, we are at our most inward place. If we are in cycle with the Moon, this will be the time our menses begin—a time referred to as our "Moon time." To have our bodily cycle synchronized with the Moon's cycle, we must be able to see the Moon so that Grandmother's light can trigger that cycle within us. As you know, light is what triggers many of our rhythms on Earth, including the migrating of birds, nest building, and other instinctive behavior. We, too, are profoundly moved by the light, yet with so much artificial light influencing us, it is more difficult to perceive these natural cycles.

In the *dark of the Moon,* as we begin our bleeding, is the time when the veil between us and the Great Mystery is the thinnest. It is the most feminine, receptive time for women, and its function is exactly that: to be receptive. This Moon time then becomes a time of retreat and calling for vision. If we women are to use ourselves well at this time, then we still ourselves to receive visions, dreams, intuitions, and other left-sided messages. Native grandmothers teach us that this time is never used for ourselves alone; it is always used to pray for All Our Relations. Praying and asking for things for ourselves is important and appropriate, but not at this time. When we are in this place of being most receptive, we must never limit what we can receive by focusing only upon ourselves.

Grandmother Moon has completely covered her face, and so can we. At this time, then, a traditional woman goes to a Moon Lodge, a place of quiet and beauty separate from the activity of daily life. This becomes her questing place, a place of protection and nurturing in contrast to the high precipices of other kinds of vision quests. During the days of her bleeding, she has the joy of doing nothing. She is not required to cook, to clean, to take care of others, to go to a job, or any other activity. Her sole purpose is to call vision for her people: to open herself to whatever the Great Spirit wishes to send through her to serve her family, her community, her world. She could receive something as simple as a new recipe to nourish her family, or a design for a rug she will weave for her home, or as grand as a call to create a national campaign for abused children or a city-wide recycling effort.

Coming out of this dark Moon time, she has cleansed her body, nurtured herself with quiet and beauty, and received her visions. And now, Grandmother begins to uncover her face. As the tiny slice of new Moon waxes fuller and fuller, the woman comes back out into the world, carrying her vision. Then as the full Moon comes again, in the time of highest activity, she is at her most yang—working actively to make that vision real in the world. She may be talking with others, giving speeches, or simply busy in her kitchen or at her loom. This is the time of manifesting what she has been given on her inward quest.

The full Moon is a time then of outward contact and connection. It is also the time of our ovulation, if we are in cycle with Grandmother Moon. This makes wonderful sense for the continuation of the species, since these would likely be nights when we dance under the beautiful Moon, connect with our mates, and create new life. Should we decide not to create a new life through our bodies, we continue this cycle with many other kinds of creations.

Around again, Grandmother begins to cover her face in the next waning phase. As we are a week or so beyond full Moon or our ovulation, many of us begin to feel a sense of draining energy, agitation, impatience, restlessness, and perhaps even pain. This is Grandmother Moon within us signaling that it is time to quiet ourselves and gently withdraw. Rather than trying to "cure" our PMS (premenstrual syndrome) so that we can continue with business as usual, it is imperative that we begin to honor our bodies and follow the Moon's suggestions. This time, then, becomes a time for doing less outwardly. Although you may still have to go to work, you can plan fewer things for the evening, as well as call nurturing and healing to you through more nap time, relaxing hours in a warm herbal bath, and receiving a massage. At this time of the waning Moon, it is important to pay attention to the fact that you are becoming more and more receptive, and that whatever environment or energy you absorb at this time will be played out in the more active, waxing time of your cycle. Take care in choosing the situations and people of your environment because of the special sensitivity of your nature as Grandmother moves toward her dark phase.

Native teachings, as well as those from ancient Eastern traditions, remind us of how important it is to our health, general vitality, and longevity to quiet ourselves during this time, and to rest completely during the yin time of our menses. Our female bodies are doing extra work, gathering the energy and life-force within our wombs so that a child can be created there. This is released as we bleed, and yet we give little thought to how we can make up that energy loss. Native grandmothers tell us that we are damaging and aging ourselves unnecessarily by not attending to our natural cycles, and taking care of ourselves with rest and nurturing during this time.

It is very likely that few of you have your Moon time in cycle with the Moon. Several things account for that, including lack of moonlight in our eyes as we walk in artificial night light and close ourselves in buildings. Another influence is stress, both physical and emotional. You are also pulled by the cycles of the women around you; many of you who work in offices or live in dormitories are aware that women living and working together tend to bleed near the same time. There is nothing terrible about this lack of rhythm with the Moon, yet you are missing the full power of the Moon cycle experience by not being in synchronicity with Grandmother. If you are bleeding at the dark of the Moon, you will be able to perceive how much your body calls you to quiet reflection, and how easy it is for you to journey within. The Moon's power is being added to your own receptive mode, making you the most powerful receiving station known in human form! Many of the amazing prophecies made by our Native people about modern times were made by women in their Moon Lodges. For example, the images of giant silver birds flying and of great spider webs covering the land—now interpreted to be airplanes and power lines—were said to have come from Moon Lodge women through their visioning. I have found that if I am bleeding out of rhythm on the full Moon, I feel split by my own body being different from the Moon. Outwardly, I am called to be up all night, drumming and dancing with friends, while inwardly I want to rest in quiet beauty. Neither part of my being can be fully honored.

$$\supset \supset \supset \bigcirc$$

There are a few things that may help you if you want to be with Grandmother Moon in her cycle:

1. Spend more time in the moonlight where artificial lights are not hitting your eyes at the same time. Let the Moon caress your face. Know exactly where Grandmother is in her cycle. Offer her small gifts such as blue stones or blue cornmeal, as you ask for help in dancing to her rhythm.

2. Your intention is very important here. Set an intention to gradually come into rhythm with the Moon over several months' time. This is where being under Grandmother's light really helps you know her cycle and thus be able to imitate it.

3. Tell the other women around you about what you are trying to do and why, so their cycles may begin to follow the Moon, and thus influence your cycle positively.

4. A less natural technique that works for some women is to create an atmosphere in your bedroom akin to the Moon's light. Leave on a relatively bright night light during the full Moon, and gradually work

down to the total absence of light in the room during the dark of the Moon. Then reverse the procedure back up to full light at the next full Moon.

5. Be easy and patient with yourself about shifting your cycle. You and many other women have been off natural cycle for many Moons, and it will take a while to re-establish the natural rhythm. However, as more and more of us do this, it will be easier and easier for all women to come into Grandmother's cycle. Honor the cycle that is presently within you, even though it may not exactly follow the Moon's cycle at first. Get to know yourself and your own rhythms, moods, and needs. As you give more attention to your body, it will be able to give you more signals about what is needed.

I know you are questioning how to actually practice this Moon way; or very likely, the life you now lead and the outside obligations you are expected to meet are not tuned to this kind of a cycle. Begin gently, not only with yourself but with those who live with you. Educate them as you learn these things for yourself. If you have not created a family in which others can take care of their own meals and other needs, begin now to do so. At work, you may be able to take the first day of your Moon time off, as a health practice rather than a sick day. Another tack to try is for women who work together to help cover each other's tasks, so that each woman has some time off during her period.

As the usefulness of Moon practice, in both creativity and the health of employees, becomes more evident through our actually doing it, we can then begin to institute one day off, and then two days off. In a generation or two, we will again make real in our lives the wisdom of the grandmothers. We will renew the Moon Lodge practice of creating beautiful places of retreat for four days a month. This will happen only as we truly know within ourselves its usefulness to us and all those around us. The first step is our own inward one of bringing our body's Moon cycle back to its place of honor and usefulness for ourselves and our society.

As for our own attitudes, it is important that we begin to change how we view not only our Moon time but the actual menstrual blood itself. We have likely been taught to think of it as dirty, smelly, unclean, or a curse; we have likely held the attitude of "putting it out of sight and mind," even trying to pretend it is not happening by using tampons and other means so that no one notices what is happening, including ourselves. This attitude of uncleanliness is the opposite of the truth about our blood. This blood has been created within us with all the magic, the energy, and the nutrients needed for the beginning of a new human life. It is rich and nourishing and very special. Traditional women gathered their blood by sitting on moss or other softened fibers, then gave the blood back to the Earth to nourish her. This blood is wonderful as a nutrient for your plants, your trees, your lawn—a wonderful giveaway to an Earth so in need of nourishment.

One way I do this giveaway when I am not in a place where I can bleed naturally upon the Earth is to use a menstrual sponge (which can be found in most health food stores, and used by simply attaching a strong string to it) for gathering my blood. I then squeeze and rinse the sponge out into a jar of water, which can then be given away to the land. My elders say that nature has shown us that the Moon time is when things are to flow out of our womb, not be put into it. Thus, their advice is not to place anything within us during our Moon time, including having intercourse. I have switched to using natural, washable pads whenever possible, and the blood can be washed from them and given away as well. In whatever way I offer my blood, I often sing a song, "Blood of Life," which is an honoring of it. "I give away this blood of life to All My Relations, and I open my womb to the light. Give away, give away, give away, give away. I open my womb to the light." (See information on the cassette, *Gift of Song,* in appendix 3, page 473.)

Something I found more wonderful and fulfilling than I could have imagined ahead of time is to actually sit upon the ground and give Moon blood directly back to the Earth. Wearing a full skirt with nothing under it, I go out and find a quiet place on the land. Then I make a pad of soft grasses or moss, upon which to sit with my wide skirt spread out around me. Meditating in this manner is a very special treat, one I hope you will give yourself.

In earlier times, Mother Earth, the Goddess, and all aspects of the feminine were honored as primary. During this time, a bowl containing women's Moon blood was often central upon the altars of her shrines. It represented the power of renewal and the mystery of giving birth to new life. Vicki Noble (editor of the women's magazine *Snake Power*) has researched the history of Moon blood, and tells me that, as the masculine gods became prominent, this practice was stopped. Rather than recognize the power of women and the feminine, those in power sacrificed other creatures (sometimes even people) to obtain this blood. In time, killing and death became the energy on the altar rather than life and renewal.

Now it is important, not only in healing ourselves but in healing our Mother Earth, for each of us to bring the Moon blood back to its place of honor in our lives. Calling our power from the Great Spirit must now replace taking from others by force. A poem by Ellen Bass that appeared in *Our Stunning Harvest* expresses this very powerfully.

TAMPONS

My periods have changed. It is years
since I have swallowed pink and gray darvons, round
chalky midols from the bottle with the smiling girl.
Now I plan a quiet space,
protect myself those first few days when my uterus lets
go and I am an open anemone. I know
when my flow will come. I watch my mucous pace
changes like a dancer, follow the fall
and rise of my body heat. All this
and yet I never questioned them, those slim white handies.

It took me years to learn to use them
starting with Pursettes and a jar of vaseline.
I didn't know where the hole was.
I didn't even know enough
to try to find one. I pushed until
only a little stuck out and hoped
that was far enough.
I tried every month through high school.

And now that I can change it in a moving car—
like Audrey Hepburn changing dresses in the taxi
in the last scene of *Breakfast at Tiffany's*—
I've got to give them up.

Tampons, I read, are
bleached, are
chemically treated to
compress better,
contain asbestos.
Good old asbestos. Once we learned not to shake it—
Johnson & Johnson's—on our babies or diaphragms,
we thought we had it licked.

So what do we do? They're universal.
Even macrobiotics and lesbian separatists are hooked on them.
Go back to sanitary napkins?
          Junior high, double napkins

on the heavy days, walking home damp underpants
chafing thighs. It's been a full twelve years
since I have worn one, since Spain when Marjorie pierced
my ears
and I unloaded half a suitcase of the big gauze pads in the
hotel trash.

Someone in my workshop suggested Tassaways, little
cups that catch the flow.
   They've stopped making them,
   we're told. Women found they could reuse them
   and the company couldn't make enough
   money that way. Besides,
   the suction pulled the cervix out of shape.

Then diaphragms
   It presses on me, one woman says.
   So swollen these days. Too tender.

Menstrual extraction, a young woman says.
I heard about that. Ten minutes
and it's done.
   But I do not trust putting tubes into my uterus each month.
   We're told everything is safe
   in the beginning.

Mosses.
The Indians used mosses.
   I live in Aptos. We grow
   succulents and pine.

   I will buy mosses
   when they sell them at the co-op.

Okay. It's like the whole birth control *schmeer.*
There just isn't a good way. Women bleed.
We bleed.
The blood flows out of us. We will bleed.
Blood paintings on our thighs; patterns
like river beds, blood on the chairs in
insurance offices, blood on Greyhound buses

and 747s, blood blots, flower forms
on the blue skirts of the stewardesses.
Blood on restaurant floors, supermarket aisles,
the steps of government buildings. Sidewalks will have blood trails,
like Gretel's bread crumbs. We can always find our way.

We will ease into rhythm together, it happens
when women live closely—African tribes, college sororities—
our blood flowing on the same days. The first day
of our heaviest flow we will gather in Palmer, Massachusetts,
on the steps of Tampax, Inc. We'll have a bleed-in.
We'll smear blood on our faces. Max Factor
will join OB in bankruptcy. The perfume industry
will collapse, who needs
whale sperm, turtle oil, when we have free blood?
For a little while cleaning products will boom,
409, Lysol, Windex. But
the executives will give up. The cleaning woman is leaving a
red wet rivulet, as she scrubs down the previous stains.
It's no use. The men would have to
do it themselves, and that will never come up
for a vote at the Board. Women's clothing manufacturers, fancy
furniture, plush carpet, all will phase out. It's just not
practical. We will live the old ways.

Simple floors, dirt or concrete, can be hosed down
or straw can be cycled through the compost.
Simple clothes, none in summer. No more swimming pools.
Dogs will fall in love with us.
Swim in the river. Yes, swim in the river.
We'll feed the fish with our blood. Our blood
will neutralize the chemicals and dissolve the old car parts.
Our blood will detoxify the phosphates and the
PCBs. Our blood will feed the depleted soils.
Our blood will water the dry, tired surface of the earth.
We will bleed. We will bleed. We will
bleed until we bathe her in our blood and she turns
slippery new like a baby birthing.

Something I would highly recommend as a support for this Moon time practice is the creation of a Moon Lodge. This is a place set aside for Moon time visioning, either just for yourself or for a group of women. A vision was given me of hoops of eight women working together with the commitment to support the spiritual growth possible through the Moon mysteries. Eight is a symbol closely akin to the symbol for infinity, and thus represents infinite power. And too, it's hard enough for eight women to try to meet as a group without trying to add more. This hoop can perhaps meet for meditation or dreaming together on the dark of the Moon, and for drumming, dancing, and sharing with other hoops or new women on the full Moon. If new women are interested in the practice, they can begin their own hoop of eight. Otherwise, quiet, meditation, and retreat within are honored within the Moon Lodge, even if several woman are using it at the same time.

Your Moon Lodge can be an extra room, a tipi, cabin, yurt, or whatever is available. Once you have the place, creating the inside of it is made easy by thinking of its use—a place to rest in quiet and beauty, a place to call the highest visions possible. Through my vision I see an open, light, and airy room with plants to give it life. There is a carpet and/or huge soft pads and pillows to sit and lie upon. In the center is an altar composed of objects that have meaning for your Moon time. Perhaps the phases of the Moon or the Four Directions symbols are on the walls. There could be a small refrigerator available for juices and nutritious drinks, although I find that I eat little during my Moon retreat. It's good to have direct access to a bathroom so that you and the others don't need to go through public areas. Also have available writing and art materials suited to your inclinations for expression.

In my vision I was shown a huge leather-bound book in which individual women recorded their experiences, their dreams and visions, and their art work. In this way each woman of the hoop may connect more fully with the inner world of the others. Often women meeting together will over time create a complete "quilt" of dream images, each piece coming from a different woman. This metaphorical quilt or tapestry will often reveal a fuller picture than any one woman can see from her own visions.

The question always comes up about Moon women being asked to leave ceremonies by traditional elders. This has caused many hard feelings, especially when these women don't have knowledge of their natural Moon function at the time, and when the elders do not give them this information. My experience has led me to suggest the same traditional thing to women—that they use themselves and their energy differently during their menses than being in large gatherings and ceremonies—yet that suggestion does not come from thinking the women are unclean or will harm anyone with their energy. I do not believe that this energy, which is so connected with life, can cause great harm. That energy is never naturally negative or evil in any way.

There are, however, some reasonable explanations for this practice of stepping aside, which I believe were understood by the women who made these rules long ago. Men have followed these rules, and perhaps become rigid with them. Yet *they* can only confuse us when *we* do not know our own bodies and cycles well enough through our own Moon experience. When we know ourselves deeply in this way, no one outside us will have to tell us what to do—we will know within.

These are the reasons experience has shown me. First of all, if we Moon women are using ourselves well, we will be retreating to quest for vision to serve our people. Part of our challenge today is that there are few ceremonies available to us. This may be the one sweat lodge you have a chance to do in months, and darn if your period doesn't show up! This makes it a difficult choice to sit out, yet if the sweat lodge was available every day, as in many Native communities, it would be no problem. Often, as a matter of fact, the Moon woman was given a sweat lodge to complete her cleansing as she emerged from the Moon Lodge.

Secondly, a Moon woman's body is already doing a deep cleansing; she is low on energy and is called to rest and quiet for reasons of her own health. The stress and energy of interaction or focused ceremony does not serve her, especially the intense stress of a hot sweat lodge. It is not only unnecessary but contra-indicated.

Thirdly, the function of the Moon time is to be quiet, to go within, to release outward things, to move through structure into more subtle levels of being. Thus, this very feminine energy could be termed de-structuring. It is not about form, it is not about rigidly set ways, it is not about anything involving time and order, it is not about anything linear. A ritual or ceremony, however, often has a set procedure and an outcome that it is meant to produce in a certain amount of time. If a Moon woman comes into that setting, her very powerful energy is moving to de-structure everything it touches, and thus she has a disturbing effect on the outcome.

All these things suggest to me that Moon women are better occupied in other ways. When it is possible at my ceremonies, I honor Moon women with their own separate lodge in which to quiet and rest and call vision. At the conclusion of the ceremony, they might be asked to come and give their special insights and thoughts.

$$\text{☽ ☽ ○}$$

A very special function which the Moon Lodge hoop can serve is in the ritual recognition of the phases of a woman's life. Initiation ceremonies can be done for young girls blossoming into womanhood, as well as for elder women moving into Moon pause (menopause).

As young women see their mothers and friends participating in Moon practices and having the days of beauty in the Moon Lodge, they will become curious about these things and ready for learning about them. Then, at their first blood, a celebration can be held either privately, or with other girls, or with the Moon Lodge hoop. I feel that it is important to let your girl decide how she would like to celebrate this event once she has the information. She should never be pushed to do something that would make her uncomfortable. Rather, she should be invited and encouraged to help with the plans.

It is said in Native ways that this first blood is the richest and most powerful a woman will ever have. On this day, she is very special and is so honored, for she is becoming like her Mother the Earth: able to renew and nurture life. Among Lakota people, this young woman is honored with a rite called "Her Alone They Sing Over," which is beautifully illustrated in Vera Louise Drysdale's book, *The Gift of the Sacred Pipe*. Other tribes do beautiful ceremonies, including the Navajo, or *Dineh*, people, who continue the practice of a special puberty ceremony for young women. (See "Carla's Sunrise" in *Native People* vol. 4, No. 4 [Summer 1991], p. 8.)

You will also want to read, even if just for yourself, Mary Dillon and Shinan Barclay's lovely little book, *Flowering Woman: Moontime for Kori,* which gives Moon time teachings for young girls through the story of a young woman who is given an enchanting initiation ceremony. A fabulous and fulfilling thing to do for your own Moon Lodge group is to take yourselves back in time, and have such an initiation ceremony for yourselves, since you very likely missed that experience as a young woman.

Acknowledging yourself as a woman who has Moon power in her body is also important. For ceremony or gatherings, wearing red and/or ragged clothing is a way of acknowledging this bleeding capacity. Premenstrual girls are often given white to wear, and Moon pause women can wear the black of the crone. Other ceremonies and Moon practices are given in two very special books: *Dragontime* by Lucia Francis, and *An Act of Woman Power* by Kisma K. Stepanich.

Another very empowering ritual I recommend is one to honor your Moon pause elders, initiating them into the Grandmother Lodge. In the Native understanding, Grandmother is a generic term used to honor an elder woman. It has more to do with her station in life than with whether or not she has grandchildren. The Grandmother Lodge is a special ceremonial place for those who have passed beyond their bleeding. These women may certainly still enter the Moon Lodge and attend its functions. But they also have their own lodge and function.

I have spoken before of the special charge that women assume when they choose a female body—the nurturing and renewal of all life. Because younger women are busy with families, careers, and so on, they cannot pay full attention to this responsibility. However, when women pass beyond the years of child-rearing, they have more time and attention for this. Our Native people rightly say that the responsibility of the nurturing and renewing of life is an enormous one, and thus requires an especially strong person to carry it off. They say the Moon pause women *are* especially strong because they retain the precious blood of life within them, and thus have extra energy available since there is no longer a need to make a place in the womb for a child every month. Although, unfortunately, we hear more about the hot flashes and problems of menopause, Moon pause women often talk to me about how powerful and free and energized they feel at this time of their life.

It takes a wise and powerful woman to stand for life and good relationship, especially in this time when so much is oriented toward destruction, separation, competition, and hostility. This Moon pause grandmother, if she has done her Moon Lodge practice as a traditional woman would have, will be a very wise and visionary woman, because she will have retreated to Moon quest every Moon—thirteen times a year—for all the years of her menses, often thirty to forty years. *This depth of spirit and developed ability to call vision means she has powerful tools to use in her guidance of the people.* In a Grandmother Lodge of eight women, there could be an average of four thousand experiences of calling vision and journeying on the left side. Just think of what that could mean in terms of their spirits, their wisdom, and power! Thinking of this kind of Grandmother Lodge responsibility is for me a powerful urging for me to do my Moon practice and gain wisdom before that change comes to me.

These women make a commitment as they are officially initiated into the Grandmother Lodge. They pledge to use all their energy in service of the nurturing and renewing of life for All Our Relations. This dedication can manifest itself in many ways, large and small. One woman might pledge to create better care for children her grandchildren's age, while another might decide to run for vice president of the United States on a peace ticket. Whatever form their actions may take, they are vitally important to the solution of our present world crises. These women not only have wisdom, they have the time, energy, love for our children and All Our Relations, and many other resources. Some have monetary resources—I know many women who are transferring this money from environmentally damaging industrial investments to fund projects that will make a better life for the grandchildren of Earth.

It is beautiful to see the light in the eyes of grandmothers who are honored in this way. For the first time they may have someone valuing them for their elder status rather than denigrating them as useless old ladies, someone glad that they are not cute teenagers, someone who cherishes them with all their wonderful wrinkles. More importantly, they begin to know their own value and understand that they still have an important function, that there is no such thing as "over the hill." This is very important to women who have been told that once their family is raised and/or they have retired from their jobs, they are useless. Although it is beautiful to see the light in their eyes, it is even more beautiful to see them at work nurturing and healing and renewing their world.

MOON TIME AWARENESS

Find a quiet time and place to do the following exercise. Your own Moon time would be an excellent occasion. Also, you might want to create a little meditative Moon Lodge for yourself, or simply make a special Moon time space in your home to work through this process of honoring yourself and your body (see step 5).

Begin by taking some time to reflect on this Moon information as it applies to you. If this is new information, does it feel right to you? You may also find that your work with some of the questions in this exercise uncovers much deeper issues than you suspected about your attitudes toward your Moon time. If so, try doing a recapitulation exercise with them (see page 252).

1. Were you raised with denigrating terms for your Moon time, like "the curse" or "being on the rag"? Have you associated your period with aggravation, the pain of cramps, and inconvenience? Is it possible for you to change your way of viewing your Moon time, to honoring it?

2. Have you been taught that your Moon blood is dirty or negative? Can you begin to view it as rich and nurturing, worthy of being gathered and given away in a ritual?

3. Can you express love and caring for yourself by the healthful practice of quieting yourself and resting as your Moon time approaches and during it, even if you cannot stop working?

4. Are you willing to open your left side during this special time when the veil between you and the Great Mystery is the thinnest, in order to serve the life around you with vision and wisdom?

5. Do you have a room that could be dedicated as a Moon Lodge? Do you have spirit sisters who might want to join with you in its creation? (I have made two cassette tapes about these teachings and about setting up a Moon Lodge, called *Moon Time* and *Moon Lodge*. See appendix 3, pages 474–475, for further information.)

6. Will you teach girls you know about these Moon practices? Buy the book *Moontime for Kori* for all of them as they approach puberty. Offer them the choice of developing their spirits through Moon questing—a choice you likely did not have and may regret not having.

7. Ask the men in your life whether or not they can understand how important this practice is for you and the other women in their life. Share with them what you choose to do to honor your Moon time. Ask them how they can envision supporting your practice.

8. As a fitting conclusion to the Moon Time Awareness Exercise, which may take some time to complete—especially if you have done recapitulation work as well—you may want to perform a ceremony of letting go of old patterns, old ideas (see chapter 5, page 105, and chapter 8, page 169). You can do this by yourself, or you can invite the sisters with whom you might like to create a Moon Lodge to participate in your ceremony.

MOON STAFF

There is a Moon practice given to me by my *hunka,* or spiritually adopted, sister Norma Cordell. It is called the Moon staff, and it can be made by you individually in your Moon time, or made together by a group of Moon women who have formed a separate circle during a larger ceremony.

1. Find a stick as tall as you are. For a group of women find a stick of average height.

2. Bring yarn, string, or cord of many colors—including plenty of red.

3. Hold the staff in front of your body, and measure on it the level of your pubis. This is where you will begin wrapping red yarn, string, or cord for a few inches down the stick. Leave an end of the red yarn hanging down from pubis height onto the ground to symbolize the blood of your body being given to Mother Earth.

4. Then, holding this symbolic thread of blood against your Moon staff, begin wrapping more yarn around them both, using whatever colors feel right to you. Be sure to wrap the first few inches and the last few in red. You may use many shades to create a pattern of how your month has felt to you. I sometimes leave little ends of string hanging out where the colors change and hang feathers or other symbolic objects from them.

5. An essential part of this practice is that you make a conscious prayer with each wrap of the yarn around the stick. Remember, this prayer is not for yourself, but for all the peoples in the Circle of Life, for All Our Relations.

6. When the Moon staff is completed, it is filled with prayers and good energy. If you have done it individually, you may keep it, collecting together all thirteen from your year. If you make the Moon staff with others at a ceremony, it may be placed in the Earth or a supportive rock base during the ceremony so that its energy might bless the area. Usually, however, sooner or later, the staffs will be burned so that the prayers they contain can be released.

This Moon practice is a way of using well the patterns placed within you by Mother Earth, Father Spirit, and Grandmother Moon, both for yourself and for others. In a time when there is little ritual and few elders to guide our spiritual development, this practice becomes an especially important tool.

You can begin with even this little bit of information, and develop a powerful practice. The doing of it will begin to teach you in itself. As you become more sensitive to the truth of your experience, you will automatically deepen this practice. And remember that you have the truth and the knowing inside yourself, placed there by Mother Earth and Grandmother Moon. Touching into the feminine mysteries is only a matter of quieting, opening your left side, and listening.

White Buffalo Calf Pipe Woman continues to call us to be women of spirit, to be holy women. What more wonderful way than to use our natural bodily patterns of Moon time to gain wisdom and vision to serve All Our Relations.

DANCING AWAKE THE DREAM

The dramatic action that we need to create a way of life on Earth
that really works will be taken
not through personal, social, or political action,
but through spiritual action.

We must now take responsibility for the oneness, this way of harmony
with All Our Relations. We must learn and make practical
in our everyday lives the law of Good Relationship.

After I had been leading workshops and doing other teaching for a good while, and after I had completed my pledged cycle of four fasts (vision quests), I began another kind of cycle in an unexpected way. I was standing in an aspen grove near Sun Valley, Idaho, on a beautiful late summer day. I'd just finished a long run of teaching engagements and was quite exhausted, so I'd retreated among the aspen groves to the home of my old friend Robyn, to recoup my energies. Being accustomed to an intense schedule that allowed very few days off, suddenly having several days to rest and relax seemed an enormous stretch of time.

On the third day, while walking among the trees along a small magical stream, I became aware of warm, intense light shining down on me. Guided by an inner awareness, without thinking, I opened my arms to the sky and said, "Great Circle of Life, let me know what you need me to do. I am at your service." Without a second's hesitation, there was an answer, which seemed to come from a chorus of ancient grandmothers' voices, "Put a spiritual block on the cutting of trees in the Amazon, and other such acts that threaten the life and breath of the children of Earth."

I was astonished by this immediate reply and by its sense of urgency, and I realized that I was in the beginning negotiations of a spiritual contract. Younger Brother had taught me that it is important to be very clear in our conscious contracts with Spirit, because those commitments are written on the record of eternity. He helped me understand that we can always turn down such a request from Spirit; there is no problem with that. If we do not feel ready, able, or willing to do as suggested, then saying "no" is essential, rather than accepting and then not fulfilling our bargain. In addition, when we do say yes, we have the power to ask for what we need. Often, especially in the case of heroines from dysfunctional families, we are too willing to take an enormous task on our shoulders without asking for help. Younger Brother reminded me again and again to ask for what I needed in the bargain, rather than expecting that my mind would be read and my needs automatically filled.

Standing in that grove, I realized I was now at the negotiation table. I thought for a few moments before replying. The hesitation came largely because I had never put a "spiritual block" on anything, and in fact did not know exactly what was meant by that. After careful consideration, I replied, "I will agree to your request if I am guaranteed two things: 1) that I will be told exactly what to do, and specifically how to do it; and 2) that I'm given the support to do it." The ancient ones spoke again without hesitation: "Proceed then."

This message came at a time when I and many others were beginning to work with the concept of critical mass, the underlying premise of what would become my ceremonial cycle. Basically, the principle states that if a critical mass of human beings align their consciousness on any one thing, this will automatically shift the consciousness of all humankind. Instruction from my elders indicated the dire need for us to gather in great circles of spiritual action, drawing in the Greater Light and aligning our intention toward a peaceful, harmonious world. My elders say that if one in ten thousand two-leggeds "stands in the light," then the Light comes for all of us. In less esoteric terms, the dramatic action that we need to create a way of life on Earth that really works will be taken not through personal, social, or political action, but through spiritual action, through simultaneous alignment and prayer from a certain percentage of the world's population.

I often think of this critical mass in terms of an enormous card on which we're all standing. In our present scenario various groups are doing their thing in each corner. Some folks are dashing about doing important things in various places, some are hanging dangerously over the edge, but the card does not flip to a new side. What is required is enough of us getting together on one corner and *jumping* so we can flip the whole card over. Change will then come for all of us instantaneously, rather than in slow, painful steps. This has been prophesied; we need only be willing to live the prophecy through our own lives. Thus, I based my ceremonial cycle on that concept: the efficacy and power of the gathering in consciousness of very large numbers of people, both those at the ceremonies and those who would join us in prayer circles around the world.

The "spiritual blockage" was to be this kind of ceremony, and I immediately began communicating with a network of people around the world, asking them to join our circle physically or spiritually at the time of the ceremony. Part of the publicity and literature going out was a detailed explanation of the ritual we would perform, so that others might join us in like form. Besides working with the concept of critical mass, this ceremonial cycle was also a teaching about the fact that everyone must begin to take spiritual action, as well as action in other arenas, to heal our Earth; no longer could we wait for "someone else to fix it." In his book, *The Vision*, Tom Brown tells of Stalking Wolf, the elder who taught him, and of his prophecies. After a certain point, said his guidance, nothing would work to heal the Earth but spiritual action. We have definitely passed that point! In the past, part of our dysfunctional victim stance in the world has been to wait for someone else to make it all right—our mother, father, governmental leaders, God—and that has obviously not worked. One of the metaphors that came to me strongly was of a new vibration coming to Earth, a new harmonious song being sung out through all the Circles of Life. If we on Earth only listen and enjoy, as our televisions have trained us, the music will soon fade, leaving us where we have always been. However, if we join in the singing, picking up the melody and the harmonies to become co-creators of the song, this action will imprint itself in our experience and in our world. The new time will then have arrived, and we will act in the new way. This new time, then, will be a time of maturing into conscious, co-creative action with Mother Earth and Father Spirit, as it becomes more and more obvious that we create the world we live in, from its smallest to its largest aspects.

It became clear to me that the time and place for the first ceremony, which I called "That We May Walk Fittingly on Mother Earth," was in autumn, at my annual Feathered Pipe Ranch gathering near Helena, Montana. The word went out through my channels and through India Supera, the owner of Feathered Pipe Ranch, who actively supported me in the creation of this ceremony. I knew there would be many people joining us, as ecological groups around the world were beginning a strong focus on the rain forests, and the movie *The Emerald Forest* had just come out. In our prayers, we invited all those concerned by the plight of the ancient forests, not only those who had read our material, to join us.

It bothered me that my assignment was stated in negative terms: "put a block against." While asking about this in meditation, I was told it was stated thus as a simple and direct way for people to understand the idea. Yet in my ceremonial work, I would use a more positive approach: not so much to stop as to awaken those involved—with love, light, and information. This positive focus felt much better to me.

The primary "mother circle" gathered at Feathered Pipe Ranch for a week of preparation and sharing. We added to our combined knowledge of the interconnectedness of all life, both through sharing recent scientific findings, and through working with Creator's law of oneness. In meditation, we looked deeply within ourselves to understand the ancient words I had received again and again, "The trees are the teachers of the law." Our conclusions were that, for us two-leggeds, the tree people are the most powerful and obvious teachers of Creator's law of oneness. When we cut down the trees, we not only cut off our own supply of oxygen, for the trees absorb carbon dioxide and other gases, and return to us the oxygen needed for life, but we also disturb the cycles of water and climate. We meditated upon the fact that without the grasses and flowers and trees having made a place for us, we would not be here upon our sweet Mother Earth.

We also remembered why the rain forests are so important. Among other things they contain an incredibly large percentage of the diverse life species and healing plants on our planet—many of which we know little or nothing about. These dwindling great forests are some of the last vestiges of forests that covered a large portion of the world's surface before mankind began to clearcut vast areas. New Zealand, now known for its rolling pastures, was once covered with forest. Europe and Africa were beautifully forested lands, and, of course, our own continent was once lush with forest from shore to shore.

Before our gathering, I gained many insights into this issue of our relationship with trees. One that moved me most profoundly came as I sat at my Sky Lodge home, looking out the second-story windows directly into the tops of beautiful long-needle pine trees. Touching into the left side, I had asked the trees to give me any information or help they cared to offer for the upcoming ceremony. My favorite ponderosa was glad to respond, but its returning query was totally unexpected.

"What are you sitting on?" the huge pine asked.

My heart sank, and I replied, "A chair. A wooden chair."

Again came a question, "What material is this house made from?"

Oh, dear, the huge pine was going to press the point. "It's made of wood," I said, looking down like a guilty child.

That giant kept up the pressure. "What about your table? Your cabinets? Your dressers? What do you burn in that fireplace? And I think it would be good if your reply was 'trees.' Wood seems a little removed to me. Perhaps you should say as well, 'live trees.'"

And I sat in my live-tree chair, near my live-tree desk, on my live-tree floor, in my live-tree house near my tree-eating stove, and cried. Before this lesson, it had been so easy to think it was "those other guys," those bad guys, who were destroying the forests. Now, I could not deny that I was a contributor to that destruction as well. Not just they, but me and you—all of us—must change our ways. I remembered that my Indian people had rarely cut down trees, and then only with ceremony. All the wood for burning was gathered rather than cut. Because of this, the forests were clean and parklike, and thus burned less quickly through lightning strikes and other natural causes.

When a tree was cut for ceremony—such as for the Sun Dance, where it represented the Tree of Life in the center of the circle—four days of ceremony and prayer were focused solely on that specific ritual. Offerings were made to the spirit of the tree who had chosen to give itself for this dance, for the renewing of all life. And when the tree was cut, four young women, who had never done harm to anything, were asked to strike the first blows. All this care given for the life of one tree—when in contrast, we now destroy acres with bulldozers in one day. In stark contrast, it pointed up to me how callous we have become, though we think of ourselves as conscious and loving.

You will very likely want to take a look at your own relationship with living trees, in your life, in your home, and in your workplace. Once this inventory is complete, it would be appropriate to find a place in nature near a favorite tree, and make an offering of thanks to the tree people for all they have contributed to your life—in products of wood, as well as clear air to breathe and water to drink. Ask forgiveness for your willingness to so casually allow the taking of the lives of many trees. Then follow this up with action, by recycling paper, furniture, and other wood products, by stopping junk mail, and by being conscious in all ways of your consumption of living trees. Be creative in finding other materials to use; even homes can be very well and beautifully made of sun-dried brick or packed earth.

With many such learnings deep in our hearts, and the cleansing of the purification lodge completed, our small group gathered with all those from our area who came specifically for the ceremonial day. We began with prayer, drumming, and song, honoring All Our Relations, and connected our energy with all those whose hearts were joining ours. We did a simple version of an animal dance, in which each person honored an animal, plant, stone, star, winged, or any other being in the Circle of Life through their unique dance. Part of this was devoted specifically to the many beings from the Amazon forests. Then we sent out a prayer, a shield of love and light pouring into the Amazon and around the whole of Mother Earth. Bells were sounded and a conch shell trumpet was blown to set the energy in motion.

When other circles reported in later, amazing stories of healing and energy were shared. In one experienced ceremonial circle two women fainted when they connected with the energy of the larger circle—it was that powerful. My friend Suzanne Lewis in Idaho told of incredible heat filling her hands as their circle joined ours, which presaged an enormous jump in the effectiveness of her therapeutic body work.

Powerful subsequent actions in the world encouraged us. The World Bank decreed it would not loan money to those destroying their forests. Brazil made a beginning step by setting aside some five hundred miles of Amazon rain forest to be protected in a national park. People began boycotting hamburgers made from beef grown on the razed rain forest land. And an effective new win-win conservation plan for buying up of national debts in exchange for the protection of forests by Third World governments was put in motion. Our prayers were being answered, and yet much remains the same.

By the time I finished this first ceremony, it dawned on me that I had actually begun another full ceremonial cycle of four. And, as I had pledged with my vision quests, I committed myself to completing all four. I began to realize that this cycle was another level of my work in the world, a level that made powerful use of my teaching skills, of my work in ritual, of my facility for helping others touch into the realm of spirit, and of the chants and drumming that were by now a solid part of all I did. They helped me put together a new way of touching people, especially of touching large groups. The large ceremonies also moved me to expand the focus of my work to more actively include All My Relations, and my work began to take on a global aspect. This cycle called me to learn about working in cooperation with others, rather than doing everything myself—a challenging but very rewarding task.

My next glimpse of the cycle came in Seattle, where suddenly three out of every four people who came to me seeking personal counsel expressed deep pain around the patterns of family relationships in their lives. The key came as they spoke of those patterns—from their parental families—being played out, much to their horror, in the lives of their children. They felt linked together by a dark chain. Link after generational link, they found themselves bound to patterns they felt unable to break. I am a part of this pattern, too. Although I'm not alcoholic myself, and though I did not suffer physical abuse, alcoholism and poor and damaging family communication patterns have been part of my childhood and adult life.

Thus, the next year's ceremony, "Breaking the Chain," would turn our attention back to us as individuals, and to our need for beginning a healing within ourselves. Understanding that to have peace on Earth, we must have peace within ourselves and our families, we danced this ceremony—again connecting with groups worldwide—to break our generational chains of family dysfunction. Nine out of ten of us have inherited, and incorporated into our psychological and emotional foundation, patterns of alcoholism, lack of nurturing and intimacy, emotional and sexual abuse, violence, and more. So this Fourth of July ceremony, gathered in the beautiful Cascade Mountains of Oregon, focused on the acknowledgment and release of these unworkable habits, and their replacement with healthy ones. We called upon the higher powers to assist us in literally melting the chains that bound us—transforming that energy into golden light to join our hearts in harmony and love.

My spiritually adopted sister, Norma Cordell—an incredible teacher and healer in her own right, who now lives in the San Francisco Bay area—helped find our beautiful camp near Eugene, and Gwendolyn Rousch, who was the only one to participate in all four of the ceremonies, orchestrated our gathering. People came from near and far to work with this issue, which was obviously deeply personal to us all.

Our camp was situated near a beautiful stream, which created a series of falls as it ran close by us, and we began our ceremony by walking barefoot through the towering trees to that clear, rushing whitewater, for purification. Then we danced, using the pattern the Dawn Star had given me on the white beach of Tulum. Our handful of men held the circle, creating the inner space for the action—something that in the past has been a feminine mode. They danced to the right, spinning the wheel around the Four Directions, chanting in voices strong and deep, "Healing Earth, Healing Spirit, Healing Earth, Healing Spirit . . ."

The large group of women began circling in a figure eight, moving in the pattern of the Four Great Winds, dancing the symbol of infinity and its power. Leading them into movement, Norma and I began in the Southeast, the place of the great masters of humankind—those who came in human form to make real on Earth the great capacity for love and truth and harmony that lies within us. We moved left across the center and up to the Northwest, the place of the *Law*—Law that is not man-made, but expresses the reality of what it is to live a fully human life with All Our Relations. Then around the top to the Northeast, where we picked up its element, emotion—motion moving outward. We worked with the understanding that anything manifest in the world is powered by our emotional feeling states—the motor of creation for two-leggeds. Charging ourselves with the intensity of our desire for releasing our unworkable habits and for developing appropriate and transformative patterns in their place, we danced joyfully through the Southwest, the place of spiritual action.

In the center of the loops of our figure eight circle, drummers kept a steady beat. And we danced for hours in the midday Sun, the women's lines echoing in song, "Oh, Mother, hear my plea: Set my people free. Oh, Father, hear my plea: Set my people free. Oh, Mother . . ." A tall trio of exquisite dancers began to reach their arms down toward the ground when speaking to Mother Earth, and up toward the clear blue sky when pleading with Father Spirit. We all followed suit, moving through the intricate pattern of crossings and relationship with ease and grace.

Earlier, we had prepared an actual chain. It was constructed of long strips of paper, upon which each person had written the generational patterns and habits they were now willing to break for themselves and for all humankind. Much emotion went into this process, as our dancers realized how many generations these chains had held their own families—jumping from parents to children, although that was the last thing either would have wished. They realized, as well, how many other people in the world were suffering from the same debilitating patterns. Glueing the links together, joining one pattern with another, we formed a chain of dysfunction, which hung in full view as we danced.

As the sun began to drop behind the trees, and the magical time of twilight approached, I received an inner signal to do what we had come to do. I led the line of women out of our figure eight into the form of an arrow—an active, aggressive and powerfully intentioned shaft. And we ran straight into the chain, bursting it apart. Then we swung back around to join in the circle of harmony our faithful men had held for so many hours, and together sang beautiful songs of freedom and peace.

Our next movement was spontaneous. We gathered the chain, every link, every tiny scrap, so that nothing remained on the ground for us to remember, and burned it in a beautiful bonfire, under the cross that stood on the hill above the meadow. Our final act was a prayer, which dispersed back to the Great Central Sun the energy that had been held captive in those chains. Through that sun, the energy could return to us transformed into brilliant golden light. The prayer was completed with the image that we each use that golden light to fashion a unique, delicate chain, with which to join our heart to the heart of All That Is. A joyful new possibility for familial relationships and patterning was before us!

We, and the people who danced with us in countries all around the world, voiced a statement in unmistakable words. The chain had been broken; what remained was to walk the new patterns into our lives. In the last several years, dysfunctional family therapeutic work, first begun by the organization Adult Children of Alcoholics, is being recognized by more and more helping professionals who have the tools to help us create in reality the loving, supportive, and clear intimate family experience we need as a beginning step in making the whole world our family. I, too, have experienced family therapy, and have attended trainings that have empowered me to become a more fully functioning adult. The program for Adult Survivors of Abuse at the Meadows Treatment Center in Wickenburg, Arizona, was an especially powerful healing for me.

The ceremonial vision expanded in Idaho during the third year. Headed by old friends Suzanne Lewis and Paul Williams, a wonderful group of people came together to sponsor "Dance Awake the Dream." In a splendid mountain lake setting near McCall, Idaho, three hundred of us gathered to create an all-night dance, in concert with the worldwide Harmonic Convergence. It was gratifying that, though my vision had initially catalyzed this ceremonial cycle, many people became its co-creators, contributing through their active participation, pieces of their own visions, and financial support.

As the focus of our dance, we shared a vision with people all over the world. Deep history revealed to us that when the Dawn Star left his active teaching in the Americas, he left something behind. It is said that his heart (perhaps the heart or seed of his message) was buried under the enormous tule tree near Oaxaca, in central Mexico. This heart of light, this seed atom of a whole new way of living for humans, was buried in Mother Earth, much as the seeds of flowers naturally fall and are buried under fall leaves and winter snow—left there to germinate for an entire age. The image envisaged in the Harmonic Convergence was the springtime sprouting or bursting forth of this energy of love and light again—a tiny piece of this awareness sprouting in the hearts of every person on Mother Earth. The commitment of many people participating around the globe was to be consciously present, to midwife the rebirth of this light-energy into the world.

After days of getting acquainted, purifying ourselves, clearing and honing our intention, and setting out the dance circles, we gathered together at twilight on the day before the birthing. Our menstruating women established their own tipi Moon Lodge as a place of centering and meditation, rest and visioning. They also had their own dance circle, at the edge of the meadow that contained the central dance circle. Since the energy of Moon women is closer to the Great Mystery, to the deep and quiet—because this is a natural time for calling things into reality from the deep, dark womb of the unknown—they were to play a central part in the drama that we unfolded. Dancing in their special circle, with Moon staffs fashioned with their own prayers, they tapped the ground and chanted a call to the light buried within the Earth. With the giveaway of their Moon time bloods to the Earth, they called for the coming of the light from its place of germination. Looking from our mother circle of 250 dancers, their small circle looked magical, with their steps dancing close around their own fire.

Our drumming within the mother circle pulled the main circle of dancers into motion. Their task was to pick up the light-energy brought to the surface of the Earth through the Moon circle, and to dance it into reality—to ground it in our lives—through the pulsing beat of our dance. Because of the number of people in this larger circle, they were far from the fire circle and the drummers in the center. During the night, the warmth and light called many to the central drums so that the strength of our rhythm never waned.

As in birthing, where a woman surrenders herself completely to her labor, part of our night-long ritual process was the surrendering of our small human egos and ideas to the larger reality of Mother Earth and Father Spirit, and we created special areas for this labor and releasing. When the dancers became fatigued, they could come within the circle to the Mother area, to rest face and belly down upon the Earth in surrender to Mother. Or they could go to the Father area to rest on their backs, and open in surrender to sky and Father. Throughout the night, the dancers exchanged places, resting in this giveaway of themselves, and then with renewed strength and clarity rising to dance again.

The dancing continued, sometimes in the exquisite silence of the quiet heartbeat drum under the bright stars above, and sometimes with chanting filling the glade. When at last the dawn star rose, everyone came out from the rest areas to make our circle complete, and to give a final pulsing of energy to our intention. Just before the dawning light, I broke the circle of the old day, had the fire of the passing age put out, and asked everyone to take a brief time out to clean up and put on their simple white vestments, each one tied with rainbow-colored ribbons. After putting on a white buckskin dress gifted for that occasion, I re-formed the circle, and called our fire men to lay a new fire.

The Moon women formed a circle around the fire pit, standing with their beautiful Moon staffs beside them. These staffs, which had called the light with their insistent tapping, were to be the kindling for the fire of the new dawning. Each Moon woman stepped forth and gave away to the fire, saying, "I give away this blood of life to All My Relations, and I open my womb to the light."

A huge roar came from the circle as the fire was lighted in the first rays of dawn light. Then we continued to dance awake our dreams, using these precious moments to give forth through our individual prayers and our circling dance, the highest and finest of our dreams—for ourselves and for all our family upon Mother Earth.

As the first rays of the sun came over the eastern mountains, dawn light glinted and sparkled on the lake to the east of us, and ospreys and eagles from the sanctuary nearby wheeled above our circle in the blue sky. A multi-cultural, multi-racial song of peace and harmony, of the golden dream for a renewed Earth, had been sent up, echoed and magnified by the crystal mountains around us. Later, as we feasted and shared the completion of our ceremony, we felt that a new day on Earth had truly begun.

I pulled away from the camp, realizing that three hundred people had come together easily and gracefully in a small forest glade. Not only had they taken care of themselves, but they had also contributed to the general welfare—we were leaving the campground more beautiful than when we had arrived. Our entire experience, not only our dance and our prayers, echoed the way of life that was our dream for mankind.

I named the fourth and final ceremony "Listening to the Great Voices: An Experience in Silent Knowledge." In communication again with an international group of supporters, I introduced its guiding vision. Almost every critical issue we face today on Earth is an issue of relationship, of our seeming inability to follow Creator's one law: You shall be in good relationship with all things and all beings in the Great Circle of Life. Whether it is we two-leggeds fighting and destroying each other in war; whether it is the massive cutting of trees that now results in desertification, destructive winds, and famine; whether it is dysfunctional relationships within the family and society; and whether it is the pollution of our life-giving waters, the tearing of our protective sky dome, the maltreatment of animals, or the chemical poisoning of our crop lands—*it is all a matter of relationship.* White Buffalo Calf Pipe Woman, Dawn Star, and countless other great masters have come among us to illuminate the solution to these issues by carrying the light of oneness for us to follow. *We must now take responsibility for this oneness, this way of harmony with All Our Relations: we must learn and make practical in our everyday lives the law of Good Relationship.*

For this final ceremony of the pledged cycle, we were given an interesting task: to be still and listen so that we might receive the silent knowledge coming to us so freely from the Great Voices within and all around us. We were being asked to bring back from the silence—the Great Mystery—a deeper knowing of oneness and its practice, so that our daily lives might shine forth as models of harmony and peace, so that the dawning light of this new day upon Earth might shine through us to All Our Relations. In making real the vision, we came to understand that the nature of our present task on Earth calls us to envision and create our reality together—and that in the process we practice the end result for which we pray.

This, the last ceremonial gathering, was seen as a unified vision quest. The mountain valley in which it took place was sweet with the scent of wild rose, sage, and evergreen. The Deerborn Valley is also full of ancient spirits of the land—a cave there holds the oldest human artifacts and animal remains in Montana, and is said to have been the magical cave of a bear shaman. We spent our first three days in preparation—of ourselves and the ceremonial grounds—through fasting, purification lodges, emotional clearing, unification and alignment processes, chanting, drumming, and dancing. One of the greatest joys there was the opportunity to keep a constant heartbeat sounding on the big ceremonial drums—both made by my adopted brother, Rodney Scott, who had recently gifted one to me. He and Pamela Tutthill had been the primary organizers of the event, as well. We had the remarkable chance to realize, through our bodies, how profound the drum's teaching is. This was especially powerful for those generations of us who lost that heartbeat at birth, when we were taken from our mother's breasts, remaining in a certain "un-bonded" state ever since. There was an ineffable energy of nurturing, trust, and oneness generated by that heartbeat, which resonated throughout the Deerborn Valley and all our hearts.

Over the past few years, most of the teachings given me have been for women, and I have been praying recently for things to share with men specifically. One very clear guidance that has come has been for men to join together in drum groups. The drum is a feminine form, which emulates Mother Earth and woman's womb; yet, as in marriage, it is often given into the care of the men. These men's groups, then, can become metaphorical caretakers of the instrument, the womb that renews all of life and is also the continuing heartbeat at the Center of Life.

Gathering together in groups of eight around a drum large enough for all to beat, to spend several hours in the resonating of that heartbeat, through the drummers and out to others, is a powerful practice (see instructions on page 127). Drum groups like this can give our young "warriors" a powerful and beneficial activity that serves their people much more effectively than the making of war parties. When the nurturing and renewing of life is held in a balanced way among men *and* women, our healing has truly begun.

We danced a circle around the altar, upon which an ancient "buffalo stone" and a bear effigy—from the altar of the bear shaman's cave—rested on a larger stone also from the cave, which had long ago been carved with bear and buffalo figures. We alternated periods of intense dancing with extended periods of deep contemplation. In the sweetness of the starry night, our dancers heard the many great and beautiful voices around us: the ancient people who rejoiced at the return of their songs; the bear shaman, watching from her hillside grave nearby; bird, wind, and river singing their melodies; buffalo and bear spirits calling from the ancients' altar; thunder rolling like tympani around the bowl of mountains; and the heartbeat of Mother Earth echoing through the continuous drumbeat in the center of our circle.

We had also heard a strong voice from the children playing there in stream and flowers, and from the children of the generations to come, asking us to create a life of beauty before us. Our Moon women again created a wonderful giveaway through their own Moon Lodge tipi, by gifting to the dance a Moon stick, which they wrapped with colored yarn to symbolize nurturance and oneness among all things. As we gathered the next morning in our final sharing circle, we realized that the messages each of us had heard individually from the Ancient Voices were very much one message. They represented each person's own path toward wholeness and healing, and also offered ways to channel their own wholeness into the healing of the large Circle of Life. We had done a mutual quest for vision, and had been answered. Our ceremony was an experience of beauty, cooperation, deep sharing, community, and strong vision—a microcosm of the oneness for which we joined in prayer for All Our Relations.

Although that gathering completed the envisioned ceremonies, there was one more step in the process that I had seen very clearly. To fulfill it, shortly after the winter solstice my partner Alvin EagleSmith, my assistant Melane Lohmann, and I went to a very special area on the eastern front of the Rocky Mountains, whose icy peaks soaring straight up out of the plains of the Blackfeet reservation I had seen as giant crystals for the magnification of my final prayers. In winter, that part of the country is often deep in snow, and buffeted by heavy winds, which make being outside for long very difficult. Yet, the day we picked to drive north had the feeling of spring in the middle of winter. We drove for hours up over the rolling hills, with the magnificent peaks rising before and beside us to the north and west. After stopping to visit elders on the reservation, we walked through the snowdrifts up the canyon I knew so well, both through vision and through spending time there in its summer meadows. We made a medicine wheel of prayer ties, which waved in the steady but gentle wind. Even with the warm day, that wind chill brought the temperature down below zero.

My experience of this simple ritual of completion was primarily gratitude—for the beauty and commitment of the very special people who had put forth the energy to participate over these four pledged years of my life, and gratefulness for my own growth and learning in the process. I have always been a person who depended upon herself, and who helped others. Cooperation and receiving help were not my pattern. These four years marked a wonderful shift for me, for I could not have done these things alone. My own commitment, as I gave thanks for the dancing of the four ceremonies, was to unroll even more fully in the world and in my life the intention of oneness: first, through working with others who teach in the same spirit as I, and secondly, by offering trainings whose focus would bring people together into small, cohesive, contiguous groups of their own. Through these groups, each person's true gifts and magnificence could be supported in daily life, and hopefully *each of them, as well as I, would truly dance awake the golden dream of peace, abundance, harmony, and the greening of the garden of Earth, a dream that lives in the heart of one and all.*

Within two days of our visit to the mountains, the temperature there dropped precipitously, and gale-force winds of 114 miles an hour whipped those canyons and plains. Railroad cars were blown off the tracks, houses were blown down, power lines fell, gas tanks froze, and havoc reigned. The old was most assuredly swept away in that storm. At home, we offered another prayer of thanksgiving for the inner guidance that led us to make that journey in the springlike weather we had serendipitously chosen. Even though the ceremonial cycle is now finished, the work has only begun.

MANIFESTING THROUGH THE FOUR WINDS

These days I see many teachings available on the four quadrants of the medicine wheel's Four Sacred Directions. These help us place ourselves in the world, and give us a framework on which to place the wide-ranging knowledge we receive.

However, I have seen very little concerning another aspect of the wheel that has been very useful to me: the Four Great Winds. The Winds are complementary to the stationary aspect of the Four Directions, through which all things naturally cycle. They are about the process of creation, about manifesting the dreams of our lives.

Go back to page 351 of this chapter and review our use of the energies of the Four Winds in the "Breaking the Chain" ceremony. This same empowering movement through the figure eight of the Winds can be used for anything you'd like to create.

1. Get very clearly in mind what you wish to manifest. Then move yourself toward its realization with the help of the powers of the four cross-quarters—NE, SE, SW, NW. Let's say, as an illustration, that you wish to manifest a new job, one more appropriate to your talents and desire for serving All Your Relations.

2. Begin this process by going to the Southeast (in meditation, dream, and study) and calling upon *the great masters of our human family.* This is not a passive, "come make it happen for me" kind of

calling. It is more a process of alignment of *yourself* with the truths they gave to humankind. So you might ask for the Dawn Star, for Buddha, or for any other wise and masterful being, to walk with you through the process. Attune yourself to the highest and finest humanity has offered—in essence, ask for the backing of the Masters. One way to do this is to meditate and study, both within yourself and through outer means, the precepts they gave for living a truly human life. When you can go to one or several of them in your meditation, and perceive them giving an enthusiastic "YES!" to your plans, then you are in that alignment that is very powerful.

3. Now do the same with the Northwest, *the Law*.

► Consider what the true laws of life are. For you, is the law represented by that moment when your father "laid down the law" and said, "I don't care if you want to be an artist. Our family has built this law practice for generations, and you are going to carry it on!" Or is the law White Buffalo Woman's teachings of oneness and good relationship—her message of the ways that help you blossom fully as who you are?

► Once again, get as clear as you can about what the laws mean to you. Pray to know them even more fully, and align yourself as closely as possible with them.

Can you imagine the power you now carry? You are walking a path within yourself that has garnered the "backing" of the masters of human life, which means that you are in clear alignment with what truly works for us as humans. And you are also following the true, deep laws of the larger reality. What a tremendously powerful place to be!

4. Next, move into the energy of the Northeast, which is where you gather your own power through *emotion*. Here you must be willing to let your enthusiasm build, to let your positive feelings and desires have full rein.

Too often in life not only have we been told to hold back the emotions our culture judges as negative—anger, hate, sadness—but we are also told to hold down our enthusiasm and excitement. "Don't get too excited; this might not even happen." "Settle down and act like a lady—stop jumping around even if you are happy and enthused." After years of this training, this begins to come from within ourselves. Having been disappointed before, we don't want to get our hearts set on something again.

► As you stand in the Northeast, take a close look at these kinds of old programs in yourself. This is where the importance of steps 2 and 3 comes in, for if you have your desires consciously aligned with the highest and finest you can perceive, then you can relax and know that you are moving in a positive direction.

▶ Now, your full excitement and joy about creating this wonderful new thing in your life can blossom forth! Imagining it fully, feeling it as true, and celebrating it create a motion outward (e-motion) into the world—knowing that something you held within yourself is now literally being propelled outward. Now envision how you will carry this new thing into your life and into the world. Remember, the more powerful the vibrations of your emotional feeling, the more powerful the motor you give this dream.

5. The final step, then, is the *spiritual action* of the Southwest. You are moving powerfully, aligned with your spirit and the Great Spirit.

▶ The time has come to take the concrete steps, do the groundwork, make the calls, tell people about your new life choices.

▶ And walk the dream into your reality.

This cycle of ceremonies not only focused my own and other people's attention on some very profound and critical issues, it served to teach me many things about working in a powerful way with larger groups; and it also magnified my understanding of how to manifest spiritual action in the world. I realized that my work had now become global. It seemed to me that the vision of the ancient dragon mother was coming true in my life—the tipi of light was spreading its healing and nurturing rainbow colors all around Mother Earth.

CHAPTER EIGHTEEN

AT CAMP ON THE DEERBORN

As Mother Earth and Father Spirit have been
my most powerful teachers,
I want to gift others with the opportunity
to learn from them directly.

The ancient ones sing in joy that you have come here
to deepen your spirit.

Spiritual warrior's pledge:
Not for myself alone, but that all the people may live.

We can come to the wilderness to feel what is possible
and naturally beautiful—but we must stand
rooted in the Earth and face the crying issues right where we live.

"The ancient ones sing in joy that you have come here to deepen your spirit," I said to my first Eagle Song training group, at Blacktail Ranch in Montana. In my mind's eye, I could see ancient spirits standing in a great circle around our tipi camp in the meadow beside the Deerborn River. Drifting down to me on the breeze I could hear a chant, a welcome song. I continued, "This valley has, for thousands of years, been a gathering place for ceremonial magic."

My dream for many long years on the road had been of a wilderness place where I could bring groups of people onto the land to train them. Although I had taught at many fine learning centers, in beautiful parts of the country, none of them were it. Then I heard from my friends Shakira and Richard about a beautiful ranch set back against the exquisite

Scapegoat Wilderness of northwestern Montana—a ranch upon which an ancient cave had been discovered. Shakira told me about Tag Rittel, the ranch owner, who had as a young man explored with zeal every foot of this land that his grandfather had homesteaded. It had been Blackfeet Indian country before then, and Tag had found everything from arrowheads to eagle catch pens, tipi rings and an ancient stone Sun wheel, aligned exactly with the solstice dawnings. Another stone circle, which seems to have been both a medicine wheel and a Sundance ground, rests in a high aspen-ringed meadow near the new bunkhouse.

Most exciting for Tag as a young explorer, and for us as we journeyed there, is the enormous cave he tunneled his way into, to find—about a quarter of a mile down inside the five miles of it he explored—an ancient altar. Lying undisturbed on this stone altar was an ancient buffalo skull, and a remarkable stone: carved in simple, elegant lines on one side, a bear, and on the other side, seemingly more modern, a buffalo. Further exploration of the cave's depths led to evidence of human habitation there over eons of time. University experts carbon-dated some of the human artifacts at six thousand years old, and other remains, such as the enormous musk ox skull and huge bears' skulls, at twenty thousand years old.

Making our way down the steep entrance tunnel, through high-domed rooms and low passages, we could feel ourselves drawn back in time, to share again with Tag the excitement of discovering the altar. In the quiet, dripping womb of Mother Earth, the altar and the stone still rest as he found them. We quieted ourselves there within the vaulted room and welcomed the darkness that helped us become one with our Mother Earth, with that place, and all that lives there in spirit. I sang songs which echoed, within each person and within the sweet darkness, their sorrows as well as their joy and wholeness.

I had discovered the richness of this beautiful retreat place during "Listening to the Great Voices," the last gathering of my ceremonial cycle. One day after that gathering, it suddenly dawned on me that this was in fact the place to begin my Eagle Song Camps, and to make my dream of a wilderness training camp come true. Blacktail Ranch had all the things I wanted. There was the setting at the end of a long road, backed against the quiet of wilderness; an ancient atmosphere of cere-mony and holiness; a meadow of tall grass and wildflowers for the tipi village; a river to play in by day and listen to at night; another small stream where the sweat lodge would sit beside a beaver pond; a herd of paint ponies to ride; and facilities to serve a group. Tag and his wife Sandra said "Yes" to my proposal, and we were on our way.

There were important reasons I wanted to create a camp for my teaching, besides the fact that I was weary of the road, and longed for a summer "office" by a rippling mountain stream. Talking about Mother Earth and Father Spirit standing in hotel rooms and conference centers in big cities—without so much as a live plant in the windowless room—brought it home to me that students would learn more by experiencing the things we could only talk about there. Now I had spoken enough of Mother Earth calling us back to her sweet cradle, and of Father Spirit alive in the birds and wind; it was time to take my students onto the land. In one of my inner journeys, a great echoing voice had said to me, "Go back to the land; everything you need is there. Go back to the land—everything you need is there." Over and over, day after day, month after month, the voice echoed, its call a continuous song in my mind. I looked into my own experience of learning and transformation, and realized that as *Mother Earth and Father Spirit have been my most powerful teachers, I wanted to gift others with the opportunity to learn from them directly.* From that understanding came my intention to create a place for my students to live in harmony with the Earth and to deepen their contact with Spirit.

The first year, with the help of my assistant, Melane Lohmann, I called together two camps: A DEEPENING OF SPIRIT and THE HEALING VISION. DEEPENING OF SPIRIT is a two-week intensive training for women already on a path of service in their lives. It incorporates ceremony, ritual action, physical toning, drumming, dancing, traditional purification lodge, and vision seeking to realize White Buffalo Woman's challenge of aligning self and community. HEALING VISION is a nine-day camp devoted to seeking personal vision through deepening students' relationships with Mother Earth and Father Spirit, and honing their awareness of the unique gifts they bring to the healing of themselves and our planet. In the years since, I have added SONG OF THE BEAUTY WAY, IN THE CRADLE OF MOTHER EARTH, and SINGING THE SACRED as well as our CONTINUING THE QUEST camps which are specifically meant for returning participants.

SONG OF THE BEAUTY WAY is designed to encourage students, through the metaphors of ritual art and Native craft, to live their lives creating beauty on their Earthwalk—integrating beading, basket making, rawhide and leather work, feather decoration, making rattles, and other crafts, with a philosophy of service. This work leads to our final act of creating a Beauty Bundle—a unique reminder of the beauty path they have committed to walk, in all aspects of their lives.

After studying with the famous tracker and survival expert Tom Brown, I realized it was important to pass on to others some of the skills he teaches. Not only could they help one stay alive in a survival situation, more importantly, they could help my students understand that Mother Earth offers a safe and nurturing cradle for us. Although we may love being in the wilderness, too often in our ignorance of Earth ways we feel unsafe there without the excess baggage of equipment and food we feel we must bring there. Tom offers an incredible range of skills given him by his Lipan Apache teacher, Stalking Wolf, to make us truly at home in the arms of our Mother, the Earth. IN THE CRADLE OF MOTHER EARTH is designed to give students a beginning knowledge of some of these attitudes and skills, as well as the philosophy of wholeness that is a part of all the camps.

Our SINGING THE SACRED camp is focused on sacred and healing work through voice, song, chanting, toning, and drumming. It is a joyful sharing of chants; an opportunity to create new songs by listening to Spirit; a chance to practice the harmony of our voices blending; and a time to heal ourselves through vibration and rhythm.

Although these Eagle Song camps vary in their content and presentation, some themes echo through them all. I'll use our work at A DEEPENING OF SPIRIT camp to illustrate the flow of activity, the bonding and the teachings, common to all the camps:

The day before camp commences, students arrive to set up their tents in the grassy open meadow adjacent to the tipi circle. With the guidance of staff, some choose the shelter of huge cottonwoods near the river, some the open sun at the meadow's center. Still others are called to the banks of the flowing, singing river to site their new "homes." Inwardly commenting on the metaphors these choices portray, and noting each new arrival's seeming level of comfort with outdoor living, the staff begins to get acquainted with the campers.

> Over the horizon something's coming.
> Something beautiful for you now.
> *Way ya, hey ya, hey ya, hi yo!*

Our camp crier sings this beautiful Cree morning song to awaken with drum and voice the sleepers in tents and tipis to a dazzling high-country morning. They then take their first of many hikes down the dirt river road to the circle-prayer of thanksgiving before breakfast in the bunkhouse. On the way they are already discovering the beauty of the land and of each other for which to be thankful.

Then back up the road to our wonderful yurt—a round tentlike building thirty feet in diameter and made of canvas stretched over wood—for the first teachings and the opening ceremony. The resounding heartbeat of my big drum, "Mother's Heartbeat Singing," calls us into circle.

The first element or theme in any Eagle Song camp is that of **unity and oneness.** It is the first experience I want campers to have—one I hope will continue as a baseline element for all of our days. Together, we will use the teachings of Mother Earth and Father Spirit to deepen our own spirits and unify our focus. We will talk very little about our pasts, our professions, what we have done. We will concentrate upon ourselves as spiritual beings, and gift ourselves with support for that part of our natures.

Thus, early on I assign people a "twin" or "buddy" with whom they check in daily and exchange special care and nurturing. I also divide the larger camp group into "hoops" of eight as learning units to give campers a sense of White Buffalo Woman's teaching about unity and support in action in their own lives. Each of these little communities is assigned its own camp staffer as a counselor, or "hooper," to provide campers with a closer sense of relationship and security.

These hoops of eight also form the basis of teachings on Moon Lodges and men's drumming circles, and they facilitate the intimate processing campers are asked to do in tipi dreaming circles, as well as such necessary chores as clean-up and tending to the dining hall. Among other things, clean-up is supervised by the staff gopher ("go-fer")—our logistics coordinator.

The second baseline element of our experiences at Eagle Song camp will be **to make our intention clear.** Each camper, as well as myself and the staff, will consciously choose to be present in this circle, leaving behind all the things that normally draw our attention. I remind campers that this is to be a time for them—not for family or friends or cooking meals or work or service—but *personal* time for each of them!

To make these first two elements more real for us, we create a group altar. Each person is called on to find something they have with them to offer for the altar, signifying their willingness to be fully present—for themselves, and in support of the group. As they place their offering on the altar, they make a commitment to stand in circle, and state their personal intention for camp. Often, rings or necklaces or pouches are placed there, but one woman gave us a wonderful laugh by putting her bra on the altar, to symbolize the freedom she sought! After building the altar, a quick talk about how to live together on this land to make life easy and enjoyable completes our time inside. Although inside the yurt is sunny and has a much more open feeling than any other kind of building, we are still inside, and are anxious to get out into the flowering meadows.

We leave the yurt, and play circle games of physical connection and bonding to get us running and breathing in the fresh mountain air. Our dog Bud, the camp mascot, "helps" in the excitement. The game of "knots," in which people cross hands to form an enormous human knot to untie, helps campers through their shyness about getting close and touching one another, and to begin to cooperate and trust one another. They learn in another game that they can support others and be supported, in a way that frees both to relax and let go. After this strenuous morning of intense focus and romping play, we break for lunch delivered to the tipi meadow, and rest among the grasses.

Through this kind of contact, and through the process of living with a group of women for fourteen intense days, campers also have the opportunity to come into more harmony with other women. Rather than conflict, jealousy, or competition, our focus is on recognizing each other as mirrors, on finding unity among ourselves, and on using our togetherness to serve ourselves and All Our Relations.

Now I ask the campers to pay attention to a different kind of bonding and oneness—one that connects them to Mother Earth and Father Spirit, alive in the entire Circle of Life around them—an awareness that will go with them on their afternoon *medicine wheel walk,* and on into their lives. In the medicine wheel walk, I invite them to "take a circle of the territory," to walk around the area in a large, sweeping circle, acquainting themselves with the area in which they will live and with the other peoples in the web of life where they are guests.

"Note who and what you see," I tell them; "pay attention to what you feel and what calls your attention. The things revealed on this walk can teach you and give you guidance." In our world today, we have few means to receive guidance from the world around us. Some part of us expects to hear spiritual messages from the voice of a white-haired numinous figure, or receive none at all. Yet Native peoples had many means to receive wisdom from the Great Mystery. A primary one involved building a symbol system through which messages could come to them. Native people closely observed the other peoples who made up the circle of their daily life, and learned of each people's unique ways—and unique gifts or medicine.

White Buffalo Woman and many Native peoples refer to each group of living things as a people—the deer people, the stone people, the star people—as a way of acknowledging their equality with us in this dance of life. For instance, a mouse living on and in the Earth sees things in detail. The eagle flying high and near to Spirit sees the long view or visionary way. The wolf has a close-knit family and works in cooperation. The otter is especially playful. To know all the many beings well allows the Native person to assign to each a meaning commensurate with its medicine gifts (see Jamie Sams and David Carson's Medicine Cards in appendix 1, page 458).

I suggest to the campers that they not only study the medicine wheel symbology I have given them, but that they also begin to form their own symbols by paying attention to what things may mean to them. Then, not only on this walk, but from now on in their lives, these animals, birds, trees, stones, reptiles, flowers, and other beings can be vehicles through which the Great Spirit and their deep self can send them messages. Thus, a yellow bird seen heading south is not just a passing event, but perhaps signals this person to awaken (gold, east, awareness) and pay attention to the relationships in her life, or to her need for humor (south, heart, relationships, laughter). A turtle slowly making its way across one's path to the east might be a reminder that there is now time to slow down and really experience things, rather than hurrying along unaware. So, when the campers are aware of these concepts, they head out, each in their own direction, for a solitary medicine wheel walk through which they come to know this place that will be home for fourteen days.

As with every gathering time, the mother drum's heartbeat calls us together again after dinner. Food takes on a new meaning to bodies hungry from hiking and breathing the high mountain air! In the evening we share stories from each other's medicine walks, then gather around the big drum to learn the correct ways to use her and care for her, and to practice the steady heartbeat that will bond the group. I introduce songs—ceremonial songs, dance songs, and songs that are wonderful for group harmony—all of which we will continue to use during our days together. The element of music—of song, dance, and drumming—becomes a vital part of camp. It is a way we bond with each other, practice our harmony, send up prayers, and bring our heartbeats into oneness. Our hearts literally come into the same rhythm when we are around the drumming heartbeat for even a short while—thus we become of one heart!

Each morning after the first day, we arise to the crier's call and join for morning exercise—a blend of several ancient movement forms whose purpose is flexibility, longevity, weight stabilization, increased circulation, and growing bodily awareness. These exercises are always included because it is of primary importance to have a healthy body if we are to do our work in the world effectively. Woven into our time together are many things that will not only begin the process of becoming more healthy and vital, but also enable campers to take home practices for their long-term health. We can attend to our physical vehicles in many ways: through eating nourishing meals of primarily vegetarian food, learning more functional ways of moving through Feldenkrais exercises, learning to listen to inner messages about what our bodies need, or hiking.

How we attend to our bodies leads us to look at how we use the whole of our attention. Science has shown that each person has only seven—plus or minus two—units of conscious awareness available to them at any time. This means many things are done outside of our conscious awareness. Consider how we learn to do complex tasks: First we learn a simple piece of the process, then put it on automatic so we can go on to the next level of the task. For example, think of the complexity of learning to walk or to drive a car. Given this fact, it becomes important to be aware of how we use our attention.

I have already shared with you the way Dawn Boy taught me a way from his tradition to think about this. The "first attention" calls us to attend to our physical bodies, for on our Earth walk they carry our spirit and soul and action. An illustration of the importance of this first attention is that, if we are attending to something else and happen to walk in front of a fast-moving train, then we won't be around long enough to attend to anything else!

The "second attention" can be used for more symbolic or representational tasks, such as meditation, imagining, or thinking about a specific topic. For instance, driving down the road, we may use several units of our first attention to watch the road beside and behind us, and to perform the physical tasks of driving. Our second attention, meanwhile, may be engaged in thinking about our boyfriend, planning the day's work, or going over the words to our favorite new song.

I use our beginning circle dance to illustrate this to our campers. To begin with, they need to use their first attention to make the circle round and even, to put their arms comfortably around each other, to figure out how to let their weight down onto the left foot at the downbeat, and to keep from stepping on a neighbor or dragging the circle by being too slow. This totally occupies them for a short while.

Once I see that they have gotten this down and are doing it quite automatically, I can talk to them about the dance step itself. I suggest that the left foot is the feminine, receptive side, and thus stepping down on it can be used to represent their connection with Mother Earth and receiving support from her. I ask them to use their second attention in a simple meditation: to say "Mother, Mother," each time their left foot comes down. As they do this, they picture themselves standing over the very center of the Earth, connecting to her heart, giving attention to her with their soft step upon her face, and receiving support and information from her. This engages a second attention. If they get too carried away with this, they sometimes let their physical circle get into a strange shape, and need to be reminded to keep a strong first attention to the integrity of the circle.

Once these two attentions are fully engaged, and the tasks they've been given become quite automatic and easy, I ask them to use their "third attention." The third attention is the attention of holiness—it consists of attending not to oneself as an individual, but to the whole Circle of Life—a global, all-inclusive consciousness. It is much like Master Kaskafayet's God realization, through which we come to understand ourselves as one with the web of life. I have our dance circle practice this by dropping away from attending to their feet or even to the meditation, to focus their awareness on the *full circle*. I ask them to dance close together so that their left step is the entire circle's left step, and they think of themselves "as the circle." This practice in holiness extends throughout our time together, growing more powerful as we use our circle to represent the great Circle of Life.

In this and many other ways, we work through our bodies to learn the principles of oneness with the life around us. Campers become more aware of how they use their attention, and thus how to choose what "to buy with it." They learn that it is leaking their power to attend to what does not work or what might happen some mythical time in the future. Their personal power builds as they use their attention to focus on the tasks at hand, and how these tasks are often metaphors that can be taken into their larger life.

In making our group altar, each person has stated a personal intention. I add my statement of intention as I talk to them about how we will move through our days at camp. I remind them of the third element of the training, one we have already worked with in the "dance of attention": **building awareness.** First of all, they will work to understand the ways in which they leak their power. We help them make a serious assessment of the ways in which they habitually waste life energy, time, and consciousness—the ways they limit themselves, either subtly or blatantly; how they live their daily lives; and how they affect those around them. Through journeying, processing, and working in small groups, each person has the opportunity to specifically identify several major power leaks, including when, where, how, and with whom they occur. We then make an assessment of the things we need to work on and improve. Once these power leaks are defined and challenged, we have more of our own power and energy available to ourselves and others.

One camper realizes she spends all her time trying to please everyone else and never does what she is good at. Another realizes she is in a job that goes against her principles. Still another realizes she nags all the time rather than asking directly for what she wants. A fourth person realizes that she needs to go back to school in order to improve her skills in her chosen field. Another understands that she spends more of her time hassling with her partner than she does in finding better ways to relate. Another acknowledges that her overweight and poor stamina keep her from doing many things she wants. On these occasions, anything in our lives that doesn't allow for the highest and best use of our full selves is up for examination.

Working in their hoops, campers distill and distill this information until they come up with three or four beliefs or habits or patterns that are basic to all their power leaks. For instance, one underlying belief might be low self-esteem; a second might be dysfunctional childhood patterns; a third might be a deep belief that nothing will ever work for them.

One highly effective way to challenge these power leaks and to move forward in becoming more of who we already are, is to make an Action Contract, in which we commit to personal "Acts of Power" and "Acts of Beauty." Power, I believe, is what we gain when we come into harmony with ourselves, our deepest truths, and our highest intentions, and flow harmoniously with all the life around us. It is the power of the river, helping us paddle downstream! Therefore, an Act of Power is an action through which we can begin to plug our power leaks, handle our issues, and become more whole and well within ourselves. It is an act of personal healing, integration, and empowerment. When we are truly empowered, we are acting from the core of our own unique being—a beingness connected with Source, with Spirit, with All That Is. Empowerment not only opens us up to the creative flow of the river of life, but also to the joy of being who we truly are—to doing what is meaningful to us, doing what has value in our lives. When we are empowered, the full force of our energy, excitement, interest, talent, intention, and choice is focused in one direction and it becomes very powerful.

Yet, being empowered must not be confused with being "success-ful." We each know many successful people who dislike what they are doing, find little of their true selves in their work, and feel little fulfill-ment even though they may be doing good things. I know top-flight lawyers who would find their true fulfillment in building exquisite cabinets; storekeepers who yearn to sit at a computer all day and create programs; computer programmers who would love to have a business of their own through which to express themselves.

Our acts of power might include devising a manageable life plan that would allow us to start losing weight, choosing to deal with childhood abuse issues by going into counseling, finding a job more in line with our calling and values, clearing up a relationship or leaving it, cleaning out and giving away all the excess piled up in our lives, taking lessons to enhance our artistic skills, or taking more time to rest and nurture ourselves.

Through working with their hoop and hoop leader, each camper comes up with something that is uniquely truthful, realistic, and work-able for her. She also outlines the precise steps and time lines she needs to accomplish these things.

Then we turn to Acts of Beauty, through which we extend our personal wholeness into the world by giving the gift we came to Earth to offer. Standing in the best place we are able to at the time, we are called to give away to All Our Relations. We are in the world not only to lift ourselves and grow but also to share our gifts and talents with others. Thus we must remember the spiritual warrior's pledge: *Not for myself alone, but that all the people may live.* Therefore I ask campers to commit to acts that will create a more beautiful way before and around them, acts that are a giveaway to All Our Relations.

Although working within ourselves is the primary task, we cannot wait until some theoretical moment when we have perfected ourselves to give to the larger Circle of Life. Giving to that larger circle can become a part of our learning and growth. So Acts of Beauty are acts of service and healing for others. One woman may commit to fully recycling in her home; another may be able to create a recycling pro-gram for her whole city. One may commit to talking with her children's classmates at school about Earth harmony; another may write an article for a national magazine on the same issues. One may commit to taking her children camping to introduce them to the beauty of Mother Earth directly; another may create an exploration program for her church youth group. Another may join a women's circle, while her sister camper may go home and lead one for the women in her community.

Some commit to tithing to socially conscious organizations; others may transfer their family investments to them. Again, each person is helped to find exactly what level they are able to contribute, what talents they have to use, and how to use them now.

Working toward actions that will take campers far beyond our Eagle Song camp days is the central intention of our time together. And we will work in many different ways toward the final ceremony where commitments are made to these acts of power. One way we focus on action contracts is through our hoops. Another might be personal meditations or journal work. One of the most powerful ways to refocus our lives is the vision quest. This time of quiet and communing with our deep selves and with Spirit adds enormous power to our personal understanding, and helps us give form to our commitments.

Yet another way we work with these acts of wholeness and service is to create a rawhide shield upon which symbols of these inner experiences can be made real in the world. Early in our first week, we spend a day making the shield itself. However, the campers will not paint any symbols on their shields until they have returned from their alone time on the mountain, and have completed writing their Action Contract— their commitment to Acts of Power and Beauty. Constructing the shield is an amazing process, during which each camper forms a willow hoop, cuts the rawhide circle, and laces it over the hoop. It is then left in a safe place, packed with sand, to dry. The shields, eight to ten inches in diameter, are then hung on the leather thong, which will also serve as a necklace, when it is worn over the maker's heart in ceremony.

The powerful element of awareness will continue with us throughout our days at camp. Not only in our inner work, but in outer interactions as well. I call campers again and again to bring themselves into the present moment and to become aware of the beauty of life and the lessons around them. We open our awareness in a new way, as we descend into the cave and Great Mystery, into Mother Earth's darkness.

After wonderful stories of introduction from Tag—about his discovery and exploration of the cave—we hop in the old school bus to be driven several miles up the Deerborn, past the magical Medicine Rock. Down into the great cave we go to explore and to rest in powerful silence and meditation around the ancient altar. Our songs echo in the cavernous rooms as we sing to Mother Earth, leave tiny offerings, and pray. Many participants find that being in Mother's mysterious womb is the most powerful experience of camp. Emmy Devine writes of our experience there, "Standing in the deepest black, within the vaulted pelvic bones of the shaman's cave, water dripping and women weeping, Brooke echoes my fears and yearnings." We have found a feeling of Mother Earth's deep love and unconditional acceptance there, which we will carry with us for a long time to come.

Outside again in the sunshine, we have lunch at an old cabin near the mouth of the cave. Then the bus heads back down the canyon, and those who want to stay behind and leisurely walk back to the ranch, playing in the streams along the way that feed the Deerborn. All are encouraged during this and any other free time to begin exploring the central ranch area for their own vision quest spot.

The fourth element of our Eagle Song work is that of **purification.** I have Mother Earth and Father Spirit as wonderful allies here. Living for fourteen days under the stars, open to the fresh breezes and open skies, sung to by birds and streams, there is a natural purification and clearing that begins to take place. The fact that campers have left their daily lives and work behind is also a clearing.

A more active process of clearing takes place when they enter the stone-people lodge for a purification ceremony that is a gift from me and my staff to our campers. The campers help make a domed willow support structure over the pit that will eventually contain heated stones. Then blankets and tarps are placed over the support structure to form a "womb" that is pitch black inside, for this lodge represents the womb of Mother Earth. When the stones are hot, we strip down to the suit Mother gave us when we were birthed and crawl into the structure, saying "All My Relations" as we enter and leave, to remind us that this ceremony of purification is not just for us but for the full circle of life.

This traditional ritual performance reminds us that we can use something physically cleansing to purify our minds, emotions, and spirits as well. We purify our bodies with steam from water sprinkled on the stones; and our emotions, mind, and spirit with prayer. When we are complete, we emerge from the lodge with thanksgiving, and experience the cleansing of fresh air, and a plunge into the beaver pond beside us on Inipi Creek. However, the ritual is not complete until we have lain face down upon Mother Earth, felt our heartbeats become one with hers, and set in our memories the relaxation, release, and clarity the purification lodge has given us.

Our days pass quickly: hiking to see the new pinto colts in the high pasture, learning the ways of the land, singing, dancing, chanting, going for a trail ride on our day off, resting in flower-filled sunlit meadows, working together to become more aware of our inner truths, and learning the ways of the Moon in the little Moon Lodge tipi set some way off from camp on the river.

Sooner than we can imagine, it is time for our ceremony to send them out for their days of vision questing at chosen spots in the bowl of the valley. **Questing for vision and guidance from our own deeper selves and from the Great Mystery** is the fifth element of the training. We have spent days getting ready for this time: learning about vision questing traditions and rituals for setting our sacred circle, getting to know ourselves so that we can use this visioning time well, and learning to enjoy being outside in the starry nights.

An intense game we use to help accomplish being comfortable in the night is called "Coup!" In this game of hide and seek, we divide into two teams or tribes who must cross each other's territory in order to get to the safety of their winter camps. A crier from each team goes to the far end of the territory and calls a special coyote, owl, or other cry to signal her team home. The tribes—identifiable by personal face paint and unique headbands, special communication signals, a chief strategist, and a scout—cross paths and attempt to count coup by taking each other's headbands. The stories that are told over hot chocolate at the bunk house later are illuminating, as we count to see which team "couped" the most headbands.

We rise early on vision quest morning. The staff prepares the ceremonial ground, while campers get their bundles ready, taking minimal but necessary items—sleeping bag, ground cover, rain gear, and water. After the blessing and purification ceremony, I perform one last ritual—painting their faces and praying over them—before they make their own way to the chosen place they will stay for the remainder of that day and the next.

During the time they are gone, the staff and I pray with them at regular intervals, and send out the heartbeat from the Mother Drum both in the morning and at sunset. We connect our hearts and minds, checking in with the questers on the left side and sending them strength and encouragement through our prayers. We know that each has formed a sacred circle around herself—a circle of protection and containment within which to build the energy of her prayers.

We know also that the questers will be working on their one right-sided task: decorating their beauty arrow. This is a forked stick they have found on the land to represent the arrow of beauty, the giveaway they will send into the world. During their quest, at a time when they are thinking or praying about this active part of their life, they will wind the beauty arrow with yarn—a wrap for each prayer. Many of them add other decorations, such as flowers, sage, feathers, lichen, or other natural items they have found at their questing site.

One of the lessons the questers learn through their days on the mountain, and in many other ways, is the power of prayer to make the spiritual way real in our daily life. We begin our day together with each woman taking a pinch of tobacco and a pinch of cornmeal for offering prayers. Each of us goes off a short distance alone and uses the tobacco to make a prayerful connection with All Our Relations—most especially those with whom we're living for these days. We then offer the cornmeal to nurture all in the circles of life around us. This small ritual helps each of us place ourselves in proper and holy perspective with all of life.

"What I got was prayer," Kristine McAllister reported. "Those prayers made me feel safe and as though I was constantly being balanced. Prayers carried us through all the difficult times and resolved my anxiety. Brooke had unquestionable faith that was expressed through the prayers, and the patience that comes from faith. I have carried these learnings into my daily life, and hold her in mind when I become anxious or impatient. Then I simply call in prayer."

We learn to use prayer as a way of asking assistance from the great forces around us, and as a way of expressing gratitude, whether at meals or in the "doingness" of our days. Dorothy Mason, a camper who became one of my Eagle Song staff, says, "Brooke has a way of praying that invokes the aliveness of the seen and unseen dimensions that work together on this planet toward heart and life. She stands in a meadow, fully connected to the Earth and Sky, and with a clear, strong voice speaks to the Grandfathers, the Grandmothers, the winged ones, the four-leggeds, the tree and flower and wind spirits . . . and my entire being listens with a single ear, fully awakened to the power of that call— knowing in a profound way in those moments the reality of oneness in the Circle of Life around me. Brooke gathers the layers of the Sacred, and with her voice and vision brings them into form to be remembered by each of us on our way toward home."

Having made their continual prayers and touched that reality of oneness with the Circle of Life around their power place, the questers come down off the mountain in the dawn light of the second day, to be greeted in a personal cleansing ritual by me, and by drumming from the staff. Silence, integration, light food, and quiet re-entry time make up the remainder of the day.

From now on time is compressed—things seem to speed up. We gather together to share briefly the highlights of each person's quest, and in the afternoon each woman has the opportunity to share privately with the staff or with me her personal questions or stories. I remind questers not to lessen the power of their experience by revealing it all to everyone, and ask them to hold their vision for themselves, that it might be something they treasure and learn from for years to come.

Now comes the time for them to paint their shields with the symbols of their wholeness on the outside, and tiny symbols on the back to remind them to be aware of the ways in which their power leaks.

Campers then return to their hoops to finalize, on paper, their Acts of Power and Beauty. This is the sixth element of our training: **choice and commitment.** When our staff divides campers into hoops, we do it geographically, because these hoops will be staying in contact with each other, and experience has shown that phone bills are not so huge if campers live in proximity. Each hoop further divides itself into two smaller groups—which we humorously call hooplets for want of a better name—to act as support groups for each other over the next six to twelve months in fulfilling the commitments each camper will make.

Each of the members of a hooplet writes out the Action Contract of her commitments—including a statement of how she may try to flake out, give up, or make excuses for not completing them, in order to plug the loopholes she may face in later months. Copies are made for me, for her hooper, and for each member of her hooplet. In this way, all know exactly what is to take place, and can give support through prayers, letters, and phone calls.

To make this Action Contract process more real, let me tell you the story of Nell. She came to us a loud, boisterous woman weighing well over two hundred pounds. And she "threw that weight around," pushing her way into every situation, acting as though being big meant that she was very powerful and special. She carried what therapists sometimes call "aggressive fat."

As we journeyed through the week, it became clear that her weight held her back from many activities—her knees would simply give out under the stress of carrying her very far on the land. She went through a lot of anger about the kitchen not serving heavy meats or sweets with our meals, threatening to get someone to take her to town for a "real meal."

As the hoop worked together, and Nell began to feel safe about expressing her true feelings, she began to claim her sadness at how she looked and how unhealthy she, in fact, was. She shared with her hoop that she had trouble being active, not only here, but in her daily life as well. And then, as sometimes happens with this issue, she began to acknowledge the sexual abuse she had received from the time she was very small. As Nell expressed it, "Becoming big and mean and ugly was the only way I could protect myself from the cruelty and sexual advances of my male relatives." Although the work at camp was not about resolving all these issues, Nell had the opportunity to see how these old patterns no longer served her—how much they leaked her power.

For her Acts of Power in her Action Contract, Nell committed to continuing the work she had begun on her childhood abuse patterns and her present unworkable patterns. She would very likely attend a self-help group, such as Overeaters Anonymous, so that she could specifically address the issues around her weight. Another part of her pledge was a gently strengthening program of exercise. The last part of her contract, her Act of Beauty, would be to begin volunteer work with abused children—work she knew would help to open, soften, and heal her heart. As you can see, the final contract may look rather simple, yet the process of coming to the specific commitments is a deeply moving and transforming one.

The support of Nell's hoop was a major factor in her process, and it would continue to be a primary support for her until she was able to build that in her own community.

The story of Lannie also comes to mind. A person who for all of her forty-five years had been devoted to raising a family and doing volunteer work in her community, Lannie had never really paid attention to her own wants and needs or to her own spiritual development. For her, the Action Contract process really began when she called to ask about Eagle Song camp and was very unsure she could leave her grown family and old patterns to venture forth. To say that I encouraged her to come is putting it mildly.

Lannie made a remarkable step in coming to camp, and spent her days there evaluating how much of her power she had leaked through being a "good girl," a helper, a fixer, and a supermom. There were moments when she cried in the arms of her hoop for the "loss of so many years" of her life, years in which she never ever thought of what she personally would like to be or find joy in doing. She longed to truly know herself and to nurture the gift of her true self now that she had the time and freedom to do it. Her Action Contract set out specific things she was going to do for herself: a new haircut; a new wardrobe that would be a personal statement in color and design of who she felt herself to be; a meditation group she had been wanting to join; and classes she would take.

Lannie's Action Contract read something like this:

ACTION CONTRACT FOR ACTS OF POWER

I, **Lannie** . . . having fearlessly examined the ways in my life in which I have leaked and given away my power and energy, now make a sacred covenant with Mother Earth and Father Sky to live a powerful life and to accept myself as a powerful creator.

In the presence of All My Relations and my Sacred Hoop, I firmly commit to the following Act of Power:

1. I will spend three weeks investigating various hair stylists for their ability, and looking through magazines to select styles I might like. By the end of the fourth week at home, I will have a new hair style that brings out my unique beauty and feels wonderful! I will send snapshots to each member of my hooplet as proof by the fifth week.

2. I will spend a month, if needed, finding someone—whether a good friend or a professional—to help me create a personal wardrobe that expresses my uniqueness, compliments my coloring and shape, and fits my budget and lifestyle. Over the following six months, I will create for myself, through my clothing, a look that expresses who I truly am. Part of this process will include going through my present clothing and eliminating everything that does not meet these criteria. Snapshots of my looking dynamite will go to hooper and hooplet as I buy the clothing for each season.

3. Within two weeks of returning home, I will be regularly attending the meditation class I began but quit because others "needed" my attention. I will attend regularly for a trial period of three months, and check in with my hooplet about whether this is meeting my real needs. At the end of that time, I may continue if it works for me; if not, I will within a month find another group that may better suit my needs and attend regularly for another three-month trial.

4. I will take the six-week study course on grieving and loss given through "Hospice" that I have wanted to attend for several years now. The next class begins a month or so after I return home, and

I will take it. I will write a three-page report to share with my hooper and hooplet the learnings I have gained.

5. I will take the Assertiveness Training class offered by the growth center in my area. I will continue to work personally with the therapist who runs it if she and I decide that this would be valuable for me.

Ways I may sabotage myself:

I will be very persistent and cunning—very sure that others need me so much that I cannot possibly devote all this time to myself. I am also likely to bring up issues of money. Don't let me get away with any of it. I am much too powerful to let these things keep me from knowing my true self!

I require the following amount of time to fulfill this contract.

I will need three months to fullfill my Acts of Power Action Contract.

I reserve the right to amend this contract and give myself permission to grow through each step in the living of my vision.

Should I fail to honor my commitment to this Act of Power, I agree to:

If I do not accomplish any of the above in the allotted time and in the eyes of myself or my hooplet, I pledge to give away my mother's heirloom ring, her most precious gift to me.

_____

Signature and Date

ACTION CONTRACT FOR ACTS OF BEAUTY

I, **Lannie**, pledge myself to actively demonstrate my gratitude to All My Relations for the blessings Spirit has bestowed on me in countless ways.

I renew my Spiritual Warrior's pledge—**"Not for myself alone, but that all the people may live."**

In the presence of Mother Earth, Father Sky, All My Relations, and my Sacred Hoop, I firmly commit to the following Act of Beauty:

Rather than leaking my power by "helping" others, I realize that true transformation begins with myself, so I will begin with me. I pledge not to give myself away in service again until I know more of

who I am and what gift I came to offer the world. I will not do volunteer work for three months. And I will check with my hooper and hooplet any time in the following three months I feel an urge to volunteer my services so they can help me decide if this would be a true expression of myself, one that comes from something other than the need to please others.

Ways I may sabotage myself:

The worst hook will be when my daughter calls at the last minute, frantic for a babysitter—it will be a great challenge to go to my class instead of rescuing her. I will help myself by giving her a clearly written statement of my schedule, and asking her to honor it.

I require the following amount of time to fulfill this contract.

I will need six months to fulfill my Acts of Beauty Action Contract.

I reserve the right to amend this contract and give myself permission to grow through each step in the living of my vision.

Should I fail to honor my commitment to this Act of Beauty, I agree to give away:

My telephone answering machine that allows me to be constantly "on call."

_____

Signature and Date

Lannie did have many times when she faltered, yet through persistent help from her hooplet—first, in remembering how deeply she wanted these changes; and secondly, in receiving their suggestions about ways to meet each challenge—she triumphed. This triumph was not only in small things, it went much deeper, for she allowed herself to walk, strong and beautiful, down the path of finding her true self and offering it to the world.

The encouragement that both Nell and Lannie received represents the seventh element of the training at Eagle Song camps—**support**. It is very clear to me that one of the primary reasons each of us may not be fulfilling our highest potential, acting from our deepest spiritual truth, and experiencing our maximum joy is that we do not have the support to do it. This is what we attempt to correct with the support of our hooplets, which continues long after camp. Although it is certainly not required, I know of hoops who get together once or twice a year, and continue to be the best and most consistent sources of spiritual support each person has!

Lannie comes to mind again, because she completed her study on grieving just before her aging mother passed away. Thus, she was able to be present with her mother in a very empowered way during the process of her dying, and with her family after her mother's death. Lannie was able to honor her own needs and feelings in this difficult time, and she also helped others to do the same. Her hooplet gave her tremendous support, and honored her wisdom for taking the study course at a time when some deep part of her must have known she would need it. Lannie came through it all with her truth shining even more brightly!

Finally comes the moment we have been working toward—our Dedication Dance of Commitment. On the last morning of camp, all don their special ceremonial clothes and line up across the creek from our ceremonial center. The staff and I are busy, laying out each camper's shield and beauty arrow in a circle around the Mother Drum. Then all is quiet except for the heartbeat of the Mother Drum, which calls us into circle one last time. Campers file silently across the Deerborn, touching their heads and hearts with water in a final symbolic cleansing. Each is smudged with sage and sweet grass before entering the ceremonial clearing.

When all are ready, the drumbeat speeds up and the campers dance into their final circle around the big drum. This is their chance to look at the beauty of the shields and arrows of their sisters, and they dance around this circle four times, calling in the power of the four directions as they do. They come to rest behind their own shield and arrow. Each camper stands and makes a personal commitment to Acts of Power and Beauty. When this is finished, I place the person's shield around her neck, hand her beauty arrow to her, and we all sing, yell, drum, rattle, and cheer in celebration of this act of completion!

The end result of this entire process—creating Acts of Power and Beauty, and completing the contract to make them real in the world—is tremendously empowering and freeing. It gives campers a chance to move through self-limiting beliefs, addictions, and many levels of fear about their own living of a powerful life. It helps them find the true next step in bringing forth the reality of their own dreams, for themselves and all those whose lives they touch.

When this beautiful ceremony is complete, we are ready for the eighth and final element of our training: that of **taking action in our lives and in our world.** In a final ceremony we take back our objects from the group altar, restating our commitment to ourselves and to the world. Earlier in the day we have spent time talking about the process of re-entry into our daily worlds—both the joys and the challenges. We complete our time together with a dance of oneness and dedication to All Our Relations, the building of an image of our continuing connection over time and distance, and a joyful sending of the wonderful energy we have built together out to the world! Then we adjourn to the lodge for a celebration dinner. The last evening we'll share in circle is spent drumming, singing, and dancing our way into the starlit Montana night. Many of us stay awake all night, savoring both the company of these women who have become sisters, and the sweetness of the clear night air under the biggest stars we have ever seen!

A parting comment from Sibylle Mayer Baughan illuminates the camp experience: "At camp I learned about this precious land on which we live. Both the land and Brooke put me in touch with the depth of my soul, with the very essence of my being."

To give you a feeling of Eagle Song camp from another person's point of view, I'd like to share with you Marion Gracen's perceptive experience at our DEEPENING OF SPIRIT camp:

When I initially came back home from Eagle Song camp and my first vision quest, I knew that people at home could never fully understand what I had experienced, or how and why the outward expression of my energy had so radically shifted. At first, as a way to get out of long explanations, I used to just jokingly say, "Well, Brooke throws a mean ceremony!" In fact, that's true.

Over and over, Brooke takes her vital and grounded physical presence, her high intentions, clear visions, and extraordinary gifts as a ceremonialist and creates a "door" for her students. This door opens out from the physical world to the numinous or the cosmic. She stands firm at this door, calling sweetly to Spirit to come and greet us, all the while challenging us, each at our own level of readiness, to come close to the door or to pass on through into our own knowing and wisdom as it is fed by and blends with the Great Mystery.

If you do choose to pass through the door, you can be sure that you have been offered preparations for this trip. Brooke will have equipped you with a symbol system that allows you to speak directly with Spirit, and Spirit with you. She will also have grounded you in a community of people and in your own body so you know that there are safe and strong places to come to once the journey is over. She also offered me a grounded and profoundly simple tradition in which to operate: a tradition in which my own teaching and wisdom could take form.

During all these preparations, Brooke asks only that you be honest with yourself. Tell the truth about what you're ready for, about what scares you, about how you leak your power and intention, about how the magnificence of "All That Is" is sometimes too much to bear, about what you already know.

Her spirit will be there waiting to greet you as you come back from the journey, too. Sometimes the childlike innocence of her greeting is enough to help you remember the shyest and smallest detail of your learnings . . . and sometimes the physical strength and power of her greeting stance call you to stand tall and own the strength and courage you've been gifted with. She's an adept, a mirror, and a wizard at inviting you to a banquet table set with your highest and best. She throws a mean ceremony!

Each time a group of campers leaves, it is clear to all of us that we have only begun our work together and our enjoyment of the beauty of Blacktail Ranch. As I looked at how to follow up on our DEEPENING OF SPIRIT and HEALING VISION camps, I realized that each camper had potentially begun a series of vision quests, and I wanted to offer them the opportunity to continue and deepen that practice if they chose. Thus camps to CONTINUE THE QUEST are offered each year.

These camps for returnees take them the next step in their personal and group work, focusing on using the talents of the entire group to benefit each other and to continue the personal growth and support that allows us to be of more powerful service in the world. Everyone comes prepared to get right to the work and fun—eager to greet old friends again and to meet new ones from other camps. Our time together is precious and healing.

As well as the Eagle Song camps at Blacktail Ranch, I love to find time in my schedule to invite individual students to my home at Sky Lodge for personal retreat. In the little cabin or the tipi nearby, retreatants can have quiet days of reflection and spiritual questing. My function during these retreats is simply to guide them, to help the retreatants deepen their practice, and to make the land available to them for exploration.

Our first day together we walk the land, and I point out where the fox lives; where the trails are; how easy it is to get lost in the spruce bogs up the creek, yet how the wildlife loves to hide there; and introduce them to our cats, the horses and mules, and to Bud the dog who will be their best buddy and hiking companion during their stay. In subsequent days we spend time clearing their intention, setting goals, and moving them toward those goals.

Most of a retreatant's time is spent alone in the wilderness quiet, looking within and touching the beauty of the land. One person went out each morning to lean against the big ponderosa pine and watch the fox on his hunting rounds. Another retreatant thrilled to a herd of elk passing nearby. Another challenged, and conquered fears of the unknown, the dark, and the cold by spending days outside in the snow with only Bud as a companion. Some have thrilled to the joy of cross-country skiing over the snow-covered meadows.

I took one woman skiing through the spruce bog in the full moonlight (our only chance to fully explore the bog is when the ground is frozen and the snow piled high). All retreatants have elected to sit alone on the mountain in vision quest during their time here—many near the ancient Grandmother tree. These Sky Lodge retreats are a joy for me, calling me out on the land and into the wind myself, and giving me a unique opportunity to interact individually with a small number of students.

This new level of my work—inviting students to spend significant time in the beauty of Spirit alive in Mother Earth—is deeply gratifying to me. I have learned that my best work takes place when I am doing what I love, and being on the land is what I love. It also gives me a wonderful opportunity to work with craft and ritual art, which is the growing edge in my own life. Although I am only a beginner in this area, ritual art is calling me as primary in the next stage of my life, and I love having a chance to learn and grow in this area, while also teaching my students.

The most powerful aspect of the work is the opportunity it affords me to be on the land. Being present on Mother Earth makes my work much easier, for rather than expending the effort it takes to transport students in imagination out of a closed room, I can spend my energy working and playing with them, offering the gifts of Mother Earth and Father Spirit directly.

ACTION CONTRACTS

I have now worked with Action Contracts in many groups, including weekend workshops. They have proven to be some of the most powerful and transformative work I have helped people do for themselves. Here I would like to suggest the steps to you, so that you, too, might benefit from this powerful tool for transformation. (You may want to review pages 372–374.) I also want to give thanks to my friend and co-worker Kim Karkos, who first taught me this kind of work, and helped me give it away to early groups.

Remember that Action Contracts are meant to help you take the actions which will help you make real in your life the appropriate next steps of personal healing and offering your gifts to the world. This can take place as you understand what has held you back previously (your power leaks), discern what you truly want to accomplish, and create concrete steps for moving forward.

Your Acts of Power will be personal empowerments, meant to bring you healing, wholeness and integration—allowing you to learn more and more about who you truly are, and to make that real in the world. It is the warrior's step of finding personal uniqueness, and developing those gifts and talents that Creator gave.

Acts of Beauty are a turning outward to gift your unique talents in service of All Your Relations. You came to Earth not only to learn and to grow, but also to offer something to the larger Self—All Your Relations. In doing this, you bring joy and healing to yourself and others, and complete a warrior's commitment.

SUPPORT HOOP

1. The first step is create a support hoop of four to eight people—friends, family, counselors, who will work with you on your action contract, or others who also wish to engage in this work for themselves.

2. Commit to regular get-togethers for group processing (twice a week is an ideal minimum).

3. Commit to supporting each other over the next six to twelve months to complete the contract process.

POWER LEAKS

Power leaks occur through the limitations we place on how we live our daily lives and the impact we can have on our world. These leaks may be blatant, and thus quite obvious to us. But most likely from our perspective they will be subtle. They are difficult to pinpoint because they have been a part of our patterns for so long. They may even be things that have worked at one time in our lives and are just not working now as we want to further our personal integration and healing, developing new habits and patterns of excellence and full expression.

1. Begin to address with each other the *ways you leak your power.* Look at areas of your life that hold you back from doing your best:

▶ Where you avoid.

▶ Where and when you deny.

▶ What may be harmful to you or others.

▶ What events make you feel hungry, angry, lonely, tired, scared, or upset in any way.

▶ What doesn't serve you well.

Ask your hoop how these power leaks strike them, how they affect them? What do they see that you don't?

Alone, or in the group, go within yourself to feel the feelings these power leaks bring up: Do you feel angry? fearful? sad?

Take time, in meditation and in group processing, to trace these patterns back as far as you can:

▶ When did they begin?

▶ How have you acted them out?

▶ How do you feel about them now that you've focused your awareness on them?

▶ What would you like to change?

2. Now take an appreciative look at the skills and attributes you possess that truly work for you:

▶ What are your strengths?

▶ What are your unique talents?

▶ What are your joys?

▶ What is your special beauty?

▶ How can you enhance these gifts:

▶ Within yourself: through affirmation, visualization, journaling, talking about them and receiving feedback on how others perceive your beauty and power.

▶ In the world: how can you walk your gifts more powerfully into the world?

3. Take these power leaks and strengths you've now identified, and

choose three or four you want to focus on in your action contract. You might want to work with your strengths as well as, or even instead of, your weaknesses; it can be a more positive approach at times. It builds your self-esteem while also grooming your power. These leaks and/or strengths may be:

Physical weaknesses or things that limit your body from full functioning.

Emotional issues or patterns you want to change.

Skills or abilities (in your work or vocations) that could be honed and polished.

A spiritual practice or awareness you want to develop.

A relationship you want to change.

ACTS OF POWER AND BEAUTY

1. Begin to think about specific actions (inner and outer) that you can take to change the several power leaks (or strengths) you've chosen to work on.

▶ As your **Act of Power**, what actions can you make to empower *yourself*—within yourself, *for* yourself?

▶ And, from this stance of wholeness, as your **Act of Beauty**, what actions can you make as a giveaway to the world: to benefit your family, community, country, planet, All Your Relations?

2. When you have a good idea of what your acts of power and beauty may encompass, go to your hoop, and with their suggestions and feedback, become *very* clear and *very* realistic about what you intend to do and achieve—to the satisfaction of yourself and all present. Decide:

▶ What precisely you will *do.*

▶ How it will be documented and evaluated.

▶ How long you give yourself to complete each task.

▶ What you need by way of support from your hoop.

▶ What object or service of value to you will you stake as a giveaway if you fail to honor your contract? Do this for both your act of power and your act of beauty, as a further stimulus to completion and growth.

3. Now you should have several very specific actions you can commit to in writing.

▶ Write these out as a formal contract—see the sample blank and filled-in contracts provided—including all the conditions and terms you've agreed upon in your hoop. Phrase it all as simply as possible.

▶ Make copies of your contract for each hoop member.

4. Gather your hoop together in ceremony. State your contract aloud, to voice and make real *in the world* your commitment to these acts of power and beauty.

▶ Arrange with your hoop members the means of continuing support from them that will best help you realize your new goals.

▶ Get to work!

5. As you frame your contract, keep these points in mind:

▶ Be specific.

▶ Be realistic.

▶ Consider the ways in which you may very well attempt to sabotage your Action Contracts. Although you will discuss these probable acts of sabotage verbally with your hoop sisters, you may also want to write something out as a reminder to yourself and to them in the months after you leave camp.

▶ Allow yourself flexibility. Know that you can amend your contract, as necessary—again, in negotiation with your hoop—should circumstances affect your ability to complete it as originally worded. . . . But complete it!

6. Make this contract a gift to your higher self. Don't think of it as an ax hanging ominously over your head. Rather, see it as a rewarding challenge that may actually be fun, and become, at each step, both empowering and enlivening.

ACTION CONTRACT FOR ACTS OF POWER

I, *[add all your names—birth, nicknames, ceremonial, spiritual],* having fearlessly examined the ways in my life in which I have leaked and given away my power and energy, now make a sacred covenant with Mother Earth and Father Sky to live a powerful life and to accept myself as a powerful creator.

In the presence of All My Relations and my Sacred Hoop, I firmly commit to the following Act of Power:

_____

_____

_____

Ways I may sabotage myself:

_____

_____

_____

I require the following amount of time to fulfill this contract.

_____

I reserve the right to amend this contract and give myself permission to grow through each step in the living of my vision.

Should I fail to honor my commitment to this Act of Power, I agree to give away:

_____

_____

_____
Signature and Date

ACTION CONTRACT FOR ACTS OF BEAUTY

I, *[add all your names—birth, ceremonial, spiritual]*, pledge myself to actively demonstrate my gratitude to All My Relations for the blessings Spirit has bestowed on me in countless ways.

I renew my Spiritual Warrior's pledge—**"Not for myself alone, but that all the people may live."**

In the presence of Mother Earth, Father Sky, All My Relations, and my Sacred Hoop, I firmly commit to the following Act of Beauty:

_____

_____

_____

Ways I may sabotage myself:

_____

_____

_____

I require the following amount of time to fulfill this contract.

_____

I reserve the right to amend this contract and give myself permission to grow through each step in the living of my vision.

Should I fail to honor my commitment to this Act of Beauty, I agree to give away: _____

_____

_____

_____

Signature and Date

COMPLETED ACTION CONTRACT FOR ACTS OF POWER

I, **Jane Elizabeth "Janney" Wilson Smith, Bright Feather,** having fearlessly examined the ways in my life in which I have leaked and given away my power and energy, now make a sacred covenant with Mother Earth and Father Sky to live a powerful life and to accept myself as a powerful creator.

In the presence of All My Relations and my Sacred Hoop, I firmly commit to the following Acts of Power:

I will complete a series of ten landscape watercolors.

I will jog daily between now and then, so that by the date below I will be able to run three miles a day.

Ways I may try to sabotage myself:

My sister helpers: You must know that I will try to worm out of my commitments in many ways, so watch me carefully. Know that I have been "trained" by five years of therapy and can talk my way out of almost anything, using esoteric terms I will hope you don't understand. I may claim that my inner guides have given me a different direction, and such things. More specifically, I will suggest illness or disability with regard to both painting and jogging.

I require the following amount of time to fulfill this contract:

I will accomplish both Acts of Power by January 1, 1993.

I reserve the right to amend this contract and give myself permission to grow through each step in the living of my vision.

Should I fail to honor my commitment to this Act of Power, I agree to the giveaway of:

My new TrakMaster exercise bike to the local nursing home.

_____

Signature and Date

COMPLETED ACTION CONTRACT FOR ACTS OF BEAUTY

I, **Jane Elizabeth "Janney" Wilson Smith, Bright Feather,** pledge myself to actively demonstrate my gratitude to All My Relations for the blessings Spirit has bestowed on me in countless ways.

I renew my Spiritual Warrior's pledge—*"Not for myself alone, but that all the people may live."*

In the presence of Mother Earth, Father Sky, All My Relations, and my Sacred Hoop, I firmly commit to the following Act of Beauty:

I commit myself to forming a women's Moon Circle, initially to be a hoop of eight women, which will meet monthly on each new Moon, for at least six months.

Ways I may try to sabotage myself:

My sister helpers: Again, you must not allow me to worm out of this commitment. When confronted with the forming of a women's circle, I may well create all sorts of technical and timing challenges— everything from typewriter breakdowns and printer delays to conflicting schedules. You will also hear, "I'm just not ready to be a teacher or leader." Please call me on all these sabotages to my higher purpose.

I require the following amount of time to fulfill this contract. **The hoop will have its first meeting at the next new Moon.**

I reserve the right to amend this contract and give myself permission to grow through each step in the living of my vision.

Should I fail to honor my commitment to this Act of Beauty, I agree to:

Give away my crystal ball to the first person who asks for it.

_____

Signature and Date

EARTH ACTION CONTRACT

A special Action Contract that I would highly recommend is to create the opportunity for yourself to be out on the land for the purpose of deepening your connection with all of life and your own spirit. It is vital that we become more aware of and attuned to the larger life around us. What more beautiful and healthful way to do it than to be on the land in a dedicated way.

1. Find a place to be on the land that is as close to pristine wilderness as possible:

▶ Investigate the possible areas near you where you could spend time alone or in connection with several others who want to pursue the same goal.

▶ Think about your vacation times as possibilities, and discover places to go at these times.

▶ Sometimes using someone's summer cabin in an off season—in the mountains, near the swamps, or at the ocean—can work very well.

2. Set up a regular schedule for yourself to be in these places.

▶ Returning to the same place helps you deepen your experience of it, especially if your visits must be short.

▶ Regular visits are very important. Regular does not mean often, so much as interspersed at similar intervals over time. If you can go out of town only twice a year, then make yourself a regular six-month schedule. If you can go once a month, follow that schedule. If you can get out every weekend or two, even better. Just do it regularly.

▶ Make your commitment to be with Mother Earth and stick with it. Sometimes working with others who will be supportive and can come together on the same schedule helps. You can all go in one car and split costs, yet spend your own quiet time when you arrive.

3. As you begin, pay attention to what things will cause you to default on your commitment, and take them into consideration as you plan.

OUTER EARTH WALK

When you are at your place on the land, alternate moving actively about and simply being still to observe and feel.

1. If you have been on a rushed schedule, you may need to walk or run about to tire yourself physically in order to slow down. Hiking alone can be quite physical, yet very quiet.

2. Unless you are accustomed to the stillness of meditation, you may notice yourself becoming impatient with the sitting. Just acknowledge this and keep sitting for a certain amount of time you have pre-established. You may need to start with fifteen minutes, and later work up to an hour or two.

3. If it helps, take a notebook to record your observations of inner and outer things.

4. A quieting activity can be using field guide books and herbals to help you identify the flowers, trees, birds, insects, animals and their tracks, and kinds of clouds. Begin to notice wind patterns and other changes around you. Find out something about the geology of the region—get to know the stone people of your sacred ground.

5. Pick an area one yard square that you can return to time after time. Offer this place tobacco to unify yourself with it, and cornmeal to nourish it. Get to know it in detail, noticing the larger things such as trees and shrubs as well as the smaller things that you may be able to see only with a magnifying glass. It's fun to think of the blades of grass as a huge forest, and to see who lives and what happens on the "forest floor." As you return again and again, note the changes across the weeks, months, seasons, years.

6. As you observe various plants and animals and other things, take time to consider what their medicine—their unique powers and abilities—might be. Or find one special thing—such as the squirrels or chipmunks—and get to know them.

Learn about their ways, their paths, their patterns, their homes, what they feed on, how they mate, how they raise their young ones. What do they have to teach you?

7. Read books by naturalists and nature lovers. See how they have approached time on the land. Read about Thoreau's experiences on Walden Pond; John Wesley Powell's exploits on the Colorado River. Enjoy the depth and beauty of Aldo Leopold's *A Sand County Almanac* and Annie Dillard's *Pilgrim at Tinker Creek.*

MEDICINE WHEEL WALK

1. Review the medicine wheel walk on pages 368–369, bringing to mind again the unique opportunity you have when you are on the land to receive messages from the voices of life around you.

▶ Review the symbology of the medicine wheel on pages 284–289, and remember your own personal symbolic meanings of animals, trees, stones, etc.

▶ Make a circle around your chosen area, taking plenty of time to observe closely what you see, feel, smell, and connect with in each of the directions. Walk slowly with soft eyes and breathe deeply and quietly as you move gently through the landscape. Take time to sit in each direction to receive the messages that are there for you.

▶ Note your observations, feelings, intuitions, and thoughts for later contemplation.

▶ Do this whenever you need general guidance. At these times, I ask Spirit simply to tell me what I need to know at present. Or, do this when you wish for information on a specific question—in this case I begin my medicine wheel walk by stating the question, issue, problem upon which I need guidance.

Bring into your awareness not only the physical things around you, and their varying energies, but your own *inner* experience as well. Keep a journal in which you record this personal information.

2. Do you notice yourself sometimes feeling afraid? What does this mean about your perception of the world?

▶ Does most of this come from unfamiliarity, which goes away in time?

▶ Does your fear have something to do with a general feeling of things not being all right, which the unfamiliarity of the land only brings up more forcefully?

3. Make note of your feelings of smallness in comparison to the natural world, your feelings of sudden blending and delightful oneness, your experiences of awe, your wonder at the chaotic order of it all.

4. Perhaps in this quiet beauty, profound issues come up for you. Rather than denying or ignoring them, take them back home to work on with your hoop or counselors.

5. Open yourself as well to numinous or extraordinary experiences of the left side.

▶ Pulitzer Prize—winning author Annie Dillard, in her lovely book, *Pilgrim at Tinker Creek,* speaks beautifully of a time when a very special tree became alive with light, and the deep learnings she gained from this and other experiences in nature.

▶ Let your eyes soften and relax. Allow the outer world forms to melt and even blur a bit.

▶ Look at the spaces *between* things rather than at the things themselves.

▶ Allow yourself to hear/feel/see with more than your physical senses.

▶ Listen to the Great Spirit through every living thing.

EARTH MEDICINE CONTRACT

The Earth Medicine Contract is based on a year's journey around the Great Wheel of Life. The medicine wheel can be used in many ways, and one of these is in making a spiritual blueprint for living in harmonious relationship with Mother Earth.

I, *[add all your names—birth, nicknames, ceremonial, spiritual],* in the presence of Mother Earth, Father Sky, All My Relations, and my Hoop, acknowledge my oneness with all life. I make a sacred pact to reconnect with Mother Earth and All Life from the depths of my being and to give action and beauty to this commitment.

Through prayer and intuition I have determined that I am in the _____ direction on the Sacred medicine wheel:

⊕ Eastern Quadrant. It is the direction of Eagle, illumination, Yellow, Spring, Daybreak, Elder Brother (Dawn Star).

⊕ Northeast. Emotion that Empowers.

⊕ Southeast. The Highest Good, the Masters.

⊕ Southern Quadrant. It is the direction of Mouse, Coyote, the Sacred Plants, Trust, Innocence, Growth. Summer, Day, Red and Green.

⊕ Southeast. The Highest Good, The Masters.

⊕ Southwest. Spiritual Action.

⊕ Western Quadrant. It is the direction of Bear, Crow, Obsidian, Introspection, Autumn, Sunset, Letting Go and Harvest, Ancestors, Black and Brown.

⊕ Southwest. Spiritual Action.

    ⊕ Northwest. The Law.

   ⊕ Northern Quadrant. It is the direction of Buffalo, Owl, Crystal, Wisdom and Essence, White, Winter, Night, Elder Sister (White Buffalo Woman).

    ⊕ Northwest. The Law.

    ⊕ Northeast. Emotion that Empowers.

As my Act of Earth Awareness I will find my Sacred Place, make myself open to its teachings, and honor it in a sacred way.

My Sacred Place on Mother Earth is _____

_____

    I pledge to go to my Sacred Place for acts of ritual communication every _____ in the year _____

    Ways I may sabotage myself: _____

_____

    In gratitude for its many blessings, I pledge the following giveaway to my Sacred Place on Mother Earth _____

_____

_____

_____

                      _____

                             Signature and Date

COMPLETED EARTH MEDICINE
CONTRACT

I, **Laura Mathis, Astralena, Little Grandma**, in the presence of Mother Earth, Father Sky, All My Relations, and my Hoop, acknowledge my oneness with all life. I make a sacred pact to reconnect with Mother Earth and All Life from the depths of my being and to give action and beauty to this commitment.

Through prayer and intuition I have determined that I am in the **Northern** direction on the Sacred Medicine Wheel:

As my Act of Earth Awareness I will find my Sacred Place, make myself open to its teachings, and honor it in a sacred way.

My Sacred Place on Mother Earth is: **between Coos Bay and Tillamok Head, Oregon, at the shore where the water is cold, the waves are strong, and the wind sings my name.**

I pledge to go to my Sacred Place for acts of ritual communication on **November first, All Saints' Day,** in the year **1992.**

Ways I may sabotage myself:

I may sabotage myself by claiming that I have little time, or that my old car is "on the blink."

In gratitude for its many blessings, I pledge the following giveaway to my Sacred Place on Mother Earth—**that three fir trees will be planted, each with a Herkimer diamond crystal, in the mountainous cliffs that overlook the shore. These trees are pledged to support the next steps of all who seek oneness.**

Signature and Date

Moving my primary work into the wilderness onto the breast of our sweet Mother Earth is a powerful metaphor for me. It symbolizes having the wilderness become a nurturing friend rather than a threat to be conquered. It symbolizes creating good relationship with all the living forms around us. It symbolizes the movement toward Earth harmony that each of us needs to make in our lives if we are to be allowed to remain in the garden of Earth. And it gives those who participate an opportunity to experience the clarity and beauty of natural, unspoiled land.

Given that experience, almost every camper and retreatant longs to move to Montana. However, *I charge them to go back to where they live and work to re-create this exquisite natural garden in their own home area, for it once flourished there as well.* Besides, if everyone moved to Montana, then the wilderness would be lost through overpopulation, and there would be nowhere to come and learn of Mother's natural beauty!

Each camper's Action Contract helps tremendously in that process of taking the learning home and making it real there. We can no longer run away to the wilderness as a solution to our problems. We can come to the wilderness to feel what is possible and naturally beautiful—yet we must stand rooted in the Earth and face the crying issues right where we live. We must make a firm commitment to the very ground we walk upon each day. The transformation can be made. Even school children are teaching us that streams can be made pure again, trees planted to reforest barren areas, parks made clean. Green belts, gardens, and open areas can be created within our cities. It's clearly time for us to move forth in good relationship and replant the garden on every foot of Mother Earth—to walk with our attention on holiness.

For me, the opportunity I now have to be on the land and to bring my students into Mother Earth's wilderness to learn is the answer to a prayer I have long held. Much of what troubles us as two-leggeds comes from our having distanced ourselves from the larger part of ourself—All Our Relations. Our short-term "solutions" to small pieces of the problem only seem to get us into more hot water. The yearning I have for the wilderness not only answers my own inner call to regain that good relationship with Mother Earth—and with Father Spirit alive within her—but it also puts me in the best place to do the work of healing that is my intention for others and the planet.

A woman asked me the other day to tell her what I do at camp so she could do it at home in the city. My reply was, "It can't be done." And it's not because she lacks some magical ability that only I possess, it's that none who live in the city have the magic ingredient—the pristine beauty and natural wonder of the wilderness. Of course we can learn many things right where we are; I taught for years in any location I was asked. But I've come to realize that there are certain things Mother Earth needs to teach us in her most primal state, and she calls us to the wilderness to learn them.

We must surrender ourselves to her under her great open skies. We must allow her to overwhelm us with her beauty and her challenges. We must give ourselves to her heartbeat if we are to learn the essential lessons necessary to meet the crises we have created. And so I give thanks for her beauty, and send up prayers that her pristine elegance be protected and nurtured by us all in as many places as possible upon her lovely face.

EMBODYING SPIRIT

My work is about bringing Spirit alive and awake within us here on Earth:
it is about embodying spirit here and now.

It has made sense to me to go as directly to Source as possible
—to pass through and beyond individual teachers
and traditions to touch the ancient source of
knowing.

Sometimes posing the questions can be as effective in teaching as
having the answers.

I have always been interested in the ways that show us how to live a truly human life, a fully human life. And I have known that these ways were given to us at the beginning of time—planted deep within the human spirit, that we might grow those seeds into fullness over the span of our human evolution.

However, as two-leggeds, we must always remember that we are only a small part of the Circle of Life. Many other peoples live in it with us: four-leggeds; wingeds; green-growing people—including the trees, the standing tall ones, food crops, and myriad others; stone people and others of the mineral kingdom; water with all the finned ones and others who live in that kingdom; and those of the starry realms, the ones who have gone beyond and those who have yet to come, as well as those who exist in the more subtle realms.

We are at a critical time on our pathway as two-leggeds: We have developed great power, a power that can as easily destroy us as move us to a whole new level of being. The choice is up to us, and we must make it now, always keeping in mind our responsibility to All Our Relations. It is time for us to embody the ancient truths of our humanness, it is time to let blossom the flower of Spirit that was planted within us. So it has made sense to me to go as directly to Source as possible—to pass through and beyond individual teachers and traditions to touch the ancient source of knowing. Taking what I have received there, I have been called to make that knowing real in the present day, to create a living tradition.

This practice has brought me to both my own growing edge, and to the growing edge of developing human consciousness—a challenging and tenuous place to be. I have been given in vision the image of being one of the atoms at the tip of an obsidian arrow point, which must pierce the veil of the old to reveal the new. Being at the tip is no better or worse than being where the arrow is set to the bow, yet it requires a certain toughness, a certain kind of physicality. I was born and raised rough and tough. My early life honed and toned me for my assignment at the tip.

My spiritually adopted sister Norma, younger than I in years and in experience on the road, used to laugh and tell me that she was glad I had gone on the road before her to take the heat—the heat of being a non-traditional, mouthy woman teacher on the road of Spirit. The heat has at times been intense, both from those critical of my path, and from my own inner experience of loneliness, lack of concrete guidance, and uncertainty.

Yet always an admonition from Spirit has come back to me. I was shown in vision that I stand on the edge of a cliff at the end of the old world. I must gather my courage to step forward past the edge, knowing that when my foot comes down, it will land on solid ground. It is as though the very act of faith and courage in moving forward is the building of the bridge to a new time, as yet unknown upon Mother Earth. The pattern, the path, is there in invisible cloth, waiting to be worn and traveled in so that it may come to know itself as real. The admonition from Spirit is, "Keep stepping!"

My steps at times have felt like stumbling, falling, then picking myself up, taking turns that proved detours. But I have kept stepping. A large part of the courage I needed to keep stepping forward has come from the supportive energy of those younger sisters and brothers walking the path behind me. Knowing they were there, knowing they expected these brave and guiding steps from me, both challenged me and enabled me to move forward. This has been one of the great blessings of my life.

In looking at my way as a teacher, the first thing that comes to mind is that I have been an elder sister—perhaps a few steps ahead in some areas of life, where I can make a map or hold out my hand to help someone step over an obstacle that I know well, having stumbled or jumped over it myself. I have stayed open and truthful about my personal challenges and growing edges, attempting to model for others a way of growing toward wholeness rather than being there. It is clear to me that I am in the same process as everyone else. My intention is to offer what I have learned from my experience, and to reach toward others to learn what they have gained from theirs.

Often my students are my teachers. I find that in working with others, what I need to learn is pointed out to me. If I am aware, I am learning all the time from what works exquisitely, and even more from what doesn't! In a continual process of taking a clear-eyed assessment of myself, I work openly with the things that are the hardest for me, the things that make me feel the most vulnerable. And I encourage my students to engage in this process as well. They not only see me shine with new accomplishment, but they also watch me as I pick myself up dirty, and brush the dust off—a grin showing through my tears. Both experiences seem necessary in moving forward.

I did not find much of this kind of teaching by example when I spent time with those who taught me, and it would have been very valuable. For instance, it would have been very instructive if Black Hand had been able to say something like this to me: "Although I'm clear that this is a part of my spiritual duty, I'm very angry at having to accompany you to Bear Butte for your fast right now because it disrupts my personal plans. I am going to do it. But I feel it is important to let you know the struggles of a medicine person—it is not always personally easy. You will likely find the same when you are devoting your life to others." This would not only have created a more real relationship between us, it would have provided a deeper and more positive teaching for me.

Because I feel that living my teaching is so important, I have included some comments from my students and Eagle Song camp participants. The fact that I am far from perfect as a teacher is quite obvious, and yet their comments help illuminate what I do accomplish in being with them, which is sometimes difficult for me to assess from just my own perspective. In asking them to share their thoughts with me and thus with you, I have again learned from those I teach.

In Lynn Peck's words, "Brooke's most significant characteristic is her willingness to be utterly human. I had not been to any sort of workshop for almost four years before attending her weekend retreat at Rowe Conference Center in western Massachusetts. When I met her there and heard her speak of her own process and problems, and I saw that she was willing to use her own life struggles as an example for us, I was sold."

Darion Gracen expressed it this way: "One of your powerful qualities is telling the truth about where you stand—honestly owning who you are and what you are about, and having that be witnessed and accepted by others. From this empowered model, your students are then able to feel the power of standing 'at the center of their own medicine wheels,' accepting their own rhythms and assets and limitations."

My friend, Holly Blue Hawkins, had this to say: "I have appreciated your openness and honesty about your own work in progress. I see that it is possible to teach by being a student oneself—that sometimes posing the questions can be as effective in teaching as having the answers. One of my biggest challenges has been to risk making mistakes. I've finally realized that it is more productive to take two steps forward and one step back than it is to wait until I'm absolutely sure I can 'get it right.' That means being willing to step into view with who I am in the moment. . . . It is scary, but also exhilarating, and ultimately more responsible and giving than it is to stay safe all the time. I see you doing that, Brooke, even though you have often become a target for doing what you believe in. And that, my friend, is your greatest teaching."

A second way I can look at who I am as a teacher is to see that I stand just inside the door to the left side, the door to Spirit, holiness, and timeless reality. I am one who holds open that door, invites people in, and welcomes them as they pass through toward wholeness and holiness. The inarticulate knowledge arising in us as humans comes through me, to be expressed in the world. I provide a model of someone who lives a life of Spirit, and yet is solidly grounded in the reality of the right side. This helps allay students' fears, so that they can journey open-eyed, alert, and curious into the territory of the left side, knowing there is a friend and guide there before them.

An image I have of myself is standing below a cliff, where a large leap is necessary for any who want to join me. I not only show them that the leap can be made, and provide arms to help ease their landing, I also sometimes kick a little dirt out to loosen the bank, thus "encouraging them" to take that challenging leap. I do this because I know that even though they are afraid, they can make it!

Thus, in my work, I ask students to look truthfully at who they are in the moment: their strengths and weaknesses, their wisdom and their folly, their gifts and their power leaks. Then I empower them to know themselves as more magnificent, more capable, more courageous than they knew themselves to be. It can seldom be said that I coddle my students. I believe in coyote teaching—the kind that lets you learn through your own experience and self-responsibility. I act as a springboard, a catalyst, a friend along the way, asking my students to stretch for their best by seeing it in themselves, waiting to be lived.

Another aspect of my stance, in both the spiritual and left side of life, is that I validate this normally unsupported aspect of my students. In a world that has become intensely left-sided, the people I work with have largely lost, or more devastatingly, never discovered the spiritual selves that are at their center. They have lived more with what a friend calls "mall consciousness"—if you feel emptiness inside, go to the mall and stuff yourself full of something. We all experience the "holes" that are left in us by our lack of attention to our true selves and to the spiritual experience that lies within us. For an in-depth study of the theory of "holes," read *Diamond Heart*, by A. A. Almaas (see appendix 2, page 464).

We fill these aching holes with an incredible array of addictions, whether to sugar, unhealthy relationships, sex, alcohol, drugs, work, or whatever. We will often try anything to temporarily (for all these *are* temporary) fill up our aching inner emptiness with something outside ourselves. This not only leads us nowhere, causing us great trauma and misery, it also ignores the very reason we came to Earth—to discover and share more and more of who we can be. I tell my students that, since there is going to be some trauma and misery anyway, they may as well spend their lives facing the challenges of growth and opening to Spirit, rather than maintaining the status quo by filling their "holes" in temporary ways. If they can face the emptiness long enough, they will discover what is truly needed in order to become whole, which is the only way to truly fill this emptiness.

These holes of ours are crying to be filled with spirit, wholeness, and holiness. I challenge my students to walk the path of a warrior—the one who discovers and manifests her own uniqueness and wholeness, and who then gifts it to the world for the life of All Our Relations. Students who work with me for more than a weekend often find the lives they have known being challenged and unsettled as they return to their homes and families. Some know that they cannot put Spirit at the center of their days before their bodies are able to "tolerate" the increased energy and vibrancy of living out their more essential enspirited selves— so their next step on their path is to attend to their bodies.

Others are challenged to deal with the areas of their lives that have been the most deeply cut off, whether it is their feminine side, or their emotional natures, or their warrior selves. They attend to whatever hinders them. They see how often they have said "yes" with their heads when their heart was screaming "no." Then they go back to their daily lives with incredible courage and determination to make the changes that will bring more integrity to their experience.

I teased my second-year returning DEEPENING OF SPIRIT campers about whether they had the courage to return for another round, after the intense changes that had come about in their lives in the first twelve months after the first camp. To my surprise, thirty out of fifty-four answered with a resounding "Yes!" Integrity was becoming more inviting than the numbness; their deep selves were beginning to have a voice.

No matter what stage of development someone is in, the "door-opening" experiences of the left side let them truly feel what becoming more of themselves is about. The integrity and expansion of their true selves is intoxicating and inviting, expanding, usually scary, and certainly grounding and empowering. Melane Lohmann writes, "The first awareness Brooke gifted me, which returned me to myself, was a belief construct, with community and cultural tradition intact, that jibed with everything I had ever experienced of Spirit in my life. First, that I find Spirit (God) in wilderness. Second, that I have a direct connection and communication with the Spirit-in-All-Things. And third, that it is good to pray and live one's life in contact with this force, unnameable: Spirit/Earth."

Part of this spiritual way of living is contacting the numinous in the ordinary, of awakening to the miracle of life in every moment. In their life on the land during camps, our campers become more sensitive to the unfolding miracle of life, because they are closer to the natural processes of Mother Earth. A concrete way of having them practice awareness is in doing ritual art work. I speak often to them about the grandmothers' ways, which are akin to a Zen way of being in the world. The grand-mothers teach that power comes, not from the magnitude of one's ceremonial prayers or from the brilliance of a one-time offering, but from moment-to-moment attention. And this, in turn, comes from a place of wholeness, prayerfulness, awareness, respect, and gratitude.

With each step they took, with each stitch they made, with each bead they sewed on, with each piece of food they sliced, with each prayer as they wrapped their Moon staffs as younger women, the grandmothers built power into the moments of their lives and all they touched. Imagine the power contained in a vest whose cloth was cut when a boy baby was born, and stitched over the years for him to wear as a man—into which a prayer for him was placed with every stitch, every bead and quill. This is the way of the grandmothers.

In these moment-by-moment prayers, and in more elaborate ways, I share a way of using ritual and ceremony as an integral part of life. Whether it is a christening and naming ceremony for a newborn, a puberty initiation for a young woman, a first vision quest for a young man, a purification lodge, the dedication of a new crystal, or a grand-mother lodge initiation, ceremony helps to bring the divine into mean-ingful combination with the ordinary.

A primary ritual in everything I do is the forming of a circle, where people are equal and equally seen. We sit in the round and speak our hearts, we dance in circles, we remember ourselves as part of the Great Circle of Life. I hope to empower my students to not only seek out ceremony but also to create it in their own families and community life.

Coming Home is another aspect of my teaching. First of all, to me, it means coming home to the essential, central part of ourselves, our deep spirit and connection with all things. Second, it is the matter of coming to understand our place in sacred history. Much as Dawn Boy showed me my place, I ground my students in the ancient knowledge and lineages of old, as well as in prophecy and a visionary look into the future. Knowing where we are in the fullness of time grounds us in the larger reality, and helps us feel a part of a great movement of human consciousness and evolution. I caution students not to let themselves be "a gray blip on the evolution of humanity," as Moshé Feldenkrais cautioned me, reminding us all that if we do not become who we truly are, and express that in the world—if we act just like everyone else, and never make any waves—then we have contributed nothing.

A third and primary way of coming home is that which White Buffalo Woman and Dawn Star have modeled. This is coming home to the land, to our true parents Mother Earth and Father Spirit, and to the larger family circle of their children: to a respectful and joyous awareness of All That Is. As White Buffalo Woman calls for her warriors to step forward, my answer is to harness the energies of many who are committed to healing and wholeness for themselves and for All Our Relations. I teach my students about their true mother, the Earth, and their true father, Sky (Spirit), and translate this ancient wisdom into ways that can be applied every day in modern life.

In addition to cultivating their sensitivity to the Circle of Life and the land upon which we stand, I encourage my students living on Turtle Island to become true Earth stewards. We can no longer think of the red nations as the ones who are to be the caretakers of the Earth. It is time we all grow into a mature "owning" of the land, as our Native people have for centuries. Owning it, not with a legal document, but with love and caring, with attention, protection, and nurturing. We who live here, whether of Native blood or not, are North Americans; this sweet and beautiful Earth is our home, and we must take exquisite care of it— whether we are black, white, yellow, or red, whether we are in a place for only several years or have a lifetime deed to the land. It is time for all people to take responsibility. My friend Holly Blue Hawkins put it beautifully: "White Buffalo Calf Pipe Woman's story, her law, her teachings have profoundly affected my life. If I'd never gotten anything else from Brooke's teaching—*You shall be in right relationship with all things and all peoples*—would have been plenty, since it has become the framework from which I've developed my own set of values. All my inner work comes from that starting point."

Walking grounded upon the Earth has also been a major part of my teaching. I know that it is our physical body that is the foundation for our Earth walk, and that attention to our bodies is vital to our full development and movement in Spirit. My way of moving in the world has been an important teaching for both myself and my students.

Daily exercises for flexibility, longevity, body tone, and general health are fundamental for walking in balance. Using Moshé Feldenkrais's principles, I move my students toward awakening each and every cell in their body so that they can be fully alive and present in all their movements in the world. Working through the healing aspects of ritual performance adds to this physical learning. In one such exercise, I have them choose partners of their body size and type. Then they press against each other in prescribed ways, attempting to knock each other off balance while I teach them how to soften into non-resistance to retain their equilibrium. My workshop student Debra Beck-Grossman reported the learning that came through such a little exercise: "I have been in a new community where there has been little friendly contact. I found that it had been so long since I had had a lot of intimate contact with anyone but my husband, that simply looking into another's eyes threw me off balance. Also, people coming at me from behind have always thrown me off. I like direct contact, direct people. I don't do well with sneaky people. When I went home I began to look at the sneaky people in my life—and to learn how to deal with them! Another thing I noticed was that I use my eyes a lot for balance. It was good for me to practice with my eyes closed—to feel my balance in a different way. In life, I have become very good at seeing things coming at me that used to throw me off, and then rolling with the punches. This kept me present and brought immediate change."

Yet another aspect of my work is the modelling of both the strength and the sensitivity of the feminine. Teaching women about their Moon time, their exquisite receptivity, and the strength of their natural intuitive, caring ways has been wonderful. I have seen them empowered by a new awareness and respect for themselves as women—for their Moon time and for their female bodies. I have portrayed women's natural beingness as different from the old images that told us we were passive, weak, silly, competitive, ungrounded, and bitchy. I also try to model the ability to carry strength, power, clarity, assertiveness, physical capability, and vibrant expression without the need to act like a man. Too often in recent years, women have tried to regain their power by acting like men.

I'm reminded of a time several years ago when I taught with a woman who is a fine Earth teacher. She spends much time on the land, and wears only old jeans and men's shirts. Beneath her rough surface is a heart as rich and warm as gold and a mind as brilliant as a star. However, at this gathering I noticed her looking at me in a rather disgusted manner as I wore my long Navajo-style skirts out on our teaching walks, and feminine blouses and dresses to dinner.

Later, when I visited her at her home in the high Rockies, she took me hiking up to fourteen thousand feet. I had no hiking boots with me, so I wore borrowed boots that made my feet very sore. Much to even my surprise, I made it to the top just fine without slowing her down to wait for me. When we arrived at an ice-filled alpine lake, held sacred by Southwestern tribes, I felt called to jump into its clearing waters and did so with gusto. Stripping off my clothes, and yelling joyously, I dashed under the cold waterfall that fed it, and then dived into the water. Emerging dripping and very cold, I dried off with my clothing and lay down in a sunny protected area to rest and warm myself.

A while later, as we were going back down the mountain, I sensed a new respect in her eyes as she talked with me, but it did not come home to me fully until we stopped to give back the borrowed hiking boots. As I was taking them off, she blurted out to her friend there, "You should see the muscles in her back! She's in incredible shape! She went right up that mountain." Then she ordered: "Brooke, take your shirt off and show the muscles in your back!"

I got a big kick out of this, realizing that she had assumed my wearing skirts meant I was weak and incapable on the land. In truth, I wear skirts because I love wearing them and I feel free in them. But I also sense that it is good modeling for women to see me moving powerfully over the land, taking care of whatever needs doing in an easy, free-flowing skirt. The basic lesson is certainly not about skirts, although my grandmothers tell me that it weakens us as women to put something like pants "between our legs." The important lesson is about being who we are as human beings in female bodies, and being powerful in our own natural ways.

As Joanie Jackson and many others have commented over the years of my teaching: "The ease, the grace, the centeredness, the power of being a woman that you embody are a real inspiration to me. In you, I see Artemis . . . huntress, restlessness, challenge, female strength cloaked in feminine swirling."

This focus on ourselves, individually, as women also extends to learning about being with other women in a good way. Having the opportunity to be with and work with women in an intimate circle over many days is a powerful teaching in itself. It helps break through old images of competition and conflict, and brings us into a joyful way of being and working together. Whether they like or dislike each other, the women in my circles hold each other as sisters during and often after our time together—and holding that vision is instrumental in breaking old patterns.

I have been told that I came into this life as a master of vibration, and I want to vibrate my students at every level to their very core. Having studied the work of Milton Erickson, a masterful medical doctor and a magician of hypnosis, as well as other research on how we learn, I know that it is important to touch people at all these levels because mental and spiritual concepts are reinforced by feeling and action, by silence and stories, by drumming and dancing.

Jack Schwartz, a fine teacher and healer friend of mine and author of *Voluntary Controls* and *It's Not What You Eat, It's What Eats You!* (see appendix 2, page 465), once told me: "It's your vibration that does magic with people, not the subject you're teaching." He explained that my personal vibration has a very high frequency, and when others are around me long enough, it presses them into movement in their lives by its very nature. "All you need to do is entertain your students enough to get them to come and stay around a while, so be sure to do whatever it is that you like doing as a teacher."

In thinking about this aspect of my energy that presses people to move, Mad Bear Anderson's words about my being a crystal healer return to me. Perhaps it is the specific crystalline energy I carry that intensifies, magnifies, and creates movement not only in my own life but in all those around me.

Many students have commented on the subtle yet concrete shifts they have experienced at my workshops and gatherings, although they could not attribute these shifts to any specific lessons. Rather, the shifts seemed to be the cumulative outcome of a deep inner resonance that began vibrating in them even before they arrived and kept building during our time together until it surfaced as a powerful change in their outer lives.

What are these vibrations, these deep resonances? Where do they come from? How do they affect us?

Vibration is the basis of all physical life. Both modern science and ancient mystical teachings tell us that each and every thing in existence, animate or inanimate, has a spirit vibration, a "hum," that is unique to it alone. This is what White Buffalo Woman and our Native elders are speaking about when they acknowledge that each thing and being in the Circle of Life is alive and is to be respected. Thus, sound, rhythm, harmony, noise, very high- and very low-frequency waves, and other vibrations may have a much deeper influence on us than we suppose.

The earliest histories of many of the peoples on our Mother Earth tell of civilizations that existed long, long ago that based their science on pure vibration and sound. For example, with their vibrational technology, they were able to cut gigantic building blocks of stone from mountainsides and quarries, to lift and move these blocks through space and time, and then to form them into structures by acting at the level that underlies the foundation of matter. It is said that the great building blocks of Stonehenge in England, and the pyramids of Egypt and South America, were cut, transported, and set in place through vibrational technology. When one examines these structures up close, this seems much more likely than using the crude mechanical technology we employ today.

From the mystery teachings of Egypt comes an illuminating understanding of vibration. They believed that the soul is the eternal part of us that journeys through time in many forms, while the Spirit is seen as the vibration that gives life to that soul in an Earthly body. If you are interested in learning more about vibrations, read *Nada Brahma: The World Is Sound* by Joachim-Ernst Berendt (see appendix 2, page 464).

Another aspect of the vibrational spectrum is something Moshé Feldenkrais reminded us of again and again—"You can't give away anything you don't have," he would say. This meant that if I wasn't relaxed and centered when I was doing individual body therapy with clients, I couldn't teach them about being relaxed and centered. His wisdom helped me to see that there is more to teaching than just standing up and talking about something. In fact, I often teach what I want to learn myself.

And I have been encouraged to keep working with my own healing as a strong part of my teaching. For example, at one point in time I began to understand how important it is for people to find peace within themselves, so that peace can then echo outward to the larger world. In talking about this with students, I saw that I too needed much work in this area before I could be any kind of model for them. I became aware of the tension I carry, of the harried feelings I sometimes have during my intense road trips, the aggravation I feel when things are not just right at home. So I started doing more healing of my workaholic tendencies and my perfectionism. I also suggested that students go to advanced masters of peace, like the Vietnamese monk, Tich Nat Hahn, who is known as a teacher of peace. *Whatever you want to learn, it is important to seek it in a place or a person who manifests in their daily life that which you seek.*

Another realization that has informed my teaching is the primal importance of drumming, dance, and song in my work. The understanding of vibration helps me to see why the simple heartbeat of the mother drum echoing for hours and days could create such transformation in people's bonding with the Earth. As I looked around me for ways to truly model the peace and harmony I wished for my students, I thought, "What could be a more powerful nervous system programming for harmony than to actually sing several-part harmony in groups?" The actual physical and emotional feelings linked to this experience are very powerful. I remember that, in my youth, some of my highest moments were singing exquisite harmony in the choirs to which I belonged. Add to this singing *dancing* in rhythm with harmony, and the student receives a joyful, yet profound teaching.

As Andrea Lyman tells us, "[Brooke] really knows how to call Spirit and move energy around! I will never forget the eagle's wing that came to touch my face and head as she centered our focus in the sweat lodge. She gifted her medicine to all of us. I have sung, drummed, and danced with her into ecstasy around her big mother drum in our circular ceremonial yurt—building the vortex of energy until it felt as if the whole place would lift off the ground."

Drumming, dancing, and song are vital to the work I do. They touch my students at the most profound level possible on the physical plane—basic vibration. The ancient teachings tell us that our lives are literally a song. And our song, combined with All Our Relations, creates an exquisite symphony. Creator sang a song to begin all that is physical when this world was brought to life, and we continue that creation through the vibrations we put forth. Helping students think of their lives in this way enables them to choose the "song their lives sing." We sing and drum and dance as a continuing part of our time together, whether formally gathered around the drum, waiting together for the next event, or singing one of my traveling songs as we walk: "I walk a path of beauty, walk a path my ancestors laid out before me. . . ."

I also encourage my students to listen deeply inside and allow the songs they hear there to emerge and become medicine songs for them. It is very gratifying to me that many of the songs in my newest album, *Visions Speaking,* were received and gifted to me by students who have vision quested with me. This resonant work, especially when coupled with the big mother drum, helps students return to a deeper, truer, more natural, more harmonious place within themselves. And this, in turn, allows them to be in deeper harmony with the Circle of Life around them.

I have always had a powerful singing and speaking voice, and recognize more and more what a gift this is for me as a teacher. On one of my vision quests at the Medicine Rocks, my inner guide spent one whole day working with my voice. My site was about twenty yards from the base of the huge granite cliffs. The voice of my guide instructed me to project my voice up against the stone wall until I could hear it bounced back to me. I did this, feeling the need to almost shout to make sure it bounced back.

"Now do that same thing with the same intensity, but with less loudness," I was instructed. So I attempted this, and after many trials was able to lessen the volume. "Keep lowering the volume until you can bounce your voice off that wall at a whisper!" my guide said. And much to my surprise, by the end of the day, I could whisper with clear intention and focus, and the whisper would bounce back to me.

This has been a very useful tool for me in working all day with large groups, and no microphone. And it is a teaching I've passed on to others: how to speak up and express their truth in a way that carries in the world. I often find that people cannot even speak up enough to be heard in a circle of twenty people. Working with their voices and their willingness to let the world know who they are is a powerful teaching device—one that makes real for them their attitudes about themselves. I suggest to all my students that they take voice lessons—oriented not toward becoming great singers, but toward freeing their natural voice and expression. Especially in this time of the nine-pointed star, where our primary challenge will be using the throat chakra (vibration) to become conscious co-creators of our world, it is important that we develop that tool.

Another function of my "voice teaching" is to encourage students to pray aloud. This is done, not so that others may hear, but so the vibration is actually made in the outer world, and can carry more powerfully. In Elaine Peterson's words: "By the simple example of her own self expression—in her very careful and precise choice of words and her clear articulation—Brooke shows the way to the essential, to the source: away from the superflous and the limited. That example has been an inspiration to the exploration and development of my own true voice."

Marion Gracen reports, "When I look at all you do, I can boil it down to vibration—kinesthetic, song and voice, as well as emotion. You work with sound vibration and rhythms, and with the silence, the open spaces in those rhythms. Your physical strength lends people the courage to tolerate and make use of some of the vibrations you call up. Your own vibe responds elegantly to the emerging vibe of the group . . . leading and pacing naturally. Your personality helps us remember not to be satisfied and to always reach for more."

An interesting and special use of vibrational quality that I employ in specific situations where I have extended contact with my students is to give them spiritual names. Especially at Eagle Song camps and with my individual retreatants, I find naming them a powerful tool. I give them active names that will serve to connect them to the power of their experience during our time together, and enable them to recall that power more fully in their daily lives. The names are also given to stimulate and draw forth from each person some aspect of themselves that my staff and I can see only beginning to emerge in their lives.

For instance, one woman came to us with amazing and powerful dreams that presaged her experience at camp. During her vision quest, the paint horses came to be with her and share their energy. Her powerful left-sided abilities were easy to see, not only in her dreams but in her art and visions of beauty for the world; yet we sensed she was unable to ground her left side in reality as much as she would have liked. We used all these associations to give her a name that has been powerful for her, "Tames the Dream Horse."

Another woman came to us who was in need of taking her own personal space in her home, and especially creating an altar, a place of spiritual meaning. She also wished to begin gathering circles of women to make a safe place for their spiritual growth and transformation. This woman we called, "Weaves a Spirit Nest," a name that has continued to empower her over the years.

A man who was becoming both a drummaker and a father, and thus actively working on his nurturing abilities, we gave the name "Shares the Mother's Heartbeat." A woman doing intense work with her inner child and learning to honor her spirit within, and who also wanted to become a mother, was named, "Bears the Spirit Child."

Another woman who did not feel she could sing with power, and yet became our camp crier—to sing us awake each morning with a truly beautiful voice—was appropriately named, "Sings the Beauty Dawn," a name that also signified her awakening to the truth of her beauty and self-worth at many levels. These names grow more and more meaningful as the qualities of which they speak are called forward to emerge in the reality of students' daily worlds.

It is important to me that my students understand that *they are the ones* who can heal themselves, and that they do have the power to do it. I create a safe place for that transformation to occur, and act as a catalyst for it—yet it is always their work, their challenge. I encourage them in this work, not only for themselves, but also because I know that the more whole they are within themselves, the more whole they can be with the larger life around them. Their healing is a significant part of the healing of Mother Earth and All Our Relations. So I call them to responsibility and ask them to walk in their own power. A vital element of this is that they take responsibility for the lessons before them. I ask them to look at each situation that is creating difficulty or denial—and to use it for all they're worth as a learning device rather than playing the role of victim or going numb around the issue.

Since I believe that we create our own outer reality through our inner reality, I ask them what a person would have to believe and carry inside themselves to create the outer life situation that they are living at present. Sometimes this helps them find those "hidden" beliefs, attitudes, judgments, and decisions that form the foundation of what is unworkable in their lives. Knowing they have the power to create their situation, they begin to bring focused awareness to the process of creating what they want, rather than letting their old "programs" run the show. Thus, what I am teaching is a healing way of walking forward in the world, not a set of rules to follow.

Based on the belief that Spirit lives within each of us, I encourage students to look *within* for wisdom, rather than depending upon outside sources or forms. I ask them to go past the form to reach the unchangeable truth that lives within each of them. I believe that through each of our experiences we can synthesize ancient and modern experience so that the deep teachings emerge.

Lynn Peck says, "Brooke's teachings are about walking in your own power, not in the shadow of some other being. She stresses the beauty and uniqueness of each of us, of the necessity to honor the differences and create harmony instead of discord out of those differences. In this lies the hope of saving this planet for future generations of *all* beings, not just the two-leggeds."

I work to create an atmosphere that is nonjudgmental and egalitarian, where one is accepted for whatever one is. My students report that they often experience this as an atmosphere of unconditional love, where their wounded inner child finds the support necessary for healing itself by opening to its own creative source. This allows them to take responsibility for themselves in the fullest sense, and in the resulting freedom they can be more open and receptive to the creative spirit.

"In the most delightful ways, my adventures with Brooke over the years have helped me in the process of remembering who I am," wrote my longtime friend and student, Wendy Walsh. "My experiences with her have always set aflame the place in me that knows I'm here on this planet to be fully alive and to offer my highest—to heal myself, to support others in their growing, and to contribute to the positive evolution of this Mother Earth. Brooke challenges me to explore the full range of my humanness—to soar on Spirit wings, and to walk grounded upon the Earth; to honor my vision and to live it in the world."

White Buffalo Calf Pipe Woman has reminded us that unity, cooperation, and harmony are vital elements in our healing process, especially in these years of such deep separation and alienation from our spiritual essence and from the Earth. This experience of unity and support is found in the groups of eight women I assign to work together in hoops at workshops as well as at Eagle Song camps. The fact that these hoops will continue to give support and nourishment over time and distance after they leave our gathering imprints upon each camper's consciousness that unity does not require someone standing beside you physically. I make clear to them the enduring connection of our hearts and spirits.

The form of the circle, in which all are equally important and responsible, is a natural way to practice oneness. Coming together, again and again, to physically maintain the perfect roundness of the circling spiritual dance is a vital learning, even when there are ripples in the circle, such as individuals wishing to withdraw or wanting to run the show differently or feeling personal discomfort with others in the group. Their ability to maintain the basic harmony of the circle, even with these challenges before them, affirms their awareness of building community together.

Everything is brought into the circle—nothing is excluded. Ideally, if there are problems or issues within the group, these things are also brought into the circle for healing. Should someone sprain her ankle and be unable to dance, she is brought to sit or lie within the circle, rather than being left out. When someone is ill, she too is brought into a healing circle whenever appropriate, rather than left to lie alone in her tent or room. The circle becomes the container of all things, all happenings, concerns, celebrations, mourning, all anger, all joy, so that no one and nothing is ever left out. It is within the circle, then, that the healing is created. It is within the circle that we create the wholeness and the holiness.

In the beginning of an extended teaching, I will often stand at the center of the circle, and obviously lead the group. But, as the days pass, I step back into the circle itself and dance with the group in mutual sharing and learning. By the end of our days together, I step out of the circle entirely—a gesture that frees the gathered hoops to dance their own dances, sing their own songs, walk their own paths. Camper Susan Winecki describes this beautifully:

> I remember one of our last days at camp. We gathered in a circle, with Brooke in the center, kneeling and drumming the big mama drum alone. We danced around her, arms linked, eyes brimming, as she looked up at us from her place on the Earth. We had changed places in those fourteen days. We began on the ground, looking up at Brooke. Now we stood tall in our woman selves as she sat small in her wisdom and joyfulness. We grew wings in those days with her. She nourished and guided us, and it was good. Now we can soar. And we are!

Looking back at the shift in my role over the years from student to teacher, it is interesting to note that although I sat at the feet of my teachers listening attentively, opening my heart and my mind, filling myself with their vibration and their knowledge, the making real of that learning came only through my putting it into practice. We are given many ways to practice our lessons, and the personal practice that Creator gave me was to turn around and give away what I had received. I soon learned that there is no better way to test what one knows than to attempt to teach it to another. When I began to focus on teaching, I saw that to do it well, I had to keep learning from my students. So I found myself sitting at the feet of both my masters and my students.

It has become clear to me that all the personal lessons I need to learn will be spelled out in the interaction between teacher and student. I am in a wonderful partnership with all those who come to me to learn. I have always known that I had few answers. Yet, I've found that walking down the path together, asking the right questions, has been much more powerful than attempting to have the answers in teaching. I think of Moshé Feldenkrais giving us the advice that, "The *worst* state a human being can be in is to be right." I am beginning to think that one of the *finest* states a human being can be in is that of curiosity. So I have carried my curiosity and my openness into my teaching, and in doing this I have found much wisdom along the pathway.

I have always been clear about wishing to teach with integrity. My main question has always been what I was able or qualified to teach. No one of my teachers seemed able to answer that question because they each taught me in such different modalities—there was no one over-arching teacher or elder to turn to. Yet, as I taught, I began to understand how profoundly useful was the advice that Master Kaskafayet had given me one day when he focused intently on me in response to a question about what to teach: "Teach only that which you know. . . . and you will know it by experiencing it." As a rainbow teacher at the edge of a whole time on Earth, these words have helped me tremendously. Because we are moving into a new level of manifesting the oneness that Creator asked of us, there is little from the past that can truly guide us. The only thing left that I am sure can be a clear beacon for me is the ancient and everlasting truth, and so that is what I seek. And when I find some small piece of that truth, wherever and whatever it may be, I live its experience into my life and then pass it on to others as I have experienced it.

Those of you who walk the path of rainbow teacher with me, will find this a powerful guide in determining what you have to give away. It will also help you answer questions posed to you about your "qualifications" by those on the path of one particular religion or tradition rather than the rainbow way. If you follow the dictum of teaching from experience, you will have a less challenging time with both of these things. When I have been challenged by some "traditionals" about what I teach, I have been grateful that I had the solid ground of "knowing through experience" to stand on. That and my intention to serve in a positive and useful way have been my grounding over the years of my teaching.

As I look toward eldership in my life, I am more and more drawn to ways of teaching that involve me fully in the doing of what I am talking about. Now, rather than being on the road, I would like to be in my garden planting when I speak to others about living in simplicity and harmony. I have long held an image in my mind of sitting at my loom weaving a beautiful piece, or of walking among blossoming fruit trees, while speaking with someone who has come to quiet herself and retreat for a while where I am. The prophecies from the ancient Native linages have told us that the true teachers of the new time will not be those traveling down the road lecturing; they will be farmers and gardeners and weavers and humble people of the land. This makes total sense to me as I look at the issues that need to be addressed. People living harmoniously with the land will be the ones giving us the direction we need. Remember that the word "humble" comes from the same root as "humus," and means "of the Earth, or land; close to or in harmony with the Earth." I look forward with joy to being a part of that sharing.

THE RIGHT QUESTIONS

Too often in our learning we experience what is termed "premature closure." We think we see how things are and find a temporary solution. Or, we get an answer from someone else and think, "Whew, that's that!" Then we hang onto that answer for dear life—and close the book. However, I think it is much more useful if we can remain curious and open, constantly looking to the next question that experience will bring us.

This makes me think of the story of the two little boys who were duped by a "kindly" old stranger into handing over a valuable scroll into his keeping so they would have a chance to play. He then makes off with the scroll, of course. Later, their master asks each child what he learned from the experience. When the first little boy says, "I learned never to trust a stranger," the master is very sad. But he is more pleased with the other little boy's reply, which is partly in the form of a question: "Master, I learned to expect the unexpected. How can I learn to be more aware in such new situations?"

And, indeed, we may well ask what we can do to become more aware in our daily lives. Some of the awareness-creating steps you might want to try would be to:

1. Take time at the end of each day to reflect on the events that stand out in your mind.

2. Choose at least one situation from your day that gave you the opportunity to learn something. Ask yourself, "What did I learn from this?"

▶ When you asked yourself this question, did you notice that you had already decided—consciously or somewhat unconsciously—what you had learned?

▶ If not, take a moment now to search out the learning. Put it into a simple phrase, something like the motto at the end of one of Aesop's fables.

▶ Now, take a close look at the beliefs inherent in your statement of the lesson. Is what you have stated really what your highest self wants to learn? Or have you actually "closed the book" with the decision or judgment you had?

3. Is there a question or something new you'd like to explore that this lesson has opened up?

4. Is there something you might do as a follow-up that will continue the learning? Too often when we go through something challenging, and thus discomfiting, the "lesson" we think we've learned is simply to avoid it. Just as the first little boy said to his master, we tell ourselves, "What I really learned is never to try that again."

Perhaps in those situations, you might come up with such questions as:

▶ "How can I approach such a situation next time with more awareness or more knowledge?"

▶ "Who can I walk beside down such a path who will help me see it in a different light? Who might help me see it more clearly, help me make better choices?"

▶ "The next time this kind of situation comes up, how can I be more prepared to deal with it with integrity and ease?"

FINDING YOUR HOLES—AND FILLING THEM

1. Take a free day and devote it to finding out about the ways you fill the emptiness in your life. It is best to do this when you are alone, or undisturbed by others.

2. Plan to do absolutely nothing! Keep a notebook or journal with you to note down some of your experiences for later contemplation.

3. As the day goes on, take note of any restlessness or agitation you may be feeling, but don't do anything to change it. Simply let your experience develop by itself.

4. Be willing to notice and fully experience your emotional feelings:

▶ Do you feel guilty about not doing anything?

▶ Does shame come up?

▶ Is there something that makes you angry?

▶ Is sadness your primary response?

▶ Did you experience moments of bliss and joy?

▶ Is it scary to just be?

5. Pay attention to exactly what you would like to do to fill the empty spaces, or to handle the agitation, or to shift the emotions you're feeling:

▶ Do you have an urge to eat or to drink something?

▶ Do you want to do anything that will keep your hands busy?

► Do you have a longing to pick up the phone and talk to someone—anyone?

► Do you want to start a "meaningful" project?

6. Hang in there with all these feelings and thoughts that come up during the day. Just allow them to be, and accept them fully. See if they sometimes change to something deeper. For instance, anger may change to sadness, and sadness may change to fear. You may be able to learn some of the truths behind the feelings that are beginning to surface. They are you. All these feelings are you speaking out about your inner needs and dissatisfactions.

7. Have there been moments during this day when you perceived something rich and comfortable and peaceful inside yourself welling up to fill the emptiness?

► In moments of inner quiet, call to the part of yourself that is your spirit, your True Self, your Deep Self.

► Ask that part of you to come forward. To come to consciousness.

► Ask your True Self to speak clearly to you. To give you guidance about filling the emptiness you feel from within yourself.

8. Remember, your True Self, your spirit, is the only real place to find that overflowing fullness.

► Touch your spirit as often as possible. Call upon it at those moments during the day when you would normally reach for something outside yourself to fill the emptiness.

► Instead of eating, or drinking, or avoiding, just be with yourself and let your inner wisdom move you.

9. Since this is a difficult thing to do by yourself, perhaps you can ask someone to help you find this deeper part of yourself. This coming to know oneself is the work of a lifetime, and the only meaningful work for your soul.

ACCEPTING YOUR MANTLE

1. I have been reminded again and again of late that it is time for me to fully accept the mantle of responsibility. This responsibility means accepting myself as powerful and knowing, whether as a teacher or as an Earthkeeper. It is also time for you, too, to consider this possibility in your own life. In order to embody what you know and make it real in your world, ask yourself:

▶ "What is it I know that others around me may not have had the opportunity to learn? How can I share that with them?"

▶ "What is the 'song' my life sings? What patterns are evident in my daily life? Am I giving others the messages I really want to share?"

2. Once you have done this preliminary work, you might also want to begin accepting your own role as Earthkeeper, as we all must do now for our sacred Mother planet. Ask yourself:

▶ "Do I 'own' the place and the area in which I live, by my caring, nurturing, and stewardship? Or, forgetting that this is the time when we must all be stewards wherever we are, do I tell myself, 'This place doesn't belong to me. I don't want to do a lot of work around here just to benefit the owner.' "

▶ "Is there an area near where I live (a park, a trail, a road, a stream) that needs to be cleaned up? Can I call together a group of people who will find joy in renewing that place and taking continuing responsibility for it?"

▶ "Even if this area 'belongs' to the city, county, state, or the nation, and they are neglecting it, can I find a way to work with the appropriate agencies to make it beautiful again?" (Often those in charge will gladly cooperate once they begin to understand that you will take responsibility for the doing, rather than adding more work for them.)

▶ "Can I begin to re-create the beauty of Mother Earth's garden right in my own area, rather than thinking of going somewhere else to escape the pollution and noise?"

3. Biologist and Earthkeeper René Dubos suggested that we all begin "to think globally and act locally." You might want to expand your sense of "local" by asking yourself:

▶ "What 'bio-region' do I live in? What other communities comprise this ecosystem along with my own? Are there ways my community can work together with the others in the region so that life is improved for all present and future generations?"

▶ "In what ways can I enlarge the circle of my personal life to respectfully include more and more of All My Relations? What or who around me can I embrace in oneness?"

4. If you live in an urban bio-region, you may want to commit to the "One Block at a Time" credo that some some city people are now following. In fact, you might want to make it into an Earth Medicine contract—one that you will share with others in your neighborhood.

EARTH MEDICINE CONTRACT:
"ONE BLOCK AT A TIME"

I, _____, in the presence of Mother Earth, Father Sky, and All My Relations, acknowledge my oneness with All Life. I make a sacred pact to reconnect with Mother Earth and All Life from the depths of my being and to give action and beauty to this commitment.

As my Act of Earth Awareness I will find my Sacred Neighborhood, make myself open to its teachings, and honor it in a sacred way.

My Sacred Neighborhood on Mother Earth is _____

_____

_____

I pledge to consciously care for everyone and everything within this square block on which I live. I will help organize those living on my block so that:

⊕ Parents will gather to create the best care for all our children.

⊕ Young people will gather to make sure that all our elders are taken care of—that their groceries are bought and carried home, and that their homes are in working order.

⊕ Pride in our block will show in the communal flower gardens that line our street.

⊕ We will also work together to turn any backyard, alley, or vacant lot areas into communal gardens and/or safe play areas. Everyone on the block—young and old—will help look out for everyone else's property and well-being.

In gratitude for its many blessings, I freely and lovingly pledge the following amount of my help, energy, and time to my Sacred Place on Mother Earth: _____

_____

Signature and Date

Why not try this on your block or in a small area around you? Reach out. See who and what answers back. See how this changes your life.

We are living at a crossroad in time. How each one of us lives our life will influence the path all of us choose to travel together. Each of us is a student, just as we are all teachers to one another as well.

In time, because we will begin to learn openly and to share fully with others what we have to give, the word "teacher" may well fall into disuse, just as there was little use for the word "holy" among the Lakota, for whom everything was understood as holy. In the future opening before us there will be little need for such distinctions, for teaching and holiness will be an integral part of the natural way of things.

To help bring this about, I continue to acknowledge myself as a student in the process of living through my questions in order to find the understandings that will move me forward. I embrace myself as a spiritual warrior, embodying the ancient knowings to the best of my ability through my unique gifts. And I accept myself as teacher, offering my experience of living tradition.

And, as you are both student and teacher as well, what is it that I, and all of us, am learning through your unique gifts?

CARRYING HER PIPE OF ONENESS

At any moment in which we are in the holiness of cooperation, unity,
oneness, and harmony with what is around us,
we are in the new age, the new paradigm.
We have stepped into that new day.

Each and every thing, whether an idea, a tiny plant, or a person, has
an incredibly deep urge to live, to grow, and
to continue on toward the light of
wholeness and holiness.

"The attitude of holiness is the most vital thing," the
Lakota grandmother said.
'The true pipe is carried in one's heart."

White Buffalo Woman has placed my feet on a path of beauty on which I intend to walk across the horizon into a new time of peace, beauty, abundance, and full self-expression. As she walked, carrying her sacred pipe of the oneness of the Circle of Life, so, carrying a practice of unity and harmony, I walk. I move toward a time when the garden of Earth is green and flowering again, when sweet water runs in every brook and stream. I move toward a time when we will all know how to manifest fully the oneness that is ours within the sacred ecology of All Our Relations.

Although we can see across the horizon to the dawn of a whole new day for Earth, we have work yet to do within ourselves before we will be allowed to walk into that new day. Dayana, a seer friend of mine who seems very much in touch with White Buffalo Woman and her ways, was speaking with us one day about taking care of our bodies. In jest she said, "Why don't you just blow through your bodies with your crazy, unhealthy ways of living, and then get new ones like you've been doing for centuries?" A twitter of recognition of this pattern spread across the room. Then Dayana became more serious and said, "No, I mustn't kid around with you about that, because in the future it will not be so easy to get a body."

In disbelief, as a chorus, we asked, "Why?"

She answered, "Because there won't be nearly so many."

"But why?" we asked again.

"Because there will not be so many two-leggeds on Earth," she said simply.

"But why?" the chorus echoed again.

"There will not be so many human people on Earth: because to stay on Earth for this new time that is dawning, each of you must sign a contract. The contract with Mother Earth and Father Spirit is a stringent one. *If you are to remain upon the Earth, you must be willing to have everything.* You must be willing to have absolutely everything."

We sat quietly considering this for a few moments, wondering why in the world that meant many people would be gone—wouldn't that be an easy contract to sign? Yet, I could feel uneasiness fill me and spring up in the room.

Our sober, questioning faces must have asked another "But why?" because our friend Dayana said sadly, "There will be many fewer people here on Earth because only a few will be truly willing and able to sign that contract. . . . And because anyone who is not willing to have everything is holding everyone else back."

We understood her to mean that if any of us wanted to stay on Earth and yet live in an old paradigm—to live in want and disharmony and struggle—would mean that those things would still be a part of people's experience in the world. However, this is not to be, cannot be, if true and full harmony and abundance are to come. Contaminating the new with the old reminds me of the Hopi story of the emergence into a new age. It was a time of change when good-hearted people wanted to live in a new and different world and leave the bad-hearted people and ways behind. They made an arduous climb through a hole in the sky into that new world. But, at the very end, there came a little girl who belonged to the bad-hearted people. There was much discussion about her coming in, but out of kindness they let her through. And this is how bad-heartedness was allowed into the new world. Once again it grew large, and remains with us today.

And we in Dayana's group that day looked inside ourselves. Could each of us give up those old familiar patterns of struggle, of conflict, of scarcity, of victimization? Could we give up our numbness, our limitations, our greed, our fear? And I looked within myself. "Could I?" Very likely the answer for each of us was that it would not be nearly as easy as we first assumed. Each of us had been through enough personal growth work to know that the shedding of old patterns, no matter how unworkable and painful they are, is no simple matter. Our highest guides sometimes urge us to stop struggling and simply make that instantaneous shift to a larger, more whole frame of reference, yet each of us knows how difficult that attitude is to maintain, even when we can momentarily experience the beauty of it. It was a quiet crew that went home from Dayana's talk, each of us chewing over this profound information for ourselves.

That question, "Am I willing to have absolutely everything? Am I willing to be truly whole? Am I willing to walk in a holy manner?" lies at the back of my mind, and moves me to seek a whole new way of being inside myself. It moves me toward a place of power, where I am in flow with the river of life, rather than struggling upstream or across it in a tipsy, unstable canoe. I know that this flowing river of life is akin to the experience of oneness of which White Buffalo Calf Pipe Woman and Dawn Star spoke.

When we are at one with things, we will enjoy not so much a sense of power, but a sense of ease; not so much a sense of good timing, but of synchronicity; not so much of conquering our weaknesses as of bringing forward our most wonderful gifts. So I am called again and again to the question of wholeness, of holiness, of unity, of oneness. It is increasingly clear to me that what is required for all of us on Earth is exactly what White Buffalo Woman prescribed—good relationship. And the way to create this lies in unity, in cooperation, in the breaking down of barriers, in the release of fear and constriction.

Yet, in my own life, this is still the most difficult thing for me. I have always been the hero-child from a dysfunctional family—a person who works alone, who faces enormous challenges in trying to be emotionally clear and expressive, and who has few workable patterns for personal intimacy. Knowing this about myself makes me feel very ungrounded—unprepared to walk into this new time. It points out to me that not only my strengths, but certainly my weaknesses will be tested during this crucial period. The uncomfortable feelings and fear that arise are a powerful motivation to work toward oneness and wholeness.

It is clear to me that *at any moment in which we are in the holiness of cooperation, unity, oneness, and harmony with what is around us, we are in the new age, the new paradigm. We have stepped into that new day*. Yet, just as surely, when we are in conflict, separation, fragmentation, and disease we are right back in the old time, back again in a time that is dying. For myself, I am moving toward wholeness through personal growth work that is based in spirit. And I am continually reaching out for ways, in every aspect of my life, to practice this oneness. I would like to share some of these things with you now, in the hope that they will stimulate you to find new ways to practice this holy way in your everyday life, that we might walk forward together across the rainbow bridge that leads into the new day.

The attitude of oneness requires something of us that has not been popular in New Age circles. In fact, it has been denied by most of them. And that is the embracing of the dark side of life—in our own lives most especially. We have wanted to be all light and love but have overlooked one of the necessary means to attaining these qualities: embracing the dark. Darkness often implies evil to many of us. Yet, a part of me knows there is no evil, there is only fear and separation. When fear and separation have been bridged into peacefulness and unity, then the dark is as beautiful as the light.

In my inner work to make oneness real for myself, I was given a vision that affected me profoundly. In my dream I saw a monstrous being with red eyes and dripping fangs—a human person degenerated into some horrible, dangerous thing. He was angry, hurtful, and destructive, dirty, greasy, bloody, and covered with soot. As he moved among the people, they scattered in horror. When he came near me I ran as far away as possible—away from the terrible stench of his rotting flesh, tightening myself in defense. A few brave souls tried to battle him and were torn asunder; his stench on their remains was a horrible thing. Everyone was terrified.

Then, someone came walking toward the monstrous being, wearing a long white robe that seemed to radiate light. It was the Dawn Star, with his Christ light aglow, his heart and spirit totally open. Without blinking an eye, he drew close to the monster and, looking with love into its eyes, put his arms around that horrible being. The monster held stiff for but a moment, then seemed to melt into those restful, supportive, loving, accepting arms.

It did not take long for that awful monster to be transformed into a young man who was crying. He was soft and vulnerable and lonely and terribly frightened. A few more moments in the Dawn Star's arms, and he was healed. His heart was mended. He looked around himself at the destruction he had caused, and beckoned the Dawn Star to accompany him. Together they picked up all who had been destroyed or hurt, and with this same love and tenderness, brought them to wholeness again.

The entire scene shone with a warm and radiant light. I knew a part of my heart had been healed, as well, by this dream.

I have had the good fortune to spend time with Hal Stone and Sidra Winkleman, who have created a beautiful kind of therapeutic work called Voice Dialogue (for more information, see appendix 2, page 465). Talking with a group of students one day, Hal spoke about the "hungry dog in the basement." He said that we sometimes treat anything that bothers us, challenges us, hurts us, or pressures us, like a bad dog that we tie up in the far back corner of the basement. We keep it there, ignoring it, trying to even forget it is there. All the while the dog gets hungrier. We neglect the dog, give it no attention, no nurturing. And the dog gets hungrier and angrier. Until finally that almost mad, ravenous dog breaks free, bounds up the steps, breaks down the carefully barred door, and eats us!

This was Hal's way of saying that whatever in our inner world we do not embrace, do not accept, do not love and give attention to, will eventually break through the barriers of our consciousness and confront us, whether this is within ourselves or projected outward through some "horrible" person or "enemy." Much of Hal and Sidra's powerful work is a process of owning those "negative" parts of ourself, dialoguing with them, and eventually embracing them as a part of the family of personalities and aspects that live within each of us.

The next step is to discover and align with that larger, more mature part of ourselves—what I call the true self or deep self—who watches over the whole family, and who can be an enlightened coordinator and negotiator among these parts of self. Much to our delight, Hal played out the part of Joan, one of their female clients who was totally involved with the joy of raising her children. Acting her part, he stepped to the right and talked about how much he loved the kids. How delightful it was to be with them every day so as to not miss the little surprises and learnings every day brings. How he loved to be up with them early in the morning, that he felt good about soothing their crying, and hopped up to attend to their needs in the night. And by gosh, he even loved driving carpools of noisy children around in the station wagon!

Then he stepped to the left, owning for this mother another side of herself, which until then, she had not been able to do. He said, "You know, I really hate the little, screaming bastards. I haven't had one minute for myself since I had the first one. I'd like to see my husband stay home with this continual riot, get up at all hours of the night, baby everyone, fix lunches, make costumes, and cook a million meals in succession. I hate that lying, stupid bitch who says she absolutely loves the children, and I certainly hate that damn ugly station wagon!"

We were roaring by the time he finished acting out her experience. And a big part of the laughter was in identification with both aspects of that mother. How much we want to be good people, how hard it is for us to tell the truth, how much we want to help other people—and how, out of integrity, we can get lost in all those "yeses" that we don't really mean.

Hal told us, then, about having the mother stand in the center as the mature one, acknowledging both personalities, both feelings, as her own. Then she was able to negotiate—to set up ways for herself to have some freedom and rest, to express her displeasure at some parts of motherhood, to ask for the help she needed from her husband and extended family.

Hal said she had come to him suffering from incredible headaches that had made her want to "go mad, and break everything and everyone in sight." Instead, these headaches put her in bed for days. They were likely her barriers to the "hungry dog"—which she could finally own as her buried anger, the dog that sometimes felt as though it would burst out and "eat" one of her children. However, when she made friends with that hungry dog in herself, when she nourished and loved and accepted this part of herself, she could become a more whole, healed person, one whose adult ego could begin to create harmony within all the formerly fragmented pieces of herself.

Sidra then told us of their work with Robert, a man who had projected his disowned parts outside himself. He came to them when the stress of six months on a job with an unbearable boss had finally become too much. Jack had been hired on as his new supervisor, and Robert had come to hate him for his presumptuous, aggressive, demanding, and demeaning ways, as well as for the disrespectful manner in which he continually hustled the women in the office. "He reminds me of good old dad," Rob remarked disparagingly.

Robert himself was a model of decorum, a hard worker quite lacking in aggressiveness, who had not been promoted to Jack's position even though he had been with the company for years. In the ensuing sessions, Robert had trouble trying to portray something besides his "good guy" side. He explained that his father had been exactly the kind of man Jack is, and that he had sworn he would never, ever be like that himself. No matter how much he longed to ask one of the women in the office for a date, he would not do it. No matter how much he felt that his point of view was valid and necessary, he would not "push it." He was never going to be like his father.

So that "hungry dog" came to find him in the guise of his boss. As Rob gradually began to allow himself to own this part of his whole personality, he began to speak up about his ideas and feelings, putting himself forward in a way that pleased Jack, and actually seemed to calm some of the boss's excessive ways. Rob had stopped throwing the baby out with the bathwater, and had empowered himself through wholeness. In these ways, Hal and Sidra's unifying work brings healing to both our inner world and our outward relationships. For more good reading on embracing the dark side, read Brugh Joy's wonderful new book, *Avalanche.*

This helped me to see that the place to begin the work of embracing darkness is within ourselves. Often we try to confront this darkness outside ourselves first, and find that we end up torn to bits. Some people find that they attempt to create a sense of their own self-worth by acting out the roles of being a self-sacrificing, misunderstood, and misused martyr. I have found that it is only when we are clear of our own fear, and have embraced our whole selves, that we can truly embrace the things outside ourselves that represent negatives.

In my own inner work, this knowledge has enabled me to see that the role of "renegade daughter" was fine with me, but that I rejected the "domineering father" aspect of myself. In the process I realized that I often identify with the Aquarian part of myself—with the spiritual, virginal aspect of myself that is the most developed. This Aquarian aspect is about universal love, the new age, global consciousness. What I have not embraced nearly so much is my Leo nature, which has to do with bringing that love into reality in daily life, in personal relationships, and in physical, sexual love.

Perhaps this is why I found myself in confrontations with many older male teachers around the issues of personal relationship and sex. I am still in the process of owning this part of myself, and smoothing my outer relationships as well. I am also learning, with Hal and Sidra's help, to embrace all the little lost and undernourished children within me, and to become the mature adult who can give them what they need. By embracing these child selves and listening to their pleas, I am directed toward the areas of growth that are most important for me.

In my work with students I am also using techniques of inclusiveness to good effect. One of these techniques comes from a traditional practice among Native people. It is the use of a consensus method of coming to agreement, where a "talking staff" or feather—a symbol of the right to speak, which is held until one is finished—is passed around the circle. While one is holding this talking staff, no one else has the right to interrupt, even if the holder is silent for half an hour, or talks unceasingly for two hours. If a talking staff is not available, the same atmosphere can be created by waiting until the speaker has said, "I have spoken," to indicate completion.

While an individual is speaking or is holding the staff in silence, others in the circle focus their attention in the center, often upon an altar or fire, in order to go beyond the personality of the speaker and find the heart of their meaning through their connection in the center. The talking staff continues around the circle until each and every person can say "yes" wholeheartedly to one of the proposed solutions: a consensus has been reached.

One experience of this proved very healing, although it was initially quite taxing for other circle members. Sarah, whose turn it was, grabbed the staff eagerly, and began to pour out her opinions, her ideas, feelings, thoughts, challenges, then her anger and childhood unhappiness, and on and on. Members of the group kept looking to me to stop her, to stop this "wasting time." At long last, Sarah jerked as though coming out of a trance, looked around and came to herself again. Blushing, she said, "Thank you. Thank you very much for hearing me out," and she passed the staff.

When it went around the circle again, each person was now more conscious of being clear and concise in order to facilitate the decision we were making through this consensus form. When it came Sarah's turn again, she spoke at length, but not nearly so long. By the time we had come to consensus, she spoke briefly, and to the point, and passed the staff.

After the group dispersed, Sarah came to me and thanked me. She spoke of how she had never been listened to with courtesy in her childhood, of her anger and hurt at this pattern, which seemed to continue into her adult years. Something in those long minutes of being listened to, of being heard, had been a point of transformation for her. She no longer needed to "hog" the floor, as she had been known to attempt to do in our earlier experience of her. In the remainder of our interactions she was much more pleasant to converse with and work with. At our final meeting, she briefly explained this to the group and thanked them. We all realized we had learned a lesson in true unity.

Another lesson in cooperation and harmony the consensus circle teaches is that a true leader is one who brings diverse opinions together, helping people in the circle find a common understanding. This leader is not like those we call political leaders, who attempt to polarize people on one side or the other, so that they can get 51 percent of the votes, leaving the other 49 percent polarized on the opposite and losing side. The great orators and leaders among our people were those who could bring agreement through proposing solutions that would satisfy all concerned. Those women and men looked for the unifying energy, the thread of agreement, the deep interest of the whole circle in reaching a workable solution, and continued to put that forward.

This is a wonderful practice for my students and for me, because in the dominant culture we have seldom learned this style of decision-making. I recommend it for every decision you must make, whether at home or in your business. When a decision is reached this way, everyone's energy, excitement, and enthusiasm is behind the decision, and their cooperation can bring it into reality in a short while.

An example of this consensus circle is the process we use in my workshops to create and carry out a Dedication Dance. The whole idea of the ceremony is to dedicate our dance to something very specific, so that everything we do focuses our energy toward that intent. Some examples of the central theme of our dances have been: bringing water to an area long devoid of rain; supporting young people in their recovery programs; calling for peace in the Middle East; and healing a person or an entire community. Since it is of primary importance that everyone in the circle be in alignment so that nothing deflects the energy, this is a perfect opportunity to go around and around the circle until we are all not only agreed on our intent, but excited about it!

Another example is the fine art of conflict resolution, which is very different from the old, outdated practice of law in which opposing lawyers fight it out, often escalating the conflict. I have seen business partners, marriage partners, and others become bitter enemies through this unnecessary and damaging process of current law. However, using conflict resolution, the dispute is resolved through working with each party to see what they truly need in all areas—for instance, in a divorce settlement, the need for a certain amount of child support, or for a feeling of working together with the children. Conflict resolution is based on respect for each person, on respect for their needs, wants, and feelings. I have seen many couples come out of this process separated, but still good friends. It is such a joy for me to see these manifestations of Buffalo Woman's ways in our daily world.

One especially satisfying piece of healing work happened for me when a student called me in a very agitated state. June is a woman who has worked for years to develop her left side, and has great facility with journeying there as she wishes. She had often been aware of certain energies or beings present in her bedroom in the dead of night, but they had always been friendly. After sustaining a minor concussion in an auto accident, however, she began to have severe headaches accompanied by a weakness that enervated her for days. These events seemed to open the doorway for a frightening visitor, in experiences over which she seemed to have no control.

June reported that, lying in bed alone one night, she woke and noticed a red light spreading across the opposite wall. Looking around, she saw no possible source for the light, and it caused her great concern. Then the light began to swirl, and grow more intense and firelike. She became very agitated. Her agitation turned to alarm when a man stepped out of the wall, right through this chaotic fire. He was a Native man, dressed and painted in fierce red.

He threatened her, telling her that he, "Red Fire," had power over her, and that he could easily harm her, even threatening her defenseless children in the next room. He glared at her and stomped around the room before leaving through the wall. The fiery swirl of light followed him out of the room.

This was like a nightmare to her, and she hoped it was just a one-time occurrence. Much to her terror and dismay, it was not. This threatening presence came to her room whenever he wanted, walking through all her energy shields, her circles of light, her lines of sacred cornmeal, to lord his power over her. The more she tried to protect herself, or to destroy this horrible presence, the more powerful it grew. Red Fire seemed to fill her whole room when he came. No prayers or pleas affected his malice, and she called me, very frightened.

Knowing her positive nature, and of her power on the left side, I was stumped and asked her to give me time to consider. At first, I was inclined to think, as she had, of better and better ways to protect herself against him, to keep him away from her, or to destroy him. Then White Buffalo Woman came to me, speaking of oneness and good relationship, and Dawn Star came to remind me of embracing the monster. They cautioned me that *each and every thing, whether an idea, a tiny plant, or a person, has an incredibly deep urge to live, to grow, and to continue*

on toward the light of wholeness and holiness. When anything is threatened in any way, it uses all its resources to protect itself, even going
"overboard" into aggression in this attempt. Thus, they helped me to
fashion a plan, and I called June to suggest she embrace this red "devil"
in the following manner:

"It has been made obvious by the results of opposing him that,
rather than fear or despise him, you must honor this one. Your primary
prayer must be for his health, growth, safety, wholeness, and full expression. Become his ally in getting what he needs and wants. For in truth,
this may very well be an aspect of yourself that is reaching out for your
attention.

"Your first step will be to find a secluded place of beauty, in the
wilderness near your home—a place that might invite a wild, free, and
powerful Native like Red Fire. There, dig into the Earth about two feet
deep and the length of a man. Line it with sweet grasses, sage, and soft
moss to make this opening in the Earth a warm, welcoming place. Once
this is done, go there and pray for Red Fire for three consecutive days.
Ask the Great Spirit to bless him, to nourish him, to give him all that
he needs and wants—to move him, as he and all creatures long for,
closer to Spirit. Pray that his path be lighted and his journey home be
made sweet.

"Then, on the fourth day, gather together a group of helpers from
your close friends who will be attuned to support you. With their help,
do an honoring dance for Red Fire and all his relations. You may want
these friends to drum, to dance with you, or to hold the energy while
you dance. Before you begin this ceremony, make a bountiful feast that
you will offer Red Fire upon the completion of your dance. When you
feel complete, go alone to the place of beauty and set his banquet in the
resting place you have so carefully prepared for him. Invite Red Fire to
come and find enjoyment there, and leave it for him. After these things
are done, talk with me again."

She said she would do so, and I didn't hear from her for well over
a week. When she did call, her voice was filled with excitement. I could
hardly wait to hear what happened at her dance. She told me she had
done as I suggested, adding many things that had felt right to her. She'd
found a lovely opening in the forest behind her house, and made a bed
in the Earth there for her challenger. She reported that her negative
feelings had turned to a gentle caring as she made this space beautiful
and welcoming. To her surprise, June found herself putting some of her
most beautiful and precious things in the bed: a special crystal, and a soft
deer hide she slept under and loved. Her prayers for Red Fire became
totally sincere, as she was enabled to truly embrace him. On the fourth

day, at dusk, four women friends joined June in preparing a dance circle, with a fire in the center. One or more of them kept a drum going, and they simply held the energy while June explored within herself what wanted to happen, paying attention on the left side. She invited the women to dance with her at times, but often danced alone, moving and swaying for what seemed hours, and finally slipping into an ecstatic dance where she moved in a frenzy. Then, suddenly, she dropped to the ground, unconscious.

The heartbeat of the drum kept steady pace, even as her friends covered her with warm blankets and sat by her, praying for her to be well, and to return. She seemed to them to be very far away, and at times they worried about whether they should touch her and try to bring her back. Yet something told them to wait, and they respected this. When June finally returned to consciousness and was able to sit and speak, she told them this story: When her body fell to the ground, she was taken under the Earth to a gathering of a Native tribe. She approached the fire in the center where all the people were coming together. The drums beat a flourish and the man who called himself Red Fire stepped into the center of the circle, looking strikingly handsome and gentle. An old woman, adorned in black, came forward and told of how this man had been dishonored, discredited, and cast aside. She told of how, after many years, the hurt and rejection he felt had turned to fiery anger. He had then taken the name Red Fire, and had gone to avenge himself.

But the grandmother said that he had done his work well, for no one had ever been harmed. She praised him for his willingness to stand up for himself, and for the power with which he acted. Now all the people rose to their feet in a joyful acknowledgment of him, as the grandmother tied into his hair four white tail feathers gifted by a fish eagle—a bald eagle—and gave him a new name: Red Wolf. She reminded him that the wolf people are the speakers and teachers, and that his new way would be the gentle way of the teacher. June found herself running forward to embrace this beautiful being, though still with some uneasiness, and to acknowledge him as her teacher. As she held him to her and looked into his eyes, she awoke and found herself on the ground among her friends. With joy and gratitude, she fed Red Wolf his feast.

"I realize now that Red Wolf is the masculine, aggressive part of myself that I had denied for years," June relayed on the phone, some days after her dance. "Many of the men in my early life have been hurtful and oppressive with that same kind of invasive, angry energy, so I had completely disowned it in myself. Now I can allow that part of me to become a teacher. Since the night of the ceremony, I have experienced no more headaches, and am feeling stronger—almost well."

After she hung up the phone, I gave thanks to White Buffalo Woman and Dawn Star for the beautiful lesson in unity and wholeness they had given both June and me.

As I thought over this incident of healing, I remembered a time I had healed myself. It was in the days when I lived on the road, and I had been working intensely for many months. That day I had finished my last workshop of the season in Denver, and was driving to New Mexico to stay with friends who made a home for me with them during the holidays each year. I was exhausted, and the drive seemed especially long. My head began to fill up with mucus and my eyes began to water. I sneezed and began to have chills. Knowing that I had worked myself to exhaustion and that my body desperately needed rest, I recognized this cold as one of my old ways to get recuperation time. However, I did not want to be sick, and I realized that I did not need to be sick. So I began a dialogue with my deep self, in which I told her that the Denver workshop had been the last one of the season and that I was going to New Mexico to rest for three full weeks. When I asked if this cold was about getting the rest I needed, my inner self affirmed it. The right side of my sinuses was filling up very painfully at this point, although the left side seemed clear. My deep self suggested that I notice which side of myself had the problem, and I acknowledged that it was my right side, the aspect of my personality that was very capable of pushing too hard and not caring for *me* enough. I then struck a bargain.

"I promise that when I get to New Mexico in three hours, I will lie down and not get up again for two full days. Then I will take it easy for another complete week, giving myself massages and hot baths and trips to the hot tub. I will make no plans, do no work, accomplish nothing—simply enjoy and nurture myself with my good friends in the sunshine. Since I will have given myself the needed rest and recuperation, I will have no need for the cold." My deep self agreed, and our dialogue was finished.

Within five minutes, several things happened that quite astonished me. The fullness and pain in my right sinus instantaneously shifted to my left, stayed there for about a minute, and then disappeared completely, leaving my head and eyes totally clear. I felt wonderful! It was as though my deeper self had taken the opportunity to show me her power, and how much she affected things. My cooperation with her that day, and to this very day, can bring great healing. As I become whole within all parts of myself, and especially in those parts that are offering me challenges or disease, I can heal myself. I have used this approach with many of my clients, and see it being used more and more in the helping professions today. Like a physical embodiment of "voice dialogue," it is truly a manifestation of White Buffalo Woman's law.

Another way I have seen the effectiveness of this embracing of the negative aspects of our experience is in family therapy. Often in dysfunctional families, there will be a child who acts out, who carries on the worst features of everyone in the family, and who becomes the "problem child." For years, social service agencies and therapists worked only with this problem child, trying to straighten him or her out, in isolation from the family. When this was done in live-in therapy situations, this child often changed radically, seeming to become a completely different and more integrated person. Yet, just as soon as the child was sent home, the same old behavior returned, often becoming worse.

Finally, those who pioneered the work with Adult Children of Alcoholics began to recognize that this problem-child was merely playing out the dysfunctional situation of the whole family. That this was the family member who was the most willing to cry for help—for all involved. Today, treatment addresses everyone in the family, including those who have held their lives together by looking good, accomplishing a great many things, and carrying the burdens, rather than acting out. This form of treatment is finally bearing fruit for all concerned. These successes point out, again and again, that we cannot push away that which seems negative. We must embrace this part of the family or ourselves and let it guide us to what is needed. For instance, many of us have pushed away the voice of the frightened or needy child within us. Unaddressed, this can create psychological or physical imbalances. Yet, if we turn our attention to this voice crying within us, learn from it, and integrate it with conscious caring, it is a powerful healing.

It has become clear to me, through inner vision and outward experience, that the answers to all our challenges lie in oneness. Our prophecies have made it clear that when we at last come into the full experience of oneness, it will turn the key in a door that leads to what we would now call extraordinary abilities. Being one with all things, we will be able to communicate over time and distance, as well as across boundaries of language—both two-legged and interspecies. When there is no need for harsh, protective personal boundaries, our interpersonal communication will be total and complete, perhaps even without words as we "feel" a complete transmission of the other's message. We will also be able to move ourselves and other things through time and distance without the polluting encumbrance of automobiles and other such primitive means of transportation. We will very likely use a powerful technology such as sound to replace mechanical energy for moving, cutting, and building. In creating what we need, we will cooperate with nature. I see us asking a sturdy kind of bush to grow itself into a chairlike form; we will feed and water that living plant form in return for its service to us, rather than killing plants to make what we need.

When we remember ourselves as family who practice sharing and cooperation, the immense resources we now spend on warring and defense will be used in mutually creating a beautiful and abundant life. Our children will be able to express themselves fully, and will be our models of how to be the new human being who is now becoming possible. (For more on this, read Carey's *Starseed: The Third Millennium.* See appendix 2, page 462.)

Knowing ourselves to be one with Mother Earth, we will awaken again to using her edible foods, plant medicines, and other gifts that we now call weeds; we will find ourselves in a cradle of abundance and beauty that has been awaiting our discovery, rather than stressing ourselves and Mother Earth with plowing, transporting, and all the mind- and back-breaking labor we have created for ourselves. Like plants, we will become more and more open to the direct nourishment of the Sun, which means we will need much smaller quantities of food. Our way of living will become a technology of opening to receive rather than destroying to take. For example, we will continue to learn about better ways to receive energy from the Sun and other natural sources, rather than tearing up the Earth for coal and oil to transport and burn.

Because we will hold an unwavering image of our wholeness, any wounds we suffer will heal rapidly and completely. Our horse, Topper, demonstrated this for me after two separate incidents of tearing his chest open in a gaping wound that could not be bandaged. I watched the damaged flesh degenerate and fall away, and then observed the natural process of healing fill in that space so that only a small tough scar remained on the surface. I was astounded by this. Yet when I understood that Topper very likely did not talk to himself about the injury, did not hold an image of his wounded self in his mind, did not "get any points" for being sick, I could see how natural the process of healing really is and what an attitude of wholeness truly produces. With this graceful kind of life-style, there will be little disease and illness. Fear and constriction will give way to love and creative expression. A truly golden time will be upon the garden of Earth.

And so White Buffalo Woman comes singing into our world her ways of unity, oneness, harmony, and cooperation. I hear her song as I move forward in my ability to use these principles in my own life and in my work with others. I hear her words in my mind, "Carry forward this pipe, this way of unity and oneness. With it you will be able to go through this time, into the new time, and on until the end of time. And I will meet you there."

This brings to mind an elderly Lakota woman who comes from a line of pipe-carriers begun when White Buffalo Calf Pipe Woman gave the people that first pipe. She has lived her life with and through the sacred pipe. At a recent gathering, I asked her the question of who should carry the pipe, and whether she agreed with some Native peoples' idea that only Indians should work with that very sacred object. She stood up and pulled her small frame as tall as possible and spoke in a clear voice. "White Buffalo Woman said to use this pipe. She said it would help all the peoples of Earth, and I know it does. I don't care what color you are, what size you are, what sex you are, or where you live. Pick up the pipe with hands dedicated to the life of All Our Relations, and use it. It will teach you what you need to know. We must make use of this pipe. It is one of the ways to our salvation."

I later talked with her about those who have no pipe, or do not feel comfortable carrying one. She reminded me that the pipe is only a symbol of the sacredness of the web of life of which we are a part. *That attitude of holiness is the most vital thing,"* she said. *"The true pipe is carried in one's heart."*

So I close the circle of this book, understanding that the spiral of our lives and our growth is not completed. Coming from a childhood home in Montana, I have returned there to live, yet I journey out in the world in ever-widening spirals. My own learning deepens as I see new possibilities for expansion and wholeness. I have plans to intensify my spiritual practice, to create more support for existing programs and teachings so that I can expand and create new ones, study with experts in how to live gently upon the Earth—as a steward and caretaker—and perhaps even creating the band of musicians I've thought about taking on tour for years.

You, too, will continue your growing. Even though we may have practiced sweat lodge, or carried a pipe for ten or fifteen years, or completed many vision quests, we are yet beginners, with many years to grow in these ways. The spiral continues.

Our joyful task is to keep making more and more connections in good relationship with each other and All Things. As the old way begins to crumble and fall away from beneath our feet, we will find ourselves dancing high on the exquisite rainbow bridge of unity—the gossamer bridge that could not even be seen until the light of the new day, and the dust of the crumbling old ways, make it evident. In that new day, we will look toward the horizon, and see White Buffalo Calf Pipe Woman come singing. And it will be good.

GLOSSARY

act of beauty an extension of personal wholeness into the world by giving to the whole Circle of Life the unique gift one came to give.

act of power a personal action made to create greater health, wholeness, and balance within oneself.

action contract a commitment to perform stated acts of power and beauty, within a specified time frame.

All My (Our) Relations *all* things in *all* kingdoms of life: known and unknown, animate and inanimate, earthly and beyond, past as well as future; a phrase referring to the fact that, in the Native philosophy of wholeness, all things are related; used in ceremony and communication as a reminder of that sacred connection and interweaving of all of life.

All That Is a phrase that refers to the wholeness of life, especially to the spirit that lives in all things.

Apsa a term used by Brooke to designate a northern Indian tribe of which she is a member.

aromatherapy the use of distilled aromas of various plants and herbs to act on the brain and central nervous system for healing.

attention modes first: attention to the body in time and space; second: after *first attention* can be put on automatic, any other units of attention simultaneously devoted to outward or inward things; third: holiness, the attention to the whole Circle of Life.

Bear Butte a small mountain near the Black Hills of South Dakota which is a traditional vision questing site of several Native American tribes.

Bear Spirit man a spirit visitor who took the shape of a man while interacting with Brooke.

beauty arrow an arrow decorated symbolically during meditation and prayers to represent one's act of beauty in the world; a symbol of one's act of beauty.

benefactor refers to a *spiritual* benefactor, or one who acts as a spiritual elder, guide, or teacher.

Black Elk a traditional holy man of the Lakota people, who died in the 1950s. Wallace Black Elk, now teaching, is a nephew of "old" Black Elk.

Bureau of Indian Affairs (BIA) a federal government agency of the Department of the Interior, basically in charge of all Indian reservations and their internal affairs.

cedar a tree whose needles are used as incense; when burned, the smudge or smoke from them is known to have properties which cleanse our emotions, clear our actions, and promote forgiveness.

chakra one of seven energy centers in the human body, described in Eastern philosophy, science, and traditional systems of healing.

Chalíse one of Brooke's sacred names, which means "A Chalice Overflowing with Light."

Chief Joseph a leader of the Nez Percé Indian people, who died in 1904.

Circle of Life, Great Circle of Life phrases which describe the phenomenon that all life is interwoven and interconnected.

Corn Dance a yearly renewal dance, held by many Southwestern Pueblo peoples, which honors corn as the symbolic and literal nourishment and sustenance of the people.

cornmeal ground corn which is used—especially among tribes of the Southwest—as an offering to symbolize nurturing, of both body and spirit.

Coup a game named after the French word for "achievement," played at night by two opposing teams who encounter each other in the darkness over unfamiliar territory; also an act of bravery and daring once performed among rival Indian tribes and warriors.

coyote principle an oblique way of teaching which doesn't give a student the answers directly, but presses the student into finding the answers through her own, often exasperating, experience.

critical mass principle if a critical mass (or certain percentage) of human beings align their consciousness on any one thing, this will automatically shift the consciousness of *all* humankind.

crying for vision calling aloud for vision, with a humble attitude—most often practiced on vision quest.

Dawn Star, Morning Star a mystical, spiritual figure of several thousand years ago, featured in Native histories, said to have united all the children of Mother Earth and Father Spirit as one peaceful, cooperative family (although each tribe or group was still acknowledged as unique).

dreamer one who has developed his or her abilities to use the altered state known as dreaming.

dreaming refers also to the waking altered state in which one is conscious of experiencing another aspect of reality, unfettered by normal time, space, and boundaries.

embodying spirit to bring spirit more fully alive in our physical body and earthly self.

Father Sky, Father Spirit the sky and spirit were often referred to similarly, since they represent what is highest in our earthly experience; where Earth is Mother, Sky is Father, overlooking and living within all things.

Feldenkrais, Moshé the Israeli physicist and healer who brought the principle of awareness into physics and modern healing; he died in 1984; founder of Functional Integration and Awareness Through Movement healing techniques.

Flowersong teachings and ways originating with the Dawn Star, about a flowering of all the children of Mother Earth and Father Spirit through cooperation, unity, harmony, and love.

four-leggeds animals and other creatures who walk on four legs.

Four Quarters or quadrants the areas encompassed within the Four Directions—E, S, N, W—used in ceremony to denote the qualities, aspects, and beings assigned to each.

Four Winds the points of the crossquarters—SE, NW, NE, SW—which symbolize a cycle of movement and manifestation *through* the Four Quarters.

Golden Seed Atom a symbolic seed lying in the left auricle of the heart, which represents that which each human brings forward from all other lives or experiences prior to this one.

Grandmother a term of respect applied to all old women, especially those who have gone through Moon pause (menopause).

Great Circle of Life (see Circle of Life).

Great Mystery that which cannot be defined or known, and yet is the central power and source of creativity and all life.

Great Spirit the spirit which lives and moves within all things in the Circle of Life; that which enlivens all which is physical.

green-growing ones the plant kingdom.

Harmonic Convergence an event in 1987 celebrating the awakening of a new consciousness on Earth, first prophesied in the ancient Mayan Calendar and common to many Native histories/prophecies.

henawat a Shinela word for "what."

holy a word which comes from the same root as healing and whole, all of which have a primary reference to wholeness, oneness: being sound, recovered from injury or disease, intact, full. Holiness, in my way, is the attention to the entire Circle of Life, and the fact that Spirit lives in each and every thing. To act in a holy way, we must enlarge our awareness to consciously include All That Is.

hoops circles created with an intention to harmonize, nurture or protect; also a frame for shields.

hunka a relative who has been adopted in the sacred Hunkapi manner.

Hunkapi a sacred rite of spiritual adoption, given to the Lakota people by White Buffalo Calf Pipe Woman.

Inipi the sacred purification ceremony given the Lakota by White Buffalo Calf Pipe Woman; stone-people lodge; referred to colloquially as "sweat lodge."

Kaskafayet, Frank a non-physical, channeled presence who returned in this guise as a teacher.

kiva an underground chamber for religious purposes, used primarily among the southwest tribes.

Lakota a nation of Indian tribes whose home country is the Dakotas, popularly known as Sioux.

left side of the world associated with the left side of the body (right brain), and also with the non-ordinary aspects of reality such as altered and transcendental states, dream, vision, prophecy, shamanic journeying, unconscious sub-personalities; not limited by time, space, or ordinary cultural/social boundaries (also see *nagual*).

lodge a tipi or other structure used for housing.

lucid dreaming being awake and aware while in the dream state.

magpie a black and white bird of crow size, symbiotically associated with the buffalo.

medicine a term with several connotations for Native peoples, the primary one referring to the special powers which Spirit gives each being, thereby emphasizing that each thing or being in the entire Circle of Life is worthy of respect and attention, because it carries Spirit within it and manifests that power in unique ways. The medicine of a fox may be thought of as cunning; the medicine of a chameleon camouflage; the medicine of the cheetah swiftness; the medicine of the owl that of navigating through the darkness; the medicine of chamomile calmness; the medicine of emerald that of healing the healer; etc.

medicine bundle an item or items, carried in a small bag or wrapped in a bundle, which have special power or meaning for an individual or a group (also see *Sacred Bundle*).

Medicine Rocks a group of rocks the Apsa people hold as special, especially for vision questing; stories tell of "the little people" (spirit helpers) living there.

medicine teacher/person someone highly developed, especially spiritually, who can help others develop their unique gifts in order to serve All Our Relations.

medicine wheel a symbolic wheel of life containing all directions, aspects, attributes, things, and beings. The stone circles which portray this symbolism are sometimes laid out in alignment with the sun at the solstices, or with other astrological events.

metis a French word meaning "half," used among Native peoples to indicate those with mixed blood; half-breed.

Moon Lodge a place of spiritual retreat for women on their Moon time.

Moon time women's menstrual time.

Morning Star (see Dawn Star).

Moshé Feldenkrais (see Feldenkrais, Moshé).

nagual a term referring to the part of our human experience which does not have to do with physical reality, but includes such things as vision, dreaming, non-ordinary reality (see *left side*).

Native American Church a Native American Christian "plant church," whose services are most often held in a tipi, with the cactus plant peyote as the central sacrament.

Native, Native American a more correct name for the peoples commonly called "Indian" (the name "Indian" was reportedly given by Columbus, who thought he was in the East Indies when he landed, but is not what the Native peoples called themselves).

Neurolinguistic Programming (NLP) a type of personal growth and transformative work which involves verbal/linguistic patterns in the nervous system; founded by Richard Bandler and John Grinder.

Nez Percé a Native American tribe whose reservations are now in Washington and Idaho.

number four (as symbol) indicates the four directions and four winds which comprise the four quadrants of the medicine wheel.

Paha Sapa: the Lakota name for their sacred Black Hills in South Dakota.

painting applying pigment ritualistically in certain patterns on the body; for example, using red ochre on one's hands to symbolize dedicating them to the life blood of all things. Also, a way to symbolically designate certain internal states or spiritual experiences.

peyote a hallucinogenic cactus plant native to Texas and other parts of the southwest and Mesoamerica, often used in shamanic ritual and journeying; central sacrament for the Native American Church.

piñon a variety of pine tree with edible nuts found primarily in high desert climates.

place of power a place which has specific significance, or offers special protection, clarity of vision, or awareness of connectedness for an individual.

plant medicines   plants whose properties help us in the healing of mind, body, emotion, and spirit.

Plenty Coups   the last traditional chief of the Crow Indian tribe, whose name means "Many Achievements"; he died in 1941.

prayer cloths   pieces of cloth of symbolic color used to represent certain prayers, activated by the movement of wind, e.g. a white cloth might be a prayer for unity.

Rainbow medicine   a sacred way of healing for the Earth, which acknowledges all peoples and things as important for the well-being of all others; includes all races of people and all cultures.

recapitulation   a technique used to review one's history regarding a specific subject, practiced for the purpose of becoming aware of the habitual patterns connected with the subject, so that one can then choose a new or alternative pattern.

renegade spiritual hoop   the term used by Dawn Boy to refer to the circle of non-traditional teachers of ancient and Native ways now travelling and working the modern circuit.

right side of the world   associated with the right side of the body (left brain) and also with the everyday world of material reality, feeling, experience, and accomplishment—contrasted with the *left side,* which refers to all other aspects of our reality such as altered and transcendental states, dream, vision, shamanic journeying, unconscious sub-personalities, etc.

ropes course   a high-challenge course consisting of individual elements designed to challenge a person's abilities and teach them new moves of being, involving height, balance, agility, and other very physical modes.

Sacred Bundle   a medicine bundle of sacred objects kept wrapped in cloth, hide, or other covering, which has special power or meaning for a group.

Sacred Lodge   the tipi or other shelter wherein a Sacred Bundle is kept.

sage   an herb often used in ceremony for the cleansing vibration it emits when burned as smudge or simply smelled; it is particularly cleansing of the subtle energies around us—our aura—and of the general atmosphere.

samurai   a noble Japanese warrior of high spiritual intent.

shaman   a Siberian word for a person versed in non-ordinary states of reality, who often acts as a healer and seer for his or her group; now popularly used to refer quite indiscriminately to anyone even remotely familiar with the use of non-ordinary states of reality (many Native elders object to being called by this term since it does not originate within their culture and has assumed such indiscriminate meaning).

shield rawhide stretched over a willow hoop, painted to symbolize "what we hold before us," which can be used for inspiration, direction-giving or guidance, and protection.

Shinela a term used by Brooke to designate a northern Indian tribe whose reservation is adjacent to the "Apsa," who are age-old enemies.

skan in Lakota, the masculine creative aspect, as *wakan* is the feminine.

smudge the smoke from herbs or incense, used in cleansing rituals.

softened eyes relaxing the eyes by focusing peripherally, allowing a more diffuse kind of sight to help distinguish movement.

Southern Seers a Native American spiritual lineage which came from the ancient Toltecs down through the Yaqui and Apache who now live south of the present Mexican border.

spiritual contract an inner contract made with Spirit and one's Higher Self.

Sun Dance a great renewal dance held in the hottest part of the summer among many northern Native American tribes, which acknowledges Father Sun/Spirit as the source of all blessings and the continuance of life.

sweat lodge (see *Inipi*).

sweet grass a grass found in northern swamps, which retains its sweetness when dried and braided, and which is burned ritually in smudge, as a prayer for sweetness and goodness in one's life and surroundings.

talking stick or staff a staff, arrow, feather, or any other object which is passed around a group gathered in circle, used to indicate that only the person who holds it has the floor to speak; used in a consensus model of decision making.

Tarot cards decks of cards used for divining and augury; the forerunners of our common playing cards.

third eye one of the seven chakras or energy centers of the human body, located in the center of the forehead; associated with nonordinary perception.

tobacco an herb whose medicine, or unique power, is to help us become one with that to which we offer it, thus considered especially useful in vision quest and other ritual/ceremony where such oneness and communication are paramount.

Toltecs an empire of indigenous peoples who dominated Central Mexico from A.D. 900 to around A.D. 1200 before the advent of the Aztecs. They are known for their central deity, "Ce Acatl Topiltzin," or

Quetzalcoatl, and for their capital city at Tula (then Tollan); their descendants now inhabit Puebla and Oaxaca provinces in Mexico.

Tunkashila a Lakota word which refers to "Grandfather Great Spirit"; sometimes associated with stone.

Turtle Island a Native American name for the continent of North America.

twisted hair a high initiate of the Dawn Star's ways, who returned from the temples of the south to their homeland in the north, teaching Flowersong on the way.

two-leggeds human beings.

vision quest the spiritual practice of seeking vision, among Native peoples often done in a high place on a mountain or in a special lodge such as a women's Moon Lodge, almost always accompanied by fasting.

wallow, buffalo a depression created by buffalo rolling and hollowing out the area in which they take dust baths; these have remained on the land long after most of the buffalo were slaughtered, still in evidence on the hills and prairies today.

wildcrafting the gathering of wild plants and herbs to use in healing and rejuvenating formulas, and for food.

wingeds those who fly; birds and insects.

Wovoka a member of the Paiute Indian tribe whose vision of the Christ energy in 1889 foretold the coming of a Messiah to restore lost lands, warriors, and buffalo, and the disappearance of the white man and the disease and misery his coming had brought. Wovoka founded the Ghost Dance, a symbolic ritual whose influence quickly spread throughout the plains and Rockies. The ritual was largely abandoned after the killing of Sitting Bull and the Wounded Knee massacre.

Yaqui a tribe of Native Americans, who live in Mexico and southern Arizona.

yin and yang symbols from Buddhist religion which roughly correspond to "feminine and masculine."

yurt a round housing structure with a conical roof, first used by nomadic Mongolian people; in modern times made of canvas and light wood, often with a central skylight dome.

APPENDIX 1:
RESOURCES AND ORDERING
GUIDE

These are a few resources to get you started—not a comprehensive list!!

ART & CRAFTS

Allard's Trading Post. P.O. Delivery, St. Ignatius, MT 59865.
Bovis Bead Co. P.O. Box 111, Bisbee, AZ 85603.
Prairie Edge. P.O. Box 8303, Rapid City, SD 57709-8303, 605-341-4525.
Prairie Visions. P.O. Box 774, Spearfish, SD 57783, 605-642-5217.
Western Trading Post, 32 Broadway, P.O. Box 9070, Denver, CO 80209-0070.
Winter Sun Trading Post. 18 Santa Fe Ave., Flagstaff, AZ 86001, 602-774-2884.

DRUMS & RATTLES

Heartbeat Drums. Rodney Scott, 3555 Singing Pines Rd., Darby, MT 59829, 406-821-4401.
Moondance Drums. P.O. Box 8592, Missoula, MT 59807, 406-721-8434.
Shares the Mother's Heartbeat. Bill Shoemaker, 4302 Center St. Apt. J302, Tacoma, WA 98409, 206-572-4696.
Spirit Song Rattles. P.O. Box 2063, Taos, NM 87571, 505-776-8533.
Tarwater Drums & Rattles. Hawkwind Renewal Co-op, P.O. Box 11, Valley Head, AL 35989, 205-635-6304.
Thunder Studio Drums. P.O. Box 1552-9, Cedar Ridge, CA 95924, 916-273-3253.

HERBS

Abundant Life Seeds. Port Townsend, WA 98368.
Flower Essence Society. P.O. Box 459, Nevada City, CA 95959, 916-265-9163.

Green Terrestrial Herbal Products. Box 41 Rt. 9W, Milton, NY 12547, 914-795-5238.

Michael and Lesley Tierra, Herbalists. 10210 California Dr., Ben Lomond, CA 95005.

Seed Savers Exchange. RR3 Box 239, Decorah, IA 52101. Attn: Kent Wheatly, Director.

Talavaya Seed Co. P.O. Box 707, Santa Cruz, NM 87567.

Winter Sun Trading Post. 18 Santa Fe Ave., Flagstaff, AZ 86001.

Wyoming Wildcrafters. Box 874, Wilson, WY 83014.

INCENSE, SMUDGE, TOBACCO, AROMATHERAPY

Aromatix. John Steel, 3949 Longridge Ave., Sherman Oaks, CA 91423.

Native Scents. Box 5763, Taos, NM 87571, 505-758-9656.

Santa Fe Natural Tobacco Co. P.O. Box 1840, Santa Fe, NM 87504.

Spirit Dancer Sage. P.O. Box 644, Sedona, AZ 86336, 602-282-7536.

MUSIC

Canyon Records. Recordings from many Native tribes. 4143 North 16th St., Phoenix, AZ 85016.

Earthsong Productions. Ani Williams, P.O. Box 780, Sedona, AZ 86336.

Earth Tree Music. Lisa Dancing Light, 0171 Handy Dr., Carbondale, CO 81623.

Harmony Network. Distributor of Brooke's recordings and others. P.O. Box 582, Sebastopol, CA 95473, 707-823-9377.

Moonbear Productions. Andrea Lyman, P.O. Box 135, Sandpoint, ID 83860.

ORGANIZATIONS

Alliance for the Wild Rockies. Box 8731, Missoula, MT 59807, 406-721-5420.

Audubon Society. P.O. Box 51000, Boulder, CO 80321-1000.

Blacktail Ranch. Tag Rittel, Inc., Wolf Creek, MT 59648.

Defenders of Wildlife. 1244 19th St. NW, Washington, DC 20036, 202-659-9510.

Global Family. 112 Jordan Ave., San Anselmo, CA 94960.

MAKA OYATE Fdtn. (support for Native peoples and teachings) P.O. Box 34, Los Olivos, CA 93441.

National Wildlife Federation. 1400 16th St. NW, Washington, DC 20077-9964.

Native American Rights Fund. 1506 Broadway, Boulder, CO 80302-6296.
Permaculture Communications. P.O. Box 101, Davis, CA 95617.
Sacred Sites Conservancy. 112 Cat Rock Rd., Cos Cob, CT 06807. Attn: Tek Nikerson.
Sierra Club. P.O. Box 7959, San Francisco, CA 94120.
The Nature Conservancy. 1815 N. Lynn St., Arlington, VA 22209.
The Wilderness Society. 1400 Eye St. NW, Washington, DC 20005.
The Windstar Foundation. John Denver, 2317 Snowmass Creek Rd., Snowmass, CO 81654-9198, 303-927-4777.
Tom Brown, Tracker, Inc. P.O. Box 173, Asbury, NY 08802, 908-479-4681.

PUBLICATIONS

American Indian Art. 7314 E. Osborn Dr., Scottsdale, AZ 85251.
Luna Press. Box 511, Kenmore Station, Boston, MA 12215.
Native American Directory. Native American Co-Op, P.O. Box 5000, San Carlos, AZ 85550-0301.
Native Nations. Solidarity Foundation, 175 5th Ave., New York, NY 10010.
Native Peoples. Media Concepts Group, 1833 N. 3rd St., Phoenix, AZ 85004-1502.
Shaman's Drum: A Journal of Experiential Shamanism. P.O. Box 430, Willitts, CA 95490.
Source Directory: Indian, Eskimo, Alwut Owned and Operated Arts and Crafts Businesses. Indian Arts & Crafts Board, Rm. 4004, US Dept. of the Interior, Washington, DC 20240, 202-343-2773.
The Permaculture Designer's Directory. Permaculture Communications, P.O. Box 101, Davis, CA 95617.
Wildfire. Bear Tribe Medicine Society, P.O. Box 9167, Spokane, WA 99209, 509-326-6561.

TEXTILES, CLOTHING

Beauty Dawn, Unltd. T-shirts for Eagle Song camps and of the medicine wheel (see chapter 14, "Around the Medicine Wheel"), by Lynn Jordan Peck. P.O. Box 128, Ovando, MT 59854.
Desert Son Inc. Moccasins—The Village, 2900 E. Broadway #182, Tucson, AZ 85716, 602-795-5168.
Ortega Weavers. 101 Main, Chimayo, NM 87522.
Winter Wolf Trading Post. P.O. Box 24, Trego, NM 59934.

TIPIS, SHELTERS

Blue Star, Inc. 5625 Expressway, Missoula, MT 59802.
Pacific Yurts. 77456 Hwy 995, Cottage Grove, OR 97424.

USEFUL TOOLS

Bitterroot Bows, Arrows, & Quivers. Robert S. Parks, Rt 1 Box 138, Troy, ID 83871, 208-835-8810.
Diet for a New America: Your Health, Your Planet. Video available from John Robbins, Earthsave, 706 Frederick St., Santa Cruz, CA 95062-2205, 408-423-4069.
Medicine Cards: The Discovery of Power Through the Ways of Animals, by Jamie Sams & David Carson. Bear & Co., 1988.
Medicine Woman Tarot Cards (1990). US Games Systems, Inc., New York, NY 10016. Attn: Magda & J.A. Gonzales.
Native American Tarot Cards (1982). US Games Systems, Inc., New York, NY 10016. Attn: Magda & J.A. Gonzales.
Prescription for Survival, video recorded at *Dreaming a New Dream Conference.* Call 415-528-6044. ($29.95.)
Sacred Path Cards: The Discovery of Self Through Native Teachings. Harper & Row, 1990.
The Master Cleanser (formula for fasting). c/o Stanley Burroughs, 8905 Crate Hill Road, New Castle, CA 95658. ($2)

APPENDIX 2:
SUGGESTED READING:
A SELECTED BIBLIOGRAPHY

NATIVE AMERICAN

Allen, Paula Gunn. *The Sacred Hoop: Recovering the Feminine in American Indian Traditions.* Boston: Beacon Press, 1987.

Andrews, Lynn V. *Crystal Woman.* New York: Warner Books, 1988.

――――. *Flight of the 7th Moon: The Teaching of the Shields.* New York: Warner Books, 1985.

――――. *Jaguar Woman.* New York: Harper & Row, 1986.

――――. *Medicine Woman.* New York: Harper & Row, 1983.

――――. *Windhorse Woman.* New York: Warner Books, 1989.

Billard, Jules B., ed. *The World of the American Indian.* Washington, DC: National Geographic Society, 1974.

Black Elk, Wallace and William S. Lyon. *Black Elk Speaks Again: The Sacred Powers of a Lakota Shaman.* New York: Harper & Row, 1990.

Brown, Joseph Eppes. *The Sacred Pipe: Black Elk's Account of the Seven Rites of the Oglala Sioux.* New York: Penguin, 1971.

Brown, Tom, Jr. *City & Suburban Survival.* Tom Brown's Field Guides. New York: Berkely Books, 1984.

――――. *Forgotten Wilderness.* Tom Brown's Field Guides. New York: Berkely Books, 1987.

――――. *Living With the Earth.* Tom Brown's Field Guides. New York: Berkely Books, 1984.

――――. *Nature Observation and Tracking.* Tom Brown's Field Guides. New York: Berkely Books, 1983.

――――. *Nature & Survival for Children.* Tom Brown's Field Guides. New York: Berkely Books, 1989.

――――. *The Search.* New York: Berkely Books, 1982.

――――. *The Tracker.* New York: Berkely Books, 1982.

――――. *The Vision.* New York: Berkely Books, 1988.

————. *Wild and Edible Plants*. Tom Brown's Field Guides. New York: Berkely Books, 1985.

————. *Wilderness Survival*. Tom Brown's Field Guides. New York: Berkely Books, 1984.

Cahill, Sedonia and Joshua Halpern. *The Ceremonial Circle: Shamanic Practice, Ritual & Renewal*. London: Mandala/Harper Collins, 1991.

Cameron, Anne. *Daughters of Copper Woman*. Erie, KS: Inland Publishing Co., 1988.

Carey, Ken. *Return of the Bird Tribes: A Channelled Book*. Overland Park, KS: Uni-Sun, 1988.

Castañeda, Carlos. *The Eagle's Gift*. New York: Pocket Books, 1985.

————. *The Fire from Within*. New York: Pocket Books, 1986.

————. *Journey to Ixtlan*. New York: Pocket Books, 1985.

————. *The Power of Silence: Further Lessons of Don Juan*. New York: Pocket Books, 1988.

————. *The Second Ring of Power*. New York: Pocket Books, 1984.

————. *A Separate Reality*. New York: Pocket Books, 1985.

————. *Tales of Power*. New York: Pocket Books, 1984.

————. *The Teachings of Don Juan: A Yaqui Way of Knowledge*. Berkeley, CA: University of California Press, 1968.

Curtis, Edward. *Portraits from North American Indian Life*. New York: Promontory Press, 1989.

Curtis, Nathalie, ed. *The Indian's Book: Authentic Native American Legends, Lore & Music*. Prineville, OR: Bonanza Books, 1987.

de Las Casas, Bartolome. *The Devastation of the Indies*. Translated by Herma Briffault. New York: Seabury, 1974.

Donner, Florinda. *The Witches Dream*. New York: Pocket Books, 1987.

Dooling, D.M. and Paul Jordan Smith, eds. *I Become Part of It: Sacred Dimensions in Native American Life*. New York: Parabola Magazine, 1989.

Dorris, Michael. *A Yellow Raft in Blue Water*. New York: Henry Holt, 1987.

Drysdale, Vera Louise. *The Gift of the Sacred Pipe*. Norman, OK: University of Oklahoma Press, 1982.

Eagle Man, Ed McGaa. *Mother Earth Spirituality: Native American Paths to Healing Ourselves and Our World*. New York: Harper & Row, 1990.

Eaton, Evelyn. *The Shaman and the Medicine Wheel*. Wheaton, IL: Theosophical Publishing House, 1982.

Erdrich, Louise. *The Beet Queen*. New York: Henry Holt, 1986.

————. *Love Medicine*. New York: Holt, Rinehart & Winston, 1984.

————. *Tracks.* New York: Henry Holt, 1988.

———— and Michael Dorris. *The Crown of Columbus.* New York: Harper Collins, 1991.

Gidley, M. *Kopet: A Documentary Narrative of Chief Joseph's Last Years.* Chicago: Contemporary Books, 1981.

Halifax, Joan. *The Wounded Healer.* Notre Dame, IN: Crossroads, 1982.

Hansen, L. Taylor. *He Walked the Americas.* Amherst, WI: Amherst Press, 1963.

Highwater, Jamake. *The Primal Mind: Vision and Reality in Indian America.* New York: New American Library, 1982.

Hillerman, Tony. *The Blessing Way.* New York: Harper & Row, 1989.

————. *Listening Woman.* New York: Harper & Row, 1990.

————. *Skinwalkers.* New York: Harper & Row, 1987.

Hoebel, E. Adamson. *The Cheyennes.* New York: Holt, 1960.

Hungry Wolf, Beverly. *The Ways of My Grandmothers.* New York: Morrow, 1981.

LeGuin, Ursula. *Buffalo Gals and Other Animal Presences.* New York: New American Library, 1988.

Linderman, Frank. *Plenty Coups: Chief of the Crows.* Lincoln, NE: University of Nebraska Press, 1962.

————. *Pretty Shield: Medicine Woman of the Crows.* Lincoln, NE: University of Nebraska Press, 1974.

Lopez, Barry H. *Giving Birth to Thunder, Sleeping With His Daughter: Coyote Builds North America.* New York: Avon, 1981.

————. *Crow and Weasel.* New York: Farrar, Strauss, Giroux, 1990.

Mails, Thomas. *The Secret Native American Pathways: A Guide to Inner Peace.* Tulsa, OK: Council Oak Books, 1988.

McCluhan, T.C. *Touch the Earth.* New York: Promontory Press, 1989.

Neihardt, John G. *Black Elk Speaks.* Lincoln, NE: University of Nebraska Press, 1988.

Sale, Kirkpatrick. *Conquest of Paradise.* New York: Knopf, 1990.

Sams, Jamie. *Sacred Path Cards: The Discovery of Self Through Native Teaching.* New York: Harper & Row, 1990.

———— and David Carson. *Medicine Cards: The Discovery of Power Through the Ways of Animals.* Santa Fe, NM: Bear & Co., 1988.

Sildko, Leslie. *Ceremony.* New York: Penguin, 1986.

Sojourner, Mary. *Sisters of the Dream.* Chicago: Northland Books, 1989.

Standing Bear, Luther. *Land of the Spotted Eagle.* Lincoln, NE: University of Nebraska Press, 1978.

Storm, Hyemeyohsts. *Seven Arrows.* New York: Ballantine, 1985.

————. *Song of Heyoehkah.* New York: Ballantine, 1983.

Summer Rain, Mary. *Phantoms Afoot: Journeys into the Night.* Norfolk, VA: Donning Co., 1989.

———. *Phoenix Rising.* Norfolk, VA: Donning Co., 1987.

———. *Spirit Song.* Norfolk, VA: Donning Co., 1985.

Sun Bear, with Wabun Wind. *Black Dawn, Bright Day.* Spokane, WA: Bear Tribe Publishing, 1990.

———. *The Medicine Wheel: Earth Astrology.* New York: Prentice Hall Press, 1980.

Swan, James. *Sacred Places: How the Living Earth Seeks Our Friendship.* Santa Fe, NM: Bear & Co., 1990.

Thunderhorse, Iron, and Donn LeVie, Jr. *Return of the Thunderbeings.* Santa Fe, NM: Bear & Co., 1990.

Walking Turtle, Eagle. *Keepers of the Fire: Journey of the Tree of Life—Based on Black Elk's Vision.* Santa Fe, NM: Bear & Co., 1987. (Also recommended for children)

Welch, James. *Fool's Crow.* New York: Penguin, 1987.

Whitaker, Kay. *The Reluctant Shaman.* New York: Harper & Row, 1991.

Ywahoo, Dhyani. *Voices of Our Ancestors: Cherokee Teachings from the Wisdom Fire.* Boston: Shambhala Publications, 1987.

ECOLOGY/EARTH ETHICS

Abbey, Edward. *Desert Solitaire.* Tucson, AZ: University of Arizona Press, 1988.

———. *The Monkey Wrench Gang.* Tucson, AZ: University of Arizona Press, 1985.

Birnes, Nancy. *Cheaper and Better: Homemade Alternatives to Store-bought Goods.* New York: Harper & Row, 1987.

Boone, J. Allen. *Kinship With All Life.* New York: Harper & Row, 1976.

Carey, Ken. *Starseed, The Third Millennium: Living in the Posthistoric World.* San Francisco: Harper Collins, 1991.

Cohen, Mike. *An Earth Kinship Trailguide.* New York: National Audubon Society, 1990.

Devereaux, Paul with John Steele and David Kubrin. *Earthmind: Tuning in to GAIA Theory with New Age Methods for Saving Our Planet.* New York: Harper & Row, 1989.

Dillard, Annie. *Pilgrim at Tinker Creek.* New York: Harper & Row, 1988.

Fox, Matthew. *The Coming of the Cosmic Christ.* New York: Harper & Row, 1988.

———. *Original Blessing.* Santa Fe, NM: Bear & Co., 1983.

Hassoll, Susan, and Beth Richman. *Energy.* Creating a Healthy World—101 Practical Tips for Home and Work Series, Snowmass, CO: Windstar Foundation, 1989.

———. *Everyday Chemicals.* Creating a Healthy World—101 Practical Tips for Home and Work Series. Snowmass, CO: Windstar Foundation, 1989.

———. *Re-Cycling.* Creating a Healthy World—101 Practical Tips for Home and Work Series. Snowmass, CO: Windstar Foundation, 1989.

Javna, John. *Fifty Simple Things Kids Can Do to Save the Earth.* Kansas City: Andrews & McMeel, 1990.

Kloss, Jethro. *Back to Eden.* Santa Barbara, CA: Woodbridge Publishing Co., 1975.

Kourik, Robert. *Designing & Maintaining Your Edible Landscape Naturally.* Santa Rosa, CA: Metamorphic Press, 1986.

LaChapelle, Dolores. *Sacred Land, Sacred Sex: Rapture of the Deep.* Silverton, CO: Finn Hill, 1988.

Leopold, Aldo. *Sand County Almanac.* New York: Ballantine, 1986.

Leslie, Robert F. *In the Shadow of a Rainbow: The True Story of a Friendship Between Man & Wolf.* New York: W. W. Norton, 1986.

Macy, Joanna. *Despair and Personal Power in the Nuclear Age.* Philadelphia: New Society Publishing, 1983.

——— and John Seed, et al. *Thinking Like a Mountain: Toward a Council of All Beings.* Philadelphia: New Society Publishing, 1988.

Mollison, Bill. *Permaculture: A Practical Guide for a Sustainable Future.* Washington, DC/Covelo, CA: Island Press, 1990.

Powell, John Wesley. *Exploration of the Colorado River & Its Canyons.* New York: Penguin (Nature Library), 1987.

Robbins, John. *Diet for a New America.* Dallas: Stillpoint Publishing, 1987.

Seymour, John and Herbert Girardet. *Blueprint for a Green Planet.* New York: Prentice Hall, 1987.

Stafford, Kim. *Having Everything Right: Essays of Place.* New York: Penguin, 1987.

Szekely, Edmond. *The Biogenic Revolution.* San Diego: IBS International, 1985.

———. *Essene Way—Biogenic Living.* San Diego: IBS International, 1989.

———. *The Teachings of the Essenes: From Enoch to the Dead Sea Scrolls.* San Diego: IBS International, 1981.

Thoreau, Henry David. *Walden.* New York: Doubleday, 1960.

Venolia, Carol. *Healing Environments: Your Guide to Indoor Well-Being.* Berkeley, CA: Celestial Arts, 1988.

Wright, Machaelle S. *Behaving as If the God in All Life Mattered.* Jeffersonton, VA: Perelandra, Ltd., 1987.

————. *The Perelandra Workbook: A Complete Guide to Gardening with Nature Intelligences.* Jeffersonton, VA: Perelandra, Ltd., 1987.

HEALING/PERSONAL GROWTH/SPIRITUALITY

Almaas, A.H. *Diamond Heart, Book I: Elements of the Real in Man.* Oakland, CA: Almaas Publications, 1987.

————. *Diamond Heart, Book II: The Freedom to Be.* Oakland, CA: Almaas Publications, 1989.

Bandler, Richard and John Grinder. *Frogs into Princes: Neuro Linguistic Programming.* Moab, UT: Real People Press, 1979.

Berendt, Joachim-Ernst. *Nada Brahma: The World Is Sound.* Rochester, VT: Destiny Books, 1987.

Black, Claudia. *Double Duty.* New York: Ballantine, 1990.

Bolen, Jean S. *The Tao of Psychology: Synchronicity and the Self.* New York: Harper & Row, 1979.

Bradshaw, John. *The Family: A Revolutionary Way of Self-Discovery.* Deerfield Beach, FL: Health Communications, 1988.

————. *Homecoming: Reclaiming and Championing Your Inner Child.* New York: Bantam, 1990.

Cameron-Bandler, Leslie. *Know How.* San Rafael, CA: Future Pace, Inc., 1985.

Diallo, Yaya and Mitchell Hall. *The Healing Drum: African Wisdom Teachings.* Rochester, NY: Destiny Books, 1989.

Field, Reshard. *Breathing Alive: A Guide to Conscious Living.* Great Britain: Element Books Ltd., 1988.

Gallegos, Eligio S. *The Personal Totem Pole: Animal Imagery, the Chakras, and Psychotherapy.* Santa Fe, NM: Moon Bear Press, 1990.

Garfield, Patricia. *Creative Dreaming.* New York: Ballantine, 1985.

Griscom, Chris. *Ecstasy Is a New Frequency: Teachings of the Light Institute.* Santa Fe, NM: Bear & Co., 1987.

————. *Time Is an Illusion.* New York: Simon & Schuster, 1988.

Houston, Jean. *The Search for the Beloved.* Los Angeles: J.P. Tarcher, 1987.

Johnson, Robert A. *Inner Work: Using Dreams and Active Imagination for Personal Growth.* New York: Harper & Row, 1986.

Joy, W. Brugh. *Avalanche.* New York: Ballantine, 1990.

Kelder, Peter. *Ancient Secret of the Fountain of Youth.* Cambridge, MA: Harbor Press, 1986.

Lauck, Marcia S. and Deborah Koff-Chapin. *At the Pool of Wonder.* Santa Fe, NM: Bear & Co., 1989.

Lee, John. *I Don't Want to Be Alone: For Men and Women Who Want to Heal Addictive Relationships.* Deerfield Beach, FL: Health Communications, 1990.

Lerner, Rokelle. *Daily Affirmations.* Deerfield Beach, FL: Health Communications, 1985.

Levi. *The Aquarian Gospel of Jesus Christ.* Marina Del Rey, CA: De Vorss, 1972.

Linklater, Kristin. *Freeing the Natural Voice.* New York: Drama Book Publishers, 1976.

Matousek, Mark. "Toward a Spiritual Renaissance." *Common Boundary,* July, 1990.

Millman, Dan. *The Warrior Athlete: Body, Mind and Spirit.* Dallas: Stillpoint Publishing, 1985.

————. *The Way of the Peaceful Warrior: A Book That Changes Lives.* Tiburon, CA: H. J. Kramer, 1984.

Peck, Scott. *The Different Drum: Community Making & Peace.* New York: Simon & Schuster, 1988.

————. *The Road Less Travelled.* New York: Simon & Schuster, 1985.

Roberts, Jane. *The Seth Material.* New York: Bantam, 1976.

————. *Seth Speaks.* New York: Bantam, 1985.

Roth, Gabrielle. *Maps to Ecstasy: Teachings of an Urban Shaman.* Sherman Oaks, CA: New World Library, 1989.

Schaef, Anne W. *Co-dependence: Misunderstood—Mistreated.* New York: Harper & Row, 1986.

Schwarz, Jack. *Voluntary Controls.* New York: E. P. Dutton, 1978.

Shield, Benjamin and Richard Carlson, eds. *For the Love of God: New Writings by Spiritual and Psychological Leaders.* Sherman Oaks, CA, New World Library, 1990.

Shier, Barbara. *Wishcraft: How to Get What You Really Want.* New York: Ballantine, 1979.

————. *Team Works.* New York: Ballantine, 1990.

Stone, Hal and Sidra Winkleman. *Embracing Ourselves and Embracing Each Other.* San Rafael, CA: New World Library, 1989.

Trungpa, Chogyam. *Shambhala: The Sacred Path of the Warrior.* Boston: Shambhala Publications, 1988.

Whitfield, Charles. *Healing the Child Within.* Deerfield Beach, FL: Health Communications, 1987.

Wilde, Stuart. *Affirmations.* White Dove, NM: White Dove Intl., 1988.
————. *The Force.* White Dove, NM: White Dove Intl., 1984.
————. *Miracles.* White Dove, NM: White Dove Intl., 1983.
————. *The Sacred Clown.* White Dove, NM: White Dove Intl., 1991.
Zukav, Gary. *Seat of the Soul.* New York: Simon & Schuster, 1989.

WOMEN

Bass, Ellen. *Our Stunning Harvest.* Philadelphia: New Society Publishing, 1985.
Bolen, Jean S. *Goddesses in Every Woman: A New Psychology of Women.* New York: Harper & Row, 1985.
————. *Gods in Every Man: A New Psychology of Men's Lives & Loves.* New York: Harper & Row, 1989.
Bradley, Marion Zimmer. *The Mists of Avalon.* New York: Ballantine, 1985.
Brant, Beth, ed. *A Gathering of Spirit: Writing and Art by North American Indian Women.* Montpelier, VT: Sinister Wisdom Books, 1984.
Chambers, Ellen. *Beyond the Eagle: An Intervibrational Perspective on Woman's Spiritual Journey.* Hamilton, MT: Wild Violet Publishing, 1988.
Christ, Carol P. *Diving Deep and Surfacing: Women Writers on Spiritual Quest.* Boston: Beacon Press, 1986.
————. *Womanspirit Rising: A Feminist Reader in Religion.* New York: Harper & Row, 1979.
Daly, Mary. *Beyond God the Father: Toward a Philosophy of Women's Liberation.* Boston: Beacon Press, 1985.
————. *Gyn-Ecology: The Metaethics of Radical Feminism.* Boston: Beacon Press, 1979.
————. *Pure Lust: Elemental Feminist Philosophy.* Boston: Beacon Press, 1984.
Dillon, Mary and Shinan N. Barclay. *Flowering Woman: Moontime for Kori.* Sedona, AZ: Sunlight Productions, 1988.
Eisler, Riane. *Chalice and the Blade: Our History, Our Future.* New York: Harper & Row, 1987.
Francia, Luisa. *Dragontime: Magic and Mystery of Menstruation.* Woodstock, NY: Ash Tree Publishing, 1991.
Greenwood, Sadja. *Menopause Naturally: Preparing for the Second Half of Life.* Volcano, CA: Volcano Press, 1989.
Mariechild, Diane. *Mother Wit: A Guide to Healing & Psychic Development.* Freedom, CA: Crossing Press, 1989.

Moon, Sheila. *Changing Woman and Her Sisters.* San Francisco, CA: Guild for Psychological Studies Publishing House, 1985.

Norwood, Robin. *Women Who Love Too Much.* New York: Penguin, 1989.

Ruether, Rosemary. *New Woman—New Earth: Sexist Ideologies and Human Liberation.* New York: Harper & Row, 1978.

————. *Sexism and God-Talk: Toward A Feminist Theology.* Boston: Beacon Press, 1984.

Starhawk. *Dreaming the Dark: Magic, Sex and Politics.* Boston: Beacon Press, 1989.

————. *Spiral Dance.* New York: Harper & Row, 1989.

————. *Truth or Dare.* New York: Harper & Row, 1987.

Stepanich, Kisma K. *An Act of Woman Power.* West Chester, PA: Whitford Press, 1989.

Taylor, Dena. *Red Flower: Rethinking Menstruation.* Freedom, CA: Crossing Press, 1988.

Von Franz, Marie-Louise. *Problems of the Feminine in Fairy Tales.* Dallas: Spring Publications, 1972.

Walker, Barbara G. *The Women's Encyclopedia of Myths and Secrets.* New York: Harper & Row, 1983.

Wind, Wabun. *Woman of the Dawn: A Spiritual Odyssey.* New York: Prentice Hall, 1989.

CHILDREN

Baylor, Byrd and Peter Parnall. *The Other Way to Listen.* New York: Charles Scribner's Sons, 1978.

Caduto, Michael J. and Joseph Bruchac. *Keepers of the Earth: Native American Stories and Environmental Activities for Children.* Golden, CO: Fulcrum, Inc., 1988.

————. *Native American Stories Told by Joseph Bruchac,* from *Keepers of the Earth.* Golden, CO: Fulcrum Publishing, 1991.

Carey, Ken. *Notes to My Children: A Simplified Metaphysics.* Overland Park, KS: Uni-Sun, 1984.

Carter, Forrest. *The Education of Little Tree.* Albuquerque, NM: University of New Mexico Press, 1986.

Esbensen, Barbara Juster. *Ladder to the Sky.* Boston/Toronto: Little, Brown & Co., 1989.

Haller, Danita R. *Not Just Any Ring.* New York: Knopf, 1982.

Henly, Thom. *Rediscovery: Ancient Pathways—New Directions.* Vancouver: Western Canada Wilderness Committee, 1989.

LaChapelle, Dolores. *Earth Wisdom.* Silverton, CO: Finn Hill, 1984.

Mayle, Peter. *Where Did I Come From.* Secaucus, NJ: Lyle Stuart, 1973.

Murdock, Maureen, ed. *Spinning Inward: Using Guided Imagery With Children.* Boston: Shambhala Publications, 1987.

Sneve, Virginia Diving Hawk, ed. *Dancing Teepees: Poems of American Indian Youth.* New York: Holiday House, 1989.

APPENDIX 3:
INFORMATION ON BROOKE
MEDICINE EAGLE

EAGLE SONG CAMPS

"Come willing to laugh, to play, to experience deeply, and to serve."

Purpose: 1} To deepen your Spirit through experiencing our finest teachers: Mother Earth and Father Sky; 2} to develop a spiritual community which will continue together in work of service; and 3} to enhance your ability to share this work with others in your area.

Setting: We will live at the beautiful Blacktail Ranch, an hour southwest of Great Falls, Montana. The cottonwood-lined valley will be sweet with the scent of wild rose, sage and evergreen; and as well be full of the ancient spirits of the land. A cave there holds the oldest human artifacts and animal remains in Montana; it is said to have been the magical cave of a bear shaman, whose stone effigies were found within, and whose bones were found on a nearby hillside. The whole area was likely Blackfeet sacred ground, and holds an ancient ceremonial medicine wheel, age-old dreaming caves, eagle catch pens, and our traditional sweat lodge near a beaver-dammed side creek. From our tipi circle, flower-filled meadows roll up through aspen groves into the high pines and rocky mountains. A colorful herd of pinto horses will be our nearest neighbors, on which we may ride through this beauty, while listening to Tag's tall tales about the days since his grandfather homesteaded the ranch.

Facilities: We have both a ceremonial tipi and a yurt for teaching and sharing. You will camp in our tipi ring or tenting meadow. In the ranch "bunk house" there are a wonderful group kitchen/dining hall, lounge areas, and full bathroom facilities for our use.

A DEEPENING OF SPIRIT
Two week Advanced Residential Camp for Women

Intention: These trainings are for women already on the path of service, who wish to enhance their ability to share with others through the deepening of their own spirit, knowledge and experience. We will create and participate in ceremony, healing through ritual action and art, awakening perception, physical toning, drumming, chanting and dancing, and realizing White Buffalo Woman's challenge of aligning self and community for powerful Earth healing.

Program: Mornings will begin with an exercise routine for health, flexibility, longevity and strength; followed by meditation and chanting. Together we will keep the Mother drum's heartbeat echoing. We will create a Power Shield (through confronting our personal challenges and calling our highest selves) and a Beauty Arrow (to confirm the giveaway of our unique gift to All Our Relations). We will use dreamtime, purification lodge, visiting Mother Earth's womb via the cave, ceremony in group, high games, and two days of solo vision questing to create these and other implements of spiritual action, some of which will return home with you as continuing practices. There will be time for exploration, hiking, and swimming to honor the needs of your own spirit. Echoing through all our doingness will be an awareness of metaphor and healing through spiritual action; and of touching Spirit and All Our Relations in a harmonious way. Upon completion of our work together, you will be initiated into a sisterhood lodge, and given your Eagle Song name.

THE HEALING VISION
Spiritual Camp for Women
(Some Years Open to Men)

Intention: Emphasis will be on deepening your relationship with Mother Earth/Father Sky in order to bring yourself to wholeness, and on honing your awareness of the unique gift *you* bring to the healing of our planet—in service of All Our Relations.

Program: Inner and outer questing—through exercise, meditation, chanting, drumming, and dancing, metaphor and ritual performance, ceremony, high games, dreamtime—daily practices to take home that will continue to guide you into spiritual action. A two-day vision quest will highlight these days.

SONG OF THE BEAUTY WAY
Ceremonial Arts Camp for Men and Women

Intention: Spirit and All Our Relations are calling us to turn our attention to the creation and sustaining of beauty in the exquisite garden of Mother Earth. We will create our own Beauty Bundle, to empower our abilities as co-creators in the healing of our world. Art and craft will be used as a ceremonial way.

Program: Our skills and perception will be enhanced through the practice of ritual art: beading, rawhide work, making leather pouches, basket weaving, and the making of fetishes. We will also share in ritual, ceremony, Earth-healing, dance, chanting, and meditation to enrich our spirits. Exercise, hiking, and playing will hone and tone our physical attention.

IN THE CRADLE OF MOTHER EARTH
Earth Harmony & Basic Survival Skills for Men and Women

Intention: To experience Mother Earth as a safe and nurturing cradle through learning a philosophy of good relationship with all life, and through training in basic survival skills (based on the teachings of Tom Brown, Jr., Tracker)—that you may begin to feel truly at home in the arms of our Mother.

Program: An introduction to 1) simple skills which can enable you to survive in the wilderness: we will learn to build a debris hut, fashion natural fiber cordage, light a fire with bow drill, gather wild edibles, and other beginning skills; and 2) White Buffalo Calf Pipe Woman's holy way of living in harmony.

SINGING THE SACRED
Healing Ourselves and Mother Earth Through Sound and Song

This camp is focused on sacred and healing work with voice, song, chanting, toning, drumming, and rhythm. The beauty of nature's song around us will be joyfully added to our own! Our time together will be a joyful sharing of chants and skills; an opportunity to create new songs by quieting ourselves on the land and listening to Spirit; a chance to practice the harmonious blending of our voices (and perhaps to record them); and a time to heal ourselves and Mother Earth through vibration and rhythm.

CONTINUING THE QUEST

Returnees will focus on continued intensive training, integration, vision questing, and sharing! We will take what we have learned to another level of usefulness for ourselves and others.

For information or registration packet: Contact Brooke's Singing Eagle office at #1 2nd Avenue East C-401, Polson, MT 59860, (406) 883-4686. Please specify which camp you're interested in.

> I look forward to walking a beautiful path with you under this bowl of sky.
> We'll sing an eagle's song!

CASSETTE TAPES BY BROOKE MEDICINE EAGLE

NEW AND WONDERFUL:

Visions Speaking: Songs Of The Sacred Quest

Brooke says, "We two-leggeds are realizing that we cannot move forward into a new and workable way of being until we stop and listen to the great voices speaking around and within us. We must come into harmony with All Our Relations—recognizing that the Great Spirit lives in each and every thing, and that the entire web of life is interconnected and interdependent, before we can be given the quality of vision which will truly guide us. Let us open ourselves to all the great visions to speak through us!" Included are a Cree wakeup song; several songs which came in vision to her Eagle Song campers, including *Mother, Send Me Your Voice, Flowersong,* and *Vision Beauty Way;* a joyful Kiowa round dance song; a Pomo Bear Chant; and many others.

Empowering The Spiritual Warrior: Walking A Beauty Path

This new tape is an *Elder Sister's* teaching of simple, yet profound, techniques and practices for empowering yourself as a spiritual warrior walking and creating a beauty path. As Brooke says so eloquently, "Our challenge in this time is to make real the beautiful dreams we each carry of an abundant, radiant, and peaceful world. We do this in many ways, by healing our own dysfunction and disharmony, touching the *Great Mystery* to empower our spiritual actions. As we purify the waters, clear the air, and regreen the earth, we too blossom into the fullness of our humanity, and step fully into the Great Circle of Life." Take the next step on *your* spiritual journey!

Drumming The Heartbeat

Brooke's first drumming tape is meant for use in meditation, ceremony and dancing. Included are one-half hour of basic heartbeat drumming, excellent for meditation; and fifteen minutes of two different dance rhythms, which can be used in your circles and ceremonies if you do not have a drum. This, too, is an excellent tape for those who are learning to drum, who may wish to practice with it. "We begin," Brooke reminds us, "as all things earthly began, with the heartbeat of our sweet Mother Earth, a heartbeat which brings us gently, safely, back into the true rhythm of our natural Earth walk."

SINGING:

A Gift Of Song

This moving collection of *international songs,* recorded with friend Anne Williams, is full of depth, joy, and poetry. Of it, Brooke says, "These songs are giveaways: to us from Spirit singing within us. They are messages of our changing, our rebirth, of walking through our fears into golden rainbow light." Included are Brooke's new *Traveling Song* for inner and outer journeys; *Cedar Song,* to sing while smudging; *Morning Song* for celebrations of newness; and a special woman's song titled *Blood of Life.* Also on the album, a Seneca moon chant, a Sufi call, two Basque songs, an African chant, and more. It will move your toes and soul. *You'll love it!*

For My People

"If you know yourself to be one of my people, this album is dedicated to you," says Brooke. This popular singing tape features songs written by Brooke and friends, including the Giveaway song, *For My People,* that came to Brooke specifically as a dedication for this album. Also included are: *Altar Song of the Ancients, Hey Ney Ya Na* (beauty song), *Waterfall Song, O La Ma Ma, Dawn Star Chant, Buffalo Woman Is Calling,* and others. Brooke has intentionally lengthened each song for you to sing along! This tape continues to be loved by adults and children.

Singing Joy To The Earth

"It's not about singing perfectly; it's about singing joyfully!" Brooke sings and teaches the *Medicine Wheel Song, Women's Healing Chant* (Na Bvay Hi Yay), *Waiting for Spirit Chant* (Hey Ah Hey Hey Ah), *Song to Call Spirit* (Way Ya Hey Ney Yo), *Long Wing Feathers* (Arapahoe Ghost Dance Song), *Peyote Songs, Song of Greeting and Farewell,* and *Song to the Ancient Mother* (O La Ma Ma).

TEACHING:
Visioning

In this critical time on Earth, retreating into silence to listen to the Great Voices within and around us is one of the wisest and most powerful things we can do for ourselves and All Our Relations. This important tape discusses that process: visions and vision questing are spoken of as natural human functions, used to guide us on the Medicine Path—the path of wholeness, harmony and connection with all things. Brooke teaches and encourages you to use this simple, profound way of retreating to the beauty of Mother Earth and Father Sky to quiet yourself and listen to the great voices of life around you, receiving personal guidance from them. She uses her own personal visions and vision questing experiences as teaching stories about the forms of questing, and as a channel to share information she received for all of us. Get together a circle and share this one. (Set of two)

Healing Through Ritual Action

Exceptionally useful for personal growth, group and therapeutic work, this tape helps you learn to use physical actions to reprogram your nervous system and be free of habits and barriers in your everyday life. It can teach you to create and act out these powerful healing metaphors, which include *"leaping off the edge, going for it, trust falling, dropping burdens, crossing a threshold, getting to the heart of the matter,"* and creating change through games. It helps you build the process of clearing and growth into everyday actions in the world. Of it, Brooke believes, "the information on this tape is the most useful of all the tapes I have made—you can create a whole new way of working with yourself that is fun and doesn't require 'professional help.' And, it's a boon as well to those who work with others."

Moon Time

This powerful tape brings women information on the spiritual aspects of Moon (menstrual) time and how to use this time to call vision each month. It is about reclaiming the lost ways of women's unique power. Brooke begins *Moon Time* with a chant given her by *White Buffalo Woman*—her call to women to carry spiritual water to the people. She speaks of our connection with Grandmother Moon through our cycle, and how we can use this special time for our own health and for receiving information about our part in the new life we're creating on Earth. She also gives information and techniques for strengthening our center—our belly—where *Mother Earth's mind* lives within us, and teaches us the part our mysterious center plays in *Buffalo Woman's* law of harmony with *All Our Relations.* She addresses menopause, the Grandmother Lodge & other related issues.

Moon Lodge

Brooke speaks of the creation of the moon lodge, the women's place of retreat and visioning, and its special use during the menstrual cycle. She offers practical suggestions for the room itself, for your group as it comes together, ceremonies for girls entering Moon Lodge and elders leaving it, a song, dances & spiritual actions that will help you begin your own lodge and connect it to the sister circles of Moon Lodges forming throughout the land. Also included is the *Grandmother Dance,* a dance to connect you with the wisdom of the Ancient Grandmothers.

FOR ORDERING: Contact Jodi Sager at *Harmony Network,* P.O. Box 582, Sebastopol, CA 95473, (707) 823-9377.

BROOKE MEDICINE EAGLE: A CHRONOLOGICAL BIBLIOGRAPHY

ARTICLES AND CHAPTERS IN BOOKS

"The Quest for Vision." In *Shamanic Voices: A Survey of Visionary Narratives,* edited by Joan Halifax. New York: E. P. Dutton, 1979.

"The Way of Healing." In *Shape Shifters: Shaman Women in Contemporary Society,* edited by Michele Jamal. New York: Arcana Publishers, 1987.

"Women and Nature: Time of the New Dawning." In *The Spiral Path: Essays and Interviews on Women's Spirituality,* edited by Theresa King O'Brien. St. Paul, MN: YES International Publishers, 1987.

"To Paint Ourselves Red." *In Shaman's Path: Healing, Personal Growth and Empowerment,* edited by Gary Doore. Boston: Shambala, 1988.

"Grandmother Lodge." In *Red Flower: Rethinking Menstruation,* edited by Dena Taylor. Freedom, CA: Crossing Press, 1988.

The Womanspirit Sourcebook, edited by Patrice Wynne. New York: Harper & Row, 1988.

"The Circle of Healing." In *Healers on Healing,* edited by Richard Carlson and Benjamin Shield. Los Angeles: Tarcher, 1989.

"Brooke Medicine Eagle." In *Childlessness Transformed: Stories of Alternative Parenting,* edited by Jane English. Mt. Shasta, CA: Earth Heart, 1989.

"Open to the Great Mystery." In *For the Love of God: New Writings by Spiritual and Psychological Leaders,* edited by Benjamin Shield and Richard Carlson, Ph.D. New York: New World Library, 1990.

ARTICLES IN MAGAZINES AND NEWSPAPERS

"The Rainbow Bridge." *Many Smokes,* vol. 14, no. 1 (Spring/Summer 1980), p. 3.

"The Grandmothers." *Many Smokes,* vol. 17, no. 3 (Elder's Issue, 1983), pp. 14–15.

"Opening the Wings of Spirit." *Shaman's Drum,* no. 1 (Summer 1985), pp. 11–12.

"The Lineage of the Sun." *The American Theosophist* (Fall 1985), pp. 350–53.

"Women's Moontime: A Call to Power." *Shaman's Drum,* no. 4 (Women in Shamanism issue) (Spring 1986), p. 21.

"Sacred Time, Sacred Way." *Shaman's Drum,* no. 5 (Summer 1986), pp. 4–7.

"Raven's Wing." The White Clouds Poetry Revue, no. 1 (1987).

"Becoming the Healed Healer: Models for a New Time." *Self Discovery: Arizona Magazine for Mind, Body & Spirit* (Fall 1987), pp. 5–6.

"Singing Buffalo Woman's Song." *Wildfire,* vol. 2, nos. 3 and 4 (1987), pp. 98–99.

"Singing Buffalo Woman's Song: Eulogy for a Nature Activist." *Woman of Power,* no. 9 (Nature issue) (Spring 1988), pp. 58–59.

"The Grandmother Lodge: Postmenopausal Power." *Wildfire,* vol. 3, no. 4 (Summer 1988), p. 19.

ARTICLES ABOUT BROOKE MEDICINE EAGLE

"Brooke Medicine Eagle: Messenger of the Heart," Karen Meadows. *Colorado Daily,* November 3, 1978; pp. 1, 3.

"Journey to Feathered Pipe Ranch," Alex Jack. *East West Journal,* January 1979; pp. 42–59.

"Changing the World Through the Body: Brooke Medicine Eagle's Aim," Valerie Moses. *Fort Collins Coloradoan—Sunday Focus,* January 21, 1979; p. 1.

"Holistic Indian Healer," Greg Luft. *The Fort Collins Journal,* January 25, 1979; p. 1.

"Visions of the Rainbow Woman: Brooke Medicine Eagle's Healing Power," Anne Fawcett. *East West Journal,* November 1981; pp. 31–37 (cover article).

"Montana Medicine Woman," Anne Fawcett. *East West Journal*, January 1982; pp. 24–33.

"Brooke Medicine Eagle: Native American Healer," Pat Hickey. *Whole Life Times*, September 1982.

"She Brings Message of Rainbow Woman," Charles Bowden. *Tucson Citizen*, February 8, 1983.

"Highlights," Anne Fawcett. *New Age Journal*, May 1983.

"Dancing Toward the Light," Jeff Kaikara. *Wind Circle, An Herbal Monthly*, June 1986, pp. 1, 7–8.

"The Goddess Interviews," Lisa Gentz. *L.A. Resources for Healing, Growth and Transformation*, Summer 1987, pp. 3, 36, 38.

"New Age: Inner Power Holds Key to New Era," Don Baty. *Great Falls Tribune: Montana Parade*, November 15, 1987, p. 1–2.

"Healer Brings Work Back to Montana Home," Sherry Jones. *Helena Independent Record*, Winter 1988.

"Native Arts & Spirituality," Jane Fritz. *Idaho Arts Journal*, vol. 5, no. 3 (Spring 1988), p. 12.

"Listening to the Great Voices," Morning Star. *Wildfire*, vol. 4, no. 1 (1988), pp. 32–6.

AUDIO-CASSETTE INTERVIEWS WITH BROOKE MEDICINE EAGLE

The Indian Medicine Way.

A wonderful and natural look at the ways of a Native American for healing ourselves and the planet. Traditional values and centuries-old cultural forms are still relevant to modern times, especially if we're open to new vistas. (Tape #1485, 1 hour)

Earth Is Our Mother.

Brooke, a woman of Native American and European ancestry who follows a Native medicine way, discusses the power of honesty in our relationships with each other and with Mother Earth. She shares insights gained from those who taught her to revere our planet as we would our own parents. (Tape #1633, 1 hour)

The Rainbow Warrior.

With guidance from medicine woman *Stands by the Fire* (known to her people as *The Woman Who Knows Everything*), Brooke has embarked upon the Rainbow Warrior's Way. This is not the way of war, she tells us, but the call of one who *heals*, who makes whole: the vision-giver-and-receiver: a way of knowing we may all need to experience, if we are to regain our rightful relationship with Mother Earth. (Tape #1714, 1 hour)

Spirit Dance.

In the sacred tradition of her medicine way, Brooke weaves a tapestry of the Spirit within and the Great Circle. She creates an energy connection between Father Sky and Mother Earth to move you forward on your path, opening doors to the wonder-filled unknown. Brooke uses her rainbow medicine nature to present the essential spirit and principles of living a fully human life. Going beyond forms, breaking old barriers, and transforming tradition all are part of the spirit dance as we deepen contact with our true Self. Brooke integrates her western academic knowledge with the wisdom of tribal elders. (Tape #1936, 1 hour)

Native Visions: Healing the Heart.

Raised on the Crow Indian reservation, Brooke combines her Native heritage with a strong grounding in psychology, and here she speaks to the challenge of the times we live in. Her natural ability to spark intuitive wisdom and inspire deeper levels of knowing comes through in this enlightening conversation. She shares her love of Mother Earth, and suggests we notice what is at center in our life. Alive and sparkling, Brooke gives us new ways to bring healing energies into all aspects of living. (Tape #1978, 1 hour)

Tales of White Buffalo Woman.

We are all one with all things, is the greatest teaching now available to two-leggeds, according to the message of the mythic White Buffalo Woman as recounted by Brooke, a grand-niece of the famed Nez Percé leader, Chief Joseph. She speaks of "the holy work," the work of wholeness, so vitally important to restoring the balance of nature and life, and of how our essence is one of relatedness to all. Brooke stresses the importance of ritual, prayer, drumming, listening, lightening up! and much more. She is a licensed counselor, healer, ceremonial leader and carrier of native wisdom. (Tape #2105, 1 hour)

Audiotapes available from
New Dimensions Tapes
P.O. Box 410510, San Francisco, CA 94141
(*or call:* 415-563-8899)

VIDEO CASSETTES OF BROOKE AND HER WORK

BROOKE MEDICINE EAGLE SPEAKS, the Kay Christopher Show, *Transformation Through Television,* from Austin, Texas, March 1991. Available from Kay at 1000 Westbank Dr., Bldg. 6, Suite 204, Austin, Texas 78746 (512-328-9380).

BEGIN THE DAY WITH CEREMONY from John Denver's Windstar Symposium at Aspen in 1989, contact Windstar, Box 286, Snowmass, CO 81654 (303-927-4777).

BROOKE MEDICINE EAGLE TEACHINGS, recorded at *Dreaming the New Dream: Choices for a Positive Future,* A Planetwork Symposium in San Francisco, 1988. Available by phoning 415-528-6044, shipped within 2-4 weeks.

APPENDIX 4:
A REFERENCE TO WORKS BY
AND ABOUT MOSHÉ
FELDENKRAIS

BOOKS BY MOSHÉ FELDENKRAIS

Awareness Through Movement

Twelve easy-to-follow *Awareness Through Movement* exercises for improving posture, flexibility, breathing, coordination, etc. After an introduction emphasizing the importance of self-education and the primary relationship of movement to sensory, thinking, and emotional life, Feldenkrais demonstrates his ideas through the ATM lessons. Hardbound.

The Elusive Obvious

This conversational book represents a summing-up of the theory and practice of both Functional Integration and Awareness Through Movement. Illuminated by anecdotes from his personal life and work, *The Elusive Obvious* deals with "the simple, fundamental notions of our daily life that through habit become elusive" and impossible to see. Hardbound.

The Case of Nora

This book is a brilliant case study of a woman who had suffered a severe and debilitating stroke. It is the most extensive account available of Dr. Feldenkrais's individual work of Functional Integration. The reader is taken on a safari through the "jungle of the brain," as Feldenkrais explains how he teaches Nora to see, read, walk, and function in the world once again. Hardbound.

Body and Mature Behavior

This clear, systematic treatment of the psycho-physiological foundations of Dr. Feldenkrais's theories is a widely respected classic. He describes in neuro-physiological and psychological terms how patterns of movement and posture are acquired and then relates movement habits to social and sexual development. This is a rich and somewhat technical book. Softbound.

AUDIOTAPES ON FELDENKRAIS'S WORK

The San Francisco Evening Class, Volume 1
Excellent for both beginners and those already familiar with Awareness Through Movement, this tape package includes ten ATM lessons recorded on five 100-minute cassettes, with a user's guide.

Awareness Through Movement, Basic Series
An easy, enjoyable introduction to the fundamental exercises included in Feldenkrais's book, *Awareness Through Movement.* This tape package includes ten 45-minute ATM lessons on five cassettes, enclosed in an album with a user's guide.

Awareness Through Movement for the Elder Citizen
These ATM exercises are suitable for everyone, but were created especially for those whose movement is limited by age, illness, or injury. The tape package includes ten 35-minute lessons on five cassettes, enclosed in an album with user's guide.

The Quest Workshop Audiotape Series
Recorded at the 1981 public ATM workshops sponsored by the Quest organization, these tapes represent extraordinary examples of Feldenkrais's teaching for the public, bringing alive his humor, wit, and wisdom.
1981 Dallas Quest Workshop
Many new and original ATM exercises, including a special series to improve function of the arms and shoulders. Twenty-two easy-to-follow exercises on fifteen 90-minute cassettes.
1981 San Francisco Quest Workshop
This workshop was designed carefully so that participants with neck and back problems could fully participate—many exercises improve the carriage and mobility of neck and head. Twenty-two exercises on fifteen 90-minute cassettes.
The Berkeley Workshop
This tape package contains the fullest representation of Feldenkrais's teaching available—a comprehensive goldmine of exercises to

help every part of your body. Recorded on forty-nine 90-minute cassettes, including seven lectures and over forty ATM exercises. Enclosed in albums, with table of contents and user's guide.

VIDEOTAPES OF FELDENKRAIS'S WORK

From eight in-depth interviews conducted for the nationally syndicated "Medicine Man" TV program, each video focuses on a specific aspect of Feldenkrais's work. Each tape includes four 30-minute TV programs in VHS format.

Medicine Man I
   A. *The Beginning*
   B. *On Teaching and Learning*
   C. *What Is Awareness Through Movement*
   D. *On Exercise*

Medicine Man II
   A. *On Posture*
   B. *On Breathing*
   C. *The Basis of the Feldenkrais Method*
   D. *On Working With Cerebral Palsy*

Books and audio or videotapes available from: Feldenkrais Resources P.O. Box 2067, Berkeley, CA 94702

BOOKS ABOUT M. FELDENKRAIS

Hanna, Thomas. *The Body of Life.* New York: Knopf, 1979.
   A new somatic approach to health: an in-depth examination of Functional Integration and other systems of body therapy used to achieve physical well-being and improved emotional health.
Masters, Robert, and Jean Houston. *Listening to the Body.* New York: Delacorte, 1978.
   A book of exercises with an introduction to the practice and philosophy of Feldenkrais's work.
Rywerant, Yochanan. *The Feldenkrais Method: Teaching by Handling.* New York: Harper & Row, 1983.
   A full presentation of the Functional Integration system devised by Feldenkrais to improve motor functioning and heightened sensory awareness.

INDEX

Aboriginal people, 301
Action
  and metaphor, 199–202
  taking action, Eagle Song
    camp, 383–85
Action Contracts, 372–73, 379–82,
    387, 391–95, 400–1
  for Acts of Beauty, 372–74,
    381–82, 389–90, 392, 394
  for Acts of Power, 372, 374,
    380–81, 389–90, 391, 393
  Earth Action Contract, 395
  Earth Medicine Contract,
    398–400
Act of Woman Power, An
    (Stepanich), 339
Addictions, 407
Adult Children of Alcoholics,
    216, 353, 442
Adult Survivors of Abuse, 353
Alcohol, 22
All Our Relations, 5, 9, 240, 356
  meaning of term, 6
All That Is, 9
Almass, A. A., 407
Altar, 49
  group altar, 367–68
  making altar, 72–73
American Indian Movement, 293
Anderson, Mad Bear, 413
Animals
  as teachers, 32
  astral projection of, 198

Apache Indians, 135, 240, 248
Apache Kid, 246, 248
Apprenticeship, 165
Apsa Indians, 17, 20, 59, 299
Aquarian Age, 295
Aquarian aspect, 435
Arts and crafts, resources for,
    455
Astral projection, 198
Atlantis, 268
Attention
  importance of, 90
  three attentions, 199, 370–71
  turning of attention, 90
At the Pool of Wonder (Lauck and
    Koff-Chapin), 142
Aunt Josie, 229
Avalanche (Joy), 435

Back to Eden (Kloss), 300
Bandler, Richard, 309
Barclay, Shinan, 338
Bear, 132–33, 135
Bear Butte, vision quest at, 77–88,
    94–105, 113–23
Bear-Clawed Hill, 85
Bear Heart Williams, 290
Beauty, Acts of Beauty, 373,
    381–82, 389, 392, 394
Beauty Bundle, 365
Begin the Day with Ceremony,
    479
Berendt, Joachim-Ernst, 414

Birth of child
  name given at, 174–75
  power of, 46
Black Elk, 4, 6, 23–25, 86, 143–44, 324
  sacred dream of, 4–6, 10–11
  vision of global dance, 11
Black Elk, Wallace, 291
Black Elk Speaks (Neihardt), 11, 143
Blackfeet Indians, 199, 364
Black Hand, 84–85, 95–96, 98, 99–104, 122, 266
Black Hills, 98
Blacktail Ranch, 363–65
"Body of the Warrior, The," 282
Body work
  balancing exercises, 410–11
  Feldenkrais method, 189–205
Bow Society, 12
"Breaking the Chain," 351
Breathing, 49
Brooke Medicine Eagle Speaks, 479
Brooke Medicine Eagle Teachings, 479
Brown, Joseph Eppes, 4, 6
Brown, Tom, 316, 347, 365–66
Bud, 368, 386
Buffalo
  symbolism of, 44, 53–54
  uses by Native Americans, 53
Buffalo Medicine, 39, 54, 70
Buffalo Spirit Lodge, 22
  blessings inside lodge, 39–40
  experience of the buffalo, 39–40, 53–54
Buffalo Woman's Womb, 119
Bureau of Indian Affairs, 267

Cackling Crow. *See* Dawn Boy
"Call of the Drinking Gourd, The," 283
Cameron-Bankler, Leslie, 310

Castaneda, Carlos, 19, 135, 225
Cedar, and smudging, 29
Cedar needles, and smudging, 38–39
Chalise, 141, 173, 181–82, 245
Channeling
  Kaskafayet training, 215–30, 232–33
  Terra, 225–27
Chants
  communication with Spirit through sacred words/sounds, 49
  heartbeat drumming, 73
  waiting song, 73
Cheyennes, The (Hoebel), 12
Chickadees, 61–62
Chief Joseph, 68–69
Children
  hero child, 182, 431
  initiation in Sacred Lodge, 45
  recognition of spiritual leaders among, 45–46
  spiritual development of, 44–45
  and wings of spirit, 44–45
Christ energy, 140, 142, 238, 241, 247
Christians, and Native people, 22, 26, 241
Circle, symbolism of, 419–20
Circle of Life, 5–6, 9–10, 13, 402, 413
  accounting for things in, 119
"Circle Round the Wheel," 289
Cleansing ceremony
  for spiritual cleansing, 49–51
  with water, 84
Coming Home, 409–10
Conflict resolution
  basis of, 439
  consensus method, 436–37
Conquest of Paradise (Sales), 239

Consensus method, 436–37
CONTINUING THE QUEST, 385, 472
Cordell, Norma, 342, 351
Corn Dance, 10
Councils, 11–13
  of the Grandmothers, 12–13
  peace councils, 12–13
  war councils, 11–12
"Coup" game, 376
Coyote, 282
  symbolism of, 286
Crazy Horse, 142, 237
Crazy Mountains, 63
Creative Dreaming (Garfield), 213
Crown of Columbus, The (Erdich and Dorris), 239
Crystals, 249–50, 257–71
  ceremonies upon acquiring crystals, 268–70
  cleansing of, 270
  and creation of Earth, 268
  energy generated, 257
  energy pattern of, 266
  filling crystal with intention, 270–71
  healing with, 257, 259–60
  and meditation, 258–59
  mining of, 268
  self as crystalline energy, 266–67
  sixteen crystal skulls, 268
Curtis, Edward, 68

"Dance Awake the Dream," 353
Dances
  Black Elk's vision, 11
  Dedication Dance of Commitment, 383
  renewal dances, 11
Dancing Buffalo Woman's Dream, 283
Dandelion root, 299–300

Dark side, hungry dog concept, 433–35
Dawn Boy, 235–36, 240–46, 250–54
Dawn Star, 11, 140–42, 238–42, 247, 277, 432
  disciples through time, 240–41, 248
  prophecy about destruction of Native peoples, 239–40
  teachings of, 238–40
Dedication Dance of Commitment, 383
DEEPENING OF SPIRIT, 365–66, 384, 470
"Deepening Your Relationship with Power," 282
Deerborn Valley, 356
Devastation of the Indies, The (Las Casas), 239–40
Devil's Tower, 85
Diamond Heart (Almass), 407
Diet for a New America (Robbins), 297
Dillard, Annie, 396
Dillon, Mary, 338
Dragontime (Francis), 339
Dragon vision, 56–58
"Dreaming the New Dream Symposium" (Klaper), 297
Dreams
  dreamwork exercises, 213
  lucid dreaming, 196–98
  and Native elders, 142
Drumming, 414
  effects of, 126–27
  heartbeat drumming, 73, 126–27
  and men, 126–27
  men and drum groups, 357
  Mother drums, 127
  resources for, 455

Drumming the Heartbeat, 73, 126, 473

Drysdale, Vera Louise, 4, 293, 338

Eagle medicine, 180
Eagles, 61
EagleSmith, Alvin, 358
Eagle Song camps, 363–90, 469–72
  Action Contracts, 373–74, 379–82, 387, 391–95
  building awareness theme, 371–75
  choice and commitment theme, 378–82
  CONTINUING THE QUEST, 385, 472
  Dedication Dance of Commitment, 383
  DEEPENING OF SPIRIT, 365–66, 384, 470
  HEALING VISION, 365, 385, 470
  information about, address/phone, 472
  IN THE CRADLE OF MOTHER EARTH, 365–66, 471
  making our intention clear theme, 367–71
  purification theme, 375–76
  SINGING THE SACRED, 365–66, 471
  and Sky Lodge retreats, 385–86
  SONG OF THE BEAUTY WAY, 365, 471
  support hoop exercise, 387
  support theme, 382–83
  taking action theme, 383–84
  unity and oneness themes, 367
  vision quests, 376–78

Earth Action Contract, 395
Earth Is Our Mother, 477
Earth Medicine Contract, 398–400, 426
"Earth Woman, Woman of Light," 283
East, medicine wheel, 284
Egyptian Mystery Schools, 229
Eight, symbolism of, 336
Elder Brother, 238
Embodying spirit, 248
Emeralds, 135–38
Emotions
  loving intention, 219–21
  resistance of, 218–19
  uncovering buried emotions, 216–18
Empowering the Spiritual Warrior: Walking a Beauty Path, 472
Empowerment, 372–73
  versus success, 373
Emptiness
  finding and filling the holes exercise, 423–24
  ways of filling up holes, 407–8
Enemies, embracing the monster, 438–42
Erhard, Werner, 223, 278
Erickson, Milton, 412
EST, 223, 278
Exercises
  absolute yes, 230–31
  accepting the mantle, 424–25
  around personal medicine wheel, 303–5
  around the medicine wheel ritual, 287–88
  assessing the right-sided world, 168–69
  breaking tree of family patterns, 107–9

breathing exercise, 210–11
calling your teachers, 30–33
ceremony for taking new
   name, 185–86
ceremony of release, 108–10
cleansing of crystals, 270
communication with Spirit
   through sacred
   words/sounds, 49
creating medicine bundle,
   148–49
creating necklace of
   connectedness, 72–74
creating sacred space, 28–29
exploring the feminine, 123–26
fasting, 88–91
filling crystal with intention,
   270–71
finding and filling the holes,
   423–24
Golden Seed Atom, 48–49
having your cake and eating it
   too ritual, 311–13
honoring the six directions
   ritual, 288–89
Inheritance Suitcase, 169–71
integrity of feeling, 231–32
Law of Seven Generations,
   106–7
manifesting through Four
   Winds, 359–61
meaning of given name, 183
medicine wheel walk, 397–98
moon staff, creation of, 342
moon time awareness exercise,
   340–41
moving blindfolded exercise,
   209–10
noticing habitual patterns,
   208–9
nurturing the crystal
   ceremony, 269–70

outer earth walk, 396
Paraphernalia purge, 110–11
power leaks, exploration of,
   388–89
purpose of, 27–28
pursuit of symbolic guide,
   147–48
reality shifts exercise, 211–13
recapitulation exercise, 251–53
reenacting a vision, 144–46
the right questions, 422–23
ritual for spiritual cleansing,
   49–51
searching for true name,
   183–85
smudging, 29–30
stringing the pearls of oneness,
   70–71
support hoop exercise, 387
taking ritual action, 322–24
tension check, 207–8
tree of family patterns, 105–6
vision in action, 149–50
walking wheel of relatedness,
   296–302

Family patterns
   breaking family patterns,
      107–8
   ceremony of release, 108–9
   Inheritance Suitcase, 169–71
   Law of Seven Generations,
      106–7
   and personal growth, 167–68
   and therapy, 250
   tree of family patterns, 105–6
Family therapy, 442
Fasting, 113–14
   cross-cultural view, 86
   and healers, 91
   Master Cleanser fast, 90–91
   one-day fast, 88–89

Fasting (*cont.*)
   significance of, 86–87
   types of fasts, 89
Fasting Place, Medicine Rocks, 63
Fasts, vision quests, 59
Feelings, integrity of feeling
      exercise, 231–32
Feldenkrais, Moshé, 189–205, 309,
      324, 410
   sources of information on,
      480–82
Feminine
   exploring the feminine, 123–26
   feminine energy, 10
   feminine principle, 119,
      123–24, 182
   meaning of feminine, 117–18
   and wearing skirts, 412
Flowering Woman: Moontime for
      Kori (Dillon and
      Barclay), 338
Flowersong, 239, 242, 254–55
"Flowersong: Walking in the
      Dawn Star's Light," 283
For My People, 321, 473
FORUM, 278
Four Directions, of medicine
      wheel, 284–87
Four Quadrants, 250
Four Winds
   manifesting through Four
      Winds exercise, 359–61
   symbolism of, 64
Francis, Lucia, 339
Frank Fools Crow, 142
Frogs into Princes (Bandler and
      Grinder), 310
Functional Integration,
      movement, 191

Garfield, Patricia, 213
"Gateways to the Gods," 283

Genocide, of Native Americans,
      22–23, 25–26, 239–40
Ghost Dance, 142
Gifting, for spiritual services,
      96–97
Gift of Song, A, 108, 332
Gift of the Sacred Pipe, The
      (Drysdale), 4, 293–94, 338
Golden Seed Atom, exercise,
      48–49
Gracen, Darion, 406, 416
Gracen, Marion, 406, 416
Grace Spotted Elk, 291
Grandma Rosie. *See* Woman
      Who Knows Everything
Grandmother Lodge, 339–40
Grandmother Moon, 327–33
Grandmothers, 115–16, 119
   functions of, 13
   peace councils of, 12–13
   teaching about power, 409
Grandmother Spider, 244
Great Drinking Gourd, 290
Great Mother, dragon vision,
      56–58
Great Mystery, 26, 62, 86
Great Spirit
   as judge, 24–25
   nature of, 10, 25
Grinder, John, 309
Guides
   pursuit of symbolic guide,
      147–48
   visions, 146

Halifax, Joan, 179, 281
Harmonic Convergence, 353–55
Harney Peak, 86
Healing
   and crystals, 257, 259–60
   and plants/herbs, 13, 242–43,
      300

Healing Through Ritual Action, 321, 474

HEALING VISION, 365, 385, 470

Heartbeat drumming, 73, 126–27

"Her Alone They Sing Over," 338

Herbs
herbal healing, 242–43, 300
resources for, 455–56

Hero child, 182, 431

"Heyoka, the Fourth Great Power," 282

Hoebel, E. Adamson, 12

Holiness
meaning of, 9
and Native American teachings, 9–10

Hoops of women, 13

Hopi Indians, 301

Humor, and teaching, 282

Hungry dog concept, 433–35

Hunka, 127, 179, 342

Hunkapi, 127

Incenses, 23

Indian Freedom of Religion Act, 18–19

Indian Hit List, 293

Indian Medicine Way, The, 477

Inheritance Suitcase, 169–71

Inipi, 291

Initiation
experience of the buffalo, 39–40, 53–54
at puberty, 44–45, 174, 176

Insects, 243–46, 248–49

IN THE CRADLE OF MOTHER EARTH, 365–66, 471

Intuition, yes versus no, 227–28, 230–31

Itsa Ma, 247

It's Not What You Eat, It's What Eats You! (Schwartz), 413

Joy, Brugh, 435

Kali, 225

Kaskafayet, Frank, 215–30, 232–33

Keleman, Stanley, 195

Kinesthetic learning, 165

Kivas, 45
See also Lodges

Klaper, Dr. Michael, 297

Kloss, Jethro, 300

Know How (Cameron-Bandler), 310

Koff-Chapin, Deborah, 142

Kulkulkan, 247

Lakota, 4, 13
See also Sioux

Lakota Indians, 78

Las Casas, Bartolome de, 240

Lauck, Marcia, 142

Law of Seven Generations, 106

Left-side world, 59, 161–62, 165, 177–78
gaining attention of, 250
and peyote, 243, 290

Leo aspects, 435

Leopold, Aldo, 396

Lewis, Suzanne, 350, 353

Linderman, Frank, 63

"Listening to the Ancient Voices," 283

"Listening to the Great Voices: And Experience in Silent Knowledge," 355, 364

Little People, 59

Lodges
   Buffalo Spirit Lodge, 22
   Grandmother Lodge, 339–40
   guardian society for, 43
   ideal characteristics of Lodge
      keepers, 22–23, 42
   initiation at puberty, 45
   Moon Lodge, 45, 327–33,
      336–39
   Sacred Bundles, 22–24
   sweat lodge, 291
Lohmann, Melanie, 350, 365, 408
Looks Within Place, 282, 286,
   288
Love, 225
   and truth, 219–21, 224, 227
Loving intention, 219–21
Lyman, Andrea, 415

McAllister, Kristine, 377
Mad Bear Anderson, 259, 265–66
Magpie, symbolism of, 61
Marriage baskets, 13
Masculine principle, 119, 180–81
Mason, Dorothy, 377
Master Cleanser fast, 90–91
Mayans, 247
Medicine bundle
   components of, 101
   creating medicine bundle,
      148–49
Medicine Rocks, 69
   Fasting Place, 63
   significance of area, 59–60
   vision quest and birds, 60–63
   vision quest of Plenty Coups,
      61, 63–64
Medicine Wheel, 108, 284–89
   around personal medicine
      wheel exercise, 303–5
   around the medicine wheel
      ritual, 287–88
   east, 284, 286

   honoring the six directions
      ritual, 288–89
   meaning of term, 284
   north, 286–87
   south, 286
   west, 286
Medicine Wheel Astrology (Sun
   Bear), 287
Medicine Wheel Gathering,
   284
Medicine Wheel Song, 289
Medicine wheel walk, 368–69,
   397–98
Meher Baba, 264
Men
   and drumming, 126–27
   gathering in drum groups, 357
Menstruation
   first blood celebration, 338
   and moon, 328–35
   poem related to, 333–35
   sources of information about
      Moon practices, 338–39
   See also Moon
Metaphor, and action, 199–202
Metis, 237
Missionary schools, 21, 26
Mollison, Bill, 301
Montgomery, Pam, 301
Moon
   being one with cycle of
      Grandmother Moon,
      330–31
   Grandmother Moon, 327–31,
      354
   Moon Lodge, 47, 327–33,
      336–39
   Moon staff, creation of, 342
   Moon time awareness exercise,
      340–41
   Moon women and ceremonies,
      337–39
   waning moon, 327–28

Moon Lodge, 475

Moon Time, 474–75

Moontime for Kori, 341

Mother drums, 127

Mother Earth
  fixing troubles of, 117
  and women, 117–18

"Mother's Heartbeat Singing,"
  367

Movement
  Awareness through Movement,
    192
  being the body exercise, 206–7
  breathing exercise, 210–11
  Functional Integration, 191
  and Moshé Feldenkrais,
    189–205
  moving blindfolded exercise,
    209–10
  noticing habitual patterns,
    208–9
  reality shifts exercise, 211–13
  tension check, 207–8

Mysticism, of Native American
  spirituality, 25–26

*Nada Brahma: The World Is
  Sound* (Berendt), 414

Nagual woman, 248

Names and naming
  of Brooke Medicine Eagle,
    178–82
  by Rainbow Woman, 178–79
  ceremony for taking new
    name, 185–86
  given names, significance of,
    183
  name-seeking, 182–83
  Native American naming
    methods, 174–76
  searching for true name,
    183–85
  spiritual names, 416–17

Native American Church, 243, 290

Native American Congress, 291

Native Americans
  and Christians, 22, 26, 241
  and coming of Europeans,
    239–41
  and genocide of people, 22–23,
    25–26, 239–40
  government's breakdown of
    culture, 22–23, 25–26
  prophecy about destruction of,
    239–40

Native American spirituality
  fasting, 86–87
  gifting for spiritual services,
    96–97
  Indian Freedom of Religion
    Act, 18–19
  modern influences to, 26
  as mystical tradition, 25
  prayers in, 55–56
  role of teachers in, 25
  spiritual development of
    children, 44–45
  vision quests, 59

*Native Visions: Healing the
  Heart,* 478

Navajo Indians, 338

Negative aspects, embracing the
  monster, 438–42

Neihardt, John, 11, 143

Neurolinguistic Programming,
  309

New age, 431–32, 435

Nez Perce Indians, 67–68

Nikerson, Ted, 78

North, medicine wheel, 286

Obsidian, 286

Old Joseph, 68

Oneness, 431–32
  necklace of connectedness,
    72–74

Oneness (*cont.*)
  stringing the pearls of oneness,
    70–71

Painting, of face or body, 102
Palenque, 242
Paraphernalia purge, 110–11
Past issues
  clearing past issues, 250–52
  recapitulation exercise, 252–53
Peace councils, 12–13
Pearls, stringing the pearls of
    oneness, 70–71
Peck, Lynn, 406, 418
People of the Morning Star, 238
Perelandra (Wright), 300
*Permaculture: A Practical Guide
    for a Sustainable Future*
    (Mollison), 301
Peterson, Elaine, 416
Peyote, power of, 243, 290–91
Pigeons, 62
Pilgrim of Tinker Creek (Dillard),
    396
Pima Indians, 244
Pipes
  pipestone, 102
  ways of moving pipe, 102
Piscean Age, 295
Plants
  and healing, 13, 242–43, 300
  for smudging, 29–30, 38–39
Plenty Coups (Linderman), 63
Plenty Coups, vision quest at
    Medicine Rocks, 61,
    63–64
Power
  contract for Acts of Power,
    372, 374, 380–81, 389–90,
    391, 393
  empowerment, 372–73
  essence of, 372
  Grandmothers teaching of, 409

Power leaks, 250
  exploration of, 388–89
Prayer cloths, 37, 54–55, 100
Prayers
  effects of, 377
  in Native American
    spirituality, 55–56
  Shinela prayers, 55
  sounding prayers, 55–56
Premature closure, 422
Priestly tradition, in religion, 25
Puberty
  initiation, 44–45, 174, 176
  name given in, 174, 176
Purification, ritual for, 375
Pyramids of Egypt, 413–14

Rainbow child status, 120
Rainbow Medicine, 120–23, 281
  meaning of, 283
  teachings of, 24
Rainbow teacher, 421
Rainbow Warrior, The, 477–78
Rainbow Woman, 116–18,
    120–21, 140–41, 178–79
Rain forests, 348, 350
Rattles
  functions of, 70
  resources for, 455
Reality shifts, exercise, 211–13
Recapitulation, 135
  recapitulation exercise, 252–53
Relatedness, walking wheel of,
    296–302
Release, ceremony of release,
    108–9
Returning, The, 3–4
Right, danger of being right, 63
Right-side world, 59, 161–62, 166,
    assessment of, 168–69
Rittel, Tag, 364
Ritual performance, 199–200,
    307–25

example of, 307–9
having your cake and eating it
    too ritual, 311–13
spaghetti theory, 310, 313
stimulation of emotion, 314–17
taking ritual action, 322–24
Rituals, dances, 10
Robbins, John, 297
Roberts, Jane, 215
Ropes courses, 315–17

Sacred Bundles, 22–24
praying before Sacred Bundle,
    39–40
Sacred Arrow Bundle, 12, 22
Sacred Pipe, 101, 293–95
Sacred Pipe, The (Brown), 4, 6
Sacred Sites Conservancy, 78
Sacred Web of Life, 9
Sage
    bed of, 100–101
    cleansing properties, 100
    and smudging, 29
Sales, Kirkpatrick, 239
Sand County Almanac, A
    (Leopold), 396
Sand Crabs, 38, 40–43, 266
Savell, Susan, 260–64
Schwartz, Jack, 413
Scott, Rodney, 127, 356
Service, Acts of Beauty, 373,
    381–82, 389–90, 392, 394
Seth material, 215
Sex
    as power, 226
    in return for spiritual teaching,
        41–46
Shamanic Voices (Halifax), 179
Shaman's time, 286
Shinela Indians, 19–20, 41–42, 78
Shot in the Hand, 68
Siddhis, 224
Silence, day of silence, 89

Singing
    power of, 414–15
    See also Chants
Singing Joy to the Earth, 73, 289,
    473
"Singing the Sacred," 283
SINGING THE SACRED,
    365–66, 471
Sioux, 9
Skan, 119
Sky Lodge, retreats, 385–86
Sleep, number of hours, 196
Smallpox, 22
Smudging, 29–30
    herbs/plants for, 29–30, 38–39
    lighting smudge, 29–30
    methods for, 29–30
    purpose of, 29–30
    resources for smudge, 456
    ritual for spiritual cleansing, 50
Snowy Owl, 289
Soft eyes, ways to soften eyes, 73
SONG OF THE BEAUTY
    WAY, 365, 471
Sounds. See Chants; Drumming
Source, 142
South, medicine wheel, 286
Southern Seers, 135, 161, 229,
    240, 248–49
Spaghetti theory, ritual
    performance, 310, 313
Spiders, Grandmother Spider,
    244
Spirit Dance, 478
"Spirit of Beauty, Spirit of
    Peace," 283
Spiritual benefactors, 236
Spiritual blockage, 346–48
Spiritual warrior, role of, 168
Staff
    moon staff, creation of, 342
    talking staff, 436
Stalking Wolf, 316, 347

Starseed: The Third Millennium
       (Carey), 443
Stepanich, Kisma K., 339
Stone, Hal, 433–34
Stonehenge, 413
Strongly Bears, 54–55, 267
Sufi master, 224
Sun, as power source, 67
Sun Bear, 283–284, 287
Sun Dance, 10, 284
Sweat lodge, 291
Sweetgrass, and smudging, 29–30

Tales of White Buffalo Woman,
       478
Tarot cards, 244
Teachers
    brother as, 163–66
    calling your teachers exercise,
       30–33
    Dawn Boy, 240–46, 250–54
    Feldenkrais Moshé, 189–205,
       309, 324, 410
    Kaskafayet Frank, 215–30,
       232–33
    mother as, 157–63
    spiritual benefactors, 236
    Woman Who Knows
       Everything, 17, 19–26, 33
    wrathful teacher, 224–25
Terra, 225–27
Testing, along spiritual path,
       49–50
Teton Lakota, 78
Teton Sioux, 291
"That We May Walk Fittingly,"
       282, 347
Third eye, 137
Tich Nat Hahn, 414
Tipis, resources for, 458
Tobacco, 250–52
    and cancer, 242

resources for, 456
symbolism of, 101, 113, 242
Toltecs, 135, 240, 247
Topper, 443
Transformed gossip, 221
Tree of Life, 11
Truth
    and loving, 219–21, 224, 227
    ruthless compassion, 224–25
Tula, 239
Tulum, 242, 246–47
Tunkashila, 302
Turtle Island, 53, 55, 237, 240–41

Vibration
    historical view, 413–14
    personal vibration, 412–13
    and singing/drumming, 414–15
    sources of information on, 414
Vision, The (Brown), 347
Visioning, 474
Vision quests, 59–70
    at Bear Butte, 77–88, 93–105,
       113–123
    of birds at Medicine Rocks,
       60–63
    Eagle Song camps, 376–78
    and fasting, 86–91
    helper on, 80–82, 94
    impatience experience in, 60
    meeting Rainbow Woman,
       116–18, 120–21
    nature of, 59
    of Plenty Coups at Medicine
       Rocks, 61, 63–64
    with Woman Who Knows
       Everything, 82–88,
       94–105, 113–23
Visions
    being active with, 149–50
    bringing to life, 148
    guides, 146

reenactment of, 143–46
vision space, 65
Visions Speaking: Songs of the Sacred Quest, 289, 415, 472
Voice, power of, 415–16
Voice Dialog, 433–34
Voluntary Controls (Schwartz), 413

Waiting song, 73
Wakan, 119
Wakan-Tanka, 295
"Walk in Balance," 283
Wallawas Mountains, 68
Walsh, Wendy, 418
War councils, 11–12
Warrior, true warrior, 5
Water, cleansing ritual, 84
Weed, Susan, 301
West, medicine wheel, 286
White Buffalo, 289
White Buffalo Calf Pipe Woman, 6–7, 9–10, 13, 24, 141, 291, 293–94, 419
White Buffalo Woman, 6, 142–43, 293, 429–30, 444
Wholeness, 10

Wildcrafting, 242
Williams, Paul, 353
Wings of Spirit, and children, 44–45
Winkleman, Sidra, 433–34
Wisdom Women, 115–16
Woho'gus, 140, 238
Woman Who Knows Everything, 17, 19, 36
    connection over time and distance, 78–79
    death of, 273–74
    as teacher, 19–26, 33
    on vision quest, 82–88, 94–105, 113–23
Women
    divisions of lives of, 124
    role of, 118, 119–20
    as separate race, 226
    See also Feminine
Wovoka, 237
Wright, Machaelle Small, 301

Yaquis Indians, 135, 240, 248
Yes versus no, 227–28, 230–31
Younger Brother, 235–36, 346
Ywahoo, Dhyani, 257–58

Linda Holbrook